GRANNY
MADE ME AN
ANARCHIST

Stuart Christie

Scribner

First published in Great Britain by Scribner, 2004
This edition published by Scribner, 2005
An imprint of Simon & Schuster UK Ltd
A Viacom Company

Scribner and design are trademarks of Macmillan Library Reference
USA, Inc., used under licence by Simon & Schuster, the publisher
of this work.

1 3 5 7 9 10 8 6 4 2

Simon & Schuster UK Ltd
Africa House
64–78 Kingsway
London WC2B 6AH

www.simonsays.co.uk

Simon & Schuster Australia
Sydney

A CIP catalogue record for this book
is available from the British Library

ISBN 0-7432-6356-1
EAN 9780743263566

Typeset by M Rules
Printed and bound in Great Britain
by Cox & Wyman Ltd, Reading, Berks

Granny Made Me an Anarchist

'A fascinating book by Stuart Christie, whose anarchist activiti s and
brushes with the law make the Sex Pistols look like
choirboys. . .provides an insight into the minds of driven individuals
who are prepared to kill and destroy to achieve their aims'
Sunday Express

'This fascinating personal account offers a remarkable picture of the
late 20th century, seen through sensitive eyes and interpreted by a
compassionate, searching soul, from the streets of working class
Glasgow to the brutal prisons of fascist Spain to the struggles against
injustice in Britain. It is a frank and revealing portrayal of the
evolution of the mind and thoughts and deeds of an anarchist
exploring the complexities and dilemmas of a life sincerely dedicated
to freedom, with lessons for all who share Christie's driving values
however they respond to the courageous path on which they led him'
Noam Chomsky

'An intriguing look at the life and times that helped shape the
dental technician and gas fitter turned politico – not to mention
the country as a whole'
Metro

'Crammed with incident that is described with no small amount of
wit. Even at the hands of the BPS, Franco's secret police, and facing
the prospect of being either 'disappeared' or publicly garrotted, he
retains a grim sense of humour. This is a highly detailed, if partisan
history of the protest movement in the 20th century and the social
and political upheavals to which it was a response'
Independent on Sunday

'An intelligent, spirited book'
TLS

'Christie writes with wit about his incident-filled life, presenting his side of a story that was often skewed by a sensationalist press and a defensive Establishment'
The Times

'With his rich mixture of the personal and the political, Stuart Christie has illuminated an important corner of recent history. This book is a treat to read'
Ian Jack, editor, *Granta*

'This sharp firecracker of an autobiography explodes with wit and wisdom. . .it reads like a thriller laced with political polemic and fused with an affectionate portrait of a tough Glaswegian upbringing under a strong matriarchal influence – granny'
Time Out

To 'B'
The next link in the chain

CONTENTS

PART 3: LONDON

The Worst Day of My Life

On Tuesday 1 September 1964, as Britain prepared to make its choice between Harold Wilson and Lord Alex Douglas Home in the General Election, I was in Madrid's First Permanent Military Court facing a drumhead court martial – a *Consejo de Guerra sumarisimo*, case No 1154-64 – charged with 'banditry and terrorism'.

Spain's secret police had arrested me eighteen days earlier in possession of plastic explosives and detonators to be used to blow up Spain's fascist dictator, Generalissimo Franco, and his inner circle in the royal box at Santiago Bernabéu during the final of the Generalissimo's Cup. The penalty for this offence was death by *garrotte-vil*, the grisly process of neck-breaking and slow mechanical strangulation by an iron collar and a bolt through the neck.

Madrid's burning September sun streamed through the tall windows into the gloomy hall, picking out the burnished brass buttons, gold braid and red, sweat-drenched face of the cavalry major pacing up and down between me and the judges. He was gesticulating with vehemence and shouting in Castilian Spanish. I hadn't the faintest idea what he was saying and no one was translating for me.

Every so often the major would stop, turn with a grand pantomime flourish, point directly at me like a demented Latin Lord Kitchener and – modulating his voice – hiss something obviously dramatic. Once, I turned, in case he was pointing to someone behind me. But there was no doubt – he was talking about me.

1

x x x

I was seated on a wooden bench with my fellow accused, Fernando Carballo Blanco, a forty-year-old Spanish carpenter who spoke no English, and guarded on either side by two armed soldiers. Facing us on the wall was a large, gilt-framed portrait of a Spanish warlord in heroic, victorious posture, perched on a white horse and surrounded by the dead and dying vanquished: Generalissimo Francisco Franco de Bahamonde. He was a hybrid Oliver Cromwell and Torquemada, with a sword in one hand and a holy relic and reins in the other, ready to smite down those who opposed him. The major was merely the conduit of his fury and divine justice.

Franco

El Caudillo: Generalisimo Francisco Franco de Bahamonde

On a high table, in front of this dark allegory, sat eleven army officers heavy with medals, five on either side of the most decorated, the court president, Coronel Don Jesús Montes Martín. Each had his ceremonial sword laid out in front of him.

Installed in the corner, at his own table, sat the tall figure of the examining magistrate from the *Juzgado Militar Especial Nacional de Actividades Extremistas,* Lieutenant-Colonel Balbás Planelles, with his highly polished bald pate and large silver-grey moustache. To my left was the table for the nervous translator, a captain – whose job was to translate anything I might say to the court, not vice versa – and prosecuting counsel, Comandante Auditor Don Ramón González-Arnau Diez, currently prosecuting. To my right was my unprepared and clearly intimidated British-Embassy-appointed civilian lawyer, Don Gabriel Luis Echevaria.

x x x

The one friendly face in the hall was my Mum's, the only woman present. The rest of the audience – sitting impassively, sweating profusely in the long, high, airless hall – was made up of military officers, secret policemen I recognised from the Brigada Político-Social, journalists from Franco's fascist press, and black-frocked priests. There were also two British diplomats, the Consul and Vice-Consul, and Niall MacDermott, QC, an observer sent by our defence committee in London.

It was unreal; as though somehow I had been transported into the final act of some grand opera without either the music or the fat lady, but equally incomprehensible. Later I learnt that the major was performing the story of how, since the victory of the 'Glorious National Movement' in 1939, Spain had been besieged domestically and internationally by the activities of anarchist organizations committed to bringing down Spain's national order through the use of the bomb and the gun – and that I was one of the agents of this conspiracy.

But I was eighteen years and six weeks old, a boy from working-class Glasgow and I'd never been to the opera. How in the name of the wee man had I ended up here?

PART ONE

SCOTLAND

THE JEELY PIECE SONG

I'm a skyscraper wean; I live on the nineteenth flair,
But I'm no' gaun oot tae play ony mair,
'Cause since we moved tae Castlemilk, I'm wastin' away
'Cause I'm getting' wan meal less every day:

Oh ye cannae fling pieces oot a twenty storey flat,
Seven hundred hungry weans will testify to that.
If it's butter, cheese or jeely, if the breid is plain or pan,
The odds against it reaching earth are ninety-nine tae wan.

On the first day ma maw flung oot a daud o' Hovis broon;
It came skytin' oot the windae and went up insteid o' doon.
Noo every twenty-seven hours it comes back intae sight
'Cause ma piece went intae orbit and became a satellite.

On the second day ma maw flung me a piece oot wance again.
It went and hut the pilot in a fast low-flying plane.
He scraped it aff his goggles, shouting through the intercom,
'The Clydeside Reds huv goat me wi' a breid-an-jeely bomb.'

On the third day ma maw thought she would try another throw.
The Salvation Army band was staunin' doon below.
'Onward Christian Soldiers' was the piece they should've played
But the oompahman was playing a piece an' marmalade.

We've wrote away to Oxfam to try an' get some aid,
An a' the weans in Castlemilk have formed a 'piece-brigade'.
We're gonnae march to George's Square demanding civil rights
Like nae mair hooses ower piece-flinging height.

ADAM McNAUGHTON, 1967

Hey Maw, throw us oot a piece!

I was born in 1946 in the working-class district of Partick, in the West End of Glasgow – a time before deep-fried Mars bars, curried-mutton pies and the urban blight set in.

Then as now, and for centuries, the city of Glasgow was segregated by religion. My family was 'mixed'. My father's family was Episcopalian and Jacobite going back at least 250 years, and I was named Stuart after Bonnie Prince Charlie, 'the only man in history to be called after three separate sheepdogs' according to fellow Partiquois, Billy Connolly. In spite of this I was brought up a Presbyterian, probably due to the fact my dad was mostly at sea – and on my Granny's insistence.

Partick, where I lived until I was seven years old, gave me my first loyalty and sense of identity. I lived happily with my Mum, Granny and Grampa in a top floor apartment of a friendly, four-storey Edwardian tenement at 52 White Street – one of the sturdy, tall, smogged-brown-red sandstone hives on the north bank of the river Clyde, surrounded by the more refined suburbs of Whiteinch, Hyndland and Kelvingrove, with industrial Govan across the river. The district was a 'Scotch broth' of the best and worst parts of the Empire's second city – our maps were coloured pink then – with its class, ethnic and religious mixture of Highland, Lowland, Irish, Italian, Lithuanian and Polish immigrants, comfortable existences rubbing elbows with bare subsistence.

White Street was located halfway up the gentle declivity that is Hyndland Street, just past the brooding Gothic red sandstone building of St Peter's Roman Catholic Church. In spite of all its sectarian bigotry, Glasgow wasn't segregated like Belfast or Derry along religious divides, but by wealth and poverty. Social standing among tenement dwellers was graded as finely as McDougall's flour, and the condescension ran downhill.

Our street, which had small gardens at the front, was considered 'better class' than the next one down the hill, Chancellor Street, but 'not quite as nice' as Caird Drive, the next street up towards the tree-lined Shangri-La of Partickhill and Hyndland Road, where they spoke with an affectedly refined, or 'pan loaf' accent. In White Street there was no 'hinging oot o' windaes', the practice in which turbaned 'wifies' in multi-coloured pinnies leant out of the tenement windows on cushions, arms crossed, keeping an eye on the comings and goings in the street, bantering with neighbours and passers-by. Walking down the canyons between buildings where hinging was practised was for all the world like walking between two giant rows of battery hens all clucking to the left, right, up and down.

A 'hing'
(Oscar Marzaroli)

A 'hing', as it was called colloquially, may have been the done thing down the hill in Chancellor Street and in my Gran's previous flat in Henderson Street, Maryhill – but not in White Street. If my Granny even twitched a net curtain, Grampa would be telling her 'tae keep away frae the windae'.

Another mark of social standing was the style of the 'close-mooth' –

the tenement entrances or 'caves in the canyons' as described by Glasgow songwriter Ian Davison. The informal agreement was that the women in the close had to take their turn at washing the close mouth, the stairs and the stained glass windows overlooking the back courts, as well as polishing the banisters and Brassoing the wee decorative brass knobs that prevented us kids using the banisters as a slide. Heaven help the woman who didn't leave the close spotless when her turn came.

In the more respectable tenements, dignity was further enhanced by decorating the close 'mooths' with fancy scrolls drawn in white pipe-clay with designs unique to each close 'mooth'. In the toilet-less 'single-ends' (flats consisting of only one room) south of Dumbarton Road, landlords didn't bother, and the poorer folks who lived there had other things on their minds. Peeling stucco, flaking plaster, broken window panes and dank, unswept 'closes' that stank of stale beer, vomit, Vimto, Irn-Bru and fish and chips identified them as the warrens of the rickety damned – and probably Catholics! If there was melancholy and despair in Partick it was down these mean streets and up these darker closes.

**Paddy's Market.
Glaswegian shopping**
(Oscar Marzaroli)

X X X

Kids of my age had the run of the street with safety. We played 'kick-the-can', 'peever' or 'raking the midgies' (looking through the middens for anything interesting that had been thrown away) from the moment we got back from school until bedtime. Interruptions for tea or a crisis were heralded from the tenement windows: 'the ba's oan the slates', or 'come oot, come oot whaurever ye ur, the game's a boagey, there's a man in the loaby!' Anyone hiding up a close or 'doon a dunny' (lying low in the dark dungeon-like tenement basements) knew the game was over and we had to go in.

We came back because we couldn't imagine not obeying. I was brought up to be God-fearing, polite, courteous and well behaved, to the point of obsequiousness and servility. Whenever I was out with my Gran or my Mum I had to walk on the outside of the pavement, nearest the road, and when we met her friends in the street I would doff my cap, say how-do-you-do and then not speak until spoken to. If I fidgeted or showed the slightest bit of cheek or petulance I'd get a clout on the back of the head and a promise of worse when I got home. If a funeral procession passed we stopped, I would remove my cap and hold it to my left breast, facing the road impassively until the cortège had passed.

We rarely swore, if ever, or used the name of Jesus or Christ as an expletive, knowing we would go straight to the 'bad fire' or be struck by a thunderbolt if God was listening or – worse – if Granny was listening. The one time I had my 'mooth washed oot wi soap' was when I was about eight and we were living in Ardrossan, a seaside resort on the Clyde coast. I had been playing with my pals on a disused railway turntable, trying unsuccessfully to turn the enormous cast-iron handle which controlled the mechanism. A couple of bigger boys who were passing tried to show off their strength, but after a few goes announced it was impossible, 'Cos it's too fucking stiff', and walked off. Surprisingly, neither my pals nor I had heard the word before and didn't know what it meant, but it sounded descriptively commanding. When I was telling Gran about this adventure, I repeated the phrase verbatim. Gran's jaw dropped and a look of horror spread over her face as though she had just witnessed the ultimate demonic obscenity. After half a second to collect herself, I was dragged across the room to the sink and a bar of carbolic soap was rammed into my mouth. When the drama was over I was given the lecture. I never swore in front of my Granny again.

x x x

This ordered, close community was our world. No one we knew went overseas on holiday; if someone went to Australia, New Zealand or Canada, they had emigrated and were never seen again. A package holiday abroad in those days meant, for Protestants, an educational tour of Palestine and the 'Holy Land' with the minister to see where Jesus was born, lived and died. For Catholics, it meant a pilgrimage to Lourdes in France or Fatima in Portugal where apparitions of the Virgin Mary had appeared to the wide-eyed locals. My mate Andy McGowan went on one of these pilgrimages to Lourdes in 1958, on the Centenary of the Virgin Mary's visitation to a young peasant girl called Bernadette. The trip cost Andy's mum £26.00, a small fortune, which she saved by putting aside ten shillings each week for a year. It was the first time anyone on the trip had ever visited a foreign country and they were extremely excited, even though all they did was go on one religious procession after another. Finally they got to the grotto where the Virgin Mary allegedly manifested. Hanging above this holy spot were discarded walking sticks and crutches and when Andy asked why these were there, he was told people cured by the holy waters had left them. In his innocence Andy asked why there were no wooden legs or glass eyes, and the next thing he knew he had been knocked to the ground by an almighty blow on the side of his head by one of the teachers and accused of blasphemy – all this in full view of hundreds of people. As he said, it was a good job he didn't ask why there were no false teeth as well.

We commiserated with him on the bizarre trial his life was set to be, having had the misfortune to be born a Catholic. The Presbyterian take on this was the minister who warned the children at Sunday School class: 'In Hell there will be wailing and weeping and gnashing of teeth.' 'But what happens if you don't have teeth?' asked one of the children. 'Then the Good Lord will provide them,' came the stern rebuke.

x x x

Mum was born in Glasgow in 1922, and when she left school in 1937 was apprenticed as a hairdresser at Bambers' Salon at Charing Cross Mansions. Bambers was Glasgow's main theatrical costumier and wigmakers to the city's many variety music halls. Chestnut-haired, petite and attractive, she loved to dress differently from everyone else. She was also slightly eccentric, and kept a pet monkey for a time, until Grampa made her get rid of the poor creature. Mum usually spent her holidays in the Rhinns village of Kirkcolm, on the west shore of Loch Ryan between Corsewall Point, Lady Bay and Stranraer, and it was here she met my father, Albert Christie.

Mum

Perhaps because I saw so little of him, perhaps because of the natural inclination of young boys, my father was the more mysterious and attractive figure to me. Dad was thirty years old when they met. He was a trawlerman from the fishing village of Torry at the foot of the River Dee, in Aberdeen, who had been seconded to the lighthouse service during the war. (After my parents married in Glasgow, on 2 June 1945, they spent the first six or seven months of their lives together in a lighthouse at Corsewall Point, at the head of Loch Ryan, where it meets the Irish Sea.)

Tall, slim-built and over six foot, he was good-looking: rakish, pensive with a wry smile and droll sense of humour. His hair was dark and he had a narrow forehead, bushy eyebrows, keen grey-blue eyes, an aquiline nose and a generous mouth set in a longish, tanned and weather-beaten face. In my memory, he always wore a faded Harris Tweed jacket, a fisherman's roll-neck oiled wool sweater and grey flannels. As a skipper he was only ashore a few days every five weeks or so and he never bothered to keep up with fashion. For weddings and funerals he wore a dark blue double-breasted serge suit, which he thought was cavalier, and a bow tie.

x x x

Dad drank heavily, but was never maudlin when drunk. He also smoked heavily, as did most men at the time, rolling his own cigarettes with a pungent Dutch tobacco. He could roll a cigarette with one hand down the outside of his trouser leg faster than tongue could tell. Presumably this was a skill acquired with one hand on the wheel or on a fishing net. I've been told he could be moody – although I never witnessed this side of him – and quick to take offence at some real or imaginary slight.

Dad, Albert Christie (about 1935).

God-fearing and superstitious, yet intelligent, he was solitary. Like many fishermen he didn't have time for small talk, but veered unpredictably between long silences and slow imaginative stories about life at sea and fishing communities in the olden days. One story stuck in my mind as a little boy. Sailing in the Barents Sea near the Arctic ice cap, he told me he once saw a tall-masted sailing ship, locked in the ice floe, drifting aimlessly through the northern seas, the frozen figure of a bearded man lashed to the wheel. For some reason I always felt he wanted to be that figure, although he often said he wanted to die by drowning, believing it to be the best way to go. He claimed drowning people did a fast memory rewind through their entire lives. This wasn't just some family or fishermen's tradition going back hundreds of years; both he and his brother, my Uncle Tom, had experienced flashbacks during near-death drownings, each having been washed overboard at separate times. Dad refused to learn to swim, like many fishermen. Where would he swim to, he argued – hundreds of miles out in the North Atlantic and Arctic oceans where the expected survival time in the water was just fifteen minutes in summer, and seven or eight minutes, at best, in winter.

x x x

Life at Corsewall Lighthouse was more bucolic, a respite from the harsh fishing life of my father's forebears. Nothing dramatic happened. At least until my Dad was drummed out of the service for assaulting the head lightkeeper under mysterious circumstances – perhaps the result of his 'moodiness', or the ancestral legacy of a hard life reasserting itself. With no money and no place to live Dad remained in Aberdeen to find work back on the trawlers while Mum and I moved in with my grandparents in their tenement apartment in Glasgow's Partick district.

In November 1950, Dad acquired his skipper's certificate and my parents tried to find a place of their own in Torry or in Skateraw further down the coast, where the family had lived since at least the sixteenth century, but fishing was poor and with nothing they could afford by 1952 they had simply drifted apart. There was no acrimony on either side as far as I was aware, although the end came curiously. My parents went with Gran and Grampa to a friend's house in Glasgow. The host, Jimmy Stewart the coalman, poured everyone a glass of sherry which my father looked at with disgust, then walked over to the sink, poured the drink down the plughole and without a word to anyone walked out the door. Everyone joked he had gone for a packet of fags, but that was the last we saw of him for twenty years.

I was about six or seven years old at the time, rather too young to know much about it, but as the years went past, it seemed a long time to be gone on a fishing trip, let alone to queue for cigarettes. Many years later when my mother and father were at last reunited, we would crack on about the last time my father went out for a packet of cigarettes and disappeared for twenty years.

x x x

Mum was now left on her own to support me on the meagre wages of a hairdresser, but fortunately she had my Gran and Grampa, who effectively brought me up until I was twelve.

When Granny Married a Catholic

My Granny was the strongest moral influence in my life. Born in 1890, into a world of penny post and carrier pigeon, of carts and horses and operations without anaesthetic, her own grandparents remembered life before Waterloo. Granny grew up in a gatekeeper's house on the grounds of Lochnaw Castle where, when she was two, John Singer Sergeant painted the portrait of the beautiful Lady Agnew of Lochnaw. In 1915, as the Edwardian age was collapsing, and with it the remains of feudalism, she married a soldier and left the castle, eventually arriving in Glasgow, along with electricity and the telephone.

Gran's ethical makeup was equal parts John Knox and village community, transported to the Glasgow tenements. Always impeccably turned out, she worked every day of her life without complaint or bemoaning the hardness of her lot. She brushed out the close, lit wash-house fires, took the ashes down four flights of stairs to the midden, dusted and polished, cleaned brasses and the nickel-plated silver, washed dishes, black-leaded grates, prepared vegetables, podded peas and baked. She always seemed to be baking. Her world was her family – and her neighbours, for whom she was forever washing or darning or making mutton flank soup. There was always a bowl of soup and bread for tramps who came knocking on the door, and if anyone in the tenement or friends fell ill or on hard times there would always be a little parcel of goodies left on their doorstep.

Unemployment and poverty were rife throughout Scotland, and even on Grampa's army pension, they had a job to survive. All his money went to pay the rent, and it was never certain there would be food on the table, but if there was it was Gran who put it there. On the day Mum was born in March 1922, Gran didn't have a penny in her purse. At least Mum survived, unlike her sister Louise, one of the estimated forty million victims of the 1918–19 flu epidemic brought over by the American troops in the First World War. Another of Gran's children, Colin, died of diptheria in 1929, aged eighteen months. Things got a lot worse after the Wall Street crash of 1929, and by 1933 unemployment in Scotland reached nearly three million. But no matter how bad the situation, Gran still managed to keep everything together, including her dignity. She worked all the hours God sent, selling newspapers in the towns and villages around Argyllshire and Lanarkshire, and worked for a time as a housekeeper in a workingman's hotel.

Agnes McCulloch Davis: Granny.

I admired not just her work ethic and her sense of community, but, strange as it may sound of a woman so shaped by her time, her independence of thought. She dealt with everyone and every issue according to her own values, unswayed by the opinion of those around her. She was always on the side of the underdog. More than anything, she loathed the sectarianism that dominated life in the west of Scotland. Although she was a lifelong Protestant in an area where religious differences were passionately and often violently manifested, she married a Roman Catholic.

X X X

Politics, like religion, were never discussed in our house, but occasionally Granny would mention the name of James Maxton, probably the leading figure in the Independent Labour Party (ILP) in Scotland. Maxton was a pacifist and had refused to be conscripted during the First World War. A hypnotic public speaker, he had been heavily involved in organising strikes against the war in the shipyards, engineering and munitions factories. Arrested in 1916 and charged with sedition, he spent a year in prison. He also played an important role in the 1926 General Strike. Mum also told me that Gran regularly went to hear Maxton speak at the small ILP meeting room in Napiershall Street in Maryhill.

James Maxton

One of the reasons politics were never discussed at home must have been that Maxton's name wouldn't have gone down at all well with Grampa, an army man through and through, who, according to my Mum, always voted Tory. Grampa's parents had emigrated to England as part of the Irish diaspora of the 1870s and he had been born in Salford. Grampa was seventy-one years old when I was born, fresh-faced in spite of his years, of medium height, finely built and slightly cadaverous looking. A war wound had left him with a limp and a slight stoop. His stare could be very intimidating. He had two suits, one for best and another for everyday wear – a 'scuffin' suit' he called it. At night the trousers would be folded neatly and placed between sheets of brown paper under the mattress. His grooming was military and meticulous; his tied shoelaces had to be exactly the same length at either end and because he couldn't bend my Gran or myself had to achieve this. Rising early, he would kneel, stiffly and laboriously, on the floor with his elbows on the kitchen table or on the bed, and say his prayers. The same procedure was repeated before retiring for the night.

X X X

Life in Glasgow between 1915 and the mid-30s was hard, and I doubt if there were many working-class women who survived the period unpoliticised. Glasgow was in a state of almost revolutionary fervour, aggravated by the huge issues of suffrage, housing and unemployment. At a couple of points this fervour boiled over. The **Rent Strikes** first of these were the 1915–16 Clydeside Rent Strikes, which coincided with Gran's move to Glasgow from the clear light of Lochnaw just after the outbreak of the First World War. Rent had increased dramatically over a very few years, and conditions had declined; the exploitative Scottish housing laws allowed factors (the landlords' agents) summarily to evict tenants in arrears and confiscate their possessions. Partick and Govan were two munitions-producing districts which were particularly hard hit by the rent increases. The Clydeside strikes were organised mostly by women, supported politically by the ILP and people like James Maxton. By the height of the rent strikes there were upwards of 20,000 tenants refusing to pay their landlords, forcing Lloyd George's government to introduce legislation which reduced rents to pre-war levels.

John Ring: Regimental Sergeant Major, 5th Batallion, HLI, 1915–1918.

The second flashpoint that must have had an impact on Gran was the strike of 1919 over the 40 hour week, the most revolutionary working-class action ever seen in Glasgow. The strikers wanted to reduce the working week to 40 hours in order to allow returning soldiers to find employment, and prevent a build-up of potential scab labour. By 30 January 1919, over 40,000 engineering and shipyard workers were out on strike, together with the electricity workers and 36,000 Lanarkshire and Stirlingshire miners. The next day, around 60,000 demonstrators gathered in George Square to hear the Lord Provost's reply to their demands. While the workers' deputation was inside Glasgow City Chambers, the police launched a brutal attack on the demonstrators outside, which led to running street battles throughout the city well into the night. Fearing revolution, the government immediately ordered 10,000 English troops into the city, with tanks deployed in the town centre and Royal Navy warships stationed in the Clyde. Grampa, who was the Regimental Sergeant Major of the Highland Light Infantry at the time, was confined to Maryhill barracks with a full battalion of Scottish soldiers. The Cabinet Office thought that Scottish soldiers would be more likely to go over to the workers' side if a revolutionary situation were to develop in the city.

x x x

In 1954 my Gran and Grampa retired to the adjoining Ayrshire seaside towns of Saltcoats and then Ardrossan, about 30 miles from Glasgow. For economic reasons, they took me with them, while Mum stayed behind. (I did not know it at the time, but Mum had been having a relationship with a coal miner called Tom Brown – or 'Tam Broon' – from the Lanarkshire pit town of Blantyre and had had a daughter by him in 1953. I only found out I had a stepsister sometime in 1955 when mum came to visit us when we were back in White Street in Partick. I was fiddling with the knobs of the wireless in the kitchen at the time trying to locate interesting new radio stations when Mum came through from the parlour with a little three-year-old girl. 'This is Olivia, Stuart, your new wee sister.' It was a bit of a surprise, but I didn't know the facts of life at the time and thought maybe that was how little sisters came, in ready-made packages. Grampa was never told he had a granddaughter for fear of how he might react.)

Grampa died in Ardrossan in January 1955, in his eightieth year. Like the old soldiers of the song, he faded away. Before he took to his bed at the end, he thanked my Gran for all she had done for him and the family.

I vividly remember the night he died. I had been put to bed early in the 'hole in the wall' in the kitchen, but I knew something was going on. Something, possibly raised voices, woke me at about 8.30 p.m. and I ran through to the front bedroom where I saw Gran and Mum struggling with Grampa in his striped pyjamas. He was attempting to sit upright in the bed recess. Perhaps he was trying to get to the toilet; they say this happens with people who are dying.

His small face, pale yellow as vellum, had shrunk tight around his skull, which was lit from behind by three bulbs. He was staring straight ahead, as though hypnotised, eyes wide, his mouth opening and closing as he tried to speak, gasping weakly in an unrecognisable language – gibberish, interspersed with fragments of English – about a beautiful lady and a light he had seen. Those were his dying moments, his life was flickering out like a candle-end. He fell back and I was quickly ushered out of the room.

His death was accompanied by unaccountable events. Weirdly, when I woke up the following morning the clock in the front room had stopped at ten minutes to nine, the exact time of his death. I thought perhaps Gran had stopped it as an old superstition, but she said she hadn't touched it; it never worked again. Mum and Gran also told me that one of the three lightbulbs above his head blew at the moment of his death. At the same time, the flames in the coal fire which had been blazing away (and which normally never went out; one simply stoked the embers and put on more coal) visibly lost their glow and expired, leaving the room distinctly chilly. The greatest superstitious flummery, however, was connected with his religion. Grampa's last wish was that his mortal remains lie overnight in the local Catholic chapel. For this simple service the priest insisted on a fee of ten pounds, which Gran didn't have. She was extremely distressed that her husband's last request was unfulfilled, but there was no moving the priest. Later, Gran managed to raise enough money for some masses to be said for his soul, though she could not afford it and didn't believe in it.

The old man's remains were brought back to Glasgow to be buried, but because his was a mixed marriage and therefore 'outside the Church', no priest came to the graveside to administer the funeral service, in spite of Grampa's devotion to the Roman Catholic faith. This blatant commercial exploitation and the hurt it caused my granny preyed heavily on my mind. It reinforced my existing prejudices against the Church of Rome and the arbitrary power of a spiteful priesthood. I did have a few Catholic friends, but I was always aware that they were different. Sectarian tribalism demanded we hate and despise Catholics.

x x x

Catholics were poor people who lived down at the shabbier end of Hyndland Street, near Dumbarton Road. They were the barbarians at the gate, the lurkers at the threshold. When visiting a new acquaintance's house for the first time, we automatically checked the mantelpiece and walls for a Sacred Heart of Jesus on Abilone Shell, the Virgin Mary or any iconic reference to Celtic Football Club. Football was the litmus test. If challenged on some strange territory as to which team we supported, the allegiance of which we couldn't identify, we would reply 'Partick Thistle', Glasgow's tiny and non-sectarian third team whose followers rejected both Roman Catholic Republicanism and protestant Unionism. Their signature song, sung to the tune of the Red Flag was: '*Hello. Hello, how do you do/We hate the boys in royal blue/We hate the boys in emerald green/so fuck the Pope and fuck the Queen.*'

None of us really knew why we were enemies to the Catholics – particularly not me, whose grandmother despised the Orange Lodge, and who hated football – except that it was the way things were in the streets. Who did they think they were, segregated from us in their Roman Catholic schools, taught by priests and nuns? Our street songs celebrated being up to our knees 'in Fenian blood' and threatened 'surrender or you'll die'. The boundaries were everywhere, and so was the fear. And, of course, the sense of belonging that hating another group of people provides.

The degree of sectarian bitterness depended largely on where you lived. There was never much orange bunting or Union Jack waving in Partick, whereas Bridgeton in Glasgow's East End was real hard-line protestant territory with orange-painted kerbs and pictures of King Billy hanging in pub windows. The Gorbals, on the other hand, was solidly Roman Catholic and pro-Irish Republican, as were other small towns such as Coatbridge in Lanarkshire.

Ardrossan was a solidly Orange town, probably because it was a port servicing the Larne ferry to Northern Ireland. My classmates at Ardrossan's non-denominational primary school were Jews, Protestants or Sikhs, and my best mates played in the Ardrossan Winton Flute Band, which provided the musical accompaniment during processions of the local Orange Lodge and the Apprentice Boys of Derry. It sounded like good fun. This was just after Grampa died and I was angry at the way Gran had been treated by the priests. My Granny was dead against my having anything to do with the Lodge or the 'bon' as the band was referred to, but this was my opportunity to get back at the priests, and I insisted. I suppose Gran thought that her refusing to let me join would push me even further into their arms, and so she relented, reluctantly, and I was initiated into politics as a wee nine year old sectarian.

x x x

By the summer marching season of 1955 I found myself beating a drum to the stirring rhythm of 'The Sash My Father Wore', marching proudly behind the Union Jack in the Ardrossan Winton Flute Band, a prospective member of the Ardrossan Juvenile Loyal Orange Lodge.

We weren't allowed to play going past the actual Chapel, but we did beat the step to let the Catholics know we were there. There is nothing quite as scary as the sound of drums marking time, particularly the deep stomach-wrenching sound of the big Lambeg drums which take two men to carry. We may not have been allowed to play, but the drum major always stopped directly outside the chapel gates and lingered awhile tossing his big stick as high as could into the air, then catching it on the back of his neck and performing various other aerial manouevres which always brought cheers and applause from the crowds on the pavements.

Our wee Scottish hearts beat faster as we thought how nearly James VII (five less for English readers) had come to delivering us into the embrace of the Harlot. The only sort of harlot we thought we knew of was old Cigarette Annie, who looked, dressed and behaved like the dirty conniving witch in 'Babes in the Wood', and danced crazily to her own mouth-organ accompaniment on the streets of Glasgow. 'Cigarette Annie's' embrace was not very tempting: if her Roman sister was similar, it was hard to see how Redsocks (as Orangemen call the Pope) would ever bring low our glorious institutions. But all we knew was that had it not been for the struggles of our ancestors, our freedom would have been destroyed and we ourselves delivered to the Holy Office of the Inquisition by a faithless king.

It was said locally that the 12th of July celebrations were always accompanied by a miracle, the divine visitation of Saint Lanlic, the patron saint of fortified wines. This always took place in Rinty's Close, a passageway between the Garden of Remembrance and the Brethern Church. Known as the Eternal Spring, it was the appearance of an endless rivulet of a pungent golden liquid which mysteriously cascaded down the passage steps whenever the Orange Lodges marched through the town.

x x x

Mum was now living in Blantyre with Tam Broon and my half-sister, Olivia. I didn't feel abandoned or resentful – kids accept these situations, especially when there's not a lot they can do about it. And so when my newly-widowed Granny found a job as a home-help in Lamlash on the Island of Arran I went too. I wasn't particularly sorry to leave Ardrossan as I was growing bored with my circle of pals in the flute band whose opinions and attitudes were beginning to jar. Arran sounded a lot more exotic and exciting. Robert the Bruce had used the island as his base to launch the Scottish wars of independence in the fourteenth century, and he returned to it after his famous victories against the English, culminating in Bannockburn.

The island had belonged to the Dukes of Hamilton since the middle of the fourteenth century: Catholics were unwelcome and were refused permission to build a chapel or organise open religious meetings. It was perfectly safe, however, for wee Orangemen like me.

This was the time I made the transition from comics to books. I was lucky. I grew up in circumstances still propitious to reading. Reading was the only alternative to shrivelling boredom on wet evenings and winter weekends.

Mark Twain's Huckleberry Finn and Tom Sawyer were the first books I remember reading from start to finish. I was charmed and absorbed by the villainies, horrors and ultimate happy resolution. I related to Huckleberry Finn more than to Tom Sawyer. Tom was privileged and slightly flaky in his instincts – more Hillhead than Partick – while Huck, with his mate Jim the escaping slave, was resourceful in coping with crises and rarely shocked by anything, but never cynical.

x x x

When the old lady my Granny was looking after died, we returned to Glasgow's West End, where Granny became housekeeper to the kindly Revd Mr Lough, a middle-aged bachelor Church of Scotland minister, at 354 Great Western Road, close to Kelvinbridge. I completed my junior school education at Napiershall Street School in nearby Maryhill, the same school my Mum had gone to thirty years earlier.

This was at the time of Suez, the Hungarian uprising, Teddy boys and the birth of Rock 'n' Roll. I was ten years old at the time and none of these things impacted on me directly, except for Rock 'n' Roll and stories of Teddy boys apparently ripping up cinema seats. But from the fast-paced Pathé News reels of paratroops patrolling the streets of Cairo, ships sunk in the Suez canal and Soviet tanks in Budapest, as well as the thought of demon Teddy boys behaving menacingly at every street corner, I began to get the sense that something was happening. Like watching those newsreels today, the world seemed to have sped up.

x x x

I remained captivated by the movies, and watched them at the cinema and on television. Although then as now, TV was dominated by US imports, the British plays and old films I saw made an indelible impression on me. I'll never forget the 'Play for Today' production of Terence Rattigan's *The Winslow Boy*, which traced the consequences of Arthur Winslow's attempts to prove his son's innocence, after the fourteen-year old is expelled from naval college, falsely accused of stealing a five shillings postal order. Rattigan himself called it 'a drama of injustice, and of the little man's dedication to setting things right.' It was gripping drama, but with all the tension of a struggle between right and wrong, law and injustice, the underdog against the high and mighty and the rights of the citizen against soulless authority.

Leslie Howard's film *Pimpernel Smith* also made a huge impact. I didn't know it at the time, but one of the bit part actors playing the role of an anarchist prisoner in a Nazi concentration camp, was later Albert Meltzer to become a lifelong friend – Albert Meltzer. Howard, a convinced anti-fascist, had insisted on using real anarchists as prisoners in one particular scene. Apart from being a cracking good yarn about resisting Nazism, the final dark and dramatic scene at the frontier railway station on the night before the invasion of Poland literally made the hair on the back of my neck stand up. In my book it ranks among the great timeless exchanges in cinematic history. The unseen Howard, now safely across the frontier, speaking through calmly exhaled cigarette smoke, the swirling fog and the shadows, says with an air of wonderful contempt to the sweaty, nervous and frustrated fat Gestapo chief from whom he has just escaped:

> You will never rule the world, because you are doomed. All of you who demoralised and corrupted a nation are doomed. Tonight you will take the first step along the road from which there is no turning back. You will have to go on and on, from one madness to another, leaving behind you a wilderness of misery, and still you will have to go on; because you will find no horizon and see no dawn; until at last you are lost and destroyed. You are doomed, captain of murderers!

The thoughts and emotions films like this triggered we kept to ourselves. It wasn't done to talk about things which moved us – apart from the observation 'Great filum!' But it seems to me that young boys love films in which justice triumphs over injustice and the goodies win over the baddies, or are at the very least easily distinguishable, even if they die gloriously. When I was growing up, goodies and baddies were crystal clear on the world stage – Hitler was defeated, and a new enemy (Communism) was becoming clearly defined on the horizon, not to mention the old one (Catholicism) close at hand – and it was a rare film that had trouble identifying who was who on screen.

Of course, as my life and the century wore on, matters became more complicated, but I have always been grateful for having grown up in a time when such an abstract notion of justice was given so strong an emotional correlative.

Scouting for Boys

Most young people at the time belonged to a voluntary association, like the Cubs or the Boys Brigade, joining for a sense of community, perhaps because their parents thought it was a good idea, and for something to do.

For many of us, the Orange Order was really just a more emotionally charged version of the same idea. But on my return to Glasgow, I joined the Wolf Cubs rather than the Orange Order. The Cubs did far more interesting things than swaggering up and down the high streets of the Protestant enclaves of the west of Scotland. They did camping, hiking and lighting fires with two bits of stick. Church parades and humourless meetings in draughty Orange Halls just didn't compare. There were church parades – no organization was without this half-spiritual, half-martial aspect – and the compensations were cheap holidays with swimming, singing and hiking in kilts, strange broad-rimmed khaki hats and staves – when we moved up to the Scouts. And we were practical: we were taught how to build trestle bridges, dig and clean out latrines, and tie every conceivably useful knot – except a hangman's noose, a slip-knot, which was apparently illegal.

The ethos of the movement was rooted in Edwardian paternalism, which the scout masters tried to teach to us from Baden-Powell's book *Scouting for Boys*. We pledged solemn vows, learning the instincts of obedience and deference to authority. Once I made the transition from the Cubs to the Scouts, I began to be uncomfortable with the weekly oath of loyalty to the Queen and what I came to see as the pronouncedly authoritarian and militaristic nature of the movement, with its adulation of Lord Rowallan, the Chief Scout. Camping and hiking were still OK, but most of our time was spent in Scout Halls chanting mantras of obedience and loyalty, tying knots, identifying strange trees and acquiring other arcane skills which would be as much use to us as algebra. This was July 1958 and my schoolmates were hanging around chip shops and the new coffee bars, listening to rock and roll on the juke boxes, talking about clothes, 'the dancin'' and girls.

X X X

My relationship with the Scouts ended during a camp at Aboyne in Aberdeenshire's Dee Valley.

The weather was wet and overcast with leaden skies and everyone was slightly down – except of course the scoutmasters. My pal at the time was a rough-and-ready working-class boy, not at all the sort of person you would expect to meet among the young toffs of Hyndland, where our troop was based. He was disliked by the senior troop leaders who constantly niggled him, singling him out for nasty jobs when our other work had been completed and we wanted to go off exploring on our own.

We were chatting by a burn which ran alongside the campsite when someone pushed my friend in the burn as a 'joke'. His response was to push his assailant in the river. Within minutes the camp was in an uproar. The result of this 'rammy' was that my friend and I were punished with fatigues. Having completed our tasks, we went off into the woods without asking permission. As we left the clearing, one of the troop leaders called us back, but we ignored him and continued on our way.

When we returned about an hour later the atmosphere was tense and my friend was still furious. Someone made a sarcastic comment to him and the next thing he was lashing out at the group who had been taunting him. Piling on top of him, they tied him up with a rope and ran off.

By the time I untied him he was in a murderous temper. He picked up an axe and ran off after his tormentors screaming blue murder. Luckily I managed to cool him down before he decapitated the cream of the rising generation of Glasgow's Kelvinside gentry.

x x x

The following morning my pal and I held an unofficial boulder-throwing competition. Inspired by the young protagonist in the film *Geordie*, the idea was to hurl the largest boulder as far as possible across the burn on to a ledge which overhung a narrow winding lane we believed to be unused.

Unfortunately, we were wrong. I realised my mistake a few seconds after my boulder reached the apex of its trajectory and started on its downward journey. Round the corner came a large red limousine, a gleaming Austin Princess. The boulder bounced from the bonnet to the windscreen, on to the roof and finally bounced off the boot. The whole thing was over in seconds and the car had not stopped. Early next day the same car drove back down the lane in the opposite direction and stopped at the spot where it had been hit. The driver – who turned out to be the laird who owned the estate – got out and shouted across the burn to the scoutmaster. To give him his due, the troop leader, who knew nothing of what happened, lied profusely in our defence. He apologised, saying that it was an accident and that I had gone straight to him immediately afterwards and explained what had happened, but he had assumed that I had missed the car as no one had complained at the time. The laird spluttered that he hadn't stopped because he thought he was being ambushed by a gang of anarchists and had driven on in fear of his life.

I asked the troop leader afterwards for an explanation of this terrible word. Anarchists, he said, were wicked individuals who went about trying to remove from their land kind, decent people like the laird. They did not believe he should keep his own property even though his ancestors had fought for it.

Anarchists were considered much worse even than Catholics as they did not believe in the law at all. Catholics only wanted to worship God in their own way, but anarchists were against God, government and good manners. At least, this is how the scoutmaster, a high church episcopalian not imbued with Orange sympathies, explained it to me. From his manner I gathered that he considered my friend and me to be taking the first steps along the fastest road to damnation.

Later that evening some of my friends joked that we should become anarchists and fight him for it. But apparently only ancestors were allowed to do things like that. The thought crossed my mind that the land might be mine as much as the laird's – my ancestors from Glen Christie further up the Dee Valley had most likely fought his ancestors' battles for him.

As for the Scouting movement, Mowgli had finally lost his magic for me, and by the end of that summer I hung up my lanyard and departed.

X X X

One of the places where I felt a thrill similar to the Orange Order, or the Cubs, or the movies, was my English class. Perhaps many young Scots did.

English was my favourite subject, but I couldn't warm to Shakespeare in the classroom. He simply had no resonance with us. The language was remote and difficult, as was the historical period, and I lacked the broader knowledge that gave Shakespeare some meaning to me later in life when I saw his plays as dealing with the struggle for power, contention between elite families, and the frequent triumph of the strong over the weak.

There was only one respect in which Shakespeare's politics were evident to a twelve year old boy from Glasgow: John of Gaunt's death-bed speech in *Richard II* (Act 2, Scene 1) seemed to me to sum up the smug, complacent, self-satisfied nature of Englishness (as though such a unified concept thing ever existed). I don't suppose there's much difference between John of Gaunt's sentiments and the more mawkish 'Here's tae us, wha's like us, damn few – an' they're a' deid' mantra of the Scotsman in his cups; the sort of Scottishness which defines itself purely in relation to things English. At an age when children are looking for their communities, Shakespeare wasn't it; but Robert Burns was. For young working-class Scottish schoolboys in the mid-1950s, nothing in Shakespeare could match Burns's spine-tingling inspiring call to liberty and resistance to oppression in 'Bruce's Address to his army at Bannockburn'.

This was not just 'our side is better than your side' stuff – it had a content and a cause. Burns, whose poems we read and discussed in English classes and whose songs we sang in music lessons, was a poet and songwriter who genuinely stirred in us a love for individualism, equality and above all freedom from tyranny. Burns was my first encounter with the emotions and ideals I've since come to call socialism. Who could grow up to be anything but a class war socialist on reading Burns' clarion call to egalitarianism in 'A Man's A Man For A' That'.

In 1950s Britain, titles, rank and station, the divisions between higher and lower classes, and priority and deference in social relations were all-pervasive. No matter how well camouflaged, it seemed to me that the war and the welfare state had done nothing to alter the fact that the whole hierarchical system existed to maintain the comfort of the few.

x x x

By 1959, Mr Lough, the minister, had decided to give up his charge in Kelvinbridge and move to a new living in Lockerbie in the Scottish borders. My Granny was forced to retire and move to Blantyre to live with Mum at 108 Calder Street, an off-cream pebble-dashed four-in-a-block council house, with 'Tam Broon' (Tom Brown) and my half-sister, Olivia. It was Tam Broon and Blantyre, strangely enough, that gave me a political framework for my thoughts and feelings.

Blantyre was founded on coal, but it had also been at one time the centre of a cotton industry. It was now a small declining pit town seven miles or so west of Glasgow, skirting the industrial perimeter of Lanarkshire with its belching chimneys, blast furnaces, canals and gasometers. Its focal points were the main shop, the Co-operative, two cinemas, two cafes (Mickey's and Vince's), a dance hall (the Co-op hall), a Presbyterian Church and a Roman Catholic Chapel with their associated schools, and the Blantyre Miners' Welfare, the hub of the community. Tam was a miner.

Gran despised Tam, although she was always diplomatic – she had to be as we were all now living under his roof – but the tension was always there. For this reason, Gran was mostly to be found visiting close friends, Cissie and Paddy Long. It was the first time since I was eight years old that I spent any time at home with an adult man and I was half horrified, half captivated.

Tam was tall, broad-shouldered, avuncular and a pipe-smoker like his hero Joe Stalin, with a sallow, waxy complexion. According to my Mum, it had been the shape of the back of his neck that attracted her to him. His hair was thick and brown, slightly wavy, and he had brown eyes and a thin-lipped mouth. Mum claimed he was considered the best-looking man in Blantyre at the time. To the outside world Tam was charming, personable, engaging and generous. He blossomed in the company of his drinking cronies, with whom he talked incessantly about politics and 'socialism'. At home, he would sit in his favourite chair in the back bedroom reading the paper, spitting relentlessly into the fireplace, usually missing and covering the tiles with congealed black spit, presumably coloured by coal dust from his lungs or distillations of the dark pipe tobacco he smoked.

When he had a drink in him – which was most nights – he was a Jekyll and Hyde character, moody, violent, petty-minded, jealous, physically and mentally abusive and, worst of all, a bully.

Tam was a near perfect negative role model for a young boy. He defined himself by his politics, which he culled from the Communist Party–influenced *Reynolds News* (the Sunday version of the CP's own *Daily Worker*), and from the beer and whisky-fuelled conversations in the Blantyre Miners' Welfare. He called himself a 'socialist' and a 'fellow traveller', but in reality he was neither. His was the ideology of the shop steward Fred Kite, played by Peter Sellers in the film *I'm All Right, Jack!* Tam never attended any political meetings other than those that happened to take place in the

Reynolds
News

Miners' Welfare when he was in the bar, but he was always discussing politics with his friends who came round on a Saturday or Sunday afternoon or after a night on the drink.

Despite what I came to see as the hollowness of Tam's political ideas, I was captivated by the ideas and stories that were bandied around during these radical conversations. They seemed to have all the energy of Robbie Burns, and the moral decisiveness of the movies, and also tapped into some basic unease I felt about the way the world seemed to be put together. When I could, I would ask questions, and their answers would lead to me wanting to know more and more about socialism and this thing they called the 'class struggle'.

My First Anarchists

Never quite satisfied with what I heard, I began to seek out books on the subject of socialism. Gradually, that emerging idea began to dominate my thoughts and my reading. And of course I wanted something to happen, for us to take some action. The Labour Party seemed to offer the means of doing that, but almost as soon as I was aware of the connection, I saw that the miners were extremely ambivalent about the party that was meant to represent them. They would no sooner vote Tory than fly in the air, but there was definitely a cynical edge to their voices when they spoke about the Labour Party. They gave it their nominal allegiance, but they did not trust it. Many spoke sympathetically of the Communist Party. For most, though, their sympathy was nostalgic.

Miners enjoyed life and were extraordinarily well-read, and for the most part their company was stimulating. There was little posturing in their lives: you could see the genuine appreciation on their faces as they listened to the songs of Enrico Caruso or the Negro working class hero and Communist fellow traveller Paul Robeson on the wireless or on the wind-up gramophones or record players in living rooms of the council houses and miners' rows. It could be felt in their voices as they sang the The Red Flag, Old Man River or Joe Hill in the Miners' Welfare or on their way home from the pit.

It was outside the Miners' Welfare and in our front room that I came across my first real anarchists, communists and socialists. I listened enthralled to fascinating and inspiring stories about the moral courage and determination of men and women who believed in 'the idea' – socialism. Although I had no idea what they stood for, I had heard and seen anarchists at street-corner meetings in Glasgow, with **Guy Aldred** my Gran, and she had pointed out Guy Aldred, the 'Knickerbocker Politician' to me on a couple of occasions. (He was easy to spot: he always wore knickerbockers.) Aldred had become the most famous Scottish anarchist of his time because of his ferocious campaigning on behalf of birth control and Indian independence, and the fact that he stood as a candidate in all the local and general elections. (As an anarchist, Aldred believed that elections achieved nothing for the working classes, but they gave him a platform to argue the case for anarchist communism and denounce parliamentary parties and politicians. On the hustings, he always urged voters not to vote for him and pledged that if elected, he would not take up his seat. He was never elected so it never became an issue.) Aldred had been imprisoned on several occasions for his beliefs, having made memorable and impassioned political defences from the dock. He died in 1963 with two shillings in his pocket, having donated his body to medical research. The name of Guy Aldred was widely known and respected around Scotland.

x x x

Some of the radical miners I came across in Blantyre were **Radical** spellbinding talkers. Their rhetoric combined sentiment with hard **Miners** fact, and their charm and patter mollified even the most bitter of adversaries – until the drink kicked in. Their intellectual powers and understanding of the world seemed more suited to a university lecture hall than the Miners' Welfare. Here were men with an enormous capacity for emotion, men full of Celtic fire who spoke straight from the heart and who could win over a hostile audience in minutes. Other names spoken of reverentially were those of Davie Kirkwood, Mannie Shinwell and the Communist Party leader, Willie Gallagher –

the so-called 'Scottish Lenin'. But none of them, especially Gallagher, could hold a candle to the socialist republican leader, the 'great' John
John
MacLean
MacLean – the daddy of them all.

MacLean, who died on 30 November 1923 aged forty-four, had acquired mythic status among the Scottish working classes, like Zapata among the peasants of Morelos. He had entered the pantheon. From a Highland Calvinist background and brought up on stories of the bitter injustices of the Highland Clearances, MacLean's opposition to the First World War – agitating, organising and educating – was inspiring to the workers and highly dangerous to the government. If revolution were to have erupted in Scotland in 1916–17, John MacLean would have provided the moral courage and inspiration. His was the authentic radical voice of 'Red Clydeside'. Jailed twice for sedition during the First World War, for resisting conscription and advocating class war against capitalism as the only war worth waging, the government was twice forced to release him because of the enormous public outcry. The second time he was released from prison – only a few weeks after being sentenced to a seven-year sentence – over 200,000 people turned out to meet him at Glasgow's Central Railway Station. Here was a man, a teacher, a passionate advocate of adult education and working class socialist leader who had been imprisoned and tortured for his beliefs.

x x x

Among the books recommended by my enthusiastic mentors were Edward Bellamy's *Looking Backward*, Robert Tressell's *Ragged Trousered Philanthropists*, Marx and Engels' *Communist Manifesto* and Marx's *Capital*. I doubt if many of them had read *Capital* themselves, but that didn't stop them peppering the discussion with knowing references to dialectical materialism, the labour theory of value, the divisions of labour within a capitalist economy – and Stalin's murder of Trotsky. The ideas they talked about were exciting: socialism, pacifism, fighting injustice, building a fair and just society, an end to poverty and want and war. The people they spoke of were brave and inspiring, and the struggles heroic: the

Clyde Workers' Committee of the First World War; Black Friday 1919, the day the tanks arrived in George Square; the 1926 General Strike; the economic depression of the 1930s; the betrayal of Ramsay Macdonald's Labour Government – and the Spanish Civil War.

x x x

The Spanish
Civil War

The Spanish Civil War had been fought more than twenty years before, between 1936 and 1939. Spain seemed a long way from Blantyre of the 1960s, but its Civil War wasn't. The Second World War had followed, and for most people eclipsed the war in Spain; but for me, and for thousands of people I was to meet over the next twenty years, Franco's victory over Spain's young Republic marked the end of the last purely idealistic cause of the twentieth century.

In the preface to the book *l'Espagne Libre* in 1946, the year of my birth, Albert Camus said of the Spanish struggle:

> It is now nine years that men of my generation have had Spain within their hearts. Nine years that they have carried it with them like an evil wound.
>
> It was in Spain that men learned that one can be right and yet be beaten, that force can vanquish spirit, that there are times when courage is not its own recompense. It is this, doubtless, which explains why so many men, the world over, regard the Spanish drama as a personal tragedy.

Some people, like Camus, saw the event as a dispiriting tragedy. Some saw it as an enduring cause. It remained personal partly because Franco lived on, the last of the Axis powers, continuing to oppress the people of Spain, but also because a number of those who themselves travelled from Scotland to Spain to fight in defence of the Republic lived on. For Tam's generation, the war had been a moral line in the sand – when Franco began his war to overthrow the elected government of Spain, thousands of idealistic young men and women from all over the world had travelled to Spain to fight in the

International Brigades against the fascists. They went – and often sacrificed their lives – not because their country told them to, but to help build a new world.

Many Blantyre miners had fought in Spain and three who had fought in the British Battalion of the XV International Brigade had died at the battle of Jarama. Their names were spoken with reverence – Tom Brannan, Tom Flecks and Willie Fox. Ethel MacDonald, a local woman from Motherwell, just a few miles up the road from Blantyre, had been a regular broadcaster on the English-language programmes of the Barcelona anarchist radio station. She managed to make it back to Glasgow, where she still lived.

SPAIN, 1936

General Franco was commander of the Spanish army based in Morocco. On 17 July 1936, under the overall leadership of General Sanjurjo and with the aggressive support of the Church, Franco and several other generals rose against the five-year old Second Spanish Republic.

The Spanish anarcho-syndicalist labour union, the Confederación Nacional del Trabajo (CNT), had been aware of the rightist plot and had been preparing for a coup for some time and while the government dithered, armed trade unionists were waiting for the soldiers to come out of their barracks at dawn on 19 July. Within a matter of days, the rising had been defeated in around half of Spain, mainly in the industrial north. Political and military power on the Republican side now lay in the hands of the popular committees.

This spontaneous action by the workers fired elemental hopes among Spanish workers and peasants –

hopes fuelled by over sixty years of anarchist
agitation – and threatened to transform Spain into a
different sort of socialist society from the Soviet
Union. Spain might just show the world the way of
free communism – of anarchy.

From the very first moment of the rising, the
initiative had passed from a hesitant bourgeoisie not
to the intellectuals, or party or union leaders – but
to the rank and file of the organised working class.
George Orwell described Barcelona in *Homage to
Catalonia*. 'It was the first time I had ever been in
a town where the working class was in the saddle.
Practically every building of any size had been
seized by the workers and was draped with red flags
or with the red and black flag of the anarchists ...'
It was this that excited people from across the world
to come and fight, not to restore the government, but
to help form a new type of society.

Soon, though, the bourgeoisie and the Spanish
Communist Party, the PCE, joined forces, sponsored by
Stalin, and by 1936, the restored central government
attempted to crush the popular revolution, claiming
to be uniting the country against the fascists.

Pravda of 17 December 1936 left no doubt as to what
Comintern policy in Spain was to be: 'As for
Catalonia, the purging of Trotskyist and anarcho-
syndicalist elements has begun; this work will be
carried out with the same energy with which it was
done in the USSR.'

By May 1937, the anarchist-led social revolution
was over. The Communist-controlled republic proceeded
to lose the war against the fascists.

What I learned was that this brief flowering of socialism and democracy had been nipped in the bud because the Great Powers of the West preferred to see a fascist dictatorship in power rather than the legally elected body chosen by the people overthrown by General Franco.

The other crucial piece of information I learned from listening to the miners' banter was that the Spanish Civil War had been lost not only because the Great Powers refused to intervene to help, but because the one who did, at a price – the Soviet Union – tried to turn the spontaneous movement into a specifically Stalinist one, going so far as to undermine and even betray those on the same side who viewed socialism in different terms. The pro-Republican International Brigades had been formed as a result of people flocking to Spain spontaneously to fight fascism and the forces of reaction. Some were Communist Party members, but many were not. But as the war went on, it became increasingly clear that the Commissars of the Communist Party were determined to win the propaganda war as much – more – than the war against the fascists. The struggle had to be seen in their terms, and as a vindication of Stalinist policy, whereas the reality was the majority of fighters on the left were there not to support Stalin but to fight Franco. They were not there to replace one tyranny with another, but to oppose tyranny. This was a political sore which would never heal, not even in early 1960s Blantyre.

The International Brigades

x x x

The irreconcilable divide between Communists, Trotskyists and what I came to recognize as anarchists manifested itself most Saturday nights at chucking out time at the Miners' Welfare, when tempers were frayed and passions running high. The arguments inevitably boiled down to responsibility for what was known as the 'Events of May' 1937 when the anarcho-syndicalist controlled telephone exchange and anti-Stalinist Marxist militias in Barcelona were attacked by Communist Party-led troops. The final loss of political innocence was the realization that jackboots were not the exclusive property of fascists. These recriminations usually ended in a punch-up.

Spain was the main story, but certainly not the only one. I also sat enthralled listening to descriptions of conditions in the pits under pre-nationalisation coal owners such as the Duke of Hamilton. Many miners had come to Lanarkshire with their families after being driven from their original homes during the Highland Clearances by people like the Duke of Sutherland. These dukes were men whose fortunes were built on the blood and tears and labour of the working class.

Some stories were heated, some wistful, the moving accounts of selfless bravery, working conditions in the mine, explosions of firedamp and mining disasters. Going down the pit was a seriously life-endangering activity. Everyone lived in dread of the ominous and continuous sounding of the pit hooter signaling death underground. Those who heard the sound would immediately rush to the pithead fearing the worst for their loved ones. Hardly a Saturday night would go by without someone launching into the heartrending account of the Blantyre Explosion, a folk song commemorating the Dixon's pit disaster of October 1877 in which upwards of 120 men and boys had died. Blantyre and the surround mining communities had experienced many disasters in the coalfields since the early nineteenth century.

THE BLANTYRE EXPLOSION

By Clyde's bonny banks as A sadly did wander
Amang the pit heaps as evening drew nigh;
A spied a young lassie aa dressed in deep mournin
A-weepin an wailin wi mony's the sigh.

A stepped up beside her an thus did address her:
'Come tell me the cause o yer trouble an pain.'
Sabbin an sighin, at last she did answer
'Johnnie Murphy, kind sir, wis ma ain true love's name.'

'Twenty-wan years o age, fu o youth an guid lookin
Tae wark doun the mine at High Blantyre he came,

The weddin was fixed, aa the guests were invited
That calm simmer's evenin young Johnnie wis slain.'

The explosion wis heard, aa the women an children
Wi pale anxious faces thae haste tae the mine.
Whan the news wis made out, the hills rang wi thair mournin
A hundred an twanty young miners were slain.

Nou sweetherts an wives an sisters an brithers
That Blantyre explosion thae'll never forget;
An aa you young miners that hears ma sad story
Shed a tear for the miners wha're laid tae thair rest.

Conversations ranged from British intervention in Suez and Cyprus to the Berlin uprising in 1953, Khrushchev's 1956 revelations about the gulags and the atrocities committed in the name of Marxist Leninism following Stalin's death, and the invasion of Hungary in 1956. The Communist Party seemed to have as bad a name as the Tory Party by the end of the 1950s, but working class loyalty to the Labour Party remained firm among most of the miners, in spite of all its historic betrayals.

But whereas the more ancient wrongs and injustices of the British class system had become part of the scenery as it were, the question of General Franco and his overthrow of the Spanish Republic in 1939 remained unresolved. The issues here seemed very clear-cut. The miners still felt strongly about the defeat of the Spanish workers and glorified the International Brigades. I simply could not understand why the Allies had permitted Franco to remain in power after 1945. Had they or their Soviet allies not overthrown the fascist governments of Germany, Italy, Hungary, Romania, Bulgaria and Japan? A good part of the rest of my life was spent coming to an understanding of that reticence.

The Berlin Wall and
Calder Street Secondary

Two events in 1960 accelerated my politicisation. The first was news of the infamous Sharpeville Massacre in South Africa, at which scores of people demonstrating against further apartheid laws were shot dead and hundreds more were wounded. The shock reached every corner of the world, and opened my eyes to the unjust and cruel nature of Verwoerd's apartheid regime. And although South Africa was expelled from the Commonwealth, it didn't seem enough. Why weren't Western (or even Communist) governments doing more to help South Africa's black population?

There was no one in Blantyre to ask. Tam and his contemporaries tended to shrug their shoulders as though this was a matter for governments or the United Nations to do something about, not individuals. Most of my own mates were bemused that I should concern myself with things like that. I should be more concerned with football and fashion and pulling birds on a Saturday night at the dancing or ice-skating rink. And although I *was* interested in all that too, I felt I had no like-minded people I could talk to about these important issues. I felt quite isolated, and heroic: it was me against the world.

The second event was the election of that great beacon of hope for liberal consciousnesses everywhere, JFK. Although we didn't fully recognize at the time what a crook he was (despite the give-away of his being a Catholic!), we should have. His support for the witch-finder general, Joe McCarthy, was no secret, and nor was the fact that he was the son of a bootlegger directly connected with organized crime, a pro-Nazi sympathizer to boot. Of course, there were some round our way who supported JFK, thinking it was better to have a Democrat than a Republican in the White House, and that this small change might lead to much bigger ones. As it turned out, Kennedy initiated a whole new era in American imperialism, playing with the fates of his South American neighbours and manufacturing a stand-off with the Soviet Union over nuclear missiles in Cuba that threatened the very existence of the world, but also merely symbolized the bipolarization that he presided over in every country between him and the USSR.

Much of this was for the future, but even by the middle of 1960 international tension had built up from Laos to Berlin. In West Berlin, in July, President Kennedy added to the sense of impending doom by pledging that America would go to war if necessary to uphold the freedom of the city. Amid mounting rumours that the East Berlin authorities were planning to seal off East Berlin, thousands fled to the western sector. In July alone an estimated 30,000 people fled from East to West, and on 13 August a barbed wire barrier was erected across Germany, to be replaced five days later by the permanent Berlin Wall itself.

x x x

While I was learning about these world events and what they might mean, I also had to go to school – Calder Street Secondary.

If the miners of Blantyre conducted my education by night, during the day I fell under the spell of my English teacher, George Bradford. I don't know if my interest in history developed through literature, or vice versa, but Bradford nurtured both, and the desire to learn about much else besides. His English classes made me want to learn about everything I could. Even the fact that he was obliged to teach Religious Education once a week didn't put me off him, as he inevitably ended a reading from the King James Bible with the words 'And you can believe that if you like!'

(Also irresistible was his skilful line in schoolboy humour. When asked by some wag whether extreme sexual exhaustion was an excuse for missing an exam, George smiled sympathetically at the boy and shook his head. 'Not an excuse. You'll just have to write with your other hand.' My Granny would have had the soap out. George's refusal to be touched by dourness made us love him even more.)

x x x

It was the technical subjects teacher who was the final catalyst for my developing socialism. Shamefully, and perhaps symbolically, I have forgotten his name. He was a Labour Party stalwart and had been a member of the Labour League of Youth, the forerunner of the Young Socialists. When I asked him to write out the words of 'The Red Flag', I

Class of 1960–1961: Calder Street School, Blantyre, Class 3A1. (I am second from the left in the back row.)

became his favourite. I felt as though I had struck emotional gold. Here, at last, was a political soulmate.

My mentor represented the majority of Scottish radical thought at the time: despite constant disappointment, he clung steadfastly to the hope that eventually the Labour Party would bring about a socialist society. He advised me that to change the world I should join the Young Socialists, the youth section of the Labour Party.

He was also an amateur magician and would select me to demonstrate his tricks whenever we had a free period. In woodwork classes my classmates were always nudging me to suggest to him a magic show rather than turning wooden lamp bases on a lathe.

The last English essay I wrote before leaving school in May 1961 was a biographical sketch of Karl Marx, together with a synopsis of *The Communist Manifesto*, outlining Marx and Engels' views of revolution as a consequence of the class struggle. Most of other students wrote about their holidays.

The Communist Manifesto was the only one of Marx and Engels' works that I could get to grips with. I had tried to hack my way into *Das Kapital* but found it mind-numbingly boring; I simply couldn't comprehend the dense complexities of his language, or the abstractions of his economic theory. Economics was not the reason I was interested in politics. I was much more inspired, as I suspect most young people interested in politics are, by the moral and ethical than the economic. Of course, Marx's key point is that economic injustices underpin all others, and much of my reading of socialist literature has been an exploration of how and why that is the case (and how it might be different), but still, the stuff that stirs the soul is the treatment of people rather than the treatment of money.

The Communist Manifesto, however, even though it was written in 1848, was moral in tone and a lot more penetrating in its identification of the bourgeoisie as the real bad guys of history. (All thoughts that seem even truer today than 150 years ago: 'The bourgeoisie . . . has left remaining no other nexus between man and man than naked self-interest, than callous cash-payment. It has resolved personal worth into exchange value, and in place of the numberless indefeasible chartered freedoms, has set up that single unconscionable freedom – Free Trade. In one word, for exploitation veiled by religious and political illusions, it has substituted naked, shameless, direct, brutal exploitation.') Marx and Engels had a slightly nostalgic view of the value of the priest and religion that I didn't share – in my view the bourgeoisie and the priesthood were bogeymen in the same conspiracy against the common good – but these were terms I felt much more comfortable with.

x x x

As Blantyre had no second hand bookshops, I spent a lot of time in the public library. I had never seen rooms and shelves filled with so many books. Apart from my own collection of *Just William*, *Jennings* and *Billy Bunter* books, Tam only had Reader's Digest anthologies and Agatha Christie novels. I was overwhelmed when I discovered that I could borrow any book I wanted (except certain ones, such as

Havelock Ellis on sex, which were kept under lock and key in the back room for an unspecified class of person that didn't include me). So much knowledge, so much wisdom, so many perspectives and possibilities. I had no idea where to begin. Finally I took out Ripley's *Believe It or Not* which I devoured overnight (a telling choice, some might say) and returned the next day to borrow something else.

Two young librarians took me under their wing. They were in their late teens or early twenties and active in the local Campaign for Nuclear Disarmament. I began to hang out with them socially, meeting them on their Saturdays off and helping out distributing CND leaflets at Motherwell and Hamilton Cross. My view of librarians and academics – they were one and the same thing in my mind at the time, I think – had been formed largely by the film of Kingsley Amis's *Lucky Jim*, so I remember feeling slightly shocked by these two young men's radical thought and borderline criminality. From then on librarians became my role models – the new bohemians – and I wanted to be one.

x x x

At the library I discovered two books that confirmed that the 'grown-up' world (or the Establishment, as I quickly learnt to call it) was as fundamentally repressive as I had always felt: Joseph Heller's *Catch 22* and J.D. Salinger's *The Catcher in the Rye*.

The Catcher was a revelation to me, as it has been to so many teenagers – almost as though some telepathic distance-reader had cracked my psychic code. It was unlike all other books I had read, which had a thread of coherent wisdom and black and white certainty running through them. Instead, *The Catcher in the Rye* focused on human frailties and unpredictability. Holden Caufield's frustration at the debasing compromises of the adult world – the phoneys – was precisely mine.

Yossarian, the protagonist of Joseph Heller's *Catch 22*, was another hero. I'd seen Joseph Heller interviewed on television around the time his book was published, and I was attracted to its anti-war inclination. What I first read as Yossarian's paranoia and Heller's sharp satire soon seemed not like fiction at all, but coded reality. The self-perpetuating nature of power and abuses of authority were not metaphors – that was truly and accurately how the system worked. It felt like a blinding flash of insight.

My librarian friends pointed me in the direction of Bertrand Russell (a leading member of CND at the time) and R. G. Ingersoll (whose arguments confirmed my own instincts about the Catholic Church – although they also forced me to relinquish my affection for the Presbyterians, whose Calvinist creed he thought was the worst of all), but the author who summed up the blend of heroism and political insight that was most powerful for me was Howard Fast. Fast's horrifying book *Eyewitness: Peekskill, USA* was an account of the riots caused by two concerts Paul Robeson, the famous black singer, gave in 1949 close to the town of Peekskill, New York, in support of the Harlem Chapter of the Civil Rights Congress. These riots were displays of racism as disgusting and disturbing as the Sharpeville massacre, and they happened in the Home of the Free. Fast's other great work, of course, was the novel *Spartacus*, which in 1960 was made into the film of the same name. For weeks after seeing the film my school friends and I would re-enact the hillside scene after the final battle shouting 'Am Spartacus'. 'Naw yer no. Am Spartacus', 'Naw yer no, Am Spartacus!' The film and the novel are obvious parables about tyranny and heroic resistance; it has always been curious to me that my friends would engage with the fantasy of Rome and slaves, but not the much more compelling reality of Spain, or America, or even Scotland.

x x x

Lady Chatterley's Lover For a boy interested in books, politics and of course sex, the *Lady Chatterley's Lover* case was a watershed. I knew that there were books we weren't allowed to read in the library, but apparently there were some that weren't even allowed to be printed. *Lady Chatterley's Lover* by D. H. Lawrence was one of these. The Internet age (although it causes frustrations of its own) has made it difficult to imagine the frustration of living in a state that decided what its citizens were fit to read. When Allen Lane of Penguin Books decided to mark the 30th anniversary of Lawrence's death by publishing *Lady Chatterley's Lover* for the first time in the UK, in defiance of the absurdly archaic Obscene Publications Act, the population was electrified. Almost everyone of my age took an interest in the case, certainly the boys (we were too embarrassed to speak to the girls about anything to do with sex), most of whom had previously little or no interest in politics, some of whom became more permanently radicalized by the event.

Ostensibly, the book tells of Lady Chatterley's adulterous affair with Oliver Mellors, the family gamekeeper, and details some of their erotic meetings. But it wasn't just Lawrence's relatively tame descriptions of the couple's sex that upset the Establishment; it was the novel's subtext – that the working class could be sexier than the upper class, crippled as it was by war and convention – that made this one of the most important political, social and cultural trials in British criminal history. When the prosecuting barrister Mervyn Griffith-Jones asked the jury in all seriousness whether it was a book one would want one's 'maidservant or wife' to read, he distilled the paternalistic Edwardian culture that was actually on trial – Griffith-Jones may have lived in the same country as the rest of us, but he was clearly from a different planet. He showed that the trial wasn't about the sex, it was about the power, and the politics. Arguably, the case came to trial because the book was going to be published in the relatively new paperback format, something the masses could buy.

The *Lady Chatterley's Lover* trial was not the end of the Obscene Publications Act; others followed such as that of Hubert Selby Junior's *Last Exit to Brooklyn* in 1967, but the trial of Lady C was a harbinger of all that was to come in the 1960s.

I don't know what the total sales figures for this book were, but because of the trial, the first print-run of 200,000 copies was sold out in days. It took me a few weeks to get hold of my own copy, which I had to buy in Glasgow, as did lots of the boys at school, just to see what the fuss was about. I wasn't particularly impressed and can remember my disappointment at the poor quality of sexual explicitness. Mellors braiding a daisy chain through Lady C's pubic

51

hair and a reference to him 'approaching Lady C from behind,' and taking her 'short and sharp, and finished, like an animal.' Not a lot to go on there for a pubescent lad.

When I did eventually get my hands on a copy, I was seen by one of the teachers, deeply engrossed in it on my way to Calder Street School. Mr Bradford had been leading an animated and interesting discussion on censorship in our English class (I can't imagine that any of the boys there thought that they should be protected from reading the book, but I do seem to remember that passions were running high). Apparently the book's publication had triggered an even more heated discussion in the school staffroom, and a section of the staff – led by the RE and music teachers – thought that this dangerously liberal English teacher was determined to corrupt the youth.

The teacher who saw me was the 'religious education' teacher, a sourfaced old crone, and after she vented her spleen at me in RE class, I wrote a short essay addressing the rhetorical question 'Why should I be a conformist?' It was full of indignation and rebellion; it was a cry to be alive and to be different. The truth was that in many ways I wasn't different. Adolescents have always rebelled against the previous generation (I presume; it certainly feels that way to me now), and they've simultaneously wanted to belong.

x x x

During my Blantyre years, I mixed with a small gang of teenagers that hung around Vince's chip shop in the Glasgow Road, and occasionally Mickey's Café near the Roman Catholic Chapel. Vince, a second-generation Lanarkshire Italian, had a juke box around which we spent a good part of our time and our money playing the latest records – Eddie Cochrane's 'Three Steps to Heaven', Del Shannon, Roy Orbison, Brian Poole and the Tremeloes, Johnny Cash, Ian Menzies and the Clyde Valley Stompers. The favoured Glasgow anthem, however, was Hank Locklin's 'Wild Side of Life'. This was our music and it set us apart from all older generations. It gave us our exclusivity.

For pocket money I carried pails of coal on Saturday mornings for Vince's fryers. I had to do this at home as well, so I was an accomplished coal carrier. Tam, being a miner, had a free ton of coal delivered every quarter, courtesy of the National Coal Board (NCB). This was dumped on the pavement outside our gate and I had to shift it to the coal shed in a pail. A milk and paper round also brought in extra pocket money. In the summer we went berry picking in the fruit-growing district around Lanark, hawking our services around the orchards and farms for a shilling a pail of gooseberries or whatever. It was painful work, particularly when I discovered I was allergic to gooseberry spines.

My pals, older than me, were mostly Catholics. One or two were Protestants but that didn't seem to matter, either to them or to us. The Catholics knew I had been in the Lodge, but they didn't take it seriously. I obviously wasn't a bigot and they weren't tools of Rome. Our concern was to 'pull the lasses', not to interpret the will of God or discuss the role of prelacy. This makes my decision around this time to join the Blantyre Junior Orange Lodge even more peculiar.

On an intellectual level, I saw the Roman Catholic Church in almost demonic terms, the sworn enemy of social justice and intellectual freedom, and the root of much of the evil in the world. I had certainly rejected any notion of God and Divine Providence by that time. The thing that seemed important to me was the struggle to be human in this world, not righteousness in the next. Strangely, even as an Orangeman I still regarded myself as a socialist. I certainly wasn't anti-Catholic or even pro-Unionist. Who knows? Perhaps it was an expression of a feeling experienced by people who join such organisations today – a frustration at one's situation in life; a frustration that nothing is changing, or certainly not fast enough, and a feeling that unless you do something the bad guys, whoever they are, always win.

In any case, my membership of the Orange Lodge was short-lived. After my second meeting, when I was being sworn in I realised just how ludicrous the whole charade was. I took the oath to the Lodge on bended knee in a darkened room. As I raised my left and rested the other on the Holy Bible (King James version, of course), a massive tome supported by a card table, the table suddenly collapsed with the bible closed on the floor and me along with it, rolling about in tears of hysterical laughter.

Surrounded in the initiation circle by the grim, unsmiling faces and tightly puckered mouths of the brethren, it was clear they were not amused by my lack of gravitas. The ill-omened incident indicated dark forces were at work. I never went back.

x x x

One Sunday afternoon, when I was sixteen, Tam came back from the Miners' Welfare in a foul mood. He seemed determined to pick a fight with me, no matter what, and started a venomous tirade. Unable to provoke me with his verbal banter he finally worked himself up to throw my treasured Dansette portable record player off the table and onto the floor, then started kicking it.

The Dansette was the last straw. I grabbed the poker from the hearth, lunged at him, knocked him to the floor and then, sitting on top of him, started beating the shit out of him with the poker Although he was bigger and stronger than me, he was drunk, which gave me sufficient advantage. I managed to restrain my anger before I really injured him and backed off, thinking he would come to his senses. However, when he recovered he picked up what remained of my Dansette and tossed it down the stairs, ordered my mother and me out of the house – and Olivia with us.

Fortunately, a few months earlier Gran had met and married an elderly ex-miners' union representative, Robert Scott, a perfect gentleman, well-read, well-travelled and dignified, in short everything Tam was not. It was a happy end to an unhappy period in my Gran's and Mum's lives. Other than widows, women without men as their main breadwinners and protectors were second-class citizens. Had Gran not been married to Robert Scott at the time, we would have been out on the street without a roof over our heads. We were in Blantyre now, and the support network Gran could have called on in Glasgow just wasn't there any more.

THE H-BOMB'S THUNDER

Don't you hear the H-bombs' thunder
Echo like the crack of doom?
While they rend the skies asunder
Fall-out makes the earth a tomb;
Do you want your homes to tumble,
Rise in smoke towards the sky?
Will you let your cities crumble,
Will you see your children die?

Cho: Men and women, stand together.
   Do not heed the men of war.
   Make your minds up now or never,
   Ban the bomb for evermore.

Tell the leaders of the nations
Make the whole wide world take heed:
Poison from the radiations
Strikes at every race and creed.
Must you put mankind in danger,
Murder folk in distant lands?
Will you bring death to a stranger,
Have his blood upon your hands?

Shall we lay the world in ruin?
Only you can make the choice.
Stnp and think of what you're doing.
Join the march and raise your voice.
Time is short; we must be speedy.
We can see the hungry filled,
House the homeless, help the needy.
Shall we blast, or shall we build ?

JOHN BRUNNER

No Nukes

Events and my reading were propelling me more and more quickly along the road to socialism. It was 1961 and I felt we were living through dizzyingly exciting times. I was impatient to travel, to experience life and earn money, and so I left school in June 1961, a month before my fifteenth birthday – much to the disappointment of George Bradford who wanted me to continue my education at Hamilton Academy. Kennedy was in the White House, monkeys and men were in space, Americans were trying to invade Cuba, the Berlin Wall had been built, and the Ban the Bomb movement was gathering momentum. I wasn't interested in Hamilton Academy.

I had worked as a messenger boy for a large dental laboratory delivering dentures while still at Woodside School in Glasgow. The process of making dentures from first impression through to delivery of highly polished wallies was creative and satisfying, and the lab technicians were friendly, well-read and interesting people, so I applied for an apprenticeship and was indentured (the literal phrase was used without hint of irony) to the owner, Mr Robert Burns Wilson.

One of my fellow apprentices was on my cultural wavelength: a bohemian youth called Dan Smith. Dan read the same books, liked the same music – trad jazz, skiffle, folk music and rock 'n' roll— and held frighteningly similar political views to my own. Four years older than me and in the final year of his apprenticeship, Dan was a member of the Glasgow Young Socialists, the youth section of the Labour Party, and he invited me to meetings with his close friend, Bill Kane, an apprentice coachbuilder.

Wandering through Kelvingrove Park towards Stobcross Street and the Clyde we would talk endlessly about politics, of jobs and apprenticeships and what we planned to do next with our lives, of sex and books and ideas. We usually ended up on the derelict Finnieston Quays, the now defunct gateway to Empire, kicking stones and cans into the cold mist-covered brown water of the Clyde. One chilling sign of Empire on the quayside toilets confirmed our belief that things had to change – they were marked 'Men' and 'Lascars' (i.e. East Indian sailors).

Although I was just fifteen, I passed for eighteen – either that or no one cared – and I was able to go into pubs for the first time. Dan and his friends drank in the '92', a spartan spit and sawdust pub in Cambridge Street, just a few doors down from the hairdressing salon where my mother worked, and so I had to be careful going in and out in case someone spotted me. That Friday I opened my first wage packet – which was about £2 – and spent more than half of it in the pub. I just managed to catch the last bus to Blantyre, drunk, and when I crept in, Gran was waiting for me behind the door. She had been sitting in the dark, and as I turned on the light she stood up and threw the cup of tea she had in her hand in my direction. I ducked and the tea went all over the wallpaper of the 'best' room, which made her even madder. What had enraged her wasn't just that I'd come home late and drunk but that I'd had the temerity to open my wages, a serious domestic offence. You brought your wages home, untouched, to the woman of the house who gave you an allowance, the amount of which she decided.

x x x

Without doubt, the biggest issue of the day, the one which did the most to politicise us – in much the same way as the Vietnam War politicised the following generation – was the ever present fear of an intentional or accidental nuclear attack on Britain, and the unthinkable and unforeseeable consequences for humanity.

In the late 1950s, some pundits had argued that our generation had no causes left to fight for, and that an affluent society had left the population bored and complacent – exactly the same line of argument one hears today. The anti-nuclear movement showed that to be rubbish, just as the anti-globalization movement has demonstrated in the early twenty-first century.

CND

The Campaign for Nuclear Disarmament (CND) started in February 1958 to co-ordinate the efforts of the smaller, local organizations, and specifically to plan the first march from Trafalgar Square to the Atomic Weapons Research Establishment at Aldermaston for the Easter weekend of 1958. The rapid growth of its membership was an index of how widespread were feelings that we deserved not to live under the constant threat of mass extinction. The CND included religious groups like the Quakers and the Methodists, trade unions and other political groups, concerned individuals, and a number of celebrities like Lord Bertrand Russell, Spike Milligan and the anarchist biologist Dr Alex Comfort, the author of *The Joy of Sex*. It quickly developed into a mass movement of popular protest.

Most rank-and-file CND members were solid, middle-class citizens, political moderates who believed totally in constitutional action, peaceful demonstrations and parliamentary pressure. They simply wanted to get rid of the 'Bomb'. We were all drawn together by a sense of moral outrage at US planes carrying H-bombs patrolling over Britain, US missiles being based in the UK, increasing military reliance on nuclear weapons as well as worries about the effects of nuclear testing.

The CND strategy was simple and concentrated on mustering popular support by orthodox methods - marches, meetings and trying to win the Labour Party and the elite over to a policy of unilateral nuclear disarmament.

Increasingly, however, the younger people like me who were being drawn into the movement didn't believe in winning over the top people. To us, the 'Bomb' was emblematic of a whole system that was corrupt and life-endangering - by definition, the system that had produced the bomb was incapable of abolishing it. We felt that influencing people was preferable to influencing governments.

Tired of CND's lobbying role and waiting for the political parties to take an initiative on the question of the atomic bomb, more committed campaigners came together on 22 October 1960 to form the Committee of 100, an ad hoc body set up to organise mass, non-violent demonstrations against nuclear and biological weapons. Bertrand Russell was one of the founder members of the Committee.

In Scotland, the peace movement sprang into life in 1960 with the stationing of the US Polaris-bearing submarines in the Holy Loch in the Firth of Clyde. The arrival of the nuclear missile fleet turned Glasgow into a prime target for any Soviet pre-emptive nuclear missile strike, and had a major politicising and radicalising effect throughout Scotland. Large numbers of people from all walks of life were drawn to the nuclear disarmament movement by this action, and demonstrations continued on the Holy Loch from the day they arrived.

Scottish Peace Movement

The style of protest that developed – direct action and civil disobedience – was radical, libertarian and extra-parliamentary. It was world-shaking. The demonstration is almost a cliché now, but when the traditional means of getting things changed was a cross letter to the MP or tea with the vicar (with the one noble exception of the 1926 General Strike), demonstrations were a fresh way to seize the initiative. And the new media – television – loved them.

The protest marches I attended from 1961 onwards were good-humoured affairs, with thousands of would-be beatniks, tweedy and tartan-skirted ladies and kilted gents, 'neds' and ordinary folk descending boisterously from the gangways of Clyde steamers onto Dunoon pier. Accompanied by a phalanx of 'lone' amateur pipers and singing along with the strolling guitarists, it was as though the fair had come to town. People with nothing else in common were brought together by their determination that things must change.

The Holy
Loch Demo Morris Blythman described the first major demo, at the Holy Loch on 20 May 1961: 'By train and by bus, in rattle-trap lorries, by hitch of thumb, the motley anti-Polaris crew made for Dunoon and the Holy Loch at every available opportunity. Also at every opportunity, the hard core was singing their protest on station platforms, on quaysides, on the march, from improvised platforms to hastily assembled loudspeaker systems, from floating craft of all shapes and sizes, they sang them sittin' doon, stannin' up, they sang them for the police, they sang them at the police, but most of all they sang them at the very baffled Americans.'

Morris Blythman, better known by his pen-name 'Thurso Berwick', a teacher and radical songwriter, immortalised the protests in his *Ding Dong Dollar* songbook and eventually on the Folkways LP *Ding Dong Dollar*, which was recorded in Josh Macrae's basement at 105 Balgrayhill Road in Springburn.

Morris was one of the key figures in the politically influential folk song revival movement of the 1950s and 60s, and his republican, anti-monarchist and anti-bomb songs were leitmotifs of the time. He did not consider song writing as specialised or elitist. He believed folk songs could be written by anyone and that everyone had at least one good song in them. Morris's own songs, many of which were often rewritten collectively in folk 'workshops', provided a cheery musical glue which bound us together.

Folk singers and song writers played a big part on those Dunoon marches, reinforcing the air of excitement and high optimism: as well as Morris and Marion Blythman, other 'weel-kent' names were Josh Macrae, Bobby Campbell, Gordon McCulloch, Hamish Imlach, Nigel Denver, Jim McLean, Jackie O'Connor, and of course the inimitable Matt McGinn.

Josh Macrae was the best-known Glasgow folk singer of the day. Tall, droll and handsome – he was a latter-day Rabbie Burns. He had had some hit records and had real national star potential, but he was satisfied and happy with life teaching art at Adelphi Street School and had no desire to move to London. Josh's light-heartedly ironic 'Talking Army Blues' did make it to number six in the 1959 Hit Parade, but his most famous record was the most decidedly un-blues-like 'Messing About on the River', written by Tony Hatch. Josh lived one house down from the Blythmans in Springburn.

x x x

In mid-September 1961, the Committee of 100 organized a weekend of major demonstrations, in Holy Loch and London. Immediately prior to the marches, thirty-two leading C100 members, including Bertrand Russell and his wife Edith, were arrested and jailed for seven days after refusing to be bound over with regard to further anti-Polaris demonstrations. The demonstration was banned under the Public Order Act, which had been introduced in the 1930s to combat fascism.

Committee of 100

This was one of the first occasions I witnessed of the state fighting back. Despite all my reading and thinking and talking, I was shocked that an ostensible democracy would act so brutally against its own citizens, engaged on a peaceful protest. We all knew the Establishment was corrupt and stifling, but it was revealing itself to be savage too. I began to realize that these old men in charge of the country were unlikely suddenly to realize the error of their ways. They were much more likely to dust off their truncheons.

Despite the pre-emptive arrests and the ban, some 12,000 people took part in the demo. 1,314 were arrested with ITV providing live coverage. The previous day, despite appalling weather at the Clyde US naval base, 500 took part, and 350 of these were arrested.

The Direct Action Committee (DAC), the forerunner of the Committee of 100, launched a campaign of non violent civil disobedience and direct action. Bertrand Russell is the elderly gentleman seated cross-legged.

Soon after, another of the state's weapons was revealed – the widest application of the laws of conspiracy. On 20 February 1962, six C100 members – Pat Pottle, Michael Randle, Terry Chandler, Ian Dixon, Trevor Hatton (the C100 Treasurer) and Helen Allegranza – were tried at the Old Bailey (by Mr Justice Havers, father of the actor Nigel Havers), on two counts of conspiracy under Section 1 of the Official Secrets Act. They had been arrested for their part in organising the demonstration at the Wethersfield RAF base in Sussex on 6 December 1961 and had been charged with conspiracy under Section 1 of the 1911 Official Secrets Act, containing the 'catch-all' indictment of actions carried out for 'any purpose prejudicial to the safety and interests of the state'.

This was the first time Section 1 had been used in a case not involving foreign spies and it was important inasmuch as for the first time it threw the onus on the defence to prove their innocence.

The trial revealed how high the stakes would be for the next fifteen years. Pat Pottle, defending himself, asked Air Commodore Magill, a prosecution witness, if he would press the button knowing it was going to annihilate millions of people. The Air Commodore replied that he would. On conviction, Justice Havers handed down the maximum sentences allowed – for organizing a protest, the men received eighteen months imprisonment each, and Helen twelve months. (Ironically, during their time inside, two of the six, Pat Pottle and Michael Randle, met and befriended the imprisoned Soviet spy George Blake and later helped organise his eventual escape from prison on 22 October 1966.)

The question of whether peaceful protest was getting us anywhere was hotly debated in the anti-nuclear movement. The London Committee of 100 was extremely divided on the issue. There was never any question that violence should be directed against individuals, but the idea that we should take the protest to another level by sabotaging military bases was gaining currency.

Sit down: of a total of more than 15,000 demonstrators, around 800 people were arrested during a sit-down demonstration at an anti-nuclear rally in London on 18 September 1961. This was seen as the peak of C100 activity.

x x x

I began to attend meetings of the Glasgow Committee of 100 in 1962, which included the charismatic Walter Morrison, an ex-Royal Scots Fusilier soldier who had been on internal security duties in India during the Gandhi demonstrations and was now an indefatigable peace-campaigner.

Walter didn't last long in the army after one particular briefing prior to a large demonstration. When the troops were told by their officer they would be expected to fire on the women and children if they refused to turn back, Walter stood up and said he would shoot any soldier who turned their gun on a woman or a child, and he would then personally shoot the officer who gave the order to fire. Unsurprisingly, the officer ordered his arrest and he was wheeched out to an armoured car to be taken to military prison.

So Walter was not easily intimidated, but even he was brought up short by one encounter with the agents of the state. Preparing for a demonstration, Morrison was setting up his tent on the foreshore of the Holy Loch when he was waved over to the nearby roadside by someone in a large American car. In the rear of the car were three men who addressed him by name, two from the Ministry of Defence's 'Psychological Warfare Group' in Dundee and the third an American of uncertain military or security provenance. They proceeded to warn Walter and his friends that they were out to get the so-called Scots Against War, a group who at the time were involved in publishing official secrets plus carrying out sabotage and other forms of direct action against military installations throughout Scotland. One of the MoD men pointed to the dark waters of the loch and told Walter that he was involved in a dangerous business and that it would be so easy for people like him to disappear, never to be found.

Joining the Young Socialists

I was youngest of the group who drank in the '92' bar in Cambridge Street, and later at the Red Lion in Renfield Street, which is where we were when we heard Kennedy had been assassinated. The others were in their late teens or early 20s, art students, trainee architects, and teachers – all very sophisticated, interesting – and earnest.

I was still living in Blantyre, but commuting to Glasgow every morning. Almost imperceptibly, my carefully coiffeured hair grew longer and curlier and my mohair suits and hand-made shirts made way for black denims, polo necks and Donkey jackets or white shortie Mac raincoats. I frequented Glasgow's main art cinema, the Cosmo, in Rose Street, where they screened continental films such as Ingmar Bergman's *Wild Strawberries* or Luis Buñuel's 1961 anti-religious and anti-authoritarian satirical masterpiece *Viridiana*. I had turned into a beatnik.

Years later my friend and fellow apprentice Malky Dow (now Professor Dow of Northwestern University, Illinois) recalled my metamorphosis: 'It seems to me that it was at about halfway thru the year at Langside College (where we were doing our City and Guilds intermediate course in Dental Technology), that you started to really change. While you already had clear left-wing political opinions, previously you were not really strident in expressing them. But now politics appeared to be growing more important to you, and it certainly dominated your conversations, and your manner of dress began to noticeably change. You began appearing in a pair of black leather knee-high boots, with your black trousers stuffed in them, and your trade-mark black polo neck sweater, and a black rain-coat that you always wore open and let it blow out behind you so it looked sort of like a cape. And your hair! Altho' nowadays it wouldn't likely get a second glance, in early sixties Glasgow it was a show stopper. Long and wavy and well past your shoulders. Nice hair, right enough, but Jesus did it, and the whole garb, make you stand out. I remember one day I was on a bus with a friend going down Sauchiehall Street when you got on looking as I've just described, and came up the stairs and joined us. My friend, John Polinski, was as I recall visibly uncomfortable with the other passengers staring at us – you, really. By then, however, you were quite used to it and apparently just ignored it. John later told me he thought you must be some kind of nutter, but I just shrugged it off and said "Naw, there's nuthin' wrang wi' him, that's jist how Stuart is."'

x x x

We felt like Dean Moriarty and his friends in Kerouac's *On the Road*: 'We were a band of Arabs coming in to blow up New York.' It's a line I've often had cause to think about. Stimulated by the camaraderie and banter and by the excitement of the possibility of helping to change the world, I joined the Springburn Young Socialists. Which political group to join had long been a question for me. In my view, the Communist Party had been completely discredited as a political instrument of the working class by a succession of bloody betrayals starting with the violent suppression of the naval mutineers at Kronstadt in 1921 and most recently demonstrated by the brutal putdown of the Hungarian uprising in 1956. I was persuaded by the argument that the Labour Party was the only realistic way to implement the ideas of socialism. What convinced me – and most of the other six million or so members – over to the Labour Party was, quite simply, Clause IV of its Constitution:

'To secure for the workers by hand or by brain the full fruits of their industry and the most equitable distribution thereof that may be possible upon the basis of the common ownership of the means of production, distribution and exchange, and the best obtainable system of popular administration and control of each industry or service.'

This proved to be a calculated piece of inspiring but meaningless rhetoric, designed to lure and entrap idealistic youth into the mire of electoral canvassing, party-building, office-grabbing and contending power agendas.

Springburn, like most other Constituency Labour Parties, was a minor fiefdom fought over by factions more interested in gaining control of the local castle (usually in the form of obscure executive committees) than coming together to win the war. These cabals were a confusing hodgepodge of social democratic, Trotskyist, Catholic, masonic and orange factions, some proscribed, some ignored and others encouraged, each cajoling, bribing, intriguing or contending for control. The number of deals a candidate had to make meant it was impossible to achieve anything when he finally gained power.

There were, of course, Labour Party members, and even one or two notably well-intentioned MPs, who did what they could to retain their integrity, but it was an unwinnable battle in the face of so many quid pro quos, compromises, double standards and plain downright dishonesty.

As far as I could see, there were several different types of people who called themselves socialists. Most were well-intentioned social democratic/liberal rank-and-file party members with a genuine passion for justice, tempered by a depressing willingness to compromise. A good number were doctrinaire state socialist – metaphysicians who put more faith in science and abstract theory than life and common humanity, and who believed that the workers' party acquiring state power was society's only possible salvation. A few were would-be bourgeois charlatans on the make, who saw socialism as their best bet for power and privilege. However, a growing number were libertarian or anarchist socialists, people who believed in self-management and mutual aid and opposed bureaucracy, party and state power.

Each group schemed in its own distinctive way. The most

militantly devious were the Trotskyists (who away from their own sectarian gatherings called themselves 'Marxists', rather as Jehovah's witnesses on the doorstep call themselves 'Bible students' – or Catholic fundamentalists describe themselves as Marists). They were 'revolutionary state socialists' who were strong on what they termed 'entryism'. This was of two types. 'Entryism' meant sending members into organizations to keep others out. 'Deep entryism', however, was the process of camouflaging oneself so completely that it was impossible to distinguish the undercover agent from any social democrat, and a Trotskyist could well end up as Secretary General of Nato or as a Cabinet Minister or in the House of Lords, having forgotten what he was elected for in the first place.

Meanwhile, the real string-pullers of the Labour Party, the extremists of the centre – the freemasons, Orangemen and the organised Catholic cliques – manoeuvred and manipulated from the wings.

I spent a lot of time and energy trying to master the names and inclinations of the apparently myriad socialist factions. South of the Clyde there was a different mosaic of Marxist cabals. Of course, most people who joined the Party were no more interested in understanding these subtle differences than the average Sunday School pupil was in understanding the difference between the 'Wee Frees' and the Episcopalians. The majority just accepted the views of the denomination in which they had formed friendships.

Initially, I was attracted to the Trotskyists 'International Socialism Group' (the IS, later to become the Socialist Workers' Party, or SWP). That I mimicked the jargon of 'scientific socialism' and Marxism and took it seriously still shames me; it was like Peter Pan asking the audience to clap their hands if they believed in fairies. These people understood only too well that Communist Russia had been a dictatorship ever since it had become a one-party state, but they were prepared to make every Jesuitical excuse in the book for it.

Militancy was a euphemism for faction building, recruiting members at the expense of your competitors. This might be 'scientific socialism' or it might not, but to me it became more and more apparent that socialism as I understood the term had nothing to do with parties or acquiring state power; it had to do with people, ethics, society and, most importantly, freedom!

x x x

I felt more and more that nothing that would satisfy my need for radical change could be done within the framework of political parties or the parliamentary system. What was the point of fighting to destroy one dictatorship in order to replace it with another – Stalinist, Trotskyist, Marxist-Leninist, Christian-Bolshevik or whatever?

What did catch my imagination, however, were the shit-stirring, disruptive, action-oriented libertarian socialist or 'anarcho-Marxist' ideas of the Solidarity Group. Founded in 1960, *Solidarity* was started by a few disenchanted veterans of other parties of the left: Dr Chris Pallis, a neurologist; Bob Potter, an Australian ex-Socialist Labour League (SLL); ex-Young Communist League (YCL) and engineering union member Ken Weller; and Andy Anderson, who worked in the telecoms side of the Post Office. Jim and Maria Fyffe (later to be the Labour MP for Glasgow Maryhill) were their people in the Springburn YS branch, and through them I began to read and promote their mimeographed publication, *Solidarity*.

Solidarity

Essentially, they advocated action and minimized meetings and bureaucracy. While everyone else was deeply involved in party building and internecine warfare for the hearts and minds of the Labour Party, Solidarity was organising community action campaigns against homelessness, leading the fight against nuclear weapons, and publishing investigative exposés of conditions within all sorts of industries. They were attempting to build a revolutionary do-it-yourself consciousness and practice, independent of any party.

x x x

Increasingly it seemed to me that party politicians and apparatchiks always had an answer for everything, but the solution to nothing. It wasn't that politicians were necessarily inveterate liars; simply that lying, dissimulation, temporising, opportunism and economy with the truth were inevitable consequences of getting to the top of the system.

Moreover, the old divide between Catholic and Protestant was more significant than political ideas in determining votes and candidates. During an election for the local Executive Committee, the more left wing (whatever that means in the Labour Party) of the two contending candidates happened to be a Protestant; those of us supporting him were issued with a list of Protestant houses to door-knock; to emphasise the point we were each given a Rangers scarf to wear. On the other side, the Catholics were doing pretty much the same thing. The one uncontested policy was opposition to contraception – the one thing that the Church of Rome and the Church of Scotland agreed upon.

I had not moved from the Orange Lodge to revolutionary socialism to play these sectarian games. Socialism to me was not about supporting the Labour Party in the political use of religion, pandering to sectarian prejudices, manipulating members and voters or organising whist drives.

I wanted out. I wanted decisive action and immediate solutions – not just to understand and occasionally disrupt the capitalist system, but to fight against it.

x x x

For me and a number of my contemporaries, the old political order imploded on the 1962 May Day demonstration in Glasgow's Queen's Park.

No To Polaris   The theme of the Glasgow march was 'No To Polaris'; the Labour Party National Executive decided that the Party leader, Hugh Gaitskell, should address us. This was not an honour, however – it was a deliberate act of provocation. Gaitskell was a vocal supporter of US bases; for the past three years he had been making vitriolic attacks on CND, 'pacifists', unilateralists and 'fellow travellers'. Now he was coming to the heartland of 'Red Clydeside' to lecture those most endangered by the bases on the 'benefits' of their being there. Gaitskell might have been clever (and brave), but he was not smart, or right.

After some anti-Polaris songs by Josh Macrae, Gaitskell was escorted onto the stage by some Labour Party dignitary who announced how proud he was to present to us the leader of the Labour Party.

The folk singer Gordon McCulloch, who was sitting directly behind me and my mate, John Samson, with his mate Bobby Campbell – another wonderful character and musician – shouted, 'Confront, you mean!' The roar of approval to Gordon's interjection and hooting catcalls shook Gaitskell: after a pause to survey the crowd of thousands of hostile Glaswegians, he launched one of the most remarkable tirades in modern politics with the memorable cry, 'You're nothing. You're just peanuts!' (This

'You're all peanuts!': outraged Labour Party leader Hugh Gaitskell shouted at anti-nuclear demonstrators at Queen's Park, Glasgow, Sunday 6 May 1962.
(Scottish Daily Record)

judgement became immortalised in one of Morris Blythman's many songs, called 'Peanuts' but better known as 'Boomerang', and sung to the tune of 'Bless 'em All, The Long and the Short and the Tall').

Gaitskell went berserk that day. He genuinely lost control, ranting and raving that we were all secret members of the Communist Party, tools of Russia, and that we should go back to Moscow and demonstrate under the Russian tanks. A Hampden-like roar of derision greeted his words and the jeers went on and on, rolling up the green slopes of Queen's Park.

Pandemonium broke loose. Hundreds of people, including myself and friends, feeling that the Labour Party's contempt for its principles and its rank and file members had gone too far, rushed to pull him off the platform. God knows what would have happened if we'd managed to get to Gaitskell, but the police and stewards prevented us clambering onto the stage. While milling around below the stage shouting abuse at the leader, I suddenly found myself taken in a headlock by a large Highland 'polisman' and unceremoniously ejected from the park.

x x x

Unfortunately, an identifiable picture of me made the centre spread of the *Daily Record* the next day and I was hauled over the coals by my boss, Mr Wilson. 'His' apprentices, he informed me in his most baronial manner, were not to get involved in politics or it would endanger the articles of indenture I had signed. He was marking my cards, effectively, that any more trouble and I would be out. I was seething with rage at the man's presumption at telling me what I could and could not do in my own time, but there was not a lot I could do about it and the union representative wasn't interested. He just wanted a quiet life and uppity radical apprentices didn't count for much in his books. My Granny was not amused and neither was Mum. Granny was reputed to be fey, that is possessing second sight, and I often wonder if what passed through her mind then was clairvoyance, or just a maternal chill of apprehension as to what lay ahead for me.

It didn't help that I was active in the union too – in fact, I was the works' representative of the Union of Shop Distributive and Allied Workers (USDAW) at the monthly Glasgow Trades Council meetings.

The fact that it was left to me, a sixteen-year old apprentice, to represent my USDAW branch indicates the low level of militancy in the laboratory, and indeed the impotence of the GTC itself, but it was nevertheless a fascinating arena of political debate. It was here I came across people like Harry McShane, a legend of 'Red Clydeside', and could imagine what it must have been like during the old Clyde Workers' Committee of 1919 which put the wind up Lloyd George to such an extent that he ordered tanks to George Square, armoured cars to strategic points around the city and naval guns on the Clyde to be trained on workers' districts.

I noted that the old anarchists who attended the Glasgow Trades Council never sought office or to dominate in any way; they appeared to see their role similar to that of the chorus in Greek drama – their role was to act as the conscience of the working class.

Really, though, this was another political mirage: the shop steward worked with the management in much the same way as the union leaders had been co-opted into the state. The unions had formally abandoned their commitment to class struggle and the overthrow of capitalism, preferring instead to work within capitalism's parameters, and were in turn admitted into the ruling groups through peerages and posts.

'. . . like a playing card on edge.'

In the early 1960s, the nuclear clock appeared to be ticking faster and faster. Commander Crabb, a naval intelligence officer, had been decapitated investigating the underwater parts of a Soviet ship during a visit by Nikita Khrushchev to Britain in 1956; an American pilot, Gary Powers, flying a U-2 spy plane had been shot down over Russia in May 1960; Russia had detonated the largest nuclear explosion yet, a massive 56 megatons in October 1961; American and Russian tanks were pointing their guns at each other at Checkpoint Charlie in Berlin and Buddhist monks were setting fire to themselves in Saigon in protest against the repressive US-supported government of Diem.

Cuban Missile Crisis   During the Cuban missile crisis of October 1962, it felt like nuclear war was inevitable. The brinkmanship of John F. Kennedy and Nikita Khrushchev over Soviet missiles in Cuba (and the less-reported US missiles close to the Soviet border in Turkey) could quite easily have led to our total annihilation. It is difficult today to convey the sense of powerlessness, fear and near hysteria which spread everywhere as that week drew to its close with the two nuclear powers in a Caribbean stand-off. Norman Mailer articulated the mood of the time: 'The world stood like a playing card on edge' during the Cuban missile crisis while the superpowers 'played poker with humanity'. No one was exempt from the sense of impending doom and latent panic. All over Europe and America, people packed their cars and headed for the hills or to the sea to watch what might be the last sunset on earth. Young lovers openly talked about dying in each other's arms. Some actually chose not to wait for the bombs to start falling and took their own lives. It was the closest the world came to the cold war endgame of 'mutually assured destruction'.

Films of the time such as *On the Beach*, based on Neville Shute's chilling novel of the same name, and *Dr Strangelove* expressed the constant, almost subliminal panic and tension. And these films – especially *Strangelove* – were not far wide of the mark. Given what we now know about players such as the air force chief, General Curtis LeMay, it is almost a surprise there wasn't a war. LeMay apparently told the president the 'big red dog is digging in our back yard and we are perfectly right to shoot him', and that Kennedy's handling of the Cuban crisis in the early stages was 'almost as bad as the appeasement at Munich'. When Kennedy and Khrushchev finally reached a settlement, LeMay denounced it as 'the greatest defeat in our history. We should invade today'.

LeMay was far from being a lone nutcase: the Director of British naval intelligence, Vice Admiral Eric Longley-Cook, was a regular visitor to the Pentagon in the later 1950s and reported that the US military were convinced that 'all-out war against the Soviet Union was not only inevitable but imminent'. One US general was reported to have remarked that the West could not afford to wait until Europe or America was devastated by a nuclear holocaust. He added: 'We can afford, however, to create a wilderness in Russia without serious repercussions on western civilisation. We have a moral obligation to stop Russia's aggression by force, if necessary, rather than face the consequences of delay.'

x x x

Perhaps more than anything else, it was the events of that fortnight in October when I was sixteen years old that made me finally decide it was self-delusional and fundamentally wrong, both morally and ethically, to stand on the sidelines of world affairs, like some unaffected and uninvolved bystander at a location where a gruesome accident was expected to happen.

The apparent imminence of global war gave coherence to our sense of common purpose and common priorities. The issues involved were so vital to our mutual well-being and the survival of mankind, that I decided that the struggle in which we were involved was one of life and death. The state, the oligarchic institutional means by which society is governed, controlled and ultimately repressed, was clearly the enemy; if we did not destroy it first, it would destroy us.

By the end of 1962, the National Committee of 100 was struggling to survive. It had failed to respond adequately to the Cuban missile crisis, and a number of its leaders were in serving prison sentences for conspiracy. In November 1962, Bertrand Russell resigned from the London Committee, after it dissociated itself from his pro-Castroite position. On 21 January 1963, Helen Allegranza, the Secretary of the National Committee, one of the six leaders tried the previous year, committed suicide. It had also been the worst winter since 1947.

Something had happened. Almost no one persisted under the comfortable illusion that the governments of the world would 'ban the bomb'. More and more people were realizing that the state was the enemy.

In response to this malaise within the nuclear disarmament movement, a few libertarian activists within the Committee of 100 published an eight-page discussion document called 'Beyond Counting Arses'. It proposed the adoption of a new approach, more oriented towards direct action, attacking the state by exposing its clandestine activities and flaunting the Official Secrets Act. It concluded: 'We do not believe in passive martyrdom. We are not in this movement to opt out of a burden on our consciences, but to fight for what we believe in.'

And so we did. We embarked on a whole new range of actions, the Spies for Peace most famous being conducted with the *nom de guerre* Spies for Peace, who caused a national sensation at Easter 1963 by revealing how the government envisaged a post-holocaust Britain being run (by fourteen unelected regional governors, holed up in top secret citadels already built across Britain).

JIM PETTER

'You can be Tory or Labour, Communist or Empire
Loyalist, Christian or Atheist, genius or moron,
tear-arse or layabout, capitalist or worker,
prostitute or Duchess of Argyle, pimp, bastard, or
bugger-boy, copper's nark or pacifist fruit-juicer,
it doesn't matter who or what. Your future can be
equally radioactive and you are all to be equally
dead. The only survivors will be a few Top
Bureaucrats with, of course, one month's supply of
uncontaminated food and water at their disposal. We
need a Kafka to write a novel about the last days in
the Bunker for Bureaucrats.'

Jim Petter, renegade scion of the diesel engine
family, ILPer, AEU shop steward, granddad and
lifelong cyclist, written in the Solidarity and
Anarchy pamphlets.

One of the last Committee of 100 actions summed up the tone of
where we had got to, the last fling of innocence. In July 1963 we began
a two-month march from Glasgow to London, carrying a 24-foot long
cardboard model of a Polaris rocket, which had been made in Josh
Macrae's basement. Of the thirty-five people who started out, I believe
only five completed the march. I didn't make it beyond Falkirk, the
first night's stop, as I had to be back at work on the Monday.

X X X

These new aggressive tactics brought the media more prominently
into the equations. The Spies for Peace revelations were front-page
news. In May 1963, a group called Scots Against War published a a
fairly provocative document called 'How to Disrupt, Obstruct and
Subvert the Warfare State' (essentially a Scottish Beyond Counting

Arses), and the Sunday tabloids and broadsheets went to town that weekend. *The People*, *Sunday Mirror*, the *Glasgow Evening Citizen*, the *Sunday Times* and the *Scotsman* denounced the leaflet as sedition and 'the most blatant defiance of authority ever made by the nuclear disarmament movement and amounted to open revolt'. In the space of just over three years the anti-nuclear movement had shifted from being an orderly, police-friendly, peace movement controlled by an alliance of middle-class liberals and party leaders into a powerful anti-state movement galvanized by anarchists, libertarian and non-aligned socialists. No one was going to support a movement that had no chance of success – passions were running higher, and determination was growing. Our sense of foreboding deepened in June 1964 when the Republican candidate for the US presidency, Senator Barry Goldwater, a major-general in the US Air Force Reserve, proposed that 'baby' nuclear bombs be dropped in South Vietnam.

Anti-Nuclear Movement

Demonstrations – which were no longer just against the bomb, but against racism, apartheid and America's growing war in Vietnam (another war orchestrated by governments without the consent of the people) – stopped being predictable, well-ordered, respectable events, where the marchers deferred to the marshals, the police and party cadres. On Easter Saturday, 28 March 1964, a young supporter of the C100 dramatically burnt herself to death in a park in Ruislip, Middlesex. As that weekend's Aldermaston March arrived in London demonstrators broke through the police cordons and charged down Whitehall with red and black flags flying, and almost managed to make it to Downing Street before police reinforcements arrived.

x x x

The question of whether we should use force for peace was increasingly pressing. A Scots Against War pamphlet we published in early 1964 called *Is Sabotage the Answer?* argued that non-violent civil disobedience had taken us as far as it could. Many people had gone to prison, but this sacrifice made no difference to the state's ability and determination to wage war. Hardline and conservative pacifism was against any use of force, the activists had reached their

Scots Against War

limits as pioneers of confrontation. But, as the pamphlet argued,'There are those who may want to do something not truly non-violent, but effective nonetheless. This could be termed as property sabotage. This type of action covers a vast number of activities from striking to stealing and spying.' Suggestions ranged from strikes and putting sugar in concrete mixers to using death watch beetles and fungi to damage floors and roofs.

Hardly a week went by between 1963 and 1966 without some Army Recruiting Office being broken into and damaged, and mysterious fires occurring at army, naval and civil defence centres all over the country, including the site huts at Faslane and the top secret military command centre at Troywood, near St Andrews, which was a labyrinthine 100-foot-deep bunker with two cinemas, a restaurant, operations room and so on, disguised as an innocent farmhouse. The Holy Loch pier itself was burned down in July 1964.

The authorities tried to ignore most of these incidents. Those who were arrested were usually fined small amounts, not imprisoned. Most of these actions were taken in the name of Scots Against War, but to assume, as the authorities did about this group and others later, that it had a conventional command structure with leaders and meetings was to miss the point. Scots Against War never existed as a regular group of members, like the Communist Party or the Labour Party. It consisted only of actions – some spontaneous, some planned – that were taken by a range of individuals to further the anti-nuclear cause. Scots Against War wasn't a title – it was just a literal description of what was going on.

The Committee of 100 opposed the Scots Against War development, but within a year all the key C100 members were absorbed into other organizations.

X X X

In Blantyre, meanwhile, I had become notorious not because of my political activities or involvement in demonstrations, but because of my long hair.

Long hair was unknown on the Clydeside then, though it was

starting to catch on with rock groups in England. The Beatles led the way, in hair and in music; after their bluesy beginnings, they were now producing sounds unlike anything that had gone before: 'She Loves You' and 'I Wanna Hold Your Hand'. As my friends and I walked along Sauchiehall Street and Argyle Street in our black beatnik outfits of oilskin jackets, polo neck sweaters, jeans and calf length cowboy boots, we were followed by catcalls, whistles and crude suggestions from people who wondered what things were coming to when you could not tell the lasses from the lads.

Even staunch Roman Catholics, who spent long hours pondering pictures of a long-haired Saviour, thought we must be lunatics to wear our hair so long it hung over our collars. The barbers and the press felt it signified a malignant, restless energy and lack of solid virtues. I was sure to come to a bad end. My Granny didn't like it, but she never pressed the matter. Mum, on the other hand, thought it was great.

We shook staid Central Scotland to the core, or so we thought. Certainly my boss became very nervous of me. Four years earlier, in 1959, there had been a strike of Glasgow apprentices, something previously unheard of in industrial relations. (The strike committee included men like Sir Alex Ferguson, Gus Macdonald and Billy Connolly, now lords or millionaires, or both) In 1963 there was anxiety that a similar thing might happen, and employers were nervous of signs of activism. The final confrontation for me came when my boss told me to remove a 'Ban the Bomb' lapel badge and the broken rifle emblem of the War Resisters' International – and to stop preaching 'red propaganda' to my fellow apprentices during work. I walked out.

Tearing Up My
Labour Party Card

I technically became an anarchist one Saturday afternoon in the summer of 1963 outside Glasgow's Mitchell Library, tearing up my Labour Party card after an exhilarating conversation with Bobby Lynn and Ronnie Alexander, a librarian and the secretary of the newly re-formed Glasgow Federation of Anarchists.

Ronnie had been converted to anarchism at a Kingston YS talk given by Gus McDonald (who thirty years or more later became Lord Gus, Transport Minister in the Labour government of Tony Blair; rumour had it he was not only a Marxist, but had read *Das Kapital* in its entirety) and Harry Selby, who was later Labour MP for Govan for a few years without ever having to reveal that he was a Trotskyite deep-entryist.

Ronnie went back to work in the Mitchell Library, dug out everything he could on anarchism. Soon he was told about Bobby Lynn. Lynn had become the backbone of the Glasgow anarchist movement after the death or withdrawal of those who had sustained it through the 1920s, 30s and 40s: resilient activists such as Frank Leech, Jimmy Raeside, Eddie Shaw, Willie McDougall, John T Caldwell, and Guy Aldred, the last two of whom had been heavily involved in helping comrades get to Spain and in publishing the *Barcelona Bulletin*, which exposed the Stalinist repression in May 1937 of the Catalan anarchists and the anti-Stalinist POUM.

ROBERT LYNN

Cherubic-faced, curly haired, small and dapper, generous and non-judgmental, Robert had left Glasgow's St Mungo's Academy at fourteen to take up an engineering apprenticeship in Yarrow's shipyards, where he became swept up in the maelstrom of political activity of the war years. Disaffected by the Communist Party members' policy of subordinating workers' interests to those of Stalin's foreign policy, Bobby began to explore the ideas of anarchist thinkers, including the German writer Max Stirner (1806-56).

Robert (on the right) and Jean Lynn with friend on a 'bus run'.

Authoritarian socialist states justified themselves by proposing that only the state can eventually engineer and guarantee the freedom of the people. Stirner, however, argued that freedom was not an abstract end in itself. Freedom was simply the means to the real end of being in control over one's own actions. *The Ego and His Own* is a powerful critique of what Stirner called 'fixed ideas', be they religious, rational, nationalist or ideological. For Stirner, all 'ideas' needed to be treated simply as that – 'ideas'; working hypotheses rather than ideologies. Ideologies always make hypocrites of us by denying our real, complex selves in the name of these 'fixed ideas'.

In opposition to statism, both capitalist and communist, Stirner appeared to suggest a 'union of egoists', a sort of anarchist federalism. But like most other anarchists he was opposed to providing blueprints for society. That was precisely what he was fighting against. Peter Kropotkin defined it thus: 'It is impossible to legislate for the future. All we can do is to guess, vaguely, its essential tendencies and clear the road for it.'

Robert Lynn interpreted this 'union of egoists' literally, as a workers' union, a way of organising freely within industry. In the post-war years, Robert became an irritant to both employers and communist-led union officials and was soon blacklisted. Unable to get work, he joined the Merchant Navy as an engineer and spent some years travelling the world, during which time he read everything he could lay his hands on.

When he returned from sea, Robert worked at Howden's engineering plant in Glasgow's South Side, and was a regular speaker at the weekly workers' forums in Renfrew Street, Glasgow, where anarchists, the Socialist Party of Great Britain (SPGB) activists, Scottish Nationalists and Trotskyists regularly debated ideas ... sometimes physically. Here, in an open air arena, ordinary working-class men and women absorbed and discussed passionately the ideas of Feuerbach, Clara Zetkin, Bakunin, Kropotkin and many, many others.

In this conversation, Bobby explained the anarchist view of democracy. Capitalist parliamentary democracy, he said, was no democracy at all. Firstly, the idea that political parties represented the popular will was clearly absurd. Secondly, the attainment of a majority was only a euphemism for the threat of force: the statement 'We have a majority' meant nothing more than 'We can fight you and win.' But might without right settled nothing. As the German people discovered after 1933, wrong principles would not work however great the majority by which they were endorsed.

The libertarian view of democracy, however, depended on the individual participation of each and every citizen in the decision-making process. The greatest obstacle to be overcome in all social and political relationships, Bobby emphasised, was not the corrupting or arbitrary nature of power, but the human proclivity to obedience and deference. Each of us needed to be an activist, constantly, in every decision we took. The tension was not between anarchism and democracy, or even capitalism or communism, but between anarchism and complacency

I was persuaded not just by what Robert said, but by the wonderful idea implicit in this view: anarchism was a way of life rather than an abstract view of a remote future. It was not a theory, a philosophy, a 'programme for life', nor yet a description of how individuals and society should one day be, but a whole new way of looking at the world we were in – a way of assessing and acting upon values, principles, moralities, belief systems, ideologies and social relationships. It was a glimpse of perfection; something against which I could measure myself in my actions right now.

After all the intellectual chicanery and tortuous doublespeak I'd heard from Marxist sophists to excuse atrocities and gain power, I was exhilarated. This was the most elegant solution I had heard so far, something which was not merely a logical attitude to the world, but noble and worthwhile as well. I knew instinctively this was the 'big' idea for which I'd been looking. Its essence, I later discovered, was captured in the declaration drafted by Michael Bakunin and signed by forty-seven anarchists during their trial after the failure of the Lyons uprising in 1870: 'We wish, in a word, equality – equality in fact as corollary, or, rather, as a primordial condition of liberty. From each according to his faculties, to each according to his needs; that is what we wish sincerely and energetically.'

At the age of sixteen, I felt like Parsifal first seeing the castle of the Holy Grail.

ANARCHISM

What was the idea that won me over so completely, at such a young age?

Anarchism encompasses such a broad view of the world that it cannot easily be distilled into a formal definition. Michael Bakunin, a man of action whose writings and example over a century ago did most to transform anarchism from an abstract critique of political power into a theory of practical social action, defined its fundamental tenet thus:

'In a word, we reject all privileged, licensed, official, and legal legislation and authority, even though it arise from universal suffrage, convinced that it could only turn to the benefit of a dominant and exploiting minority, and against the interests of the vast enslaved majority,' Lyons, 1870.

Anarchism is a movement for human freedom. It is rooted in normality as opposed to eccentricity – that is anarchism is not some cult of bohemians and nihilists. Its central tenet is that the fundamental problem of human society is power and the quest for power. Anarchists do not take a particularly optimistic or rosy view of human nature, in fact they do not trust that nature as they see more clearly than most the immanent dangers of the drive for power and the need to curtail it.

Its ideas can be traced back to the Greek Cynics where it was associated with a critism of the basic institutions and values of human society and a questioning of human motives. Its key texts have developed since the sixteenth century, with a philosophy and a defined outlook that have evolved and grown with time and circumstance. These include: Etienne de la Boetie's essay *On Voluntary Servitude* (1577); William Godwin's *Enquiry Concerning Political Justice* (1793); Jean Pierre Proudhon's *What is Property?* (1840); Michael Bakunin's *The Reaction in Germany* (1842) and *God and the State* (1870); Max Stirner's *The Ego and His Own* (1845); Peter Kropotkin's *The Conquest of Bread* (1892), *Fields, Factories and Workshops* (1899) and *Modern Science and Anarchism* (1913); Robert Michels' *Political Parties* (1915).

Anarchism opposes both the insidious growth of state power and the pernicious ethos of possessive individualism, which, together or separately, ultimately serve only the interests of the few at the expense of the rest. In anarchist theory, the first premise is something which the American anarchist Josiah Warren (1798–1874) called the sovereignty of the individual and from this it follows that human freedom and the rights of the individual are paramount. The argument against the state is that it, and its apparatus of maintenance, the government, are everywhere in the hands of a small ruling group, a privileged body separated by its formation, status and organisation from the population as a whole. This group collectively monopolises political decision-making. In some societies it may constitute an entrenched and self-perpetuating class. Indeed, this was the character of all states until a few centuries ago. In other more modern systems, such as democracy, there is a greater circulation or regular turnover of membership in the ruling group, so that dynasties or other kinds of closed classes of rulers do not ordinarily occur. This, of course, contributes to the illusion of equality of power in a democracy and obscures the division between rulers and ruled.

Democracy adds to the illusion of freedom and equality by proclaiming the idea of majority rule. However, this is a rare occurrence in any democracy. A large percentage of the population do not vote because they are either indifferent or frustrated. And where there are several candidates the winner receives only the largest of all the votes, which is most of the time only a minority. Then there is the more fundamenal problem of the rule of the majority. Why should 50.1% be able to impose their will on an opposing 49.9%? What is sacred about a majority and what is ethical about forcing a minority to accept majority opinion?

Above all, the state and governments are organisations for war. To quote another American anarchist, Randolph Bourne (1886–1918) in his essay, 'War is the health of the State':

'Fundamental to both government and the state is the use of violence to enforce the law and advance and defend its international interests. This may be viewed as either the imposition of the will of the ruling group, or as a device to maintain order. States and governments fulfill all these functions by enforcing the law, which their jurists draw up and interpret.

'With the shock of war, however, the State comes into its own again. The Government, with no mandate from the people, without consultation of the people, conducts all the negotiations, the backing and filling, the menaces and explanations, which slowly bring it into collision with some other Government, and gently and irresistibly slides the country into war.

'For the benefit of proud and haughty citizens, it is fortified with a list of the intolerable insults which have been hurled toward us by the other nations; for the benefit of the liberal and beneficent, it has a convincing set of moral purposes which our going to war will achieve; for the ambitious and aggressive classes, it can gently whisper of a bigger role in the destiny of the world. The result is that, even in those countries where the business of declaring war is theoretically in the hands of representatives of the people, no legislature has ever been known to decline the request of an Executive, which has conducted all foreign affairs in utter privacy and irresponsibility, that it order the nation into battle. Good democrats are wont to feel the crucial difference between a State in which the popular Parliament or Congress declares war, and the State in which an absolute monarch or ruling class declares war. But, put to the stern pragmatic test, the difference is not striking. In the freest of republics as well as in the most tyrannical of empires, all foreign policy, the diplomatic negotiations which produce or forestall war, are equally the private property of the Executive part of the Government, and are equally exposed to no check whatever from popular bodies, or the people voting as a mass themselves.'

Anarchism is both a theory and practice of life. Philosophically, it aims for the maximum accord between the individual, society and nature. Practically, it aims for us to organise and live our lives in such a way as to make politicians, governments, states and their officials superfluous. In an anarchist society, mutually respectful sovereign individuals would exist in self-regulating non-coercive relationships within naturally defined communities in which the means of production and distribution are held in common. Kropotkin's *Modern Science and Anarchism* (1913) describes his model of how an anarchist society might work:

'The anarchists conceive a society in which all the mutual relations of its members are regulated, not by laws, not by authorities, whether self-imposed or elected, but by mutual agreements between the members of that society, and by a sum of social customs and habits – not petrified by law, routine, or superstition, but continually developing and continually readjusted, in accordance with the ever-growing requirements of a free life, stimulated by the progress of science, invention, and the steady growth of higher ideals. No ruling authorities, then. No government of man by man; no crystallisation and immobility, but a continual evolution – such as we see in Nature.'

All this may be seen as utopian and impossible to work, but anarchists are not dreamers obsessed with an abstract ideal. We are very well aware that the perfect society may never be won and that the struggle may last forever. However, the ideal provides the energy to challenge things as they are, and attempt to make them what they might be.

Ultimately, only struggle determines outcome, and progress towards a more meaningful community must begin with the will to resist every form of injustice. This means challenging all exploitation and defying the legitimacy of all coercive authority. If anarchists have one article of unshakeable faith, it is that, once the habit of deferring to politicians or ideologues is lost, and that of resistance to domination and exploitation acquired, then ordinary people have a capacity to organise every aspect of their lives in their own interests, anywhere and at any time, both freely and fairly.

Anarchists do not stand aside from popular struggle, nor do they attempt to dominate it. They seek to contribute to it practically whatever they can, and also to assist within it the highest possible levels both of individual self-development and of group solidarity. Revolutionary Spain between July 1936 and August 1937 provided me and countless others with the most shining model as to how an anarchist society could and did work in practice.

The anarchist theory of revolution holds that human society is divided, not as the Marxists contend, purely by a class struggle between property owners and the dispossessed, but also by a struggle and tension between governors and subjects, between

> freedom and authority. Its guiding principle – based
> on the experience of centuries that on every occasion
> when the people have entrusted their fate to
> authority, that authority has ended up enslaving
> them – is the belief that 'liberty' and 'justice'
> cannot be upheld through state power or any authority
> principle, even by the most apparently enlightened
> and radical political leadership.
>
> It is the fundamental and uncontainable conviction
> of anarchism that social power held over people is a
> usurpation of natural rights: power originates in the
> people, and they alone have, together, the right to
> wield it.

I began attending Bobby's legendary regular meetings in Ross St – a journey literally through the dark to get to the light. I'd never experienced this sinister side of the city before. When I first got off the tramcar at Glasgow Cross and as I hurried up the empty street under the railway bridge towards the Barrows, I suddenly found myself squeezed between two razor-scarred Glasgow hard men who appeared from nowhere and pushed me towards a close mouth.

'Wherr ur you goin',' said one. 'Tae see a friend', said I. ''Zat right', said he. 'Whaurr's zis freen live?' said the other. 'Ross Street', says I, trying not to sound fearful. 'Whit's his name, then, pal?' said the first one. 'Robert Lynn', said I, and with the mention of Robert's name the mood changed as though the sun had come out from behind a dark cloud. The second one said, sternly: 'A wee boy like you shouldna be walkin' the streets o' the Calton on yer own', and with that they escorted me right to the door of 4 Ross Street, chatting away as if they had known me all their lives.

The Glasgow Anarchist Group met in this derelict ground floor single-end at 4 Ross Street, off the Gallowgate, next to the Barrows. The room doubled as a 'shebeen', an illegal-drinking house

Glasgow Anarchist Group

where people came to drink or buy cheap South African fortified wines.

I entered through a dark hallway. The scene was pure *film noir*, except it was in colour. The room, lit by a naked lightbulb, was bare except for a long table around which were seated the unlikeliest looking collection of people I had seen in my life. Old 'Red Clydesiders', William Clarke Quantrill's Confederate Army guerrilla raiders and 'The Hole in the Wall Gang' had been mysteriously transposed to a bleak single-end in Glasgow's Calton.

x x x

Robert's interpretation of anarchism gave meaning and legitimacy to the often questionable activities of some Hogarthian local characters. Many of these were regular participants in the Ross Street meetings and these were the faces around the table on my first night in the company of anarchists.

At the head of the long table sat Robert, who immediately made me feel welcome with a smile, a wave, a brief introduction to those seated at the table, a chipped mug of sweet brown fortified wine and a chair.

The ominous hush that had descended on the room when I made my entrance immediately lifted and the lively debate picked up where it had left off.

Some of the men looked awesome: massively built with heavily scarred faces. They appeared to me to be unusually aggressive towards each other, even for men who looked as though they had stepped out of the pages of *No Mean City*. One in particular, Scout O'Neill, had hands like a Belfast ham. If guns were to be bought in Glasgow, it would be here. In fact, Peter Manuel, the last man to be hanged in Scotland, in July 1958, was convicted because Scout had turned Queen's Evidence when he discovered Manuel was a suspect in a series of seven murders in and around Glasgow between 1954 and 1958. Scout had sold him a gun, a Webley revolver, supposedly for a robbery he said he was planning.

There was nothing doctrinaire or politically correct about these meetings; everyone spoke as they found, but all of them had the heart of the matter in them – socialism, in its truest sense. The heated and sometimes bellicose discussions about syndicalism, trade unionism, egoism, individualism and collectivism were constantly disrupted by wee wifies coming in with empty jugs to buy wine from Robert or his partner Jean.

After the meetings we would usually go across the road to the Saracen's Head, Robert's local, one of the oldest and, at the time, one of the most notorious pubs in Glasgow

Robert's favourite leisure pastime was organising 'bus runs' and he and Jean would put these on regularly for us and the couthy folk of the Calton. The 'bus runs' were a 'rerr terr' (Glaswegian for 'top form') and we all had a great time with our 'cairy-oots' and 'sannies'.

Occasionally we would stop at a café or restaurant for lunch and Scout O'Neill's party trick, when the plate of steak pie, peas and potatoes arrived at the table, was to put his massive hands over the dinner plate and thus completely cover it. Scout always led the singing; in fact he acquired his sobriquet because he was constantly singing the Dave Willis song with the refrain I'm a scout, scout, scout.

x x x

Anarchism was new to me, but as I learned at Bobby's meetings, it was by no means new to other people struggling for justice across the world.

After the Spanish Civil War, one of the world's most high profile revolutionary struggles was in Cuba. Hundreds of Cuban anarchists had played a significant role in the overthrow of Batista, both in the protest campaigns and armed uprising, and enduring persecution, torture, death and exile. But once Fidel Castro gained power, he was interested mainly in keeping it, and the anarchists turned into a problem. It was not at first apparent to everyone that Castro was a Marxist – some saw him as a democratic socialist, even as a revolutionary socialist – but as he eliminated members of his first revolutionary government who opposed accepting aid from the Soviet Union, his basic allegiances became clearer. Soon after the fall of Batista he began a clandestine series of purges, but it was JFK's failed invasion at the Bay of Pigs that gave Castro the opportunity to liquidate domestic opposition.

The Cuban consulate in Glasgow was one focus of our attention in the summer of 1963. Another was the occupation of the Greek Consulate in Glasgow, over the visit that July of King Paul and Queen Frederika of Greece. Both Greek royals were figures of hate. Frederika had belonged to a Hitler Youth group, had publicly defended Nazi Germany and three of her brothers had served in Hitler's army. But the main bone of contention was the fact that Greece's right wing government had tortured and jailed thousands of political prisoners, some for over fifteen years.

These demonstrations happened wherever the royals went, and were particularly significant for two reasons. It was the first time in centuries the British royal family – who had been accompanying the Greek king and queen at public occasions and on royal processions around London – had been booed in the streets. Over 200 protestors were jailed. Back in Greece the protests had a big effect and brought about the downfall of the prime minister, Karamanlis. They also led to the release of nineteen political prisoners in an attempt to restore Greece's international image.

The second main significance was the public exposure of the state's response to the protest movement when Detective Sergeant Harold 'Tanky' Challenor, an ex-SAS trooper and a CID officer with a reputation as a hard nut in London's West End, planted a brick in the pocket of Donald Rooum, an anarchist cartoonist.

Rooum had been arrested during one of the demonstrations outside Claridge's Hotel in London, where the Greek royals were staying. Challenor struck Rooum a violent blow on the ear and arrested him, saying: 'I've got a desperate one here.' Challenor hit Rooum again in West End Central police station in Savile Row, said 'Boo the queen, would you,' then hit him three more times. Finally the CID officer produced a piece of brick, saying 'There you are me old darling. Carrying an offensive weapon can get you two years'.

But Rooum had his wits about him and refused police bail to ensure he was kept in custody overnight so that he would be able to go direct from the police station to an independent forensic expert next day. When his jacket was examined, there was no trace of brick dust on it or in any of his pockets.

'Tanky' Challenor had planted his last piece of evidence on those he saw as 'the deserving guilty'. He suffered a convenient mental breakdown, was found unfit to plead and never stood trial. Three young constables who worked with him were each jailed for three years. Even so, it was difficult for Donald Rooum to prove his innocence. Robey, the magistrate at Marlborough Street, clung to the belief prominent at the time that the police were always right, and convicted others on the same charge, even after Rooum proved his innocence.

x x x

By the summer of 1963 the national press had begun to pick up on the growing influence of anarchists and anarchist ideas within the peace movement. A large part of the Glasgow Committee of 100 had come round to the anarchist view. Many older anarchists had become exhausted by the years of largely fruitless struggle. My generation felt that times were different now – the world was clearly changing in the 1960s, the established forces so obviously corrupt and acting against the interests of their own people, that were we to push hard enough, the system would have to break. Anything was possible.

Peace and Non-violence

The idea that those of us with the most radical views were the most likely to be violent began to be reported. In July 1963, prior to the Greek royal visit, the *Sunday Telegraph* pointed out that the Metropolitan Police Special Branch feared that 'anarchist extremists, acting independently of any organisation, will become violent' during the Greek royal visit. The paper went on: 'The Anarchist movement in Britain is non-violent, but it is known that there is a minority of dissenters. At present, a controversy on the use of force is being carried out in the correspondence columns of the anarchist journal *Freedom*.'

The debate in *Freedom* revolved around the question of the choice of tactics – passive resistance or non-violent confrontation with the police. As for the younger Glasgow anarchists, the question of violence or non-violence wasn't a problem – it didn't enter into the equation. It would have been as pointless as discussing the number of angels who could dance on a pinhead. The only thing that mattered was the extent to which we were provoked by the police. The older ones, like Bobby, rarely went on demonstrations. They were too easy to pick off.

x x x

The *Sunday Times* ran a Focus feature on Canon Collins, leader of the CND, who was quoted as saying: 'As an anarchist fringe has recently been very prominent in the movement, the task (presumably of keeping control of the rank and file of CND) is all the more difficult. Inevitably this means that we sacrifice a good deal of support from what you might call the more normal public.'

Professor Ritchie Calder, vice chairman of CND, added that he did not approve of widening the movement's terms of reference beyond the nuclear issue: 'Anarchist elements have always been latent – now they are coming out. You've got to remember this generation has strontium in its bones and sputniks in its eyes; older people can't understand.'

The *Sunday Times* piece concluded:

'Nuclear disarmers of all shades of opinion agree on one thing – frustration, and hence hasty and extreme action often results from increasing attempts by authority to restrict their protests. Canon Collins, speaking with great passion, should have the last word. "I think the authorities are mad, quite mad to bottle up this kind of frustration and you can quote me on that. It will only get worse. There's always a risk that in the face of provocation people will despair of democracy."'

The marches, in fact, were usually good-humoured. The only time violent confrontations occurred was when the marchers were provoked by arbitrary and unilateral actions by the police, such as attempting to stop us demonstrating or shunting us down side streets where we didn't want to go. There was no question of violence being a tool of ideological choice or part of a planned strategy. When trouble broke out it was inevitably because the police started it. Unless handled diplomatically, when people get angry the situation can quickly get out hand and become violent. Those Calder spoke for simply did not understand that for us anti-nuclear protest could not be neatly compartmentalized separately, away from every other aspect of the role of the state and its need for war – or at least enemies. Our mantra was :'War is the health of the state!' and to us the ability of the state to wage war and kill indiscriminately in our name had to be confronted at every possible opportunity.

x x x

But while the influence of anarchist ideas may have been strong, in numerical terms the threat of anarchist hordes was greatly exaggerated. In 1963–4, there were probably only about 500 or 600 anarchists across the nation active in groups in cities like London, Glasgow, Aberdeen, Dundee, and Bristol, and in a handful of universities. Including individual anarchists who kept their own counsel, there may have been perhaps in total around 2,000, but that, of course, didn't include sympathisers and 'fellow travellers'. The print-run of the anarchist paper *Freedom* in 1964 was around 3–4,000, but not all its readers were anarchists.

One group, the Syndicalist Workers' Federation (SWF), centred around the Freedom Press and Freedom Bookshop at its Dickensian premises in Angel Alley, off Whitechapel High Street in Aldgate, East London, a property owned by Vernon Richards, one of the more contentious anarchists of the time.

Vernon Richards and Freedom Press

Richards was the son of Emidio Recchioni, an Italian anarchist shopkeeper who owned the well-known 'King Bomba' delicatessen in Soho and had been friendly with the Italian anarchist Errico Malatesta. The *Daily Telegraph* had named Recchioni as the financial backer of a 1926 assassination attempt on Mussolini and caused 'King Bomba' to be investigated by Scotland Yard's Special Branch. Recchioni sued the *Telegraph* and won a large sum in damages which, legend has it, was used in further attempts on Mussolini.

Vernon Richards did not go to Spain to fight in the Civil War.

Instead he married his friend's daughter, the charismatic and beautiful anarchist writer, Marie-Louise Berneri, and went to London University to study engineering.

From 1936 to 1939 he edited an English-language newspaper, *Spain and the World*. After the collapse of the Spanish revolution, he changed its name to *Revolt!* then, when World War II broke out, to *War Commentary*. He also applied to be registered as a conscientious objector, but this was rejected – not that it mattered all that much as he was in a reserved occupation working for the railways.

Released from a nine month prison sentence in 1946 for conspiring to 'contravene Defence Regulation 39A' by inciting soldiers to disaffection, Richards changed the name of the paper again to *Freedom*. Richards ran 'King Bomba' after the war and then sold it in the early 1950s after his mother died. For the remainder of that decade and the early 1960s Richards had his own travel agency, actively promoting tourism to both Spain and Russia. In 1968 he acquired the lease of the building at 84b Whitechapel High Street, in Angel Alley, which housed the printshop, bookshop, library, storeroom and meeting rooms.

As well as the weekly *Freedom*, The Freedom Group published the journal *Anarchy* (edited by Colin Ward, an architect whose reputed claim to fame was designing Milton Keynes), pamphlets and books. *Freedom* was edited by a group arbitrarily co-opted by Vernon Richards. Funds to support these ventures were raised mainly through Richards' network of generous old Italian comrades, mainly in the United States.

There were a few other anarchist groups such as the *Freie Arbeiter Stimme* (Free Voice of Labour). These militants were the last remnants of the hundred-year-old Jewish anarchist movement in London which still hung on by a thread at that time in the East End of London, but everything they did, socials, publications, and so on was in Yiddish, the common language of East European and Russian Jews. As a result, contact with the Spanish and English-speaking movement was sporadic to say the least.

There were also Stirnerite individualists; anarcho-communists (who believed that the community was society's centre, not the individual); pacifist anarchists; anarcho-Marxists, (people who tried to fuse libertarian Marxist with anarchist theories, mainly from the Solidarity Group and the Independent Labour Party); and also Catholic anarchists.

ANARCHO-SYNDICALISM

Briefly, the anarcho-syndicalist concept of a federal society is based not on geographical communities, but on factories, workshops and industries. The syndicate, or self-organised labour force at the place of work, provides both the instrument to seize control of the means of production – farms, factories, shipyards and so on – in an expropriatory general strike, and to run them to provide for human need; this would be the economic basis of the new society.

Wage labour would be abolished and production in each workplace managed by an elected committee subject always to immediate recall and responsible to the general workplace assembly, the syndicate; the syndicates would link up in federations, factories joining with factories, industries with industries in a coordinated network driven from the base so that the workers retain responsibility and control.

Basically, it would be the full participation of all within a free, communistic society with strict accountability of committee delegates to the rank and file. It was a system which had developed naturally and worked successfully in revolutionary Spain between July 1936 and August 1937 when its exemplary flame was, to all intents and purposes, suffocated by Stalinist and social democratic forces in the name of 'anti-fascist unity'.

PART TWO

Spain

'Freedom was more than
a word . . .'

'Freedom was more than a word, more than the base coinage of
politicians . . .'

The Nabarra, C. Day Lewis

For all of these groups, the Spanish Civil War was the great
galvanizing force that showed an anarchist society was possible. And
our great demon was General Franco, unbelievably still in power, over
twenty-five years later. Had it not actually happened, it would have
been inconceivable that the last of the Axis powers had survived in
Europe for a quarter of a century; that this relic of the age of Hitler was
still around for the Beatles.

The Spanish people had been bludgeoned by twenty-five years of
propaganda telling them Franco was a wise, just and benevolent ruler,
a message aggressively supported in this very religious country by the
Roman Catholic Church. The two great enemies of the state were
freemasonary and communism. (In fact, Franco was possibly more
rabidly anti-Masonic than he was anti-communist. In his mind
freemasonry was the instrument by which the British had destroyed
the Spanish empire.)

The Roman Catholic Church in Spain presented Franco as the
captain of the besieged Numantine fortress, the new El Cid

Franco's
Spain

103

Campeador, the great crusader, and the Sentinel of the West all rolled into one. Adulation was nearly divine.

Bread and gold, as well as the circuses of the bullfight and football, played their parts in the sustenance of the Franco regime. The most important prop was the hierarchy of subordinates – Franco's loyal band of retainers, praetorians, prelates and bureaucrats. A lot of people made a handsome and permanent living out of the proceeds of Francoism. By the early 1960s, as happened in the then Soviet Union and other totalitarian regimes, there were possibly as many people to whom Francoism seemed advantageous as those to whom liberty seemed desirable.

Axis to grind: Hitler greets Franco on his arrival at Hendaye on the French-Spanish border, 23 October 1940.

The problem facing the anarchists and, more widely, the other anti-Francoists, was how to get the people of Spain to withdraw their coerced consent for the government, and the international community to face up to the moral illegitimacy of the regime.

Calls for civil disobedience and mass resistance as a method of overthrowing Francoist tyranny had been out of the question until the early 1960s. But by late 1958, Spain faced a profound economic crisis. Close to bankruptcy, the country was forced to call in the International Monetary Fund (IMF), much against the will of Franco, who feared it might demand political reforms – or even his resignation.

True to form, the IMF recommended no such thing. Its plan for stabilisation was to cut domestic consumption, massively devalue the peseta, reduce public spending and freeze wages. This led to bankruptcies, sackings and a countrywide shortage of basic consumer goods. The economy had begun to recover by the early 1960s; tourism, emigration (with workers sending back their earnings), 'external aid' and an implacable repression had allowed the regime to minimise its domestic risks, making Spain an obvious target for foreign investment.

An unforeseen consequence of foreign tourists coming to Spain and Spaniards working abroad was that ideas from Western democracies began to permeate Franco's fortress. Under pressure from the pro-Europeans in the Franco Cabinet, there had been a slight relaxation in the tight controls on unionization, and this had led to increased militancy among Spain's ungrateful workers. And a significant section of the Spanish middle class, who had previously relied exclusively upon the regime, began to make money in other

The victors: ecclesiastical, political and military leaders of the Francoist rebellion outside the Basilica of Santiago de Compostela, 25 July 1937. (Left to right); Monseñor Antonio Gracia, Archbishop of Tui (Galicia); José María Peman; Monseñor Rafael Balauri, Archbishop of Santiago; General Antonio Aranda Mata; General Dávila; Monseñor Eijo y Garay, Archbishop of Madrid-Alcalá.

ways, and therefore withdraw its consent for the regime. But what the IMF hadn't counted on was the speed and ferocity with which the regime closed the lid again on Franco's Pandora's Box.

In 1962 there had been a well-publicised 'silent demonstration' of women at the Puerta del Sol in central Madrid in solidarity with a series of miners' strikes for improved wages and conditions. It was the first time it became apparent that even twenty-five years of bitter and bloody fascist repression had not broken the spirit of the Spanish people. This demonstration signalled the revival of working-class resistance to the Franco regime. Arrests of anti-Franco dissidents rose by 80 per cent in 1962 to almost 2,500, and by the summer of 1963, Spain was in a state of serious political and industrial unrest.

The wave of strikes in Asturias, Vizcaya and Guipuzcoa, which marred Franco's '25 Years of Peace' celebrations in the spring of 1964, spread quickly to other regions and was repressed savagely by Franco's secret police (the Brigada Político Social, or BPS) which had been set up and trained by the Gestapo in 1941.

The Civil War had moved a whole generation of idealistic men and women from across the world to risk their lives in Spain to fight in a selfless cause. Now, in 1964, it looked like it might happen again.

x x x

Franco's unhindered existence became the predominant obsession in my life. On one occasion, in the autumn of 1963, I had reason to go to Hamilton to see George Williamson, the Secretary of the Glasgow Committee of 100. George had gone off to the Locarno dance hall, but his mum Annie, a rather douce and proper West of Scotland lady who did not entirely approve of George's activities, invited me in for a cup of tea and a chat. Apparently I made such an impression on her – one so young going on so seriously about Spain and Franco – she said 'Dae ye no' think ye'd be better aff at the dancin', son?'

George told me later that after the news broke of my arrest in Spain she gave a deep sigh and said: 'Ah wish tae Gawd that wee boy hud taken ma advice and gawn tae the dancin' an' fun' a nice wee girl instead!'

But much as I liked girls and the dancing, I felt it was impossible to remain silent and inactive in the face of a fascist dictator's repression of his country's people. Right then – even as I sat having my cup of tea with George's mum – miners were being arrested and tortured, their families brutalized, and everything I believed in crushed by the actions of one man. In Glasgow the anarchists organised regular demonstrations against the arrest and torture of Spanish labour militants to the office of the Spanish Vice-Consul, which more often than not ended with our occupying the building, and handing over petitions.

But it wasn't enough. All this effort, all this talk and passion and endless injustice, and things just weren't changing.

I felt I had to do something more.

x x x

I may not have been wise or competent in what I did or the way I went about it, but I did not have the benefit of hindsight. I felt it would be hypocritical to choose the easy option of marches, pickets and leafleting and not try to destroy the evils of Francoism, once and for all, with whatever means I could. I could not stand aloof. I wanted to be a participant – not a bystander. My Presbyterian conscience would be assuaged by nothing less than total involvement in the armed struggle against Franco and his supporters, even if the results were only to make them uneasy or embarrassed.

As the philosopher Jeremy Bentham observed in his study *On Government*, sometimes violence is the only way the oppressed 'can obtain a particle of relief'. I may not have qualified as one of Bentham's 'oppressed', but I felt I had to do something positive to show my solidarity with the Spanish people.

x x x

Remember, violence and direct action are techniques, not an ideology or philosophy. For the Resistance they were tactics of last resort to counter Franco's disparity of power. The means used were proportional to the ends: the use of small explosive charges against property – not with the intention of killing or injuring anyone, but to grab the press headlines to show the world that some people at least were still fighting the Franco regime. The other objective was to kill Franco. They were fighting not to advance the aims or principles of anarchism, but because of an overwhelming injustice, that a grotesquely anachronistic regime was able to continue to oppress its

Spanish Resistance

people unchallenged, as it had done since launching its genocidal military-theo-fascist coup in 1936.

Also, the anarchist strategy must be seen in the context of the time. In the early 1960s, with the example of Cuba, Algeria and the other national liberation movements that were sweeping away reactionary colonial regimes across the globe, it seemed for a time that that the use of spectacular direct actions might stand a reasonable chance of success, of triggering a popular movement that would overthrow the dictator and his regime. What the anarchists were not prepared to do was launch a wave of reactionary and indiscriminate violence targeting innocent bystanders. The prime consideration in the campaign was proportionality between means, ends and morality.

The inescapable problem with violence, however, is that no matter how just the cause or selflessly idealistic the motives, there is the ever-present danger that it can quickly become a brutal, self-serving and self-perpetuating process which fatally undermines and destroys any possibility of the intended beneficial outcome. Pursuing moral and ethical objectives by violent means can be a very fine and dangerous line to walk. It is not an easy line to draw,

The central justification of violence is self-defence and righting great wrongs which have no other redress. It is always an act of last resort and has no part in promoting anarchism. Ideas can only be advanced through argument, debate and persuasion. In fact, one of the main planks of anarchism is the removal of coercion and violence from all human relations. How you get change is by pushing at the boundaries with whatever methods are available to try to ameliorate things – writing to your MP, demonstrations, petitions, pickets, civil disobedience and occupations. Violence only comes into the equation when people reach the limits beyond which the powers-that-be will permit no more reform. It is then up to each individual whether or not they should turn back or go beyond those limits. But, to paraphrase Mrs Beaton and Noam Chomsky, you first have to reach those limits.

x x x

While the rest of the world turned a blind eye to Franco the anarchists and the Basque nationalists were the only ones who took the decision to act. As far as we were concerned, the limits of legitimate protest against the Franco regime had long since been reached. Our sense of morality and dignity told us we had a clear duty of defence, not only against attack but also against a regime which used torture, imprisonment and physical force to keep people in a state of servitude.

I decided I could do nothing useful in Scotland. To achieve anything, I needed to be in London where I would be closer to the action and to the people who made the action happen.

✗ ✗ ✗

London was only a staging post. My plan was to move to France, find a job and a flat in Perpignan as a base for whatever I had to do in Spain, only a few miles down the road. I 'skippered' with two comrades, Brian Hart and his companion, Margaret Haines, in their ground floor room at 57 Ladbroke Road (where a steady stream of Glasgow anarchists followed), and then with Mark Hendy, in nearby Ladbroke Grove. Mark worked as a copy editor for a London publisher, and also sub-edited and helped print the SWF paper *Direct Action* in a damp cellar in Cross Street, Islington.

In London, the battle appeared closer than in Scotland. Notting Hill Gate in the early 1960s was not only a seedbed of radical libertarian and bohemian culture; because of the high numbers of black West Indians, the Gate and Ladbroke Grove were also focal points of white racist and neo-Nazi 'culture'. The tension had simmered down from the Notting Hill and Bayswater riots over the 1958 August Bank Holiday, but this was still the centre of British Nazism.

Arnold Leese House at 46–48 Princedale Road in Holland Park was its epicentre. Conspiracy theorists and flagging right-wing groups and parties, including the League of Empire Loyalists, the Union Movement, the British National Party, the Racial Preservation Society and the Greater Britain Movement were all located in that seedy, run-down tenement, as were the 'Britons' and 'Augustine' publishing houses, publishers of the book *Darkness Visible*.

COLIN MACINNES

'Despite the frenzied efforts of politicians of all
hues to persuade, bully and frighten us into their
parties - or at least acquiesce in their activities -
I believe the vast majority of the human race
detests, mistrusts and despises the purely political
animal - where it is safe for them to do so. Yet I
also believe, with the anarchists, that the instinct
to unite with others - at any rate, at some point and
for some objects - is equally widespread among
mankind.

'The anarchists are the only non-political -
indeed, anti-political - party in existence. They're
not even, in fact, a party - you can't join, take out
a card, pay a subscription (though donations would be
welcome), and anything you do or don't do is because
you want to. The only way you can become an anarchist
is to wake up one morning and find you are one.

'From what I have read of anarchist lives, and
observed of those I know, they have also the
peculiarity among political groups of behaving, in
their private lives, according to their philosophical
doctrine. They don't love the masses from afar (which
has always seemed to me a way of hating and fearing
them) - in fact, they're not interested in 'the
masses', but in creating a mass movement based on
self-persuaded, not converted, individuals; and if
they do like particular persons, then they will work
with them and for them. Temperamentally, they are
informed, versatile and resourceful, indulgent of
human weakness, but set high standards for
themselves. Like all political groups they have

sectarians and extremists, but fewer than other
parties, because they nod kindly to these wayward
brethren, and then get on with the business.'

Colin MacInnes (author of *Absolute Beginners*), from
'The Anarchists', *Queen* magazine, 1962

Arnold Leese, a former vet, an anti-Semite and admirer of Hitler, had been a founder member of the Imperial Fascist League in 1928. Released from prison in 1944 on grounds of ill-health, Leese became the principle star in the 1940s British fascist firmament, attracting to him all the leading national socialist players of the 1950s and 1960s, including Cambridge graduate and schoolteacher Colin Jordan. When Leese and his wife died, the house was left to Jordan who turned it into the base for his 'White Defence League' (WDL), the instigators of much of the racial confrontation in Notting Hill in the late 1950s. In 1960 the WDL merged with the National Labour Party to form the Hitlerite British National Party and then the National Socialist Movement, founded by Jordan and John Tyndall on what would have been Hitler's 73rd birthday, 20 April 1962.

The paranoid wackos of this seedy West London tenement had one thing in common – the conviction that Jews, freemasons, homosexuals, gypsies, Jesuits, anarchists and Communist Party members were all agents of subversion under the control of a ruthless global elite directing world events to their advantage.

The swastika-emblazoned Arnold Leese House was regularly under attack, mainly from the '62 Group' – a hard-core, secretive Zionist offshoot of the multiracial anti-fascist Yellow Star Movement – so the ground-floor bookshop had steel shutters and its windows were screened with thick wire mesh.

x x x

The Jewish anti-fascists had an excellent communications system as many of their members and sympathisers were London cabbies and whenever one of their number identified a possible meeting in progress they would turn up shortly afterwards, mob-handed in cabs, and ambush them. As the Notting Hill Anarchist Group, we would regularly attend any anti-fascist rallies or demonstrations, but by that time Colin Jordan, the national organiser of the National Socialist Movement, was in jail on charges under the 1936 Public Order Act and the Nazis were trying to keep a low profile while they regrouped and reorganized.

Neo-fascism in Europe

Neo-Nazis and extreme right-wing activists were making their presence felt throughout Europe in the early 1960s. One of these – Stefano Delle Chiaie, a 24-year-old former member of the Italian Nazi organisation Ordine Nuevo, and founder of the neo-fascist group Avanguardia Nazionale (AN), who was to become the most notorious of these over the next three decades – came to London in 1962 to discuss the setting up of a fascist 'Black International' with, among others, Colin Jordan.

British Nazis are shouted down by anti-fascists in Trafalgar Square.

What Jordan and his colleagues did not know was that Delle Chiaie was an agent for a department of the Italian Interior Ministry, and had been since 1960. He also worked for the Italian Foreign Military Intelligence Service, SIFAR, from at least late 1963, and possibly even earlier.

This did not mean that he was there to gain evidence against these right wing groups. On the contrary. The early 1960s was a high point in the Cold War, and some of the more reactionary elements in the

Italian industrial and state apparatus recognised the advantages of using Delle Chiaie's fascist gangs as 'plausibly deniable' forces deployed against the left. Delle Chiaie was operating in both capacities.

In the 1963 Italian elections, the Communist Party won 25% of the vote. This was construed as a huge threat to some large corporations, not least US oil interests in the Middle East. Washington's State Department believed that if a Communist government came to power it would upset the business climate America wanted in its local client states, and throw the US Sixth Fleet out of Naples, its most important Mediterranean base. The very first US National Security Council Memorandum (NSC1) is, in fact, about Italy and the Italian elections. It stated that if the Communists came to power in the election through legitimate, democratic means, the US must declare a national emergency: the US should launch subversive actions in Italy, overthrow the Italian government, and that the US should begin contingency plans for direct military intervention. Italy and the subversion of the Italian political process was to remain the main target for the CIA's global operations until at least 1975.

Delle Chiaie was probably the most significant player the post-WWII neo-fascist movement has produced, and his name is inextricably linked with just about every major right-wing conspiracy, scandal and terrorist outrage in Italy, Europe and Latin America since 1960. In Italy, the so-called 'strategy of tension' aimed to discredit the left in general and the anarchist movement in particular by indiscriminately bombing public places such as Milan's Piazza Fontana in 1969 and the Bologna railway station in 1980. Many people were killed in these incidents, but fortunately it did not have the impact hoped for by the architects of terror. The election in 1978 of the highly thought of anti-fascist and socialist Sandro Pertini as President of the Republic did much to strengthen and restore faith in democratic values. Pertini became the most popular President the Italian Republic ever had. In fact, by 1983 Bettino Craxi became the first ever socialist President of the Council of Ministers, giving the right-wing Christian Democrats their worst electoral result since 1948.

x x x

The neo-fascists in Britain were not as sophisticated or Machiavellian as their Italian and French colleagues. They had a much more thuggish and short-term view of their role in the great scheme of things. More importantly, for all their faults, neither the Metropolitan Police Special Branch nor the British security or intelligence services had quite such a large number of reactionary personnel or the same geopolitical agenda as the Italians and their CIA sponsors. In fact, with one or two notable exceptions such as George Kennedy Young (MI6's number two until 1961), Peter Wright and elements in the media-manipulating 'Special Political Action' section of the Special Intelligence Service (SIS), most members of the British security and intelligence apparatus were committed anti-fascists who had fought the Nazis in World War II, unlike many of their Italian counterparts who been unrepentant fascists under Mussolini – and remained so in the post-war Christian-Democrat era.

Of course, not all anti-fascists are necessarily liberal (as demonstrated by Israel's treatment of the Palestinians). Some '62 group' members regularly exchanged information with MI5 and Special Branch on non-Jewish radicals in return for information on fascists. And in February 1980, the *New Statesman* exposed Gerry Gable, the editor of the anti-fascist magazine *Searchlight*, as a long-time informer for the Security Service, MI5, and the Metropolitan Police Special Branch.

In fact, all this activity in the early sixties had led the Metropolitan Police Special Branch to form a dedicated political sub-branch, which liaised with the Home Office and MI5. It quickly discovered that conventional surveillance wouldn't work with the left: firstly, groups tended to be non-hierarchical and decentralized, so it was difficult to identify 'ringleaders', as the police love to do; and secondly, very few of us could afford a telephone. It was almost impossible to listen in and make connections between a known activist and other, unknown likeminded people. Most of what the state knew about us they gleaned from reading the newspapers, ours or the nationals.

But they did what they could, busily opening mail, making lists from newspapers, and taping the few phones that were in the hands of subversives.

To test their acuteness – and wind up the authorities – in November 1963, John Brailey, a convenor of the London Committee of 100, organised a round robin of phone calls to members saying they should be at the US Embassy on one particular night at 6 p.m. Four Committee people turned up to find around a hundred police protecting the Embassy entrance.

Sometimes police documents were left in opened mail after it had been resealed. This may have been a deliberate Special Branch ploy in an attempt to intimidate and frighten off the recipients, but it was more likely to have been a blunder. This gave rise to another wind-up: our letters would mention small enclosures such as a lock of hair, though none had been actually sent; the police on finding them missing, obviously panicked and imagined they had carelessly discarded them in the opening process, so to cover their tracks duly provided substitutes.

Special Branch officers also attended all demonstrations and public meetings they considered of interest. It wasn't difficult to spot them; they were either smartly dressed with ties and raincoats or else were the scruffiest 'student types'.

But their most advanced and persistent method was infiltration. Around the time of the RAF Wethersfield demonstration on 9 December 1961, a chap by the name of Darren produced some loose change from his pocket to pay for something prior to the march, and among the coins was an RAF Regiment button. When asked to explain it he blushed suspiciously and began blustering, then hurriedly left the room never to return.

The Branch's anarchist–libertarian fringe specialist was Detective Sergeant Roy Cremer, whom I encountered at a demonstration in Trafalgar Square against the sentencing of Nelson Mandela in June 1964. It was the first time I had been arrested (for shouting abuse and not moving on when threatened by the police), and was waiting for the Black Maria to take me away when this pale, cerebral, somewhat

Special Branch: Detective
Sergeant Roy Cremer,
Scotland Yard's
'anarchist' specialist.

cadaverous-looking man appeared. He introduced himself, and began a rather sophisticated discussion of the merits of anarchism over Marxism, non-violence and persuasion over violence. He knew how to disguise an interrogation as a chat and his thought processes were as relentless and silent as the mainspring in a watch. He was reassuring, flattering and appeared to be sympathetic to anarchism. I suspect, in an intellectual way, he was. He was certainly liberal-minded, anti-racist and hostile to apartheid and the racist South African government of Dr Hendrik Verwoerd. Over the next decade, I got to know him. And, I suspect, he got to know me better

x x x

The Libertarian Movement

The Notting Hill Anarchist Group introduced me to the exiled Spanish anarchists of the *Movimiento Libertario Español* (MLE), an umbrella name for the various sections of the Spanish anarchist and anarcho-syndicalist movements.

The MLE in London had been in a bad way for a long time. The long years of exile in an alien environment had taken their toll, and the Franco dictatorship seemed stronger than ever. Its main activities had been demonstrations and pamphlets, and maintaining contact with other exiles. For years they had been becalmed, pinning their hopes on signs and portents that turned out not to mean what they thought. There was a sad nobility about the more elderly Spanish exiles who had been involved in the Civil war. I suppose it was what

Federico García Lorca described as *duende* – the enigmatic pathos which can be felt, but is difficult to explain. For a short time they had lived through an intense period of brotherhood, disinterested selflessness, self-sacrifice and solidarity. For many the few months of the Revolution between July 1936 and the early summer of 1937 were the happiest of their lives.

Hunted down in Spain, France and North Africa, they had come to Britain to nurse their dreams and wait for their day; and hand on the torch of faith and hope. Concha Liaño, a co-founder of Mujeres Libres ('Free Women') said: 'Sometimes I wonder if it was worth all the pain, all the sacrifices, all the suffering, but then I think, really, we taught the world a lesson. Insofar as we were able, we set an example of the

July 1936: Miliciana on Barcelona's Ramblas.

possibility of living without government, because there was no government, yet the collectives were working and everything was working.'

After successfully fighting off the military and the fascists and having tasted what libertarian socialism really was, many had been reduced to going through the motions of militancy after years of exile within an indifferent host nation in an unfamiliar culture and a depressing climate.

But now they were energized again.

January 1939: Franco's victims cross
the Pyrenees into exile.

x x x

Brian Hart had introduced me to two activists of the Iberian
Federation of Libertarian Youth (FIJL) in Bristol in 1964. These were
the Gurucharri brothers, Bernardo and Salvador, both closely
involved with the organisation's clandestine planning group, the
Defensa Interior (DI). Brian himself had gone on at least one secret
mission to Spain on behalf of the FIJL, as had two other SWF
members on separate occasions.

Salvador, known as 'Salva', had only recently returned to London
following his release from a Paris prison that February, a release
forced on the French authorities after a hunger strike and a massive
popular campaign led by well-known French intellectuals and artists.
He had been arrested at the request of the Spanish Security Services,
accused of being a key member of the now illegal FIJL. The fact that
the French authorities would do the bidding of Franco's secret police

was another veil falling between me and the truth – the theoretically liberal democratic governments of Europe were actively engaged in preserving the Francoist regime.

When I told Salva that I wanted to play a direct part in the resistance movement he said he would pass my offer on to the CNT's Defence Commission in Paris. My youth, my enthusiasm and my history of militancy in Scotland – and the fact that I wasn't a Spaniard – meant it was unlikely I was a police agent.

After a discussion about the serious and dangerous nature of what I was doing, which I brushed aside, pig-headedly refusing to countenance the possibility of disaster, Salva told me that an operation was being planned and I would be contacted when the final preparations had been made. I had to be ready to travel on twenty-four hours notice.

Excited by the prospect of at last doing something positive, I hitched back home to Blantyre to collect some belongings and tell my Mum and Gran I was going on a long hitchhiking tour of Europe and that I would be writing to them regularly to let them know my whereabouts.

During this short visit, the local paper, the *Hamilton Advertiser*, interviewed me on the subject of my long hair, which was still a point of curiosity. Their storyline was that I was putting barbers out of their jobs. They inquired about my plans for the future and I told them too I planned hitch-hiking through Europe. As I waved my Mum goodbye from her doorway at Calder Street I wondered to myself if she suspected there was more to my trip than I had let on. Maybe all parents say goodbye to their children wondering to some degree whether they'll ever see them again. I returned to London to wait.

x x x

Why did I, for the most part an unaggressive and easy-going person, commit myself to going to Spain to engage in an unspecified but violent campaign against the Franco regime? I didn't know exactly what was involved, but I guessed it would probably be as a courier carrying explosives and weapons. Apart from not knowing the language, I was too young and inexperienced to do anything else, but who knew what the future might bring? It was, as Longfellow wrote, complex:

> 'A boy's will is the wind's will, and the thoughts of
> youth are long, long thoughts.'

It was, undeniably, the act of an adolescent. I was at the time, like all young men, immortal – El Zorro, Superman, Audie Murphy and The Bowery Boys rolled into one. Now it will seem to many a foolish, naïve, impulsive act, and perhaps it was. I cannot claim, either, that it was entirely altruistic – my motives were certainly in part a desire for excitement and adventure.

I was far from alone in these youthful sentiments. They were all around me in the Orange Order, centuries of hatred channelled through the energy of youth and directed against one's neighbour, all over a disagreement about how to worship the same God, or a right to march down a street – a fight for the sake of a fight. Growing up in that atmosphere, how infinitely preferable it was to find my heroes in the Spanish Civil War and my enemy in a fascist dictator. (Living in a time when youth's idea of adventure is an 18–30 holiday binge-drinking in Faliraki, I have some sympathy with my teenage self.)

The Civil War struggle was still going on, but the working-class heroes who had gone to stop fascism were now either dead or elderly and had done their bit. We needed new volunteers to take their place and, hopefully, change the world. That was to be my mission. Something had to be done and no one else was doing it so it was down to me. As my Granny used to say, 'If you want something doing, do it yourself.'

x x x

I wanted to change the world because the world needed to be changed. Right in the middle of Europe, Franco was running one of the most brutal and repressive regimes in modern history – he had killed more Spanish people than Hitler killed German Jews – and the

Western democracies were now helping him to survive. Even now, while the civilized world was humming along to the songs of the Beatles and the Supremes or listening to Martin Luther King, the number of political dissidents being arrested and tortured by Franco's secret police was steadily increasing.

What redress was possible in the face of such injustice? The West was effectively condoning the regime. In the immediate post-war period, Western governments simply ignored Spain and left Franco to his own devices, but all this changed in 1959 when President Eisenhower visited Spain, effectively welcoming Franco back into the fold.

In 1964 the Francoist regime celebrated 'twenty five years of peace' (or '*paz! paz! paz!*' as the Spaniards said, in which I – and they – heard the sound of gunfire) with a series of major cultural, sporting and industrial exhibitions. Edward Heath, then president of the UK Board of Trade, made an official visit to Spain to open a British industrial fair in Barcelona, and was received enthusiastically by Franco on 2 April. The following month French Foreign Minister Maurice Couve de Murville bolstered Franco's standing even more with a three-day official visit. In June the European Community (EC) opened talks with Franco's government to discuss its application for membership of the EC. Tourists were also flowing in, some 14 million alone in 1964, compared with 11 million the previous year, all of them helping to fill the coffers of the Francoist treasury.

For me and my fellow anarchists and anti-fascists, it was as though our world was stepping through the looking glass with Alice. We were welcoming this mass murderer and Hitler collaborator, still wearing his jackboots, into civilized society, redeemed somehow by his anti-communism. The Spanish Civil War – indeed the Second World War – seemed to have been all for nothing.

A Rebel with a Cause

Of course there are many ways to act for a cause. For years – indeed, for decades – we had been demonstrating, picketing, urging boycotts, and all the while our protests were ignored as more and more Spaniards were being arrested and killed. The only out, I felt, was to somehow break this frustrating cycle of meaningless protest and find an alternative way through. This was how I came to make the conscious decision to commit to the anti-Franco movement as a fighter rather than as a helper of Franco's victims. It was end of tether time – to do otherwise would not only have been moral, psychological and intellectual cowardice, I felt; it would have been a form of collaboration. Seeing someone injured and doing nothing to help is to act negatively; as my Granny said, 'we are not bystanders to life.' I would have felt hypocritical choosing the easy, safe, useless and ineffective options of marching on demonstrations, going on picket lines and leafleting instead of challenging Franco head on.

x x x

I am not defending my actions, just trying to explain them. Presented with the same question today, with a little more wisdom, I'm not sure that I would do the same thing. I didn't know exactly what I was signing up to. I thought I knew the risks I was running personally (although, as it turned out, I had underestimated the odds against me) but I must confess, I did not spend much time considering unforeseen consequences – the possibility of innocent victims or the unleashing of an even more horrific repression on the people of Spain. I was no Hamlet. Not for me plunging into the moral quandaries and endless debates of the 'to be' or 'not to be' of direct action, I just gave them a nod of recognition and stepped lightly round them. Wrongdoers had to be held to account and there was little chance of Franco sitting in the dock facing the justice his countless victims demanded; so it was all down to me and others who shared my commitment.

My view was morally clear-cut. I had an obligation to intervene on behalf of past, present and future victims of Franco and his regime. It was a just war and a just cause against a clearly defined enemy – the last of the Axis regimes. My authority was my conscience and the ghosts of the countless victims of Francoism since 1936.

The objectives of Defensa Interior's campaign were not military; they were social, moral and psychological. Unlike, say, ETA or Al Quaida today, we did not seek to terrorize the population into changing their ways. Our aims were to draw attention to the nature of the regime and to try to precipitate its downfall by weakening its economic base, the tourist trade, and highlighting its human rights abuses; we thought of the small bombing campaign which ran in Spain between June of 1962 and August 1963 as spectacular, dramatic and well-directed propaganda actions of last resort. These were certainly violent actions, but they were not ferocious. They targeted Francoist property and institutions, as opposed to people. They were acts of desperation by frustrated people, as one might call the actions of Hezbollah today, but still, we felt, contained and humane. The exception was Franco himself. Killing Franco, the one person capable of reconciling the various contending interest groups, appeared to be the only available and appropriate agency of regime change for an anarchist. Not for us B-52s over Madrid or terrorizing and murdering the population with the tanks and humvees of the 82nd Airborne.

x x x

Anger at injustice, frustration that nothing was changing and excitement about getting involved were what drove me to Spain. By

1964, these feelings seemed to be shared with a wider British public. The social revolution of the sixties had begun. Cold War tensions were increasing, as was fear of the bomb and the feeling that parliamentary politics were incapable of pulling us back from the edge of the precipice. Two other events seemed to bring about a crisis in public confidence in the British ruling class.

The Profumo Affair The first of these was the 1963 scandal surrounding the Profumo affair. This bedroom farce involved John Profumo, the charming and urbane Conservative Secretary of State for War, a call-girl, Christine Keeler, and Captain Eugene Ivanov, a GRU officer (Soviet Army Intelligence) from the Soviet Embassy. The affair remains a byword for scandal – not because of how much sensitive information may have passed along this chain, but because it symbolized the moral failure of the upper class and brought about the collapse of the Macmillan government and the end of Harold Macmillan's political career. A few years earlier the story would probably never even have made the newspapers. It would have been confined to banter in smoke-filled Establishment clubs, but this was the post-Lady Chatterley trial era of political and social satire, of magazines like *Private Eye* and the television show That Was The Week That Was, which pursued the case relentlessly, pouring scorn on the morality and integrity of the upper classes. The programme scored a direct hit on the hypocrisy of the Establishment with a parody of the old music hall number, 'She was Poor but she was Honest': 'See him in the House of Commons/Making laws to put the blame/While the object of his passion/Walks the streets to hide her shame.' TWTWTW's weekly debunking of religion, politics, royalty and sex attracted what was then a colossal audience of some 12m viewers and was a powerful popular opinion former.

The photograph of Christine Keeler – the object of Profumo's passion – naked, straddling a chair, was to become the icon of the swinging sixties. But what captured the public imagination were the stories of orgies and debauchery at parties where a high-ranking member of the Establishment, a Cabinet minister, served guests naked except for a mask, and ate his dinner from a dog bowl.

Matters came to a head in March 1963 when Profumo lied about his relationship with Keeler to the House of Commons and then a few weeks later was forced to admit 'misleading' the House. Remember, this was a pre-pill, pre-promiscuity age, when unmarried pregnancy was a matter of deep family shame, and backstreet abortionists thrived. The tabloids may have been brash but they were still polite and deferential to politicians. All that began to change after the Profumo affair. The *status quo* ceased to be a condition to be respected and became, instead, a rock 'n' roll band.

X X X

The second symbolic event happened in 1964 with the graduation of the first generation of students from the University of Sussex. In the 1950s and 60s, a number of new universities were founded to broaden the availability of tertiary education beyond the elite academic citadels of Oxbridge, St Andrews and the like – Brunel, Sussex, York, East Anglia, Essex, Lancaster, Warwick and Kent were the first of these 'redbricks'.

The University of Sussex at Brighton with its focus on social studies was the most popular of the redbricks. By 1964, three years after its first undergraduates had arrived, *The Economist* could say: 'To have a child at the University of Sussex is beyond question the most absolutely OK thing in Britain now'. By this point it had over a thousand students and by 1968 it was to have almost 3,000.

The type of graduate the redbricks were producing, and the type of graduate it was now 'OK', or cool, to be, was from a working or middle class background, well educated, but without the investment in the Establishment that previous generations of educated working-class youths had had. They were the first generation equipped with the tools of the Establishment who felt comfortable using them to undermine the Establishment's foundations. The number of these more liberal thinkers increased rapidly throughout the sixties, imbued with democratic, egalitarian and individualistic expectations that the political system could never hope to meet.

The Student Movement

A similar process was also at work on the industrial front where the authority of the trade union leadership was being challenged by a rebellious rank and file. Wildcat strikes called by militants beyond the control of the trade union leadership became commonplace as more and more workers realized that their leaders were being co-opted by the state once they were elected to Parliament, or put on some government planning body. They began to resolve their own problems through collective processes which bypassed the traditional political system altogether.

The electorate may have been uncertain as to what they did want, but they were becoming increasingly certain about what they did not want – the Tory old guard who had propelled an old fashioned earl, Sir Alex Douglas Home, into Downing Street. Harold Wilson's election with a narrow Commons majority of just four seats on 16 October 1964 led to the axiomatic mantra in political science circles that in parliamentary elections people voted against a party rather for another. Labour's slogan '13 wasted years' appears to have found some resonance in what the electorate clearly felt was a new age. It was the first time Labour had been in office since 1951.

According to ex-Major General Richard Clutterbuck of the right-wing Institute for the Study of Conflict and Lecturer in Politics at the University of Exeter, people were now voting from fear: 'People who fear a Conservative government fear industrial confrontation and a society disrupted by unrest. People who fear a Labour government fear bureaucracy and economic collapse.'

x x x

In mid-July Salvador and Bernardo told me I should be ready to leave for Paris by the end of the month. Everything was now in hand for my trip to Spain.

Shortly before I left for Paris, I was invited to appear on what later turned out to be, for me, an almost disastrous chat show called Let Me Speak, on the recently launched BBC2. Chaired by Malcolm Muggeridge, the programme was slotted into the religious hour on Sundays. Muggeridge had recently hit the headlines as a result of a negative comment on the Royal family, which in turn had led to hostile tabloid press stories and physical attacks on him and his wife by members of the League of Empire Loyalists. To make matters worse, he had declared himself sympathetic to anarchism.

Having invited a small spectrum of anarchists, with me and another young lad called Vincent Johnson representing the 'revolutionary anarchists', Muggeridge asked me if I was sincere in my revolutionary aims. Clasping his hands in prayer-like fashion he asked, would I, for instance, given the opportunity, assassinate Franco? It was an unlucky shot in the dark, for that was pretty damn close to what I was hoping to do. What could I say but yes? By the time the programme was due to be broadcast, however, events had moved on, and I was in a Spanish gaol. My contribution to the programme was edited out by the intervention of Sir Hugh Greene, the then DG of the BBC, and of Muggeridge himself.

An unlikely friendship had been forged and for years afterwards Muggeridge and I exchanged Christmas cards. He even offered to stand bail for me seven years later in the Angry Brigade trial at the Old Bailey. Wynford Hicks and Ian Vine from Bristol were also part of the anarchist panel.

Immediately the recording of the broadcast was over I returned to Mark Hendy's flat to pack my rucksack. To Mark, John Rety and my other friends I said I was going to pick grapes in the south of France and would probably meet them at the international anarchist summer camp near Toulouse, during August.

Among my belongings was a Christie tartan kilt. There was no chauvinism intended. The year before I had gone on a short hitch-hiking holiday through Belgium and France with my mate and fellow apprentice Malky Dow, and had discovered that hitchhiking on the Continent was a lot easier for kilted Scots, for whom the French entertain a certain admiration. This was possibly because the Scots made war on most of their own kings and put so many of them to death – or maybe it had something to do with the lack of underpants.

It was 31 July 1964, just three weeks after my eighteenth birthday on 10 July 1964. I went home to pack my Bergen, folding my kilt ostentatiously on top, and made the final preparations for my trip to

Paris. That same week the Beatles' 'Hard Day's Night' was Top of the Pops, sharp-suited scooter-riding Mods were battling it out on the beaches of Hastings and Brighton with leather-clad bikers, and thousands of young working-class students with high expectations were preparing for their new lives on the redbrick university campuses.

Me? I was off to Spain; like George Orwell in 1936, because at that time and in that atmosphere it seemed the only conceivable thing to do.

'Our regime is based on bayonets and blood ...'

'Our regime is based on bayonets and blood, not on hypocritical elections.'

> Francisco Franco (quoted in H. L. Matthews,
> *Half of Spain Died*)

I took the tube from Notting Hill Gate to Victoria Station where I bought a single ticket for the morning boat train to Calais and Paris. (As things turned out, this was a prophetic piece of Knoxian prudence.)

I had visited Brussels and Paris briefly on my first hitchhiking holiday the previous year, during the Glasgow Fair – the traditional annual summer holiday, in July, for working-class Glaswegians. As I stood on deck and watched the tumbling wake of the ship snake back towards the white cliffs around Dover harbour, my veins were piping pure adrenaline. When my small remaining funds were converted into a little over a hundred new French francs by the ship's purser, I knew there was no going back. I'd lose out on the exchange rate.

At Calais, I boarded the train to Paris, and arrived at the Gare du Nord in the late afternoon. Paris was sweltering its August heat. As I made my way through the islands of luggage and small family groups preparing to flee to the coast, I was overwhelmed by the noisy excitement and the pungent aromas of black cigarette tobacco and roasting coffee.

I finally found the metro and looked for my station on the map – the Jacques Bonsergent metro station at the bottom of the boulevard de Magenta, near the place de la République.

It had been on this boulevard – outside M. Véry's restaurant at number 22 – that the French anarchist, François Koenigstein, better known as Ravachol, had been arrested in 1892 for blowing up the homes of a judge of the French supreme court and the deputy prosecutor of the Republic. The restaurant itself was the target of a bomb attack by anarchists shortly afterwards, presumably in the belief that M. Véry had something to do with Ravachol's arrest.

Ravachol

I was in Paris.

x x x

Emerging from the metro, I crossed the boulevard with its hooting, impatient streams of traffic into the relative quiet of the rue de Lancry and the apartment of Germinal García, one of the 'safe houses' of the anti-Francoist resistance organisation in Paris.

Germinal lived at number 12, beside an old and noisy printshop. I stepped through the fortress-like double doors into the half-lit gloom of an enclosed courtyard, and when I asked for 'Monsieur García', the concièrge brusquely indicated a narrow dark circular flight of stairs off to the right, muttering 'premier étage à droite'. I discovered subsequently that both the concièrge and her husband had got the job – and apartment – because they were FIJL members and friends of Germinal.

A square-faced man answered the door. He was in his early forties, with jet-black hair and a pencil-thin moustache, and dressed in shorts. Despite his informal clothing, he carried himself rather stiffly.

'Allo. Je cherche Monsieur García. Vous est lui, non? Je swee Christee. Zoot alors!'

I don't know where I got the last bit from; I must have thought it was how all French conversations ended, a bit like 'over and out'. In any case it broke the ice and Germinal immediately smiled, extended his arms in a warm gesture of welcome and motioned me inside.

The flat was small – bedroom, kitchen, bathroom and lounge – and furnished spartanly, with tall windows, louvred shutters, and a small balcony, just like I had imagined all Parisian apartments. Germinal took me through to the kitchen where he sat me down, poured two glasses of wine and opened the fridge, pulling out all sorts of continental goodies, some of which I'd never seen before, chorizo, saucisson, hard-boiled eggs, Emmental cheese and a baguette from a breadbin. We exchanged a few mutually unintelligible pleasantries – Germinal's knowledge of English was only fractionally better than my command of French and had been culled from French *films noirs*, gangster films and cheap novellas.

x x x

My host was a Spanish anarchist with a long history. Although a member of FIJL and trusted confidant of Defensa Interior, Germinal avoided direct involvement in the armed activities of the clandestine organisation and kept his participation to a strictly supportive role. The French security services, however, were aware of Germinal's part in the anarchist network. Anxious to avoid potential embarrassment or trouble from the anarchists during Soviet premier Nikita Khrushchev's state visit to France in 1962, President Charles de Gaulle's police and security services knocked on Germinal's door early one morning and told him to pack a bag quickly as he was leaving the country. They drove him to a military airfield on the outskirts of Paris where other Spanish and French anarchists had been rounded up. They were then put on board a French air force plane and flown to Corsica. The French government apologised to the anarchists' employers, and put them in first class hotels for a month with all expenses and salaries paid. Germinal enjoyed the free holiday enormously.

The rue de Lancry apartment had been a Parisian safe house for DI meetings and countless anarchist activists, fugitives and partisans over the years, including the most famous Spanish urban guerrilla of them all, Francisco Sabaté Llopart – 'El Quico'. One of El Quico's more spectacular actions took place in September 1955 during a visit to Barcelona by Franco. El Quico hailed a taxi and blithely drove

Germinal Garcia

El Quico

around the Catalan capital firing anti-regime leaflets through the sun-roof from a mortar on the back seat.

x x x

After a painfully slow conversation over glasses of wine and a stroll around the nearby place de la République, Germinal set up a camp bed in the lounge. Before bidding me goodnight Germinal explained, mainly in sign language, that this was the very bed in which El Quico had slept, with his Thomson sub machine-gun beside him under the sheets.

I woke the next morning, Sunday, slightly stiff, to the unfamiliar sounds of early morning Paris through the open window; the noisy phut-phuts and throaty whines of unfamiliar vehicles, the banging of doors, snatches of loud aggressive conversations in French and the hunger-inducing whiffs of freshly baked bread. Germinal came in with some loaves and lit the gas under the octagonal aluminium coffee percolator while I went to the toilet. The bathroom perplexed me because I had never heard of a bidet before, let alone seen one, and I was genuinely puzzled as to its purpose.

x x x

Over the next two days I wandered the streets of Paris, enjoying being aimless in a great city, and trying to read its thoughts and moods. I visited Notre Dame, explored the medieval rabbit warrens of the Ile de la Cité where fugitives from feudalism used to huddle within the city walls, strolled along the banks of the Seine looking at the stalls of books and the ranks of paintings, wandered around the place de la République, saw the Arc de Triomphe and sat on the terrace of the Café de l'Elysée, a few feet from the endless roar of traffic as it advanced relentlessly along the avenue des Champs Elysées. I sipped a beer and scanned the kaleidoscope of faces, musing to myself that if such an innocuous looking character as myself was about to go into Spain as part of an attempt to kill Franco, what dramatic stories could each of these busy and purposeful passers-by tell?

x x x

On the evening of the second day, three FIJL members collected me from Germinal's apartment and we drove to a small bistro in Belleville. One of these was Salvador 'Salva' Gurucharri.

Belleville and adjoining Menilmontant were at the heart of old working-class Paris; the place where the communards of 1871 had made their last stand against the troops of the Versailles government. On the benches of the boulevard sat brown, wrinkled old women in long skirts, black cardigans and headscarves, staring pensively into space. Now it was the home of Tunisian Jews, Algerian Muslims and the ageing remnants of the Parisian apache gangs of hoodlums and their women. The CNT had its offices in the area.

Salva had met El Quico and the four younger anarchists (Francisco Conesa Alcaraz, Antonio Miracle Guitart, Rogelio Madrigal Torres and Martín Ruiz Montoya) who had accompanied him on his last ill-fated guerrilla incursion into Spain in January 1960. El Quico's demise proved Salva's argument that the situation had changed substantially since World War Two. The days of the maquis crossing the mountains on foot and engaging in armed confrontations with Franco's security forces were over. Such actions were boundlessly rash and a completely new approach to resistance was needed.

The two with Salva were the boyish-looking Antonio Ros Monero, who spoke no English, and Nardo Imbernón, a smartly-dressed comrade who worked for Aerolineas Argentinas. Nardo spoke good English, having lived in London from 1956 to '58. (Nardo's mum, Angeles, was in effect the DI's treasurer.) All three had been among the twenty-one Spanish anarchists arrested the previous September and held for five months' preventive detention in Fresnes prison for their membership of the FIJL, which had been declared an illegal organisation in France the previous October.

These were committed protagonists of the new wave of armed struggle. To them, like countless other Spanish exiles, the Civil War had not ended on 1 May 1939. On that, both the victors – by their relentless hunt for enemies, and their brutal and ongoing repression – and the vanquished, by their suffering and resistance, were in agreement.

x x x

Yet even for the Resistance the ethical lines in this battlefield were sometimes messy and unclear. No one exemplified this more than one of the DI's financial backers, the extraordinary and daring Laureano Cerrada Santos. I met Cerrada briefly, but as neither he nor most of the others spoke English, communication was confined to a nod and a smile. Cerrada had fought with distinction in the militias and the regular army during the Spanish Civil War, and then in the French Resistance, liaising between the clandestine guerrilla groups, organised arms dumps for the maquis, escape networks, safe houses, the printing of propaganda and false documents and so on. After the Liberation, Cerrada continued these operations against the Francoist state, while also becoming one of the most notorious currency forgers in France. He was betrayed to the French police in 1951 while working on a plan to flood Spain with false bank notes. On his release from prison Cerrada found himself shunned and sidelined by many of his old friends and comrades in the CNT and FAI, and he was eventually expelled from the CNT for what was described as his 'unacceptable methods'. In spite of this rejection and enmity, Cerrada remained totally committed to the Spanish Libertarian Movement and put all his resources at the disposal of the DI during the early 1960s.

Cerrada was re-arrested in France in 1970, aged 60, and served four years in jail on forgery charges. He was shot dead coming out of a Belleville *Zinc* in October 1975 in a gangland style execution by a former CNT member, Ramón Benichó Canuda (aka Ramón Leriles), who escaped with suspicious ease to Canada.

x x x

Later that evening we drove to a planning meeting at one of the two workshops owned by Pedro Moñino Zaragoza, another of the DI's backers – a lame bespoke shoemaker who supported the DI financially and whose large workshop and storeroom provided a discreet venue for sensitive meetings. It was here that evening that I met great legends of the anarchist struggle, men whose whole lives had been spent in the struggle for freedom, veterans with the glamour of the underground struggle and the Civil War still attached to them. For them, everything was at stake.

The person who impressed me most was Cipriano Mera Sans, the near-legendary anarchist who, along with Buenaventura Durruti and Dr Isaac Puente, had been a member of the revolutionary committee which declared Libertarian Communism in 1933. For five days the economic and social life in substantial parts of Aragón, Rioja and Navarre was transformed in accordance with anarchist principles of social justice. But the rising proved short-lived and was brutally repressed, leaving an estimated eighty-seven dead, many wounded and some 700 militants jailed.

Introduced to Mera, suddenly and unexpectedly, I was quite tongue-tied. This shabby-looking 64-year-old man with intelligent twinkly eyes set in a craggy face burnished by rich experience and weathered by years of prison and the building sites of Paris – where he still worked as a bricklayer – was a truly historic figure; a man assured of his place in the history of freedom fighters. It was hard to believe I was meeting him in the flesh.

x x x

These men and women were not fanatics. They were ordinary no-nonsense rational and dignified people who lived deliberately and passionately, with a vision and a tremendous capacity for self sacrifice; they had been abandoned by the Allies in the 'post-fascist' world of the Cold War and deprived of diplomatic or democratic means of resisting Franco's state terror. Propagandistic force – spasmodic and small-scale – was the only strategy and agency of change left open to them. They weren't looking for short-cuts; they simply had no other instruments of change. To me their idealism was inspirational, particularly in the face of the devastating high political cynicism displayed by the great powers.

Hans Magnus Enzensberger, the German anarchist poet, portrayed them sympathetically in *A Brief Summer of Anarchy: The Life and Death of Buenaventura Durruti*:

They are not tired, nor neurotic, and they don't need drugs. They do not complain. They do not bemoan their fate. Their defeats have not made them cynical. They know that they made mistakes, but they do not try to wipe out the memory of them. These old and still revolutionary men are stronger than all who came after them.

It was in these first days that I met Octavio Alberola Surinach – 'Juan el largo' or 'El Méxicano' – who was the charismatic prime mover and coordinator of Defensa Interior, and on whose shoulders lay the responsibility for killing Franco.

Octavio Alberola, Franco's 'public enemy Number One'.

Alberola, an engineer and journalist, was thirty-six years old at the time. Originally from Minorca, his family had gone into exile in Mexico in 1939 where he became involved with Castro, Guevara and many of the Latin-American anti-dictatorial movements of the time. The complications and dangers of Alberola's clandestine life in Europe had meant his wife Irene and two children had been forced to return to the relative safety of Mexico.

My first impression of Alberola was that he looked remarkably similar to the 1930s screen actor Basil Rathbone, famous for his portrayal of Sherlock Holmes. He was tall for a Spaniard, about 6 foot 2, slim, with a distinctive pencil-thin lip-hugging moustache, aquiline features and intelligent, deep-set eyes. He was always immaculately dressed.

He welcomed me with a warm embrace. Volunteers were thin on the ground, particularly non-Spaniards who would be much less likely to be suspected. The Spanish police agents knew the identities of all the young Spanish FIJL activists throughout France and Belgium

136

and they would have been arrested immediately they set foot inside the country.

x x x

By 6 August, everything was ready for my mission. The explosives and detonators were ready to be collected and my ticket had been booked on the night train to Toulouse. Salva, Nardo and I met at the place d'Italie, and from there we walked down the rue Bobilot and into a narrow and neglected side street with grubby slate grey tenements.

Checking again to ensure we had not been followed, Salva gave a prearranged knock on the curtained street-floor window and, when the door opened, we filed quickly through the dark and narrow hallway and into the front room of the apartment. The Spartan furnishings in the room indicated that no one lived here; it was the quartermaster's stores where the weapons, explosives, forged documents and all the accoutrements and paraphernalia of clandestinity could be kept with some degree of safety and ease of access.

Three people were already in the room. Two were seated, Octavio Alberola and Antonio Ros Moreno. The third man, referred to as 'the chemist', was standing by the sink wearing rubber gloves, measuring and pouring chemicals. Octavio organised some coffee and we sat round the table making what small talk we could until the chemist was ready for us.

Being thirsty, I went to the sink for water, and was about to put a glass to my lips when the chemist turned round and saw what I was doing. He and Salva shouted at me to stop and rushed across, removing the glass carefully from my hands, explaining that it had just been used for measuring pure sulphuric acid. Shaken, I stood back to lean on the sideboard and went to light a cigarette. This triggered another equally volcanic reaction from the chemist as he explained that the sideboard drawer was full of detonators and the cupboard underneath held highly flammable chemicals. Embarrassed by my errors, I retreated to the table, and was very cautious after that, asking first before making any sudden movements.

The chemist placed on the table five slabs of what looked like king-size bars of my Granny's home-made tablet (a crumbly Scottish toffee similar to butter fudge) and a number of small aluminium tubes, some with red wires protruding from the end, five small, dark-brown 250ml medicine bottles filled with a liquid, five replacement caps for these bottles and a bag of what looked like sugar but was in fact potassium chlorate.

Through Salva, he explained that each of these slabs contained 200 grams of plastique (plastic explosive) and the tubes were detonators. The ones with the wires sticking out of them were electrical and detonated by a battery while the plain ones were detonated by extreme high temperature caused by the chemical reaction of sulphuric acid and a mixture of sodium chlorate and sugar. The bottles contained sulphuric acid and the extra caps had been specially modified, and were to be exchanged for the original caps when the explosives were ready to be primed and planted. Until recently, Octavio explained, they had used World War Two time delay detonators, but these had proved unstable, presumably because they had been stored for at least twenty-five years in God-knows-what conditions.

x x x

Alberola went through the details of the operation while Salva translated. My job was to deliver the explosives to the contact, together with a letter, addressed to me, which I was to collect from the American Express offices in Madrid. It was better not to have the letter on me in the event of something happening to me before I reached Madrid, as it would have compromised the operation.

Operational details

The rendezvous was to take place in Madrid in the plaza de Moncloa, on the pavement opposite the Air Ministry at the intersection of the calle Princessa with calle Meléndez Valdés. The time was between 7 p.m. and 8 p.m. on any day from the 11th to 14 August. The contact would identify me by a handkerchief wrapped around one of my hands. He would approach me and say, in Spanish, 'Que tal?' ('How are you?'), to which I was to reply 'Me duele la mano' ('I've a sore hand').

I spoke no Spanish, so to avoid the embarrassment of forgetting my lines and unloading a kilo of high explosives on the first friendly Spaniard I met, Octavio wrote the words down for me, along with all the instructions. (This was, with hindsight, extremely foolish.) Once the contact had identified himself correctly, I was to hand over the parcel containing the material, together with the letter and was then to leave immediately and not make any conversation with the contact. If he said anything I was merely to reply 'Soy alemán' (I am German), and give him to understand that I did not speak any English.

How I crossed the border was down to me. Alberola handed me an envelope containing 350 new French francs, which was a fair bit of money at the time, so I had the choice of taking the train or flying from Toulouse. I had, however, made up my mind that the safest method would be to hitchhike.

Alberola placed an automatic pistol on the table and asked if I wanted a weapon. The appearance of the gun suddenly brought it home to me that this was not a simple breaking and entering into a British Regional Seat of Government or the consulate of a tinpot dictator in the relative safety of Britain. This was real life, and death – mine or someone else's – was a real possibility. Alberola and Salva advised me against taking the gun on the grounds that were I to be arrested I might be tempted to use it, which could have been suicidal. Also, if I was not carrying a gun they would be unlikely to apply the 'ley de fugas', Spain's notorious fugitive law that allows the authorities to shoot anyone on the grounds they were 'attempting to escape arrest'. I decided against taking the gun.

From the 'laboratory' we drove to the apartment of another comrade, where we had supper and went over the details of my journey for the last time. It was getting close to the time for my train to Toulouse so I rolled the explosives carefully into my sleeping bag, packed my Bergen and we drove to the station.

By 10.30 p.m. we were on the crowded platform by the carriage door, under the station's huge glass roof.

My Journey to Madrid

The train pulled into Toulouse station shortly before dawn on Friday 7 August after a clammy and uncomfortable night. I was still tired, having dozed only fitfully during the night, waking often to check my rucksack and for anyone suspicious-looking in the corridor.

After a hurried coffee and croissant I caught the local Michelin, a smaller local train, which took me on the final stage of my journey across to Narbonne and then down the Mediterranean coast to Perpignan. Here I prepared myself for crossing the border; I would hitchhike the rest of the way to Madrid. This was the part of the journey I was most worried about. The best way to take the explosives in, I thought, was on my body, not in my rucksack in case it was searched by a punctilious customs officer.

In Perpignan, I found the public baths and paid for a cubicle. After a hot soak and still naked I unpacked the slabs of plastique, and taped them to my chest and stomach with Elastoplasts and adhesive tape. The detonators I wrapped in cotton wool and hid inside the lining of my jacket. The bag of potassium chlorate, the base of the chemical trigger, was too bulky to hide on my body, so I emptied it into a packet of sugar with a layer of sugar on top, and left it in the rucksack.

There was one tense moment when the lady attendant came in unannounced with clean towels, having opened the cubicle door with her keys. She appeared surprisingly nonplussed by the sight of a naked, skinny young man from whose chest and stomach were protruding what appeared to be either full colostomy bags or brown paper poultices. Not realising she was in the presence of a Glaswegian kamikaze, she muttered something in French, presumably apologising for intruding on someone so modest and afflicted and quickly backed out, closing the door hastily behind her.

With the plastic explosive strapped to me, my body was improbably misshapen. The only way to disguise myself was with the baggy woollen jumper my granny had knitted to protect me from the biting Clydeside winds. At the risk of understatement, I looked out of place on the Mediterranean coast in August.

With a couple of remaining slabs of plastique stuffed down my underpants (which prevented me from wearing my kilt but made my crotch bulge heroically) and a big hairy jumper on one of the hottest days of the summer, I looked like Quasimodo and Esmeralda's lovechild. 'Like some rough beast, its hour come round at last', I began slouching the last twelve miles towards the sunlit peaks of the Pyrénées Orientales and my destination, Spain.

x x x

I walked through the outskirts of Perpignan until I came to a junction with a road sign pointing to Spain. It was a straight and wooded road where prospective lifts could stop easily and safely and I could shelter in the shade of a tree. I placed my rucksack on the roadside with my kilt protruding as ostentatiously as I could manage and sat close by, waiting patiently under a tree hidden from the raging heat of the August sun.

After what seemed like hours, a car pulled over. It was driven by a middle-aged English commercial traveller from Dagenham. He was going all the way to Barcelona.

It soon became apparent that his charity was driven to a large extent by enlightened self interest. Every few kilometres the old banger would chug to a standstill and I would have to get out in the full blast of the August Mediterranean sun and push the bloody car up the foothills until we got it bump-started. Between pushing a car uphill and Granny's jumper, the sweat began rolling off me.

Waterproof tape was yet to have been invented, and the cellophane wrapped packets of plastique began slipping from my body. I had to keep nudging them up with my forearms.

Traffic was heavy when we reached Le Pérthus, near to the Catalan border town of La Junquera, the busiest of Spain's frontier mountain passes. This was where we would have to clear a customs check. On the other side was fascist Spain. After queuing for a bowel-churning eternity we were summoned up to the parking ramp for customs examination. I had to push the car on to the ramp while my companion steered. I pulled my jumper taut and waited with my heart in my mouth while two dour-faced Civil Guards in sage-green uniforms with shiny patent leather three-cornered hats and sub-machine-guns at the ready looked me up and down. I handed my passport over to the border guard while the customs officers examined the boot and searched behind the seats of the car.

'Why have you come to Spain?'

'Turista!' I replied, hoping my accent didn't make it sound like 'terrorista'.

A pair of dark eyes looked at me suspiciously for a moment before the stamp finally descended on the passport.

A tremor of excitement passed through me as the grim-faced Civil Guards ushered us on our way south down through the fresh smelling mountain pinewoods and high terraced fields of the Catalan Pyrenees. It was near here, at Castellnou de Bages, just a year earlier, in August 1963, that the last anarchist guerrilla Ramón Vila Capdevila – Caraquemada ('Burntface') – had been shot in a Civil Guard ambush, thereby finally ending the Civil War in the mountains.

The winding roads looked at first like a continuation of France, but we began to notice a certain subtle difference in the terrain, range after range, as we descended through smaller step-like hills covered with rocks and fir trees, until at last we emerged into the ancient and crumbling golden-brown landscape of Spain. Even the soil appeared to be of another colour. Louis XIV's theory that Europe ended at the Pyrenees was beginning to make sense to me.

The car made it as far as Gerona's main square, where it broke down again, this time in the middle of the rush hour at what felt like the main arterial confluence of the whole of northern Spain.

As I struggled single-handedly and nervously to push the car through a set of traffic lights – with a long queue of impatient motorists shouting abuse behind me – I felt a packet of plastique slip and almost fall out of my jumper, virtually at the feet of the Policía Armada directing traffic and shouting at us to get a move on. In my anxiety, it seemed as though that in my short time in Spain I had not heard Spanish spoken once; it was clearly a shouted language. Clutching my stomach, I murmured an excuse about a sudden attack of diarrhoea and rushed off to the nearest toilet to make good the damage, leaving the driver to fend for himself.

Eventually we got going again and before I knew it we were driving through the dilapidated red-roofed outskirts of industrial Barcelona.

'I never thought we'd make it,' said my companion.

'Neither did I,' was my reply.

We said goodbye and went our separate ways.

x x x

Rebellious and industrious Barcelona was the city of anarchism. The Barcelona great anarchist union, the Confederación Nacional del Trabajo (CNT – National Confederation of Labour), had been founded here in 1911. It was the site of so many great events, which I had read and spoken so much about, but now that I was finally here, my senses were stretched close to their limits. I felt nervous and paranoid. It seemed inevitable that my inexperience and nervousness would betray me.

I wandered Barcelona's Hogarthian back streets for an hour or so looking for cheap lodgings and trying to take in the atmosphere and sounds of the city. I remember its Mediterranean smells of sea ozone, rich black tobacco, garlic sizzling in hot, smoking olive oil, and long-simmering meals mingling with the occasional discordant odours of stagnant drains and sewers. I finally found a place I could afford in a black-stone, fortress-like tenement in the *barrio gótico*, the old gothic quarter, just off the Rambla de Santa Monica. This was at the lower and seedier, southern part of the long bustling artery that leads from the centre of the city to the docks and the sea. Its rows of plane trees provided dappled shade to island promenades dotted with bootblacks, noisy street traders at colourful kiosks and stalls which sold everything from flowers to caged birds.

Handing over my passport, I tried to ask for a room with a window. Instead I was given a featureless room in the centre of the place with no windows at all. I could have been in London, Paris or Berlin; the only touch of Spain was a picture of the Virgin Mary and Child hanging above the bed.

The rat-trap of a room did nothing to calm my feelings of anxiety, but by this time I was too tired to complain, so I took it. I locked the door behind me and threw myself on the bed, fully dressed and wrapped in explosives, and dozed off, drifting in and out of sleep.

After a half-hour nap I undressed, packed the explosives into my sleeping bag, and took a shower. As I dressed I heard someone moving in the corridor outside my door. I opened it hesitantly to discover the little girl who had shown me to my room earlier. Had she been watching me through the keyhole? I shooed her away, but she kept hanging around the door. Perhaps it was my collar-length hair that fascinated her.

I went out to find something to eat. As I stopped at the desk in the lobby to drop off my key, a loud and pushy American heard me speaking English to the concièrge and introduced himself. Proudly showing off his sun-tanned arms, he said he had just driven down from Paris in an open sports car. Somehow it came out that he lived in Notting Hill Gate and we had some common friends. He also claimed, unreasonably loudly I thought, given where we were, to be an anarchist, which made me even more nervous. He called his wife down from their room and insisted we all go out together for a meal.

While this compromising discussion was going on in the foyer, two sinister-looking men in plain clothes were checking through the passports, including my own. As we passed they gave me a sideways glance while continuing their discussion with the concièrge. Outside my companions told me they were secret policemen come to collect the passports of that day's guests. It was normal procedure.

x x x

The Americans took me to an old-fashioned restaurant, Los Caracoles, in the heart of Barcelona's red-light district. On the corner wall, in the street, rows of sizzling, dripping chickens were being grilled on a jerky mechanical spit. The house speciality was snails and bouillabaisse, but I settled for barbecued chicken and salad, washed down with sangria.

Bad move. No sooner had I finished eating when my stomach and lower intestines twisted into a Gordian knot and my bowels turned to water. Rushing to the restaurant toilet I discovered it was a stinking and unflushed human slurry pit in the floor so I returned to the table, made my excuses and power-walked back to the pension, tense and tight-arsed. I was also anxious to check out if my room had been disturbed in my absence. The 'coincidence' of meeting people with mutual friends under such circumstances added uneasiness to my queasiness. It was a troublesome first night in Spain.

x x x

The possible dates for my rendezvous in Madrid were from Tuesday the 11th to Friday 14 August. I left Barcelona on Monday the 10th, this time keeping the explosives in my bag and taking a taxi to the city limits, on the N11, the road to Madrid. I could have flown or taken the train, but I enjoyed hitch-hiking and it also meant I would have a bit more money in the event of any emergency.

By late afternoon I had only got as far as the bizarrely-serrated mountainous outcrop of Montserrat which broods behind Barcelona. Just as I had made up my mind to return to the Catalan capital and take public transport to Madrid, a lorry pulled over. The driver said he was going to Madrid so I carefully passed up my Bergen, clambered into the cab and we were off.

I wasn't long in the cab when several things about the driver began to strike me as unusual. Hadn't he stopped to pick me up on a steep incline, something heavily laden lorries seldom do? Whenever we pulled over for something to eat or drink, he insisted on paying for the meals, drinks and cigars from a thick roll of thousand peseta notes. His generosity – or my paranoia – in such an impoverished country made me uneasy.

It was an eight-hour or so, hot and dusty but interesting 450-mile journey across the plains and mountains of Catalonia, Aragón, Castille and León to La Mancha and Madrid. The ever-changing landscape of sparse, yellowy-brown unfenced horizons with dark brooding shadows which glided along chasing sunny peaks and ridges was punctuated by fleeting glimpses of medieval villages, Moorish towers and the picturesque towns of Lérida, Fraga, Zaragoza, Calatayud, Guadalajara, Alcalá de Henares and Barajas. In spite of my growing anxiety, I was totally captivated by the colours and texture and shapes of the country, and its pervasive sense of history.

We lumbered along a chalky grey road that snaked far ahead through the dun-coloured plains of Castille until it met a clear blue sky. Around us was a stony vista of mountains and tablelands dotted with rocks and giant boulders. It was a poverty-stricken soil out of which jutted ancient, stumpy blackened trees. We passed clusters of flat-roofed, whitewashed pueblos and ruined castles clinging precariously to steep hillsides. Large and tiny women dressed from head to foot in black carried pails of water from village fountains, washed clothes in streams or shepherded tinkling herds of goats and sheep along the roadside. Black bereted, nut-brown, wrinkly old men played chess by the roadside or drowsily plodded along on mules with mangy-looking dogs jogging behind them.

Eventually, Madrid's rooftops appeared on the horizon. Madrid is built on a high plateau overlooking the Manzanares valley in the geographical centre of the Iberian Peninsula. Castille's trees had been chopped down centuries before and little of the topsoil remained. Squinting down through the harsh rays of the August sun I could just make out the jagged roofline of the city spread out across the plateau before me. Puncturing the heat haze was a mosaic of spires, domes, and irregular planes. Beyond was a parched landscape which encircled the town. It was an encampment in the desert.

As we approached the city the roadsides were bedecked with

massive commemorative banners and posters displaying pictures of Franco with slogans proclaiming '25 Anos de Paz' – 'Twenty Five Years of Peace' – the pax Franquista. The triumphalist posters should in fact have read 'Twenty Five Years of Victory!' These were interspersed with colourful, dramatic, bullfight posters promoting past and future corridas of matadors such as El Lítri and El Cordobés. Bloody repression and bloody circuses.

When we came to the new, high-rise apartment blocks that overlook the shantytown of Vallecas on the outskirts of Madrid, I indicated to my generous driver that I wanted to be dropped here. He looked at me a bit strangely as if to say 'are you sure?' but when I insisted he nodded and pulled over.

X X X

Vallecas is to Madrid what Castlemilk or Drumchapel is to Glasgow, a peripheral ghetto designed to keep the workers in their place. It was where the *chabola* people, as they are called, lived in self-built shacks without running water or sanitation. According to government statistics, 1964 was the year Spain ceased to be an agricultural country. Vallecas was a direct consequence of this policy; it was where most of the immigrants from the poorer southern agrarian provinces of Extremadura and Andalusia ended up, a bit like Glaswegians around London's King's Cross and Euston or the Irish in Kilburn.

My reason for asking to be dropped off here was that were anyone following me I would soon spot them as I wandered around the relatively empty back streets. It was like opening an oven door as I climbed from the cab and was immediately engulfed by the scorching mid-day sun and the heat rising from the road. The place was deserted. It was like Edward Thomas's description of Adlestrop railway station, where 'no one left, and no one came.'

After meandering around for about twenty minutes, I managed to hail a taxi and asked for central Madrid. In contrast, the cab driver dropped me at the Puerta del Sol. This is Spain's 'kilometre zero,' the hub of Madrid's wheel whose spokes are the ten main arteries of the city and the convergence of all Spain's highways from the farthest reaches of the nation: the Atlantic coast in the north-west, the Pyrenees in the north-east, Extremadura and the Portuguese border in the east, the Straits of Gibraltar in the south and the Mediterranean in the west.

I bought a street plan of Madrid from a kiosk, a packet of Celtas cigarettes and a box of matches, then found a café. It was a relief to lay down my rucksack and for a little while step aside from its contents. It drew my attention constantly, like touching a bruise, or the throbbing heart beneath the floorboards in Edgar Allan Poe's 'Tell-Tale Heart'. I was fascinated by it, but also wanted to be rid of it – give it to my contact, or even, in a rush of blood, leave it under the table.

I sat and took my bearings.

x x x

The oval-shaped Puerta del Sol was dominated by the brooding presence of the Ministerio del la Gobernación (Interior Ministry). The buildings, boulevards and fountains around it bore the stamp of the Austrians and Bourbons, but nothing of the Moors who had occupied most of Spain for 700 years. I was intrigued by bundles of old and desiccated palm leaves tied to the balconies around the Plaza. Later I discovered that these came from the date palm at Elche, in the south-east near Alicante. Every Easter these palm leaves were tied into bundles, blessed by the priests and sold all over Spain as a protection against lightning.

What I also didn't know was that the café, the Café Rolando, was the 'local' of the Spanish secret police, whose headquarters were across the road. ETA blew up the café ten years later.

The Seguridad was also where one of the bombs had exploded the previous July which led to the summary court martial and executions of Delgado and Granado less than three weeks later. Joaquín Delgado Martinez (29), the son of Spanish exiles in France, and Francisco Granado Gata (27), an economic migrant in France, were the two anarchists arrested in Madrid and charged with causing the explosions. They had been identified by a police agent planted within

Delgado and Granado

the FIJL, but in fact both men were innocent, and had no idea even that an operation had been planned. Of course, I couldn't be certain at the time they were innocent, but I had been assured that they were by the comrades in London and Paris, and I chose to believe them. Not that it would have made much difference to my subsequent course of action anyway. As far as I was concerned, Franco had claimed two lives for actions which had killed no one, but had struck at the heart of his terror organisation, the Brigada Politico Social (BPS).

Only later did I discover that I had, in fact, met the two men responsible for the Madrid bombings for which Delgado and Granado paid with their lives in the dawn of 17 August 1963: Antonio Martín and Sergio Hernandez. One reason I was doing what I was doing in Spain was the imminent first anniversary on 17 August of the judicial murder of the two innocent men. It was our response to their deaths, to ensure it did not pass unmarked. Their executions and that of the Communist Julian Grimau a few months earlier on 18 April 1963 had been important factors in my decision to join the resistance. I felt I needed to give some reason to their deaths and those of the countless others who had died or sacrificed their freedom resisting the last of the fascist dictators.

x x x

I sipped my beer, fascinated by the black figures of priests and nuns and the cool smartness of the other passers-by: the clean-shaven, cotton-suited men in highly polished patent-leather boots. Most sported sunglasses and wore their jackets draped around the shoulders, like cloaks. Despite the heat, the women in brightly coloured summer frocks were usually hatless, showing off their perfectly coiffeured hair, their long, pale, oval faces, their great black eyes and pomegranate-red mouths. They were strikingly beautiful.

In stark contrast with this sophisticated elegance were the beggars roaming the street: the legless pulling themselves along on home-made bogies (carts) with castors or pram wheels; the one-legged on home-made crutches with arm supports made from rolled-up rags; the mentally damaged wandering aimlessly, dead-eyed and twitching spasmodically. Some begged with dignity, others did not; their dignity having evaporated with whatever trauma it was which had changed their lives for the worse. They may or may not have been direct victims of the Civil War, but to me they were the vanquished reminders of Franco's 'Twenty-Five Years of Peace'.

x x x

My destination was the American Express office, not far away. Instead of going to the railway station for a left luggage locker and leaving my rucksack there, which is what a more experienced anarchist would have done, I swung it onto my back and strolled down the carrera San Jerónimo to collect the letter for my contact.

It was siesta time and most Madrileños were either on holiday, at lunch or asleep. The streets were quiet and the plaza de las Cortes appeared empty apart from a few men standing about in doorways reading newspapers in the shade.

Turning the corner to enter the American Express office, I was immediately aware of three smartly-dressed and tight-lipped men in heavy-rimmed sunglasses standing, self consciously, by the entrance muttering among themselves. Their well-cut jackets were firmly buttoned. Although I was already extremely alert, my stomach and chest muscles immediately contracted. I knew instinctively by the way they looked at me that they were policemen. If I was right, though, were they there for me? If so, when would they make their move? Would I be able to give them the slip? I breathed deeply and tried to control my anxiety. There was nothing to show I had been compromised. I forced myself to go on, repeating silently to myself the mantra 'don't panic'. I hadn't come this far to abandon my mission on what may have been simple paranoia.

Walking past this group, I went into the American Express office where I asked for the poste restante desk. A clerk pointed me in the direction of a desk at the far end of the L-shaped room.

Handing my passport to the receptionist I asked whether any letters were waiting for me. At this same moment I noticed out of the corner of my eye two men and a woman sitting in an alcove to my right. Again, I knew immediately they were policemen. The blood and lymph drained from my face and heart. My stomach churned. Something had gone badly wrong.

The girl with my passport found my letter among the tightly packed trays behind her and pulled it out. As she did, I noticed it had been marked with a pink piece of paper the size of a bookie's slip. The woman from the alcove, a supervisor, approached the girl, now bringing the letter to me, said a few words to her and removed the slip.

All my senses were working at twenty-to-the-dozen as I tried to marshal the thoughts buzzing round my brain. What was in the letter? How much did they know? Would I be arrested there or would they wait until I had met my contact? But if they knew about the Amex pick-up, they probably knew the details of my rendezvous as well. Too many imponderables, too many unknowns.

I was close enough at this point to notice the pink slip was stamped for that day – 11 August. The supervisor handed the slip to the girl, indicating she should take it across to the two men in the alcove. The supervisor then handed me the letter and my passport. I turned to see the two men from the alcove quickly walking out. I made a mental note to shaft American Express at every conceivable opportunity, if I were ever again offered an opportunity.

My diaphragm tightened even more and my heart thumped like a tight Lambeg drum. But in spite of the emotional maelstrom going on inside me, I felt curiously detached as I took a deep breath and walked out of the office, trying to keep my face expressionless. Mustering all the self confidence I could manage, I paused at the doorway to look at the group of five men now standing to one side of the office entrance. Until I appeared at the doorway they had been deep in animated conversation. They stopped briefly, exchanging what to me were pretty obvious knowing looks with one another, and carried on. Although only one looked me directly in the eye, I was acutely conscious of the awareness of the others. By this time I had no doubt my hunch was right – somehow the police had known I was coming. These men were the agents of the Grim Reaper himself.

Attempting the jaunty air of a well-heeled tourist who had just cashed his letters of credit, I walked back up the way I had come, and as slowly as I could. I had draped my coat over my arm to hide the tightly crumpled-up letter in my hand, but then a pang of alarm shot through me. What if this gave the impression I was carrying a pistol?

I had only gone a few yards when the knot of men began to follow me up the street, still talking among themselves. My eyes darted everywhere, desperately searching for any opportunity to escape. I continued up the carrera San Jeronimo back towards the Puerta del Sol, stopping to peer in all the shop windows I passed, as though I was window shopping, but in fact to see how far they were behind. They had allowed me a good twenty yards start before moving on behind me, and they kept to that distance.

An empty taxi pulled in to the pavement beside me, but when the driver appeared to invite me to get in, I knew it was an undercover police car. I was being hemmed in.

The men paced me from behind, slowly unwinding across the full width of the pavement like the Earp brothers in Tombstone, relishing, it seemed to me, the melodrama, knowing I had spotted them. By this time I had reached the corner of the busy calle Cedaceros. As I steeled myself to make a dash through the crowds I was suddenly grabbed by both arms from behind, the anorak ripped from me, my face pushed to the wall and a gun barrel thrust into the small of my back. I tried to turn my head but I was handcuffed before I fully realised what had happened. It was all over in a matter of moments.

'Is There Something Wrong
With My Passport?'

Still stunned that they had finally broken through from my paranoia into reality, I only absorbed part of what followed. I was aware of detectives surrounding me on all sides, waving guns in my face. My legs were spread-eagled and I was forced against the wall while they patted me down for weapons.

In spite of the sense of complete helplessness that had descended upon me, I mustered all the pompous indignation I could under the circumstances. With an ingratiating smile and croaking like a frog, I demanded of the short fat arresting officer, whom I later came to know as Don Juan García Gelabert, why a respectable British citizen was being treated like a criminal.

'Do you have any identification papers?' I asked, weakly.

'We don't need papers,' he replied, sneeringly, in English. 'We have some questions we want to ask you at police headquarters.'

'Why?' I exclaimed, trying to control the twitching I felt must be visible in my cheek and the fragile dismay in my voice. 'Is there something wrong with my passport?'

One of them punched me hard in the face, telling me to speak Spanish and that I was 'un hijo de puta', a lying son of a whore. I had been pushed and hit by the police before on demonstrations in the UK, but this first blow in a foreign country was much more terrifying than any violence at home. This was a portent of real trouble.

'No', said Gelabert, 'But you are a young anarchist of the

Juventudes Libertarias.' He stuck his face into mine then pulled back and belted me unexpectedly on the side of my head. 'You have come to kill Spaniards. We'll see about that when we get you back to police HQ.' The words 'young anarchist' reminded me of something. Malcolm Muggeridge's BBC2 programme 'The Question Why' was to be shown within the next fortnight. On it was my confession of guilt.

I was led through the gathering inquisitive crowds and bundled unceremoniously into the back seat of the taxi I had snubbed earlier. Don Juan García Gelabert sat in the front with the driver. It raced through my mind that they seemed to know a great deal about me, my name, my political views, and why I was there. How had they known about the letter? Sooner or later I would have to say something – how much did they know, and how much could I lie? Would I be able to meet this great and trying moment in my life as my Covenanting forebears had done, with nobility of gesture and defiance? I doubted it.

We drove the few hundred yards to the Seguridad in complete silence. The car entered through an innocuous arched passageway at the rear of the building and emerged into a large central courtyard. Less than an hour before I had been outside enjoying a beer and a fag, watching the world go by and looking at this building from the outside. It was said that from here Franco's secret police could see the Pyrenees, Gibraltar and, it appeared, Notting Hill Gate.

x x x

During an official visit to Spain in October 1940 SS Reichsfuhrer Heinrich Himmler advised Franco to set up a secret police force which would allow him to contain his political enemies and to consolidate and strengthen his power base. Himmler helped Franco out by sending his most senior Gestapo officer, Commandant Paul Winzer, with a team of advisers to Spain to train the new organisation. Franco's secret police – the Brigada Politico Social (BPS) – was set up under the Law of Vigilance and Security of 8 March 1941.

Franco's
Secret
Police

The BPS operated with impunity and enjoyed absolute discretionary powers to ensure the safety of the state. While technically under the control ofthe civilian Interior Ministry, the BPS in fact operated under military jurisdiction. According to Edouard de Blaye, the Agence France-Press correspondent in Spain in the early 1960s, the BPS establishment numbered around 8,500 superintendents and inspectors, all of whom operated in plain clothes. The Seguridad was the epicentre of their operations.

x x x

Pushed from behind and pulled from the front, I was hustled out of the taxi. I glanced up at the sky for what, it occurred to me, might possibly be my last time. With the walls rising around me on all four sides I felt as though I was at the bottom of a deep well.

The atmosphere inside was clinical, like a a hospital or a dental surgery. As I was marched through brightly lit passages we passed small 'consulting' rooms through the doors or windows of which I caught fleeting glimpses of people seated at tables faced by the proverbial men in suits. Some were being shouted at and one was being pushed around the room and being beaten. The building seemed full of little rooms where people were being subjected to all sorts of brutality. I wondered whether they were putting on a show for my benefit.

From one room I heard what sounded like an American voice, and for a moment I wondered if the couple from the Barcelona pensión had been arrested. But no reference was ever made to them during my interrogation.

On the top floor, we came to a long, open-plan, beige-coloured room extending the full width of the building, and punctuated by groups of police. A window at the far end overlooked the noisy Puerta del Sol; the other opened on to the courtyard. The sounds of the city going about its normal business seened to come from a parallel universe. In the far corner was a smaller room with a desk and a couple of tubular chairs. I was thrust into one of these while the detectives emptied the contents of my pockets: some pesetas, French francs, a snotty tissue, a packet of fags and a box of matches.

Gelabert sat back at his desk and addressed me in flawless English 'Well, then, Mr Christie. What do we have here?'

The Registry Office of Franco's secret police where files were kept on all the regime's enemies.

They emptied the contents of my rucksack onto the floor. First they discovered the bag with the potassium chlorate and sugar mix. Gelabert tasted with his finger and grimaced.

'What is it?' he asked, in English. 'It isn't sugar.'

I should have said strychnine, but I didn't. Instead, I replied that I had bought the sugar in France and had not yet used it, despite the fact that the bag had been opened.

In my rucksack were two books I had bought in Paris. One of these, Voltaire's *Candide*, they confiscated triumphantly, presumably on the grounds that it was explosive in its own way. The other they let me keep – the Olympia Press edition of de Sade's *Justine*.

News of my arrest had spread quickly and the outer room was now filling with curious bystanders, some in uniform but most in plain clothes, all straining to see the foreign terrorist in the flesh. There must have been fifteen to twenty of them hovering around before they were finally ordered out by a tall man with a slight stoop and a face that could have been painted by Velazquez. He turned out to be the senior BPS officer, Comisario Jefe, Don Saturnino Yagüe González, the officer in charge of my case.

x x x

Once things had settled down, Yagüe removed his jacket and took Gelabert's place at the desk opposite me. He removed the automatic pistol from his shoulder holster and placed it on the desk between us while he rolled up his shirtsleeves. The barrel of his gun was pointed ominously towards me. It felt as though he was daring me to grab it. (I discovered later that this was a popular BPS trick. These guns, apparently, were not loaded.) He said nothing, but his eyes darted between his officers going through my possessions on the floor and me.

The searchers finally came to the sleeping bag. From the moment of my arrest I had undergone the emotional bends, racking my mind for a credible story to explain what was in that bag. Had I been older and wiser I would have known to say nothing. But had I been older and wiser, perhaps I wouldn't have been there.

My shabby orange sleeping bag was unrolled to its full length on the floor while they prodded it with their fingers. At the foot of the bag they felt around the outline of the incriminating packages, and whisked them out in triumph. Five 200-gram packets of plastique were laid out on the desk.

All eyes turned to me. I tried to look surprised. It didn't work.

Two of the detectives grabbed tufts of my hair and yanked me backwards until the chair was balanced on its two back legs. I was held in this position while a third man slapped me about the face. There didn't seem to be a 'good cop' around. The leering faces closed in around me, shouting menacingly in Spanish and in English that I was an anarchist come to kill and maim the happy and peaceful people of Spain.

After a few minutes of this softening up, the top man of BPS, Comisario General Eduardo Blanco, entered the room. He had probably been watching events from behind one of the two-way mirrors. Everyone except me stood up abruptly, but greeted him rather casually. Blanco sat at the table beside Yagüe, looking pleased with himself. My arrest was a great triumph for him – soon after he was made head of the Spanish Security Service, the DGS, with the rank of General.

Blanco was a dapper wee man with greying hair, a jowly anaemic face and hooded eyes behind his thick yellow-tinted glasses. He bore a remarkable similarity to General Franco. They all did. But he was more Goya than El Greco, a man used to absolute power. With a nod Blanco introduced himself and his colleague, Don Saturnino Yagüe González.

x x x

The secret police chief didn't strike me as demonic. He wasn't a Beria or a Himmler, more Joseph Fouché, Napoleon's sinister Minister of Police. His security organization was ruthless and brutal but it did not have – or at least it did not exercise at that time – the power to arrest and hold prisoners indefinitely, or to make people 'disappear'. Those powers, and worse, were left to their lackeys, the 'plausibly deniable' commercial 'security' firms such as Otto Skorzeny's Madrid-based Paladin Group. They were still, in a manner of speaking, governed by the law.

Blanco and Yagüe were professional secret policemen. I was about to be given a master class in the art of interrogation by the inheritors of the Holy Office of the Inquisition. They were not overtly aggressive during that first confrontation; they left that to their minions. Both men addressed me as Stuart throughout. Yagüe, whose English was good, began by asking what I had been planning to do with the plastique on the desk in front of us like slabs of my Granny's toffee.

I was in a dilemma. Sooner or later I knew I would talk. Heroic gestures of defiance would merely be gestures. I knew they were better at this than me. The question was, should I tell the truth (at least about that which I could not deny), say nothing or come up with what I thought would be a plausible story? The evidence lying on the table was pretty convincing – there was even a chance that this would allow them to put me in the frame for other recent explosions in Madrid.

The BPS had the explosives and there was also the incriminating letter collected from the American Express office, presumably containing the details of the planned attempt against Franco. They also had the note with directions, dates, times and the coded recognition signals for my meeting with the Madrid contact.

x x x

I said I was a member of the youth section of the Glasgow Labour Party; a friend had put me in touch with someone to stay with in

London, who in turn gave me the address of someone to stay with in Paris, someone called Geronimo or a name very similar. I couldn't remember the address, but it was close to the place de la Republique (I assumed they probably knew where I stayed in Paris and with whom, and Germinal, knowing nothing about the plan, had nothing to give them.) Geronimo, in turn, introduced me to a man who asked me to deliver a package containing anti-Franco propaganda to Madrid, in return for which I received 350 new French francs. Only when I reached Barcelona did I discover that the parcel contained explosives. I feared dumping them in case a passer-by discovered them and was injured; I feared being arrested if I handed them into the police. So I chose to complete the delivery. Blanco and Yagüe listened attentively at first and didn't take notes or interrupt, unless I got side-tracked, confused or lost my train of thought and started gabbling. Yagüe would then pull me back on track by asking what I did next or why I did such and such a thing.

That was the easy bit. After going through my story, with linking bits which I made up as I went along, I was given a cup of coffee and a cigarette. They then moved into more serious interrogatory mode. Blanco ordered everyone out of the office, apart from the men searching my belongings on the floor.

They went back over my story, point by point, this time taking notes and asking the same questions over and over again. What disturbed me most was that they never really challenged my account of events or took me up on any of the blank spaces or conflicts in my story. But their questions showed they knew what was fact and what was fiction. The interrogation appeared to be a formality. The spell of infallibility was broken only once, when Yagüe said he knew I had been trained in weapons and explosives at the 'terrorist training school near Toulouse'— a town which I had only passed through briefly once, without stopping.

While I was getting into the swing of my story, convincing myself in the process, there was the sound of sharp intakes of breath behind me. The searchers ripping up my green corduroy jacket had discovered the detonators in my jacket lining together with the instructions and directions for the rendezvous with my Madrid contact.

x x x

What I had done, Blanco observed, was classified in Spanish law as 'Banditry and Terrorism'; a charge that came under military jurisdiction and automatically incurred the death penalty by the garrotte. He then revealed his hand.

'Don't think the British government will protect you,' he warned. 'We have a lot of information on you from Scotland Yard's Special Branch as well as our own people in Britain and France. We've been waiting for your arrival since nine o'clock yesterday morning. Our machinery is so efficient, both here and abroad, that anyone who moves pays the price. Sometimes we don't even bother the courts, if you take my meaning.' I took his meaning only too well. But his mention of the BPS's close relationship with Scotland Yard both irritated and dismayed me. It shouldn't have surprised me, but it felt like a form of betrayal.

He pointed to a large organisational chart on the wall, that showed the workings of the Spanish Libertarian Movement (MLE) – boxes and flow lines of the organisational structure with the names and photographs of known organisers and militants. Anarchists, he said dismissively, were badly organised. They did not understand the concept of security and were easily kept under surveillance; they were far too open for anything they planned to succeed.

I had to agree. Some people were geared to deception. Most people, including me and most anarchists I knew, were not – that was one of the reasons we were anarchists. Blanco then showed me pictures taken of me and Spanish exiles at Speaker's Corner ('your temple of free speech', Blanco said, in what can only have been a joke). He produced other snapshots of Octavio Alberola, Joaquín Delgado and Francisco Abarca and asked if I had met any of these men. They were particularly interested in Alberola, whom he referred to variously as 'the Mexican' and 'Juan el largo'. These looked like someone's personal photographs. I wondered where they came from, and if they had been found on the two garrotted anarchists, Joaquín Delgado or Francisco Granado, when they were arrested the previous July. A few photos were not posed but appear to have been taken by professional surveillance experts. I said I did not know any of them, nor had I met them.

'That's unfortunate' said Yagüe. 'You know that lying will get you nowhere'. Neither he nor Blanco pursued the matter.

The author: Speaker's Corner, Hyde Park, 1964.

x x x

I was genuinely taken aback at how much they appeared to know. I had only just turned eighteen and still retained some lingering naïve idea that whatever the faults of our state, it was at least anti-fascist because it had fought Hitler and Mussolini in World War Two. Most of the Spanish Resistance fighters I had come across held the same illusions about Britain. I became a marginally wiser person at that point.

In that room in the centre of Madrid I felt real fear, heightened by the fact I felt isolated, betrayed, confused. I was facing the unknown. No one knew where I was, nor was there any hope of help or rescue. In cowboy films this was when the US cavalry appeared on the horizon. In real life there was never a Cavalry troop when you needed one.

I now had serious doubts about the comrades in Paris. I wondered just who I was protecting, other than myself. But strangely, my sense of fear had now faded. The shock and surprise must have numbed my emotions, like Novocain, and I was prepared for anything. This was exactly the state of mind my interrogators wanted.

x x x

The questioning continued throughout the rest of that Tuesday afternoon, evening and into the early hours of the morning. Guns were on display all the time. Whenever Yagüe and the others left the room, two Policía Armada armed with sub-machine guns stood guard by the door.

Every time Yagüe returned he wanted more details.

Unfortunately, the effect of making a statement based on partial truths is that you have to keep adding to and amending it, all the time giving away a bit more than you intended.

By the end of the day, having pored over a large-scale street map of Paris, I had given them the rue de Lancry, but not the number, which I genuinely could not remember. I still referred to Germinal as Geronimo – I suppose I was thinking of cowboys and Indians again.

The interrogations stopped about 11 p.m. They handed me my sleeping bag, a strange irony; I rolled it out on the floor of the interrogation room, eased myself in and was asleep within minutes. It was a welcome but short-lived escape. Just over an hour later, around half-past midnight, I was jerked suddenly awake by a detective. He indicated I was to get up and go with him. Held by the arm, I was then escorted, groggy and bleary-eyed, through the dark and empty labyrinthine corridors of the Puerta del Sol to a starkly-lit room for more questioning. Night-time is the secret policeman's best friend. He knows it is the best time to break his victims down, when they are at their most vulnerable, half asleep and lacking the confidence that comes with daylight.

Again I had to go through my story chronology in meticulous detail as they probed for my 'pressure points', shouting questions, with the occasional appearance from Yagüe or his deputy. Again, Alberola – the 'Mexican' – was the focus of their questions. Yagüe insisted he had been the key figure in the operation – the handwriting on the note detailing the Madrid rendezvous was the same as that on the letter at the Amex office.

Eventually I was allowed back to sleep.

I was woken again at 7 a.m. My stomach knotted as the harsh fluorescent-lit room gradually materialised around me and I took in the ring of hard faces looking down on me. It had not been a nasty dream after all.

x x x

After a few bouts of questioning alternating with sleep, I was woken by a group of BPS detectives who told me that we were going for a ride. My heart raced. I was about to be taken out and shot under the infamous *ley de fugas*, the Francoist tradition of shooting a prisoner dead and claiming they had been killed attempting to escape.

I was squeezed between two detectives in the back seat of the police 'taxi' that had brought me to the security HQ on the day of my arrest. I melted with relief when Yagüe, seated in the front with the driver, turned to tell me we were going to the rendezvous. They wanted to use me as bait to capture my contact – clearly they didn't know who that was. Perhaps they were forced to arrest me before I made the rendezvous because they knew I had spotted them.

The taxi drew up by a busy café and Yagüe sat me down at a pavement table while he sat at an adjoining table. As far as I could see, most of the café seats were occupied by plainclothes BPS men and women. Up and down the pavements on both sides of the street I saw other BPS officers I recognised, *paseando* – strolling arm in arm – among the crowds; parked by the pavement were cars with policemen, all waiting for my contact to appear. There was certainly no shortage of secret police in Spain. I was instructed to remain there until approached by my contact. If I drew attention to myself in any way, Yagüe said his men would shoot me. I took my place, like a lemon, and waited for something to happen.

x x x

I hadn't told the police about the recognition signal. I was meant to be carrying an English newspaper. I hoped whoever my contact was, he or she would smell a rat when there was no newspaper, and avoid me. I sat for two hours drinking cup after cup of *café solo*, nervously scanning the river of faces passing before me for some flicker of recognition.

Yagüe was becoming increasingly edgy. He whispered that if I had tricked them I would suffer for it when we returned to HQ. Finally he decided he had had enough and told me to finish my coffee and walk up and down the pavement a few times and then head for a police car waiting at the next corner.

I wandered nervously and somewhat conspicuously up and down the pavement in front of the café, all the time praying to myself that the contact would not appear. But August was not a lucky month for me. Nor was it lucky for my contact. The moment I moved towards the car someone tapped my shoulder. I turned round, hoping it was policeman, but it was a short and wiry dark-haired man of about thirty with a weather-beaten face. Pointing towards my hand he asked me something in Spanish. Without saying anything I looked at my watch and shook my head as though he had asked me the time, at the same time giving him the most imploring look I could, trying desperately to signal with my eyes that he should get out of there, pronto.

Fernando Carballo Blanco.

It was too late. BPS men waving guns surrounded us while the few pedestrians and people seated at the café tables who were not secret police backed away, staring with horrified incredulity. I was handcuffed again and dragged off to one car and my contact was dragged off in another, back to the Ministerio. I was taken to my usual interrogation room. My contact, whose name I later learned was Fernando Carballo Blanco, was taken somewhere else.

x x x

Now that they had come closer to proving the conspiracy, the gloves came off. The questions and the violence increased. (I was at one point savagely accused of being an 'existentialist'. Perhaps it was my green corduroy jacket that gave him this idea.) Comisario Yagüe's job now was to pave the way for a confession that would convince not just a Francoist military court – which didn't need any convincing at the best of times – but also the outside world. The last thing he wanted was a martyr. Yagüe was an infamously brutal interrogator devoid of any

compassion, but he did not put me through anything so dramatic or painful as physical torture. I suspect this had more to do with my foreign nationality than his sensitivities. He also knew I was shortly going to stand trial and the attention of the world would be focused on how he and his men had handled me during my arrest and pre-trial detention. The authorities didn't want a repetition of the international outcry that had followed when people saw the state Grimau was

Arrest of an anarchist.
(Fundación Anselmo Lorenzo)

in when he went to trial. But in addition to repeated petty violence from his henchmen, he did try to break me psychologically.

Julián Grimau García

On one occasion, I was being taken downstairs when my BPS escorts suddenly rushed me to an open landing window. They twisted my arms behind my back and a paralysing grip on the back of my neck forced the top half of my body out through the window above the small street which runs along the back of the Seguridad, the calle de San Ricardo. Gelabert, holding me tightly, hissed in my ear that in case I was toying with the idea of jumping, I should know that this was the very window out of which they had bundled former commissar Julián Grimau García. Grimau, a Spanish Communist Party member, was recovering from this fall when he was taken from his hospital bed and executed by firing squad the previous April for 'war crimes' during the Civil War.

I wasn't thinking of jumping. So they showed me what they could do to me if they so chose. As bad or worse was what I was forced to witness. During an interrogation session a day or so after Carballo's arrest, I was dragged across the room and held by the arms, neck and hair and forced to look through the one-way mirror into the adjoining room. As I watched, Carballo was dragged in and tied to a chair. One policeman took a coil of rope from a drawer and expertly bound Carballo's ankles to the chair legs, passing the ends of the rope round his waist and arms. The other man lashed Carballo's hands and forearms to the arms of the chair. Then, pulling out his automatic pistol one of the policemen proceeded to hammer Carballo's wrists with the butt, while the other systematically punched him in the kidneys and stomach.

Although I was horrified at the sight of this cold-blooded, professional and ruthless brutality, it did not make any difference to my answers. The reality was I could not talk because I knew nothing about the people and the mechanisms of the anarchist organisation. There was nothing I could add to what I had already told them about the people who had given me the explosives or where I had met them. My interrogators knew as much and probably a lot more than I did, and they knew it.

X X X

I was surprised to discover that detainees in Francoist Spain could not remain in BPS custody for longer than seventy-two hours without charges. But they had their ways round this.

On my fourth day in custody, 14 August, Carballo and I were taken downstairs and handed over to the Madrid Police who occupied the ground floor offices and whose cells were the infamous *sotanos*, the subterranean dungeons. Here we went through the process of having our fingerprints and handprints recorded, first the fingers of one hand, then those of the other. This was reassuring in a way. At least now we had been registered by the Inspección de Guardia – we were 'in the system' so it was unlikely we would 'disappear' to be found later in a ditch with bullets through the backs of our heads.

We were moved to the dungeons. These were built in the middle of the nineteenth century and had been unimproved since then. Dim, naked light bulbs cast a weak light and dark shadows down damp stone passageways hewn from the solid rock. The air reeked of blocked drains, urine, acrid sweat and damp. It was also surprisingly noisy.

The cells were narrow, dark and damp; primitive rock tombs with a stone slab for a bed, straw-filled hessian mattress and a foul-smelling rough horsehair blanket for warmth. What tragedies had their walls enclosed over the centuries? In my small way I was connected to this saga of misery, the tale of human beings at their worst. I settled back on the lumpy straw mattress and dozed into unconsciousness.

Woken by the raucous jokes of the women cleaning the reception area, I became aware that a voice from a crackly radio outside was mentioning my name. Intrigued, I asked the guard in what I hoped were understandable pidgin Castilian grunts and sign language what the report had said, but he looked at me blankly.

When we were returned upstairs to the BPS, Yagüe's attitude had changed. He had swung from coldly professional to manic hysteria, exploding like a tornado, pushing his face into mine, shouting that I could have killed innocent women and children. (It didn't seem the right time to argue that throughout the whole of the current FIJL campaign no one had been killed – apart from the two innocent anarchists Delgado and Granado, whom they had murdered – or even seriously injured.)

He went to his side of the desk, opened a drawer and produced a typed confession that he pushed in front of me to sign.

x x x

The previous four days had taken their toll. My physical and mental resources were exhausted and I was now resigned to the consequences of my action. I did not really care if they shot, strangled or imprisoned me. I was tired, disoriented, bruised and worried, but my overriding concern was how my Mum and Gran would take the news. I had had to watch Carballo being pistol-whipped repeatedly. All I wanted to do was sleep and put as much distance between myself and my tormentors as possible.

Yagüe must have realized that I had no further information to give him. He was a professional policeman who knew when to go with rather than against human nature. His tools had been stress, guile and good intelligence. My 'torture', if any, had come from within my own mind – fear of what might happen to me – as opposed to anything he did.

Even so, I read the statement they gave me to sign. The final paragraph showed an odd emphasis on Alberola's letter – they had me insisting I didn't think it unusual that I hadn't been given the letter to bring with me, along with the explosives. I wondered whether they wanted to show that the plan was thin on cunning. Were they saying I'd been set up to fail, or at least sent by a demoralised organization knowing the mission to be hopeless? Perhaps like Charlton Heston at the end of *El Cid*, I was a dead man tied to a horse with a sword strapped to his hand and a pole up his arse, sent out to rally the troops.

Whatever it was, it didn't matter now. After four days I signed the statement they put in front of me, my confession of guilt.

x x x

After I signed my 'confession', I was returned to the dank subterranean cells of the Seguridad. We descended deep into the underground caverns until we eventually came to an L-shaped white tiled room. At the far end was a brightly-lit and sinister looking chair with straps and clamps attached to its arms, legs and headrest.

Along the centre of the passage was a small channel in the floor running from one end of the room to below the chair itself. It was covered with wooden boards. A tall lever stuck out of the floor close to the door, facing the chair. It looked like a points lever by a railway track or in a signal box. This was the garrotte – they were going to execute me then and there! Now they had my signed confession they could do anything they liked. Despite my growing sense of panic I allowed myself to be clamped and strapped into the chair, wondering whether or not this was the right time to shout something defiant and noble.

My escort walked back along the passageway, behind the extremely bright lights, to stand by the lever. All I could see was his face and hands gripping the lever and behind him other vague faces in the dark. Beside the man holding the lever was someone adjusting another device on a tripod. The atmosphere was electric. All I was conscious of was the thumping of my heart.

Suddenly someone shouted 'listo' (ready), and there was a blinding flash from the tripod as he pulled the lever and I heard the sound of clanking gears. I thought to myself, 'This is how it ends, me old china' – not with a bang, but a clunk and a click.

My seat suddenly swivelled around ninety degrees on its axis like some demented Dalek, and there was another bright flash. Then it dawned on me what they were doing. I was in the Gabinete de Identificación. They were taking my police mugshot, the one that was to be flashed around the world that weekend, full face and profile. I tried blowing my cheeks out in the hope of disguising my appearance, but it was pointless; all I got for my trouble was a slap across the face from an irritated police photographer's assistant who had his own views on client satisfaction, and another session on the Dalek.

x x x

The final stage of our indictment was a brisk examination by the recently appointed examining magistrate of the Juzgado Militar Especial Nacional de Actividades Extremistas, Lieutenant-Colonel Balbás Planelles.

This was my first real contact with Carballo. He was surprisingly cheerful, I thought, given what I'd seen him go through, but he was clearly in pain where they had beaten him in the kidneys and pistol-whipped his wrists. I felt relieved and slightly guilty that as a foreigner I'd received preferential treatment. I couldn't see the same distinction being made in a British police station.

Perhaps he was glad of our luck. Balbás had only recently replaced the soulless and sadistic 'inquisitor colonel', Don Enrique Eymar Fernández, reputed to have been personally responsible for the torture, executions and murders of more than 12,000 people. Extraordinarily, Eymar had been a Republican army officer during the Civil War and had been briefly imprisoned in 1939. He was the original poacher turned gamekeeper, and all the more malevolent in his persecution of his fellow Republicans. His retirement had been forced after the international scandal over the deaths of Julián Grimau and the anarchists, Joaquin Delgado and Francisco Granado. Eymar had presided over all three executions.

Balbás was a different kettle of fish – pompous, militaristic, but not essentially skewed in his soul. He was over fifty, but still in his prime; a tall, imposing, square-jawed figure in riding breeches and highly polished boots, a highly polished bald pate with close-cropped white hair at the sides and a large silver-grey full military moustache.

My 'examination' took place in a room with only a desk and three chairs – one each for him, his interpreter-secretary, a captain, and myself. A portrait of a tight-lipped Franco hung on a wall behind him. Balbás amiably told me I was being charged under the Decree Law of 1960 on Military Rebellion and Banditry and Terrorism (Decreto-Ley 1974/60 de Rebelión Militar y Bandidaje y Terrorismo). When reading, Balbás had a curiously disarming habit of adjusting the gold pince-nez clamped to his nose, a gesture which somehow made him seem less intimidating.

Our examinations lasted a few hours and involved going through the police statements and my confession and amplifying them where he felt it was required. Then it was Carballo's turn, after which we were both ushered into police cars and driven under military escort, with jeeps and motorcycle outriders, to the notorious Carabanchel Prison on the outskirts of Madrid.

When we were handed over to the prison authorities on the Saturday afternoon, I was in an unemotional and trance-like state of exhaustion. The events of the previous week now seemed very distant. My destiny was now in the hands of others. Looking back, it seems strange, but at the time I felt quite indifferent to my circumstances and seemed only to see the surreal side of things.

'Blantyre Youth Held
on Suspicion'

I had heard so many horror stories about Carabanchel that my chest
was tight with foreboding when I arrived.

Carabanchel is laid out like a cartwheel, its four main galleries (two
more were still yet to be built) feeding out from the saucer-domed
central nave to the high walls
which formed the outer rim of
the prison. The main
administrative office with its
panopticon view of all the
galleries was located in the
nave, below the dome. And it
was a nave – four dominating
stained glass windows made it
architecturally clear how
closely intertwined were
Roman Catholicism and
Francoist legitimacy. At the
centre was the altar – a twenty-
five foot rotunda housing
records of every prisoner held
or executed in Carabanchel since the mid 1940s. Every Sunday, its
roof became a literal altar, on which priests celebrated high mass.
Below the rotunda, I later learned, were the cells where condemned

Sunday Mass.

The Prisión Provincial de Madrid clings like an enormous Martian red spacecraft to the slopes of Carabanchel Alto in the southern suburbs of the city. Built by forced labour in the 1940s to contain the massive number of defeated victims and opponents of the newly victorious military regime, Carabanchel was Spain's central remand (preventive) prison and the jewel in Franco's repressive crown. It had been the epicentre of post-Civil War terror in the 1940s; by the 50s and early 60s it had established a reputation for ferocious brutality and inhuman conditions. By 1964, however – although still unfinished – it was being presented to the international penal and judicial community as a model prison. They needed to show a new face to the world in light of their attempts to join the Common Market. But it was still the dictator's redbrick university where students matriculated with honours degrees in either crime and corruption or politics and dissent. Prisoners didn't normally remain in Carabanchel longer than eighteen months or two years.

men spent their last few hours of life before they were strapped into the garrotte-vil.

When I entered the rotunda for my arrival to be processed, the room fell silent. A screw put down his paper and made some humorous crack, obviously at my expense, at which most of the clerks laughed. Victor, the clerk dealing with my file, told me in passable English that he was a writer 'on the street', a bit of an intellectual and, he whispered, a 'radical'.

My file was open in front of him; on it was stamped in red ink

'Terrorismo y Bandidaje: Vigilancia!' Having gone through his checklist of questions he gave me a prison number and gallery. Then, looking around to see if he was being watched, he produced the fichas (index cards) of Delgado and Granado. The sight of these had a chilling effect on me; they were normal A5 size card indexes with the stark words '*ultima pena*' underlined in red ink across the release date box. I took his showing me these documents as an act of friendship, a gesture of clandestine solidarity.

Victor quickly explained that because I was awaiting a summary court martial on a charge which automatically carried the death penalty, I would be kept in solitary confinement as a maximum security prisoner in the *septima galería* (seventh gallery) until my *Consejo de Guerra* (Council of War). In a clumsy attempt to comfort me, he added that I wouldn't have long to wait. No one would be allowed to communicate with me without the written permission of the military examining magistrate and the Dirección General de Seguridad. I would be on 24-hour watch, which meant my bed, bedding and all my belongings would be removed following the first morning recount (*recuento*) and not returned until the last recuento at night. My light would be on 24 hours a day and my cell would probably be inspected two or three times every hour.

I would not be allowed out of my cell during the ten-day quarantine, known as '*el periodo sanitario*'.

Victor wished me luck and then, loaded down with my bedding, plastic cup, aluminium plate and spoon, I was taken to the septima galería, 'home' to prisoners charged with 'blood crimes', *crimenes de sangre*, socially dangerous criminals, PSs or *peligrosos sociales*, Spain's incorrigible recidivists – 'scum' as they were called in Partick. I wondered how long I'd be among them.

x x x

With a sinking heart I recognised the chief prison warder on our floor – Don Pedro, or the infamous 'Pedro El Cruel', whose reputation for brutality was the stuff of national and international legend. The warders were all Falangists and most had fought in the Civil War. The

Pedro El Cruel

crème de la crème had been Falangist volunteers and fundamentalist Catholics who fought in the Blue Division with Hitler's SS at Leningrad, against the Russians. Their services to the *patria* had been rewarded at the end of the Civil War with sinecures, particularly in the prison service.

Don Pedro was a character straight out of *Weird Tales*. Apart from the fact that one of his eyes was set disconcertingly at thirty degrees to the other, he bore an uncanny resemblance to Ernest Borgnine as the sadistic jailer Fatso in *From Here to Eternity*. He wore a dark blue shirt that marked him out as a Falangist of 'the first hour'. On his left sleeve he wore a curious badge with a swastika. I discovered later that this was the emblem of the Hermandad de la Division Azúl.

As I was marched to my cell to begin my ten days of periodo, Don Pedro shouted something in Spanish. I looked quizzically at the humourless orderly, shrugging my shoulders, saying 'No hablo español'. The orderly escorting me translated in halting English, with a sardonic grin, that by the time I left Spain I would be a 'proper Francoist'. The door slammed behind me with an echoing crash, double-locked and bolted with two heavy clunks.

(Strangely enough, Don Pedro appeared to take a liking to me. Although our later discussions often became heated, he argued with me without getting apoplectic, unlike some of the other Falangist warders. He 'didn't mind' anarchists, he said, and in fact anarchism, in his view, was part of what he called the 'picaresque' character of Spaniards, but he hated communists and Marxism, which he saw as anti-Spanish and an imported 'foreign ideology'.)

Apart from health controls, periodo was also a means of preparing prisoners psychologically for their new life behind bars. It also gave us time after the first shock of arrest to reflect on imprisonment, loss of freedom, love and affection. There was certainly nothing else to do in the bare cell. The only movement in the room was that of the slow shadow of the bars across the cell walls and floor.

An enervating tiredness overwhelmed me. The sense of desolation was enough to depress even the most clinically cheery. All I wanted to do was lie down and escape into sleep. As I stretched out on the hard stone-flagged floor I imagined myself encircled by the ghosts of unfulfilled and truncated lives. How many people had been taken from this very cell and been shot or garrotted? Men and women whose crime was resisting Franco, the ecclesiastical tyranny of a medieval church, feudal landlordism and one of the most reactionary middle classes in Europe.

I lay awake for a long time that first night on top of the bed, thinking about how the police had known, should I have done things differently, who was the traitor? Regrets, I had a few, but it was way too late to worry about them now. As I dozed, I was also vaguely conscious of the sound of the *chivato* cover on my cell door being raised and swinging shut as curious funcionarios peered in to check that this mysterious foreigner about whom they had been reading hadn't topped himself.

The *cabo* of the gallery, a scion of the Moroccan royal family, had been charging three pesetas to let prisoners have a look at me through the chivato.

x x x

The Story in the Papers

The Spanish media had a field day with my story. Accounts of my arrest had preceded me in lurid newspaper headlines and word-of-mouth stories that passed into prison mythology. Particularly colourful and prevalent was the one about me entering Spain wearing a kilt. For almost a fortnight the media had published the most extraordinary stories about the kilted anarchist assassin who had come to kill Franco and murder the best part of the population of Madrid, if not Spain. One Spanish paper had me crossing the border in full highland regalia, skean dhu (short sock dagger), feathered cap and all. Presumably the skean dhu was to be plunged into Franco's flaccid belly. Some thought all Scots habitually wore the kilt anyway. By the time the stories reached Buenos Aires, I was dressed as a woman, a mistranslation of *la falda escocesa* (the Scottish kilt).

Journalists stated quite matter-of-factly that I had been paid sums ranging from quarter of a million to five million pesetas for this assignment, and had been specially trained at a anarchist 'terrorist' camp in the French Pyrénées.

It did not dawn on me for a long time that perhaps the Spanish authorities circulated the kilt story for the same reason that they were so prompt to claim their agents were active in Britain: they wanted it thought that they were following me because I was a cross-dresser or a transvestite in order to hide the co-operation between Scotland Yard and Spanish fascism, which was an even more potent form of political dynamite than the stuff I was carrying.

Still, the Spanish Ministry of the Interior (Gobernación) took the unusual step of announcing to the media that the success of my arrest was due to the 'excellent information' supplied by Spanish agents operating in Britain. This may or may not have been bullshit, but it was almost unprecedented for a government to admit cheerfully and openly that they are operating an espionage network in friendly territory, something usually regarded as an embarrassing secret. How would the press have taken it had the Russians openly admitted that their spies had been photographing and collecting information in Britain designed to lead to the arrest of a Briton in Moscow? But they made no reference to collaboration with the British police.

The story made a major impact in the British press, both tabloid and broadsheet. At first they could not believe that an eighteen-year old Glaswegian had been involved in something as outrageous as an anarchist plot to kill the Spanish dictator. In the famous swashbuckling style of the Beaverbrook Press, Charles Graham of the *Scottish Daily Express* declared:

'Even James Bond would have been hard put to keep a straight face about the tales of terror and imagination – mainly imagination – circulating about the anarchist movement in Glasgow. Yes, anarchists, from Drumchapel and Hillhead and small towns in Lanarkshire; anarchists allegedly plotting international espionage and the overthrow of governments, also allegedly under the expert surveillance of the Spanish Secret Service. This is the tale Spanish spokesmen put out after a Blantyre youth, Stuart Christie, was held on suspicion of plotting violence and accused of carrying explosives . . .'

There was not much the press could say about my arrest until my trial, but the story was a front-page splash with most papers for a few days after the news of my arrest broke before being relegated to the inside pages. The complicity between agents of the British government and fascist Spain continued after my arrest. Prior to my trial, Special Branch in Glasgow interviewed my English teacher in Blantyre, George Bradford, asking to read through my school essays in order to get some insight into the development of my political ideas. George refused. No doubt the police of two countries were annoyed to find a stand on academic freedom and confidence between teacher and pupil should be made, not in a historic university, but by the dominie of a secondary school in Blantyre.

x x x

For these first days of imprisonment, I paced the cell – five paces from end to end, pivoting around on the last step in such a way as to keep the rhythm even. I found this somehow hypnotic and soothing. I whistled softly to myself as an aid to concentration and confidence. I tried a series of mathematical rituals – counting the miles I'd walked or the number of tiles on the walls – but other thoughts kept crowding my brain. Eventually I was reduced to the main pastime of those in solitary confinement: pacing.

Occasionally in the sweltering night I would have a sudden panic attack, woken by the sound of the *chivato* cover swinging open. Someone was watching me – someone was coming in. Were they going to make me disappear? Would I be shot under the infamous fugitive law, while trying to escape? But the cover would slide shut, and the footsteps become more distant.

Time in prison is only measurable in terms of successive events, most of them undistinguished and all of them marked by the bugle call of the *corneta*. There were no clocks. *Díana* (reveille) was at 7 a.m, followed by the cacophonous racket of cell doors being unlocked, unbolted then slammed and bolted again as the jailer counted us on his hurried way along the landing. If the count had gone well and no one had escaped, hanged themselves or been miscounted, a milky brown coffee was was brought to the cell door at 7.30 a.m.

Another bugle call at 8 a.m. signalled cleaning duties. These had to be carried out with the cell door open. Bedding had to be rolled, the cell brushed out with a broom made from twigs, the symbolic brass tap polished (there was no water to be had from it) and, finally, the floor washed. We would then have to stand by the door, outside the cell, until the gallery warder had made his inspection.

The 8.30 a.m. bugle announced morning association in the patio. On the first day, I shifted around hopefully behind my cell door, peering through the chivato to see if mine would be unbolted. It wasn't. But I did see prisoners strolling about quite nonchalantly.

Carabanchel operated what was called an 'open-door' regime. Cell doors were unlocked from first morning recuento until lunch and the obligatory two-hour summertime siesta from 1.30 p.m. to 3.30–4p.m. when they were open again until after supper around 9 p.m.

I also learned that the prisoners were mainly responsible for running the prison. The *funcionario* appointed an *encargado*, a chargehand, to run the gallery from among the prisoners and delegated much of his power to him. The encargado could use the funcionario's hotplate to cook his own meals and he could get more or less what he wanted from outside. The encargado, in turn, imposed his own order in the gallery, allocating cushy jobs to his friends or those prepared to pay him or provide some service in return. Less salubrious jobs like cleaning or distributing parcels went to those to whom he took a dislike. He was also responsible for appointing the cabos de planta, or machacas, the prisoners responsible for each landing.

The lack of regimentation surprised me. Perhaps it wasn't going to be so bad after all.

x x x

My natural optimism soon returned. I had seen films showing how to play up the Germans in Colditz. Like the Colditz prisoners, I was privileged. I had the opportunity to play up this vicious dictatorship and get away with a great deal more than others. At least I was young and had no personal commitments or family attachments other than my Mum, Gran and sister, and they weren't depending on me financially. For breadwinners with wives and children to support it was a far greater sacrifice.

On my first Sunday, the prison governor, Don Ramón García Labella, visited with his English-language translator to ask if there was anything I needed. This was surely something unique in the history of the prison administration! An anarchist being treated like a VIP. Books, cigarettes and writing material would be nice, I said. I added that I would also like my money which had been confiscated by the Brigada Política Social. Even in the short time I had been in Carabanchel, I had realised that without money it was difficult to get very far, even in prison.

To my surprise, Costas turned up later with cigarettes, a freshly baked *bocadillo* (a roll) with Manchego cheese and *chorizo piquante*, real coffee and a freshly made pastry from the gallery coffee shop. He also brought a few dog-eared Agatha Christie paperbacks.

I felt as though I was starting to get into the swing of things. I asked if he could make sure Carballo had what he wanted as well, but I was the only one with whom he was allowed to communicate. The *cabo* Risooni, however, took some cigarettes and pastry from me to Carballo later that morning.

When the paper and biro arrived I wrote to my mum to reassure her that I was in good health and was being treated reasonably, under the circumstances. My main concern was how my plight was affecting Mum, Gran and my sister, Olivia. I had been allowed to write a few lines to my mother on a postcard of Madrid from security HQ, saying briefly that I had arrived safely and would write to her in more detail as soon as possible. The card arrived the morning the news of my arrest broke in Britain.

x x x

The governor was the first of three visitors. The second was the priest. The hatred of prison priests for political prisoners – whom they denounced regularly at mass as 'red scum', 'murders' and 'the godless host' – was not always rhetorical. In one notorious incident in the prison at Castellón de la Plana, a group of political prisoners told the prison *capellan* that they were non-believers and were immediately beaten and humiliated for their 'intolerable insolence'. One Sunday, during Mass, when the bell signalled the congregation to go down on their knees, they remained standing and as a result they were brutally punched and kicked as they were dragged out by the funcionarios. Most horrifically of all, after the Mass was over the refractory politicals were taken out into the patio and shot in front of the other prisoners.

The priest was accompanied by his trusty and interpreter, José Pineda, a tall, dark-complexioned and effete young man with a distinctive hawk nose and long lank black hair brushed Hitler-like, diagonally across his forehead. Pineda dressed according to what he believed was the Andalusian take on Oxbridge fashion: a white collar, an old school tie, blazer, cavalry twill trousers and shiny patent leather loafers. All he lacked was a felt Córdoba hat. José Pineda was an Andalusian gigolo, a pathological liar, an *embustero* (a 'show-off'), and the bane of my life in Carabanchel.

The priest put his questions to me coolly, but through Pineda they came across in a blustering and patronising manner:

'Can you really be an atheist? It is not possible!'

'Yes.'

'But you are really a Protestant? In what religion were you brought up?'

'In the Church of Scotland.'

The remark angered the priest. 'The Church of Scotland, ridiculous! There is only one Church, that of Christ our Saviour! That is not a Church, it is a heretical Protestant cult.'

His parting shot, delivered through Pineda, was 'At least one good thing will come through your stay here. We shall make you a Christian in spite of yourself. You will confess the Catholic creed before you leave.'

I replied, through Pineda: 'Perhaps', then muttered Galileo's famous remark, *Eppur si muove* ('but it does move'), with as insolent a tone as I could manage.

He appeared to grow paler with anger at this reminder of the astronomer's forced recantation. For a moment I thought he was going to land me one there and then.

X X X

It would have been unfortunate for the priest if he had given way to his impulse. The last visitors waiting for me were the British vice-consul, Mr Harding, and an affable Spanish clerk from the British Embassy. They weren't conducted to my cell, though – I was brought to them. It was Monday, the first day the Embassy could send someone to see me since the news of my arrest broke on the Saturday, the day we had been transferred to the Madrid prison.

As a high-security risk, I saw my visitors in a small private chamber, separated by a large glass window, rather than the main visiting gallery. After introducing himself and asking how I had been treated, Harding told me how the outside world was reacting to the news of my arrest – it was a major international news story and there had been demonstrations in my favour all over the world, except Spain of course. Both Jean Paul Sartre and Bertrand Russell had signed petitions in my favour. The unusual circumstance of a Scot being held in a Spanish prison on a charge of terrorism had made a few people wake up to the fact that there were also a great many Spaniards in prison with me.

Harding told me my mother had been in contact with the Foreign Office. He said Carballo and I would be tried by a summary Council of War, a Consejo de Guerra, within the next few days, and that my friends in London had formed a defence committee. They were planning to send a QC to the court-martial as an observer. He assured me that the Embassy itself would organise a barrister for me.

The defence committee's QC turned out to be Niall MacDermott, an idealistic lawyer and Labour MP who had also been a syndicalist for a time. MacDermott was an 'Old Rugbeian' who later that year became Financial Secretary to the Treasury in the first Wilson government. At this time, he headed up the Geneva-based International Commission of Jurists (ICJ) and its British branch, 'Justice'. During the war, he had been a major in MI5 and incurred the vindictive enmity of MI6 for refusing to back off in his attempts to expose Kim Philby, the senior SIS officer who was also a Stalinist spy. MacDermott was finally forced out of Wilson's government in September 1968 when 'D' branch of his own former employers, MI5, accused his half-Russian and half-Italian wife, Ludmila, of being a Soviet spy.

MacDermott visited me in Carabanchel a few days before my trial. I explained to him, off the record, that I knew exactly what I had been doing, but he struck me as being slightly bewildered by the situation, as was everyone, including me.

He could do little more than be there, a symbolic moral presence, and argue his case to the press – I was an immature youth and that anarchists in Britain were a small and innocuous group, a slightly weird but morally laudable section of the peace movement, who had nothing to do with dangerous international anarchist revolutionaries – from the Continent. What else could he have said? There was little point arguing with him; I was in no position to make any contradictory statement to the press had I wanted to, but I did tell him that if he did make such a statement it would be against my wishes and would not be an accurate reflection of my feelings or my position. He even talked about a defence for me based on a supposed 'fugue state' – a temporary loss of identity. Thanks, but no thanks!

x x x

The military had appointed army defence counsels for Carballo and me. Mine was Captain Alejandro Rebollo, an infantry officer who had defended both Guy Batoux, a French anarchist arrested almost two years earlier, and the unforunate Julián Grimau, apparently with gusto, but without success. Fortunately, the British Embassy insisted that I be defended by a civilian lawyer, Don Gabriel Luís Echevarría Follos, to which the army finally agreed. This was the first time a civilian barrister had ever appeared as counsel in a Council of War.

The days dragged on. A comforting letter came from Mum telling me that everyone was well and that she would be coming to Spain for the trial. Mr Harding turned up again, this time with my Embassy-appointed lawyer with whom I went through my defence, what there was of it, with the assistance of an Embassy translator.

By this time I was resigned to a guilty verdict. They had me bang to rights. Apart from refusing to recognise the court, or haranguing the court martial and demanding to be tried by my peers, I had very few options. My only vaguely sensible defence case was that until I crossed the frontier I thought I was carrying propaganda. What was worrying me now was the sentence. I could only draw hope from the fact that at least my trial would focus world attention on Franco's fascist regime in Spain – and that my youth and the fact I was British might ameliorate whatever sentence they might impose.

x x x

Finally our ten-day *periodo* ended, and Carballo and I were allowed out into the exercise yard, under heavy supervision, while the rest of the prisoners had their siesta.

It was about 1.30 p.m. and the August sun burned from above and bounced back up from the concrete below. I sat with my eyes closed, shirt open and face turned towards the sun – in true British tradition in Spain, I was determined to get a tan. Carballo sat in the shade, close by, anxiously indicating that I should do the same, and somehow communicating a little about his role in the plan. Apparently Carballo, a carpenter, was to collect the explosives and final instructions from me, prepare the bomb and place it in the Royal Box at Santiago Bernabéu Football Stadium, or in the Stadium car park, close to where Franco's car would arrive. As a joiner he had clearance to access the area. The device was to be detonated during the cup final, when Franco would present the cup to the winning team. Not only would the bomb take out Franco, but eliminate many of his close staff and cronies as well. The venue was highly appropriate.

Franco's Team

Football – Real Madrid in particular – was a crucially important element in Franco's governance. In the same way that the Romans used the bloody spectacle of the gladiatorial Games, and in more recent times Mussolini fixed the 1934 World Cup final, and Hitler used the 1936 Olympics and the 1938 World Cup, Franco used Real Madrid to co-opt a popular non-party movement to win popular consent, and help give his regime domestic and international legitimacy. Real Madrid FC represented for Franco the political dominance of Madrid within Spain. He also understood the awful unifying power of the game whose successes provided the spiritual alchemy which, apart from the unsporting malcontents and cynics, made the idea of the regime inseparable from the prestige of the nation under Franco.

I wasn't the man with the plan – nor did I know the target – but had it been successful and killed Franco and his closest associates, I felt it would have been worth it. At least that was my view at the time. I like to think that the targeting would have been pretty precise, but if that turned out not to be the case my second line of rationalisation was that anyone in the box with Franco was likely to have been fair game. The people with him would have been guilty by association, I suppose, including any players who happened to be there when Franco was presenting them with the cup. The truth is I tended not to think in terms of the unintended and unlooked for consequences of killing Franco in such a manner. That came later.

After a few days of this sun, often spent playing handball with Carballo's home-made ball, I realized why the Spaniards sought the shade. I woke one morning with a severe headache, feeling weak and so dizzy I was unable to get out of bed. When the medical orderly arrived, and after much arm waving and curt exclamations, he rummaged in his medical bag and triumphantly produced what looked like a creamy-coloured bullet encapsulated in plastic. I looked at it inquisitively, wondering what on earth it was – were they now going to produce a gun and would I be left to commit suicide with some sort of untraceable poison? Seeing my incomprehension the medical orderly started making gestures towards his fat arse, as though scratching his sphincter. The full horror of what they wanted me to do with the 'bullet' suddenly sank in and froze my Presbyterian soul to its core. They wanted me to stick this thing up my bottom! Was there no depravity the Catholic Church was immune to?

Somehow I was able to deduce from the gestures and Spanglais noises that I had contracted a mild case of sunstroke and this *supositorio*, as they called the device they were waving about, was a stopgap measure until I could be transferred to the prison infirmary where they planned to monitor me for a few days.

x x x

This was the same infirmary in which Julián Grimau Garcia had spent his last days. Grimau had been betrayed as a senior member of the Communist Party and arrested by the BPS in Madrid on 7 November 1962 for war crimes and 'military rebellion', charges dating back to the Civil War. He was so badly beaten by the BPS officers during his interrogation that that they threw him from a second floor window (the same one they hung me from) in the hope of explaining away his injuries, claiming he had been trying to escape. Carabanchel prison's medical authorities initially refused to accept him because of his terrible state, but finally took him under pressure from the Ministerio de la Gobernación. No one really believed he would be executed, including the prison staff, friends and relations. He was kept there throughout his court martial, right up to the moment he was marched out to face his firing squad on 20 April 1963.

The scale of Franco's post-Civil War pogrom against his opponents and 'enemies of the church' may never be known. The most conservative figure for executions between 1939 and 1946 is around 50,000; others estimate the number as high as 370,000. All that can be said is that local authorities in Spain are still excavating the mass graves of Franco's victims, the Republican *desaparecidos*, sixty-three years after the end of the war. There was also the still unanswered question of the fate of the unknown number of at least 10,000 children of anti-Francoists taken away by the regime's social services, priests and nuns and never heard of again.

It was always hoped that 'next year' (with the amnesty, some time by Christmas, or Easter, on the twentieth anniversary of this or the twenty-fifth anniversary of that) the regime would be liberalised. Some people believed that the new emphasis on tourism, industrial investment and the mass emigration to the Common Market countries meant that those days were over. But with the execution of Grimau the regime showed that it had learned nothing and forgotten nothing.

However, Grimau's death did benefit the Spanish and other European communist parties politically. By giving them a martyr, it helped restore some of the party's lost support and membership after the Soviet repression of the Hungarian uprising.

Restored to good health and back in my cell after a week in the infirmary, I was wakened early on 1 September and told to collect my belongings. Carballo and I were to be tried that morning by a Council of War of the First Military Region. I was eighteen years and six weeks old.

The Consejo de Guerra

Massive security precautions were in place. Exaggerated stories had been circulating about the kilted hit man and the nature of our mission. Rumours included a story about an anarchist commando planning to ambush our convoy, and the authorities were taking no chances; a decoy convoy had apparently left the prison before us. But the 'anarchist commando' never materialised so we ended up at our intended destination.

The Consejo de Guerra was held at number five calle del Reloj, the military headquarters of Spain's 'First Military Region'. Escorted through a waiting detachment of soldiers who acted as a barrier between us and a few curious bystanders, pressmen and photographers on the pavement, we were marched up the white marble stairs to the first floor into a large hall and then into a side room to await the arrival of the military panel. Police, Guardia Civil and soldiers milled around by the doors and windows.

Echevarría, my embassy-appointed lawyer, popped his head around the door looking quite preoccupied, and told me the prosecution was not asking for the garrotte but twenty years for me and thirty years for Carballo. It is easy to imagine what a huge relief that piece of news was, even so casually delivered. It felt like I had already been acquitted. Two Civil Guards arrived soon after to escort us into the courtroom.

Still handcuffed, we were marched to a wooden bench facing the dais where the presiding officers would sit. Behind us was a barrier beyond which were the 'public' benches for selected pressmen, policemen and Falangists.

The doors opened and a mass of people flocked in, anxious to be nearest the front. Within minutes all the seats in the hall were filled. Then in came the military prosecutor and my barrister who took their places at opposite ends of the dais facing each other. I looked behind me at the faces in the public gallery and smiled warmly when I saw my mother sitting next to the British consul, Mr Simon Sedgewick-Gell. Mum replied with a comforting smile, but she was clearly under a great deal of strain and was doing her best to appear her normal cheery self for my benefit. Sitting beside Sedgewick-Gell was Niall MacDermott, QC.

A soldier entered through a door on the dais and announced the presiding officer, Illustrissimo Sr Coronel de Infantería Don Jesús Montes Martín. Everyone stood as he marched in, resplendent in full military ceremonial dress followed by a chorus of the hard-faced, tight-collared captains. They lined up along a table draped with a Francoist flag, removed their caps and unsheathed their swords from their scabbards, placing them ceremoniously in front of them.

x x x

The trial started after a few ceremonial formalities. The prosecutor, comandante Don Enrique Amado del Campo, opened proceedings with an impressively theatrical peroration, apparently demanding the maximum sentence for both of us. No chance of a fine and being bound over to keep the peace here, I thought. An army captain, Don José Bellído Serranco, defended Carballo. The case against my co-defendant flew by; there was no translator for me, so I didn't understand a word. Then it was my turn. I knew this because my lawyer stood up and said something. He could have been saying his rosary for all I knew, but I discovered later he was asking for clemency on the grounds I did not know what I was doing or carrying.

My memories of the proceedings are hazy. I felt like a detached, invisible observer looking out through the windows of my brain into

the middle of a film set or centre stage in some Grand Guignol play.
It was fascist theatre and I was the villain. I was unaware of time
passing – I seemed to be in a slow-moving dream, uncomprehending
and unmoved.

The prosecution case turned out to be a brief history seminar on
contemporary Spanish anarchism. According to the transcript of the
trial, which I received later, the prosecutor stated that mine had been
the latest of numerous attempts to undermine and destroy the

CIL

'Anarchism, formalised in the First International
held in London in 1862 under the name of the
International Workingmen's Association, first
appeared in Spain in 1869 with the formation of the
Spanish section of the International. At different
times in its history this section of the First
International has adopted different names ... and is
now manifesting itself in international informal
affinity groups among which we find the Consejo
Ibérico de Liberación (CIL) to which Christie and
Carballo belong. This group, along with many other
anarchist bodies, continues the tactics and
activities of the First International which are
directed toward the violent subversion and the
destruction of the political, economic, social and
judicial organisation of the state, and the
repeatedly proclaimed social ideas which reject
outright the whole concept of authority as contrary
to the idea of individual liberty, and accepts, as
irreconcilable, the antagonism between Society and
the State with the belief in the violent suppression
of the latter.'

'Glorious National Movement' begun by General Francisco Franco in 1939. The most consistent offenders against this 'Glorious National Movement' had been the international anarchist movement of which I, irrespective of my youth, was an evil example. The prosecutor went

on to describe anarchism and its history with an insight that would have put to shame most British investigative journalists, political commentators and academics.

When the court called on me to give evidence and be cross examined I told the prosecutor that I believed I was carrying printed propaganda until I unwrapped the parcel in Barcelona and discovered it contained explosives and detonators. Having come so far, I was afraid to hand the explosives over to the police in case they didn't believe me. I couldn't dump them in case someone was killed. I felt there was no alternative but to carry on and hope for the best. I didn't mention my Granny's role in making me an anarchist. Blaming one's Granny would not have gone down well in such a matriarchal society.

Mum arriving at Madrid airport for the trial (preceded by 'Stashy Dan' – Wilson Russell – of the *Scottish Daily Express*).

My evidence was translated for the court by a paratroop captain, Don Francisco Martínez Pariente. I felt embarrassed for the man. It was either my thick Glaswegian accent or his lack of English vocabulary, but the way he was struggling for words he had obviously been suckered into the job against his better judgement, or else he had been drawing a foreign language allowance under false pretences and was now having to prove his worth.

The military judges retired at lunchtime. The trial had lasted all morning, about three hours. My lawyer told me that the proceedings were now over, but that the sentences would not be pronounced for a day or so.

x x x

We were taken for our lunch to a small side-room with the door open and curious people peering in at us. Carballo and I had to make do with a piece of dry bread and cheese. Balbás came in with my mother and said how charming she was and told our guards that she could have a few minutes with me, but not alone. Mum had been flown to Madrid by the *Scottish Daily Express*, and this was the first time I had seen her since my arrest. I kissed her as best I could given the restrictions of my handcuffs and my Civil Guard escort. I introduced

Benedict Birnberg: the pre-eminent British radical lawyer of the 1960s-90s.

my mother to Carballo who was manacled to my wrist. I could not help but feel that she believed that it was all his fault.

It was a pity Carballo's mother was not there to balance matters, but she was dead. Being a dignified lady, however, Mum asked him – in English, and with genuine compassion – how he was bearing up. The dialogue was more in keeping with a Kelvinside drawing room than a Spanish court martial.

I was so pleased to see my Mum and tried hard to impress upon her that I was all right and things would work out all right in the end. Personally, I had no real problems with my situation and was sure I would come through the ordeal eventually. As they say, what doesn't kill you makes you stronger. But although I was OK, the emotional pain and worry both Gran and Mum were going through during that period must have been almost unbearable. Her main concern was that I had not been tortured and was being treated properly, which I assured her had been the case. I also had a brief meeting with Niall MacDermott QC, who was due to report back to my London solicitor, Benedict Birnberg, and the hurriedly

Christie-Carballo demo leaves Speakers' Corner, Hyde Park, August 1964.

formed Christie-Carballo Defence Committee.

Fortunately, Mum was able to stay in Spain for a few days and she had been told by the embassy and by Balbás that she could visit me whenever she wished. I saw her each of the next couple of days before she returned to Blantyre.

x x x

On her first visit Mum told me what happened the day she received the news that turned her world upside down. It had been her half-day, a sunny Saturday afternoon, and she had just sat down with a cup of tea to read a postcard from me from Spain. There was a knock on the door and when she opened it, two reporters from the *Scottish Daily Express* told her that I had been arrested in Madrid on charges of 'banditry and terrorism'.

Not surprisingly, she couldn't take the news in at first. But as soon as she collected her thoughts she put on her coat and hat and hurried down the road to catch the bus to Lesmahagow, the home of her constituency MP, Tam Fraser, the then Minister of Transport in the Wilson government. Fraser had been opening a local fête when she found him, but when he heard the news he quickly took her to his home and telephoned the Foreign Office, who said what they always said in these circumstances: 'not to worry' and not to make a 'fuss'.

By the time Mum got back to Blantyre the dung-beetles of the Scottish press were out in force and the normally traffic-free Victoria Street where my Gran lived had cars parked nose-to-boot on either side of the road. Mustering as much dignity as she could manage, Mum made her way through the wall of flashing lightbulbs and aggressive notebook-wielding reporters into the besieged house. Gran was not one to take a knock like that lying down; that night she pulled herself together, put on her best suit and hat and went off to the old folks' whist and beetle drive at the Blantyre Miners' Welfare as though nothing had happened.

Free Christie!

Olivia, my sister, was too young to understand fully what was happening. She had been sent out to the pictures that Saturday night and it was only on her way home when she saw the 'Free Christie!' slogans now appearing on walls and bridges and the reporters in their cars outside the house that she realised something serious had happened to me.

News of my arrest had broken on Saturday 15 August and within hours anti-Francoist demonstrations were being organised in a number of countries. Glasgow was among the first with a march and a picket held the same afternoon the news was announced. (Ian Mooney, an IS member, burned a Spanish Falangist flag outside the offices of the Spanish Consul in Glasgow. Unfortunately, he was extremely near-sighted, and instead of dousing the flag with petrol he accidentally soaked his trouser leg, so when he lit the match that was what went up in flames.)

There was concern in the BBC about my contribution to the Muggeridge programme, still yet to be broadcast, admitting that if given the chance I would settle Franco's hash. With one exception, all those who had taken part in the programme asked for it to be pulled or at least that my contribution to be cut. At the last minute, with the full agreement of Sir Hugh Green, controller of the new BBC2 network, I was edited out of the programme.

Two friends from the Scottish Committee of 100, Walter Weir and Walter Morrison, hitched-hiked from Glasgow to London when they heard of my arrest. In a sequence of events that spoke for the times, Walter Morrison telephoned Scotland Yard to ask permission to hold a fast outside the Spanish Embassy. The senior officer on duty told him it would be all right so long as it was peaceful. No sooner had Walter settled down on the pavement outside the Embassy than a Black Maria drew up and three or four policemen dragged Walter inside it. A PC Guppy on duty in Belgrave Square that evening claimed he had arrested Walter for shouting 'Down with Franco' at a group of pro-Francoist Spaniards who complained about his behaviour. Instead of being charged and taken to the police cells as normal, Walter was taken to what seemed like a large gym hall where three men sat at a table, one in uniform and the other two in civvies. They began questioning Walter about his relationship with me, about the Committee of 100 and the activities of the Scots Against War group. When Walter was taken to the cells, two stooges pretending to be fellow prisoners tried to engage him in conversation on the same subjects. His treatment was only a little more subtle than mine had been in the Seguridad. (The situation was redeemed slightly when PC Guppy ostentatiously fainted in court after Walter claimed the officer had told him, inside the police station, that he was framing him for bad-mouthing Franco.) Walter was an old hand at being arrested and locked up, but these strange events shook him up so badly in fact that he resigned for a time from the Scottish Committee of 100.

x x x

A British anarchist arrested in Spain was unusual (in fact unique), but over the years a number of French and Italians had been arrested for their role in the resistance, some of whom had been given the most barbaric treatment with the minimum of diplomatic or media concern. My arrest came just at the moment when Spain was plunging into the gold rush of international package tourism on a gigantic scale. Had I been given the death sentence, the prospects of big business backing tourism might have gone the same way. The story in most of the British press was that an innocent teenager doing no more than was normal in Britain, handing out leaflets, had been hauled in, threatened with a death sentence, and might finish up doing twenty years in a fascist prison. It was not at all the sort of thing that went well with Iberia Airlines' pretty brochures.

It was suggested to me that everyone would save face if I made a plea of temporary insanity. But that would be to betray everything I believed in. I felt I was justified in trying to save myself twenty years in prison by lying about what I thought was in the package, especially as the case would still cause a major aggrevation for Franco. But it seemed monstrous to suggest that anyone involved in attacking the regime should be thought even slightly abnormal. Abnormality to me consisted in allowing a man such as Franco to continue unchallenged in power.

x x x

Although I had been sentenced on Thursday 3 September, I didn't receive official confirmation until the following day when a slip of paper with that day's date on it was pushed under my cell door, after lights-out. The captain general of the First Military Region had confirmed my sentence at twenty years imprisonment. Minor reclusion, they called it. Had it been twenty years and one day it would have been reclusion *mayor*, a whole different tariff. The date of my release, it stated blandly, was 1984. Jesus! I thought to myself, I'd be 38 years old when I finally get out. Will it be into a 'Brave New World', and after twenty years behind prison walls, would I recognize it if it was?

Scenes from a Spanish Gaol

A few days after the trial, Carballo was transferred to another prison to serve out his 30-year sentence. We were in the patio when the *cabo* came to tell him his order of transfer had come through and he was to pack his belongings immediately. We said our goodbyes, embraced, and he was led off through the barred gates. It was an emotional moment for us both. I never saw him again.

I was left in Carabanchel, presumably for reasons of state and international diplomacy – it being much easier to monitor and control me in Madrid than in the provinces. I was, after all, a potential source of great embarrassment to the regime were something untoward to happen to me. But I was always aware I could be moved at a moment's notice, as Carabanchel was essentially a remand and short-term prison.

x x x

Carabanchel Prison in the 1950s and 60s was the sociological black hole of Spanish society. Locked behind its high redbrick walls were a multitude of redoubtable individuals and picaresque rogues from among the widely differing communities of the peninsula: Galicia, León, Old and New Castille, Navarre, Astúrias, Aragón, Catalonia, Extremadura, Murcia, Andalusia and the Basque country. This was all the Spain Franco didn't want the world to see – and quite a learning experience.

For all that, there was little violence and tension in the prison. The only serious violent incident I recall is a child murderer being thrown to his death from the fourth landing of the gallery. The only time I encountered genuine anger myself was during heated discussions over the morality of bullfights.

Over my first few months in prison, I began to feel a deep affinity and sense of kinship with Spaniards. In terms of cheerful temperament and generosity of spirit they were on a par with the Irish. They also took pride in their individuality, were full of delightful paradoxes and contradictions, had a great sense of humour and were naturally antipathetic towards officialdom. It may even have been genetic. Who knows, I might have been the descendent of a survivor of Philip II's great Armada, shipwrecked on the wilder shores of Scotland during the storms of 1588.

Flaubert, who fell in love with Egypt on his travels in 1849, suggested a new way of defining nationality. It was not by country of origin or where one chose to settle, but according to the place to which you were attracted. I was definitely Spanish.

Spanish lights were not hidden under bushels. No other nation on earth was, in its own members' eyes, so inventive or had such a rich history and culture. (Until then I had understood that the Scots had been the creative driving force of modern civilisation.) But although the Spanish were aggressively patriotic and proud of their common culture, with all its faults and animosities, they were also intrinsically parochial, and defined themselves primarily not as Spaniards but in terms of their own village or urban district. George Orwell observed in *Homage to Catalonia* that during the Civil War, the political loyalties of individual Spaniards often depended on which *pueblo* or *barrio* they came from.

Many of the Spaniards I came across had only recently moved from their villages, and from working the land, to the factories or unemployment in the big industrial cities of Madrid, Barcelona and Bilbao. Their cultures and appearances varied from cosmopolitan and sophisticated European Barceloneses and Madrileños; Moorish Malagueños and Murcianos; gitanos, gypsies from the labyrinthine cave city of Guadix and the Sacrimonte; Celtic cantabrian Gallegos from Vigo and La Coruña; mountain men and miners from the Asturias, the *quinquis* (tinkers), and, of course, the mysterious Basques.

They claimed to defer to no one, including Franco. The Aragonese were fond of quoting the oath of loyalty sworn by their nobles to the Spanish king. It bore remarkable similarities to the sentiments expressed in the Scottish Declaration of Arbroath, written in 1320, six years after Robert the Bruce's victory at Bannockburn:

'We, who are as good as you, swear to you, who are no better than us, to accept you as our sovereign lord, provided you observe all our statutes and laws, if not, not.'

They were largely ignorant of the world of the *extranjeros* (foreigners) beyond the Pyrénées. They seemed to find me as exotic as I found them. The attitude of most of the comunes, the non-political prisoners, towards me was friendly. My *nombre de patio* (patio nickname) was '*el bombero escocés*', 'the Scottish fireman', or '*el petardista*', 'the bomber'.

Although they tended not to bear grudges, a few proud Spaniards, including some bitter anti-Francoists, resented that I had taken it upon myself to intrude in what they saw as a purely Spanish affair. Some I managed to persuade that I had acted on principles that should be common across humankind, not restricted to nationality; others thought I did it for money. They had me marked down immediately as a *jilipolla*, a stupid foreigner; nice but dim – and slightly inferior.

x x x

Most of the Spanish '*comunes*' (criminal prisoners) were opportunists who were inside for small-time robberies and burglaries. One lad had been sentenced to three years for stealing a jacket in winter. There were no Professor Moriarties or criminal geniuses. There were a few highly imaginative villains, but by definition not intelligent enough to avoid capture in the long run. They were victims of their own over-reaching temperaments and sheer bad luck. Only a few Spaniards were inside for the more creative and larger-scale crimes such as fraud, embezzlement, high-value thefts, cigarette smuggling and bank robberies.

Murderers were the sorriest bunch. The majority had killed people they loved most in a moment of hysteria, madness or jealous rage and now lived with their guilt as best they could every moment of every day. A very few were psychopaths devoid of conscience or sense of guilt. These had killed or maimed not because they didn't know what they were doing, but because they didn't care. The other prisoners avoided these characters. There must have been 'nonces' (sexual offenders or child abusers), but I never came across these and I suspect they were kept in solitary confinement in the *tercera* (third) gallery.

Two of my fellow inmates were in for what were to me unusual bullfight-related incidents. These men were *espontáneos* whose crime was to have jumped into bullrings during *corridas*. One was an eccentric Gallego who had been sentenced to six years for recidivism in interrupting bullfights. He would vault into the ring at 'the moment of truth' brandishing his Galician bagpipes, push the matador to one side and confront the bull – just as the former (or the latter) was about to make his kill – blasting away at the banned Galician national anthem for all he was worth. I learned from him that the word 'toreador' had in fact been invented by Bizet because 'matador' did not scan with the tune in 'Carmen'.

The second was a mischievous, troll-like Asturian. His trick was to leap into the ring the moment the bull bounded in and confront the bull himself. On the last occasion, he had accidentally stuck his sword in the eye of one of the matadors who tried to escort him out of the ring. His actions didn't seem political. Were he to have been operating in the UK, he would certainly have been naked.

The changing population of Carabanchel was a barometer of the rising pressure of strikes, political discontent and crime in the rest of Spain. In 1961, six million tourists visited Spain; in 1965, fourteen million. And as more Spaniards wanted their culture, their music, their politics and their money, more of them ended up behind bars.

Spain was also open to tourism of a different sort. Because of its lack of formal extradition treaties with most of the rest of the world, Spain in 1964 had become not only a centre of right-wing conspiratorial intrigue; it was also a safe haven for global criminals and desperados with nowhere left to run. The poorer, more careless, or unlucky ones inevitably ended up spending time in the prison of the national capital.

In the early days, after a long and intelligent conversation in the yard with a new acquaintance, thinking I had made friends with a nice chap, I was always surprised when I discovered he was an SS or Gestapo officer awaiting extradition on charges of mass murder, or an OAS terrorist, a South American gangster, a professional assassin, an arms dealer, a rapist, a swindler, a pickpocket, or a pimp. I suppose you will see the better sides of pimps and dictators when they are deprived, respectively, of whores and minions in much the same way as you will see the better side of drunks when they are sober.

x x x

Before I went to prison my world-view was black and white, a moral chessboard on which everyone was either a goody or a baddy. But the ambiguities in people I came across in prison made me uneasy and I began to question my assumptions about the nature of good and evil. I came to recognise that apparently kind people sometimes had a duplicitous side, while those with a reputation for cruelty sometimes showed themselves capable of great selflessness and generosity of spirit. Pedro 'El Cruel' was a man with a well-documented history of cruelty and bloody-mindedness, yet during my *periodo* he had been surprisingly kind and considerate. Ian Dixon and Trevor Hatton of the Committee of 100 had found a similar thing when they were banged up in Springhill Prison with Colin Jordan, the British national organiser of the National Socialist Movement.

Also, it was hard to fan the flames of righteous anger in the face of the sheer ordinariness of people. The ethical template in my head no longer seemed to fit reality and my clearly drawn moral blueprint became smudged and fuzzy when I was brought face to face with what

Hannah Arendt termed 'the banality of evil'. As far as I could tell, there was no psychological or sociological equation between intelligence and bravery, conviction and courage, ideology and humanity or class and generosity of spirit.

The experience didn't make me cynical, or reject what I believed in. In fact, the contrary was true. The fact I met very few people who could honestly be called 'evil' made me more inclined to look for the reason they had committed evil acts. I became less judgemental of individuals, and more committed to oppose a form of society that inclined individuals to commit crimes against each other.

x x x

One of the prisoners who occasionally joined me on my ruminative patio marathons in the weeks after my arrest was an Austrian by the

name of Joachim, the *encargado de galería*, the 'trusty' prisoner responsible for the day-to-day running of the gallery. He was a tall, formal and austere sort of man, a bit schoolmasterish, with a square lantern jaw, high forehead and dark, greying hair. He was intelligent, well-read and spoke good Teutonic English. Even though he was always anxious to help me out in little ways, he made me slightly uncomfortable. Perhaps I knew subconsciously what he was. Why would a German of his age be in a Spanish jail? His only friend among the prisoners was another Belgian war criminal.

Otto Skorzeny in his Madrid offices, mid-1960s.

I later discovered Joachim had been an SS officer in a Nazi

concentration camp and was fighting extradition back to Germany for war crimes. But I still could not say that I felt myself in the presence of unadulterated evil. Joachim had powerful friends and was visited regularly by Otto Skorzeny, the Spanish coordinator of Odessa (Organisation der SS Angehoerigen or Organisation of SS members), the post-war escape network that provided new identities and shelter for wanted Nazi war criminals and collaborators and organised their escape to the Middle East, Latin America or South Africa.

One day Joachim just disappeared. I never found out if he had been extradited or if Skorzeny and his chums had managed to obtain his release.

I felt more comfortable with a French ex-legionnaire from Marseilles. Jacques was a professional criminal awaiting trial on charges of burglary and armed robbery. He had broken into the apartment of a wealthy Spanish financier and was arrested trying to blow open the safe. Unfortunately, he used too much explosive, knocked himself unconscious with the blast and blew the windows out instead of the safe door. On another occasion, he and his friends had been unable to open a safe so they dropped it out of

Patio of Yeserias prison hospital ward, winter 1965.

the first floor window of the office they were robbing, stole a wheelbarrow from a nearby building site and wheeled the safe through the streets of Paris back to their garage where they finally managed to torch it open – burning all the money and securities that were inside at the same time.

Jacques told riveting stories about the French underworld, the

Gaullist gangsters of the Service d'Action Civique (SAC) (set up by de Gaulle's security services to neutralise the activists of the OAS), and the Corsican Mafia. His constant topic of conversation was his plan to rob the vaults of the Société Générale Bank in Nice. He wanted me to come in with him on this project when I was released. He had the plans of the bank, the vault of which was built at the turn of the century close to a main sewer, making it an easy target. Access to the sewer could be gained from an underground car park directly opposite the bank.

Jacques was sentenced to ten years imprisonment and disappeared into the outer reaches of the Spanish prison system. Interestingly, the Société Genérale Bank in Nice was robbed in 1976, twelve years later, by precisely the method described by Jacques. The gang managed to get away with sixty million francs in cash, bonds and jewellery, having welded the vault's doors shut to delay discovery of the crime. The French police arrested three members of the gang, but of Jacques there was no mention.

x x x

A week or so after I received my sentence, a hospital orderly escorted me to the 'anthropometry' room that adjoined the infirmary. It was a grey room, furnished and smelling like a dental surgery. Starkly lit by fluorescent tubes it had an adjustable chair, scales and glass cabinets in which sinister-looking stainless steel instruments were laid out in neat rows. I had never heard of anthropometrics before and had no idea what was involved, or its purpose.

A small, balding, and precise-looking man dressed in a white coat and steel-rimmed glasses was writing away on a clipboard. He nodded to me as I entered and pointed to an examination table. For a moment I panicked, thinking I was going to be trepanned or subjected to some other form of sub-Pyrenean psycho-neurosurgery.

After a brief introduction the man in the white coat began making notes on his clipboard. The form he was completing had pre-printed outlines of cranial and body parts, full-face, profile and plane, which he was checking off. The form also had my police mugshot attached to it. He clamped a pair of steel callipers at various points around my head. 'Jesus Christ,' I thought to myself, 'I'm being measured for an iron mask.' In fact, this was the alleged science of determining a person's criminality by measuring the appropriate parts of the body.

The distances between each and every conceivable part of my head were noted, as was the size and shape of my nose, the tilt of my forehead and the distance between my eyes. He peered closely at my skin looking for scars and blemishes, meticulously recording every detail on his form. He noted my height, head size, the extent of my outstretched arms, the length of my left forearm and left middle finger, and the circumference of my wrist. His crowning moment came while he was examining my ears and discovered I didn't have any earlobes. His thin, dark face became animated and he let out a sharp intake of breath. He had discovered anthropometric gold.

x x x

For the first few months of my imprisonment my main problem was my inability to communicate with my fellow prisoners. It took me almost a year before I could think in Spanish, although I did manage to make myself understood before that.

I attended literacy classes with the Andalusian fop and prison governor's translator, Pineda, who had been appointed my chaperon. Dressing in what he imagined to be the 'English' style, he looked look like a cross between Lord Peter Wimsey and a Monégasque ponce. He claimed to have degrees from both Oxford and Cambridge. He stuck to my side every waking minute of the first month or so after my *periodo*. He was my Spanish teacher, 'moral tutor' and personal spy, reporting to the chief prison warders on whom I associated with and what we talked about.

Spain at the time was a Roman Catholic country in much the same way that Saudi Arabia is Muslim, and the Church was all-powerful in the classroom. Lessons began with a prayer and swearing an oath of loyalty to the Caudillo. I was obliged to stand up, but managed to avoid taking any oaths. This was followed up with the teacher delivering an exaggeratedly venomous and perverse attack on the forces of anti-Catholicism. I was aware that education in Spain had always been in the hands of the clergy, but when I first opened the textbooks I couldn't believe my eyes. The first page showed recorded history beginning with an illustration of the fall of man in the Garden of Eden.

After two or three months I explained my frustration with Pineda to a sympathetic warder who had words with the governor and, much to my astonishment, I was released from Pineda's custody. One consequence of this snub was to make me his enemy. Anything and everything I did he reported immediately to his friends among the Falangist warders.

Contact with the Outside World

My letters home were in English, and so brought me into contact with a special censor, another Blue Division veteran whose name – Don Benigno – belied both his appearance and his character.

My early letters to Mum were full of complaints about the food and the armies of unusual insects and parasites with whom I had to share my cell, my bed, and my food. (One morning I opened my eyes, disturbed by something moving on my face, to see the blurry form of a scorpion marching across the bridge of my nose. I froze, my eyes following its delicate progress, until it eventually dropped off my cheek and continued on its way over the side of the bed.)

I wrote quite forcefully and dramatically to Mum about how I would lie awake at night, unable to sleep listening to the sounds of cockroaches scuffling in the corner. Next day I was called to Don Benigno's office where he handed me back my letter and told me to rewrite it, this time without mentioning prison conditions. I argued with him that if I could not write about the prison, what else could I say apart from the weather and my health?

Clearly not the other incidents in the life of the prison. Shortly after I had been released into the normal prison regime, our gallery went to see the 1959 sword-and-sandals film *Hercules Unchained* in which there was considerable seduction, slaughter and plunder. The sight of Sylvia Lopez as Queen Omphale of Lydia hanging on to Steve Reeves's knees must have triggered something in the mind of one of my neighbours, an elderly man jailed for strangling his beautiful young actress wife in a jealous rage; that night he hanged himself from the window bars sometime after the last count. His body was discovered at recuento the following morning. I mentioned this incident in a letter home to my mother, and later that morning was summoned again to appear before Don Benigno. He was angry and accused me of trying to bring Spanish prisons into disrepute and needlessly worrying my mother. He assured me that if I continued to denigrate the penal system he would see to it that I would never be released.

The only letters I was allowed to receive during those early months were those from my Mum and Gran. But I knew through prisoner friends working in the censor's office that bags of letters, magazines, newspapers and books were arriving for me every day. Fortunately, I soon discovered that in return for 25 pesetas a week, the trusty would bring me all my correspondence before taking it on to Don Benigno. I had a couple of hours to read all my letters and cards before returning them for censorship. Eventually the trusty gave up giving them to Benigno and left everything with me.

This went on for almost a year until my man was caught performing the same service for another prisoner. After that the censor's office moved to the administrative section outside the main body of the prison. But it didn't take long to find an alternative method of getting hold of my mail. Don Benigno's new trusty was an avid collector of stamps, so I arranged for my Mum to send me a cheap package of used foreign stamps with each letter. I gave him these in return for his services. This system continued throughout my period in Carabanchel until I was finally transferred to the political gallery, where it was more difficult to move around and maintain contact with my former network.

X X X

By the end of 1966 and in the early months of 1967 the books, magazines and newspapers I was receiving showed that a cultural renaissance was taking place in Britain. From where I was, it felt as exciting as the birth of rock 'n' roll, ten years earlier.

When I left the UK in 1964, before the Wilson government was elected, society was still relatively grey and conservative. But now even popular music in Franco's Spain was changing. That much we had been able to pick up from listening to the funcionarios' radios and the weekend radio broadcasts played over the patio tannoy system. The counter-culture was on the march.

Tangible evidence of these changes came in the form of parcels of complimentary books which started to arrive in 1965, presents from the avant garde publishing house of John Calder. These books, mainly in the Jupiter series, were cerebral manna from heaven, particularly the comic novels of Samuel Beckett: *Murphy*; *Watt*; *Molloy* and *Malone Dies*. These extraordinary, surreal and time-stopping dark stories about the hilarious and tragic antics of decrepit characters who find themselves physically and psychologically disintegrating were a revelation. I had stumbled upon what were to me unknown masterpieces, and a literary encapsulation of the human condition, describing with real warmth and humanity our humdrum progress through time and space. With his presents of these books, John Calder became a terrestrial angel who brought inspiration and laughter to the cells of Carabanchel and for that alone he deserves his place in the panthéon of literature.

Radical journals and newspapers also started arriving around the same time – without the system of bribery, they would never have made their way past Don Begnino. *Heatwave*, edited by Christopher Gray and Charles Radcliffe, was one of the intellectually stimulating duplicated magazines that reached my cell.

The content and layout of these publications showed that the pace of events outside was quickening. The Wooden Shoe, a new bookshop in London's New Compton Street run by an Australian, Ted Kavanagh, and the veteran London anarchist Albert Meltzer, began sending me their new publication *Cuddons' Cosmopolitan Review*, with a clutch of articles by exciting new (to me) writers such as Tuli Kupfberger and news about ideas and events, particularly about what the Dutch 'Provo' movement was doing in Amsterdam.

This was the same team who also published the one-page

Radical Culture in the 1960s

broadsheet *Ludd* which created a bit of a furore around the time of the seamen's strike in the summer of 1966, the first national strike organised by the National Union of Seamen (NUS) since 1911. Prime Minister Harold Wilson and Ray Gunter, his hard-line anti-Communist Minister of Labour, had been obsessed with Communist-Trotskyist and anarchist agitators and conspirators who were 'stirring things up'. In June 1966, Wilson made what turned out to be one of his most infamous McCarthyite speeches, claiming the seamen were being manipulated by a 'tightly knit group of politically motivated men'.

The strike had been forced on the NUS by its rank and file members. Anarchists were among those active in the Seamen's union and in the British merchant fleet, but none were sympathetic to the NUS leadership, which was referred to disparagingly as the National Union of Shipowners. One of these anarchists, George Foulser, who was a key contributor to *Ludd* and who played an important part in the seamen's strikes in the 1950s and 60s, wrote:

> The general run of merchant seamen are dominated by a rat organisation with members of the capitalist-class as its so called officials, and voting-rules which make sure that no seamen will ever get official positions in the National Union of Seamen. Since I was born the N.U.S. has never had a single instance where the union officials have taken action against the shipowners. It was for the genuine seamen, the rank and file without a voice in their own trade union, to take action in order to retain the good name of British Seamen . . . The N.U.S. is often referred to as the National Union of Shipowners; and sometimes as the National Union of Scabs. It is because the N.U.S. follows the shipowners' aims that it fights tooth and nail against ships' committees for NUS members.
>
> In Australia, New Zealand, Canada, the USA, Holland, Norway, Denmark, Finland, France, Italy, the Republic of Ireland, and in all the communist countries, merchant seamen have had legally recognized union representation aboard ship for years . . . Now that seamen have realised the value of their rank and file movement, I

think that we shall obtain our freedom and our legal ships'
committees – but no thanks to the British government whether
Labour or Tory. And certainly no thanks ... to the shipowners and
their N.U.S. lapdogs. (Foulser 1961: 64–5)

Foulser, G. (1961), *Seaman's Voice*, London: MacGibbon and Kee

The content and tone of these new radical publications which were
reaching me in Madrid were light years away from the old-fashioned
Freedom and *Direct Action* papers I had left behind two years earlier.
They were amalgams of the best of the old anarcho-syndicalist ideas
melded with dadaist and surrealist texts, together with a new social
critique propagated by a group calling itself 'Situationist'.

'Situationists' were a small but influential French-based circle of
intellectuals who had developed a critique of 'alienation' and
'recuperation' based on what its leading light, Guy Debord, described
as 'the Spectacle'. Basically, they were radical and bloody-minded
advertising copywriters and graphic artists manqué who argued that
images had come to replace the real and that people had become
conditioned players in a global film or TV advertisement. They
wanted to break down what they saw as the borders between life and
art in order to live with 'imaginative intensity'. This they proposed to
do by creating dramatic situations that could be anything from an
artificially created riot to vandalism to suicide. What they did,
however, was produce lots of witty and trenchant posters, parodies
and slogans that caught the mood of the period and – if it did nothing
else – provided amusing and thought-provoking graffiti and artwork
for a new generation of radicals.

Perhaps the most important and wider cultural influence and
barometer of late 1966–7 was the appearance of *International Times*
(IT). *IT* was an intriguing newspaper which became the English-
language voice of the new counter-culture, the harbinger of the
hippies. It was professionally produced, printed on a letterpress
machine with an innovative layout. Edited in its early period by Tom
McGrath, *IT* avoided political analysis; it was eclectic, non-
judgemental, anti-Vietnam War, libertarian, hedonistic, sybaritic,

Situationism

International Times

211

drug-oriented and sexually liberated. It carried articles about music, legalising cannabis, William Burroughs, Alexander Trocchi, underground events, women's issues, blacks, CIA conspiracies, UFOs and hippies. To me, locked away in the Castilian sierra it was a clear sign that something new and exciting was happening on the outside, but quite what I hadn't the foggiest idea.

x x x

Don Alberto was my conduit to the outside world. He seemed unsuited to the job of prison warder. To him it was just a good job, something scarce in Spain where wages were extremely low. He was also responsible for issuing the twice-daily wine ration to prisoners, two glasses of wine at one peseta each. Two prisoners accompanied him, one carrying a wooden tub with the wine and the other carrying a small demijohn to fill the tub as it emptied. As long as we were discreet about it, we could have as much wine as we wanted. His charges for other services were two pesetas on top of the cost of the stamp for a letter, the same for my Sunday papers and about five pesetas on top of the cost of a bottle of whisky, brandy or whatever drink we wanted. These had to be brought in plastic containers, lest someone grow suspicious at finding empty spirits bottles in the prison dustbins.

Don Alberto lasted only about nine months in Carabanchel. One of the prisoners tried to get out of a spot of trouble by grassing up Don Alberto. When Don Alberto clocked on for duty the following morning, he was stopped by the chief of services and two security screws and asked to open his case. Inside were two bottles of scotch, a bottle of vodka, five hundred grams of hashish and bundles of letters for prisoners.

About six weeks after my court martial the governor, Don Ramón García Labella, summoned me to his office to tell me that the system had plans for me. I was to be transferred to the *quinta* gallery, which was considered more salubrious with a 'better class of prisoner', and that I would have to work in order to 'redeem' or reduce my sentence. (According to the governor, I had been sentenced by a military tribunal therefore I was not classified as political; only those sentenced by the civilian Tribunal de Orden Público (TOP) were considered political prisoners, and were kept together on the *sexta*. I knew this not to be the case, but accepted his judgement for the moment.)

By this time I knew that with the exception of the political prisoners, most inmates in Franco's jails usually served around a quarter of their sentences. Up to half a sentence could come off if a pope died and even more when another was elected. That year, 1964, Francoist Spain was celebrating 'Twenty-Five years of Peace' and on 15 September Franco authorised an *indulto*, a reduction by a sixth part of all prisoners' sentences, including those whose death sentences had been commuted. I now had 16 years and nine months left to do.

Life in the *Quinta*

Apart from the occasional *indultos*, a further third could be deducted from one's total sentence by 'redemption' or working. This meant that for every two days a prisoner worked, one day was deducted from what remained of their sentence. I would have preferred not to work for Franco – it was bad enough being kept a prisoner by him, and until then my time had been spent enjoyably, learning Spanish, talking, drinking coffee, sunbathing behind the washing lines, and playing *pelota*. But I was to have no say in the matter. Also, it was getting on for the middle of October, and the winds blowing down from the Sierra de Guadarrama were turning colder so the option of exchanging a bitter, damp and grey patio or cell for a warm workshop had an appeal.

When I left the *septima*, Don Pedro 'El Cruel' hid his emotions well as he waved me farewell, with an admonition to behave myself otherwise he would be after me. He knew where I lived!

x x x

A single cell on the ground floor of the *quinta* had been set aside for me. I was privileged. Most prisoners were banged up four or six to a cell.

Don Benigno called for me the following morning after the 10 o'clock recuento to take me on a guided tour of the *talleres penitenciarios*, the prison carpentry and print workshops. I was going to work in the printshop, a strange trade for a fascist dictatorship to teach an anarchist. The attitude of Franco's regime to learning had been summed up in 1936 with the fanatical General Millán Astray's cry of 'Muera la inteligéncia!' (Death to intelligence!) during a speech critical of the new regime by Miguel de Unamuno y Jugo (1864–1936). Hadn't these book burners learned anything about the power of the printed word over the past forty years? Weren't they aware that the printing trade had been a radical and libertarian stronghold for many years, particularly in Spain?

Don Benigno left me with the printshop owner, a plumpish and cheerful businessman by the name of Don Carmona, who had jumped at the opportunity of cheap labour and minimum overheads in return for low capital investment. Once or twice a week Carmona held classes in graphic arts in his office and at the end of the first course I came top of the class. This was not due to any particular cleverness on my part, but to the fact that I was one of the very few of the machine minders in the workshop who could read. Most of the other apprentices were *análfabetos*, illiterates.

Operating the noisy Heidelberg press was a tedious eight-hour day. The only time the trance was broken was when a sheet of paper misfed, whether induced or accidental, or something went wrong with the platen and we had to strip the machine. This happened two or three times a day.

I was one of the lowest paid in the workshop; my monthly wage amounted to a couple of pounds, about 200 to 300 pesetas, while the chargehand, also a prisoner, earned nearly £20 a month, a lot of money at the time. This was still a far cry from the pittance British prisoners earned in a supposedly more progressive penal system. Fortunately, I was not dependent on my wages. Mum sent me £5 every month from home – a lot of money out of a weekly wage of £12 – and I also had 1000 pesetas a month from the CNT prisoners' support committee in Toulouse.

The camaraderie of the printshop was good, but I persuaded the governor to let me work Tuesdays with the dentist, on the basis of my apprenticeship as a dental mechanic. The dentist, Don Mariano had a dental practice in Madrid, and he agreed to my helping out because he wanted to improve his spoken English. Working with Don Mariano gave me access to the whole prison and regular contact with the three CNT members in the sixth gallery: Francisco Calle Mancílla, ('Florián'), José Cases Alfonso and Maríano Agustín Sánchez, and the one FIJL member, Alain Pecunia, the young French anarchist. The only other occasions to meet with them were during Mass, visiting times, during Saturday cinema or sneaking off from the printshop.

x x x

Anarchists were in the minority among political prisoners in Carabanchel, with about fifteen or so scattered around the four cellular galleries that had been built at that time. Most of the political prisoners were communists. The rest were Basque separatists from ETA, the Basque Nationalist Party, the Basque Workers' Union, and about ten members of the Roman-Catholic-influenced Frente de Liberación Popular (FLP), including Nicolás Sartorius, Nicolás Redondo and Alfonso Guerra. There were a similar number of Maoists from the Frente Revolucionario de Acción Popular (FRAP) and pro-Cubans as well as students and academics arrested during the 10,000–20,000-strong student demonstrations of 1964 and early 1965.

I became friends with one French anarchist in particular, Alain Pecunia. Alain explained the circumstances of his arrest and those of his two fellow-accused. They bore remarkable similarities to my own. The BPS had been waiting for the seventeen-year old French lad on his return to the French border at Cerbère in April 1963, after he had planted his small explosive device on the Barcelona–Palma de Mallorca ferry, the *Ciudad de Ibiza*. These attacks on the railway lines were not intended to kill or maim, simply to disrupt the rail infrastructure as part of the anti-tourist campaign. All three men had been allowed to cross into Spain on missions that were already compromised.

Although Pecunia's background was vastly different from my own, the process of our politicisation had been similar. The son of a senior naval officer who had served on de Gaulle's staff in London during

World War II, Pecunia's passions had been aroused not by the anti-nuclear movement but by the conduct of the French war in Algeria, particularly over the use of torture by the French army. He began by throwing himself into anti-war demonstrations, gradually becoming more deeply involved in anti-OAS activities with the Algerian Front de Liberatión Nationale (FLN). He had been a Young Communist for a short time, much as I had been a Young Socialist, but had then discovered anarchist ideas through the French Anarchist Federation (FAF) newspaper, *Le Monde Libertaire*.

The three young French lads were sentenced to twenty-four, thirty, and fifteen years respectively for acts of 'banditry and terrorism'. Had they been Spaniards the probability is they would have been garrotted, even though they were responsible for no loss of life.

Alain was the first of the three to be released. His father carried considerable clout in Gaullist circles and, according to Pecunia, Franco had insisted on a personal phone call from de Gaulle on the matter. The people involved in negotiating Pecunia's release sounded like a character list in a Dennis Wheatley novel: the Duc d'Aumale, French and Italian fascists trying to negotiate an exchange of OAS prisoners (in France), even Otto Skorzeny was asked to intervene by a former French member of the *Abwehr* (Hitler's army counter-intelligence service), a German collaborator. Stories also circulated about secret clauses in ongoing financial accords between France and Spain. The French Foreign Ministry official responsible for the Southern Europe desk at the Quai d'Orsay, a certain M. J. de Folin, told Pecunia later that his freedom had cost the French government two Mirage jet fighters. Pecunia was released on 17 August 1965, exactly two years to the day after the executions of Delgado and Granado. He had served twenty-eight months in prison.

x x x

From time to time in this undemanding existence, I would fall to speculating what might have been had I caused the death or deaths of innocent people. A shudder would run through my body. It would have been a terrible burden to bear if I had managed to escape the garrotte-vil. As one of Solzhenitsyn's characters comments, memorably, in *The First Circle*:

'What is the most precious thing in the world? It seems to be the consciousness of not participating in injustice. Injustice is stronger than you are, it was and always will be, but let it not be committed through you – a crippled conscience is as irretrievable as a lost life.'

Alan Ladd said much the same thing in the film *Shane*: 'There's no living with a killing.'

I also wondered about the possible negative consequences of successfully assassinating Franco: would it have liberated Spain, or led to a more severe and bloody repression and the emergence of an even more brutal dictator? But by what means other than resorting to violence can ordinary people challenge a state apparatus which is evil, corrupt and repressive, whatever its excuse may be; where there is no fair play, no respect for justice and freedom; which is not subject to legal or social strictures, and is unresponsive to reason, appeals to morality and international diplomacy?

Franco's regime was a rogue state supported by tourism, emigré wages and the overwhelming economic and diplomatic clout of the USA. Like the regimes of Hitler, Mussolini and Stalin it scorned the give-and-take of negotiation as evidence of weakness or Marxist or masonic manipulation. It ignored the protests of its own people and those of its opponents around the world, convinced in its own self righteousness that its use of terror and repression would ultimately allow it to win through to being accepted as a European power on its own terms. Franco was a military man who respected only one thing – overwhelming, devastating and lethal force.

Even so, the decision to kill a man to prevent greater violence and evil was a tragic and burdensome choice. Unlike the hanging judge who relies on the executioner, or the bomber pilot who drops bombs on innocent bystanders from 30,000 feet, or the F16 fighter pilot who fires a 'surgically targeted' missile into a residential apartment block in Gaza from 200 metres, I did not see it as merely some 'unpleasant duty' to be performed. Those of us outside the institutions of state had no club or regimental officers' mess to return to for a port and brandy and absolution, or reassurance that 'collateral damage' – that weaselly euphemism for massacring the innocent – was the unavoidable price that had to be paid in the 'national interest'. We anarchists had only our uneasy consciences to answer to.

Ultimately, what matters is that evil must be kept from destroying the good. Jimmy Stewart – the idealistic eastern liberal who wanted to counter evil with reason and law in John Ford's *The Man Who Shot Liberty Valance* – found this out at the end of the film: 'When force threatens, talk is no good.'

As for my debate with myself, I concluded that my arrest had been the best possible outcome. I had now become a regular reminder to the world of the nature of Franco's Spain. 'All is for the best in the best of all possible worlds'.

x x x

Two executions took place during my time in Carabanchel. I saw the last stages of the gruesome ceremony preceding one of these, that of a *quinqui* by the name of El Lute.

There was no love lost between the gypsies and *quinquis* and the Guardia Civil. They had been sworn enemies since the formation of the rural paramilitary force in the previous century. El Lute had killed a Civil Guard who had tried to arrest him.

El Lute's Execution

On the evening before the execution everyone in the prison, including all the trusties, were locked up until El Lute had been brought from the isolation cells below the sexta galería through the quinta to the condemned cell which adjoined the execution chamber. I was medical orderly of the quinta at the time, so my door was the only one unlocked.

That night I lay in bed reading and re-reading Oscar Wilde's *The Ballad of Reading Jail*. It seemed the only way to understand what was about to happen.

With an execution imminent the prison was on high alert, all prisoners tense and a full complement of jailers in attendance. The macabre ritual of institutional murder required the presence of the captain general of the region, attended by senior Francoist civil servants, general staff officers, ecclesiastical dignitaries, the arresting civil guard or police officers, the prison governor and high funcionarios.

The condemned man was led out of his cell in the *calabozos*, the punishment cells, and took his place in the grotesque procession which would march through the prison on its way to the execution chamber. The dignitaries of Francoist justice waited in the gallery of the punishment cells to fall in line behind the manacled prisoner as he was taken on his own funeral procession. From the condemned cell they filed slowly along the *camino de la muerte*, the death road, past the sexta, up the stairs past the infirmary, through the quinta and the rotunda, then down stairs to the tiny chapel where the priest was to hear his last confession.

I was able open my door a foot or so to witness part of the condemned man's last journey. He was brought through the quinta just after 11 p.m. Looking down the gallery through the chivato I could see this horrifying troupe advance slowly on its processional path through the gloom of the dimly-lit gallery. As they trudged closer I heard the deep, slow, rhythmical chant of the creed. The march bore the stamp of a medieval auto-da-fé. This macabre, mumbling, procession was preceded by the priest dressed in gold-embroidered brocade reading from a missal; then came an acolyte brandishing a cross high above him, then other church functionaries with the sword, and the olive branch, symbols of justice and mercy. Accompanying the cross bearer were two more acolytes chanting and swinging incense burners. Behind them marched more familiars, bearing other banners, crosses and lighted candles.

Behind the priest and acolytes walked the condemned man in a white open-necked shirt, his head and shoulders held high and his hands manacled behind his back. He towered above the two small funcionarios, Don Fernando and Don Tomás, both dwarfs, who waddled along incongruously on either side of him.

He was followed by a phalanx of perhaps twenty or so military, legal and lay official witnesses led by the Captain General in his dress uniform complete with ceremonial sword. Through the chivato I looked closely at the face of the condemned man as the staged tableau passed my cell, trying to read his emotions and thoughts. I thought of the two innocent anarchists, Delgado and Granado, who followed the same calvary only a year earlier, and then I thought of myself who could so easily have been in the gypsy's position. He was the only one not chanting the creed.

> *'And strange it was to see him pass*
> *With a step so light and gay,*
> *And strange it was to see him look*
> *So wistfully at the day,*
> *And strange it was to think that he*
> *Had such a debt to pay . . .'*

Executions took place at five o'clock in the morning, precisely. Few prisoners slept the night before an execution. The hour before the execution dragged by. I paced up and down my cell, smoking cigarette after cigarette, reading Wilde's harrowing poem, line by line, verse by verse, feeling intensely emotional and attempting to empathise with the man I had seen pass by a few hours earlier.

A tangible sense of melancholy descended on the prison in the final minutes before the execution.

> *'We waited for the stroke of eight!*
> *Each tongue was thick with thirst:*
> *For the stroke of eight is the stroke of Fate*
> *That makes a man accursed,*
> *And Fate will use a running noose*
> *For the best man and the worst . . .'*

I don't know how we knew the time, without clocks or watches, but at five o'clock, a hellish timpani broke the silence of the dawn. Prisoners banged on their plates and rattled the window bars with their spoons while others kicked the cell doors in unorchestrated unison. Their cries of abuse against the executioners and jailers rose up to the heavens, a cacophonous noise that echoed through the galleries and over the prison walls. That outburst of impotent frustration, despair and anger cost us 24 hours without exercise or privileges.

> *'Out into God's sweet air we went,*
> *But not in wonted way,*
> *For this man's face was white with fear,*
> *And that man's face was grey,*
> *And I never saw sad men who looked*
> *So wistfully on the day.*

I had been pushing for a transfer to the sixth gallery, but every time I petitioned the governor or the Dirección General de Prisiones my application was rejected. The CP and Maoists opposed my transfer on the grounds that I had been convicted of 'banditry and terrorism' and was therefore not a 'genuine' political offender. (Coincidentally, this was the same reason given by the then fairly recently formed Amnesty International when asked to intervene in my case. I was not, they said, a 'prisoner of conscience'. Perhaps they believed I had been paid to carry the explosives.)

The more likely reason was that another anarchist in the gallery would change, even ever so slightly, the balance of power. The CP prisoners also refused to call Pecunia and the CNT members 'comrades' (which was normal practice among all the political prisoners), but addressed them instead as señor. Nor would they *tutear* any of them, the familiar way of addressing a friend or comrade. They always used the more formal *Usted*.

Life in the quinta was not arduous – the prison had changed a lot since the horror days of the forties and fifties. When the old dentist died, the new doctor shared the job of practice nurse between me and his favourite, a man called Zurro. An important perk that went with the job was the use of an electric hotplate. Ostensibly, it was for emergencies where boiling water was needed, but its main use was culinary. Zurro was a wonderful cook who introduced me to the delights of Spanish cuisine, 'Fundador' brandy and Rioja wines which he had smuggled in on a daily basis.

Watching Zurro with a melon was an education. He would carefully select one from the *economato* and place it delicately on the palm of his left hand, raising its bottom ever so slightly and pressing the centre with the thumb of his right hand. He never once looked at the melon but kept his eyes upon an invisible point in the distance. He rarely bought the first melon he pressed; sometimes as many as a dozen melons would pass through his fastidious hands before he made his final, triumphant, selection – much to the relief of the man in the economato and everyone in the queue behind us. Sometimes if they were feeling generous they would give him a round of applause after he'd made his choice!

The doctor's consulting room was an adapted cell equipped with cupboards, filing cabinets, a desk, an examination couch, chairs and a sterilising unit. When Zurro and I were cooking a meal in the evening we would sometimes make use of the old steriliser to boil the spaghetti to save time, but we always made sure it was cleaned out after use, in case of emergencies. Certainly no one became ill as a result of the culinary uses to which we put the instruments of medical science, at least not to my knowledge.

x x x

One curious and ostracized group I now came into reasonable regular contact with was the *maricones*, homosexuals, who were kept in virtual total isolation on the fourth landing of our gallery. The only work they were permitted to do was cleaning, and they cleaned the consulting room. The older ones redeemed their sentences by taking in washing, sewing and ironing.

Maricones were for the most part cheery and full of coquettish and flirtatious banter. They brought a little colour and life to the day-to-day drabness of the prison. Most of them had been convicted under the vagrancy laws, *la ley de vagos y maleantes*, and were usually homosexual male prostitutes and therefore offensive to the church, threatening the sexuality of 'nice' society.

When they could, they dressed up in clothes of the brightest colours and often there would be a hint of lipstick, rouge and eye shadow. When questioned by a screw as to how he had got hold of the make-up he was wearing, the *maricon* replied that he had smuggled it in his cunt, meaning, of course, his arse.

A tremendous patio pastime was watching the bullfight *aficionados* re-enact what they considered the best corridas of their heroes: Manolete, El Cordobés or El Viti. One played the part of the torero and the other the bull. They divided this ceremonial slaughter into three acts – the *tercios*: the *picadors*, the *banderillas* and the act of death, the *faena*.

It was hypnotic and depressing to see them practising their mock elegant manoeuvres in slow motion, *capeas*, dextrous and intricate passes with an imaginary sword and cape. It was one thing to watch these guys play out the circus of the *corrida*, but I found it impossible to hide my distaste for the barbarity of the event itself. Bullfighting was the one issue that caused me most arguments with Spanish friends. They simply couldn't believe that anyone should think the baiting, torture and slaughter of a dignified and sentient creature was not great sport. They didn't see it like that at all.

x x x

In 1964 and '65, the colonial powers were having their grip loosened on their colonial possessions. Increasingly, liberation movements in these subject or satellite countries were being targeted by mercenaries recruited from among the zealots associated with the Organisation de
The OAS L'Armée Secrète (OAS – a clandestine terrorist organisation set up by rebel French Army officers in 1961 to resist the collapse of French settler power in Algeria). These were plausibly deniable neo-fascist and ultra-right wing groups used as cover by the Portuguese, Spanish and US intelligence services and secret police organisations, the most notorious being as the Lisbon-based Aginter Press and the Madrid-based Paladin security consultany group of former SS veterans run by Otto Skorzney and Dr Gerhardt Harmut Von Schubert, formerly of Goebbels' Propaganda Ministry.

x x x

In 1964, Jean-Jacques Susini's Z commandos (ultra-rightist pied noir students of the Nationalist Front) attempted to assassinate de Gaulle in Toulon; in October 1965 Moroccan anti-colonialist politician, Mehdi Ben Barka was kidnapped and murdered in Paris by French gangsters working on behalf of the CIA and renegade officers of the French secret intelligence service. These and other acts were part of a new wave of revanchist terrorism, and prompted the French government to pressure the Francoists to act against the OAS high command in Spain.

Most of the Spanish-based OAS leaders had been forewarned by sympathetic colleagues in the BPS of the crackdown and had fled to offer their murderous skills elsewhere. Some sought sanctuary under the protective wing of the extreme right-wing military regimes of Latin America. Others went to Italy where they were protected by pro-fascist and anti-communist elements within the Italian security and intelligence services. Portugal was another country where they found a sympathetic employer with need of their terrorist expertise – Salazar's secret police, the PIDE.

OTTO SKORZENY'S PALADIN GROUP

The Madrid-based 'Paladin Group' was an agency and strategic centre for the recruitment of mercenary killers and terrorists. This company, headed by Otto Skorzeny, specialised in sabotage and assassination operations in the Maghreb, sub-Saharan Africa, Latin America, Asia and Europe. Its personnel also carried out deniable killings and acts of terror on behalf of General Eduardo Blanco's Dirección General de Seguridad and were probably responsible for the murder of José Alberola Navarro, Octavio's father, in Mexico City on 1 May 1966.

225

In the weasel vocabulary of intelligence and security agencies, companies like Skorzeny's permitted clandestine state agencies to 'respond to a crisis without transgressions of administrative jurisdictions'.

**José Alberola Navarro:
murdered 1 May 1967.**

In other words, it allowed them to murder troublesome dissidents and political opponents without fear of comeback. In a letter from SAS founder David Stirling, a friend of Skorzeny for many years, to Charles Foley, the author of *Commando Extraordinary*, a biography of the infamous SS colonel Skorzeny's war years, the author noted that since the early 1950s the Nazi had 'been toying with the idea of setting up an international directorship of strategic assault personnel whose terms of reference would enable it to straddle the watershed between paramilitary operations carried out by troops in uniform and the political warfare which is conducted by civilian agents.'

The political turbulence and proxy wars in satellite states which marked the mid 1960s meant that Skorzeny's paramilitary security organisation flourished. In the Argentine, Skorzeny's company provided the personnel for ad hoc killer groups such as José Lopez Rega's Argentina Anti-communist

Alliance, the notorious pro-Peronist AAA death squads. In Spain, with the tide of angry opposition rising month by month and the increasing number of actions against military and political pillars of the Franco regime, Skorzeny was given a contract by the Dirección General de Seguridad to deal with its enemies, particularly the Basque separatist organisation ETA.

The public face of the Paladin Group was that of a legitimate security consultancy, but the reality was that it provided cover for its primary function which was to recruit and run mercenaries and killers for dictators and failing colonialist regimes around the world.

In France and Spain its covert activities were implemented under a variety of names of convenience: among others these included the 'Spanish Basque Batallions', Mariano Sánchez Covisa's 'Guerrillas of Christ the King' and the 'Apostolic Anti-Communist League'. Aldo Tisei, an Italian neo-fascist supergrass and associate of the Italian terrorist eminence grise Stefano Delle Chiaie, told an Italian examining magistrate many years later: 'We eliminated ETA members who had fled to France, and did so on behalf of the Spanish secret services.'

Some of those who failed to escape to Latin America, Italy or Portugal with the other OAS leaders – such as Pierre Lagaillarde and Yves Guérin Serac – during these periodic diplomatic clampdowns in Spain ended up in Carabanchel.

In the spring of 1965, five OAS leaders were arrested and charged with the attempted assassination of a French general in Germany. This turned out to be one of the last *attentats* in the bloody history of the

OAS. Two of these men ended up with me in the *quinta*, a Colonel Raymond and Pierre, a chubby, white-haired, balding, Pickwickian academic who had been a professor of oriental studies in Algiers.

Colonel Raymond, the man responsible for the attentat, was an imposing military figure. He had been a company officer with the première Régiment Étranger Parachutiste (1e REP). He was well over six feet tall with an athletic build, closely cropped blond hair and a rugged and scarred Teutonic face. He had escaped from Germany to Italy, where he had been arrested, released, and then passed through the Cité Catholique network of monasteries that run from northern Italy through France to Spain. This Roman Catholic escape line was essentially the same as that set up by the pro-Nazi prelate Bishop Alois Hudal to smuggle war criminals and Nazi collaborators out of Europe. Raymond was quite indignant at being arrested on an international warrant in a 'friendly fascist' country. Despite his age, military experience and sophistication, he still had not understood the fundamental reality that states have reasons that override all private or partisan moralities. I had also found that out too late and to my cost.

Both men spoke good English. They were cultured, sophisticated, had a dry sense of humour and enjoyed debate. They were fully paid up Catholics and held very right-wing conservative views of the world. It was paradoxical to see the humanity in these men run in parallel with their capacity for authorising, justifying and participating in cold-blooded murder. These were passionately idealistic and driven men who took the loss of what remained of the French empire badly and personally. The surrender of Dien Bien Phu and the loss of French Indo-China in 1954 had been bewildering and humiliating blows to what they saw as France's 'honour'. It was this loss that had made them all the more determined to hang on to Algeria, which they were planning to reinvent, along with the Francoists and Salazarists, drawing on the original fascist ideas of José Antonio Primo de Rivera.

They claimed that they and their colleagues had been forced into doing whatever they had done as a result of the non-negotiable nature of the war for 'unconditional surrender' and the horrendous massacres by the FLN of innocent French settlers and loyal Arabs before and after independence. Also, they had faced the vicious and murderous Gaullist parallel police, the Service d'Action Civique (SAC), '*les barbouzes*', professional criminals and thugs totally devoid of any morality or compassion.

Raymond and Pierre agreed that the means they had sometimes used appeared savage and that innocent civilians had been killed by the OAS – 'collateral damage' – but in their eyes the ends were redemptive. It was, they said, the 'Z Commandos' run by the more doctrinaire Jean-Jacques Susini, that had been responsible for much of the extreme violence in Algeria. Susini and his men turned what the more old-fashioned colonists Raymond and Pierre felt was a defence of French honour and Christian values into a self serving, Mafia-type operation by murderers and criminals. But then all power structures, colonial empires in particular, have tended to resort to barbarism when the ruled cease to be compliant and start to organise, such as Britain in Kenya and the Portuguese in Angola – the template for them all being surely the Black and Tans in Ireland. The likes of Susini are always on hand when the occasion demands.

As Catholic traditionalists, the colonel and the professor justified what they had done in much the same way as David Livingstone and other British missionaries rationalised their activities. They were on a civilising mission in which the cross followed the flag and vice versa. As well as being old-fashioned chauvinists, my French patio companions were also obsessive anti-communists. They saw themselves as misunderstood victims of a global power struggle to defend Western civilisation against godless Communist barbarism. Perhaps the reason they related to me so frankly and sympathetically was the fact that as an anarchist I was hostile to Marxist ideology and the Communist Party.

The only time I saw them angry was when an old enemy arrived in the gallery in January 1967 – an exiled former leader of the Algerian FLN, who had been arrested in connection with the shooting in Madrid of Mohammed Khidir, an associate of General Oufkir.

x x x

The Calvinist albatross hanging round my neck compelled me to use my time in prison constructively, so I decided to apply to take English, Spanish and History A Levels. I wrote to Mum to ask the Associated Examining Board in England for advice on how to proceed in my situation. They wrote back almost immediately. Not only did they overcome all the problems presented by the Dirección General de Prisiones and the Carabanchel administration, but also Mr Mackintosh, the man with whom I liaised at the AEB in London, generously sent me all the expensive textbooks I needed free of charge.

I found it difficult to study. Having left school four years earlier and with a sixteen-year sentence facing me I had little sense of urgency or focus. Reading was a way of passing time enjoyably; reading to study was a chore.

The set Spanish A Level text that year was Pio Baroja's *Zalacaín el Aventurero*, but discussing this title with the Madrid university students, academics and writers imprisoned during the cycle of demonstrations of 1965–6 led to more stimulating patio seminars about Spain's classical and contemporary writers.

My enthusiastic prisoner-tutors introduced me to writers such as Lope de Vega, Calderón de la Barca, and nineteenth- and twentieth-century writers like Pedro Antonio de Alarcón, Benito Pérez Galdós, Vicente Blasco Ibáñez, Miguel de Unamuno, Ortega y Gasset, and the later writers such as Ramón Sender and the Andalusian genius

Federico García Lorca Federico García Lorca.

What was inspiring was the fact that although Lorca was a banned writer, many otherwise cynical and even illiterate prisoners could quote large chunks of his poems. His *Romancero Gitano* (Gypsy Ballads) was of course particularly popular with the gypsies. It was this collection which made Lorca hated by the Guardia Civil and which led to his murder at the outbreak of the Spanish Civil War. In one of his poems Lorca appears to have foreseen his own fate. His body was never found.

Franco's prisons were the only places in Spain where there was genuinely free and frank discussion on politics, history and contemporary literature. Here was the real Spain whose creative spirit was captured by the shepherd poet Miguel Hernández in his poem *The Winds of the People*. In addition to the crash course in Spanish literature, culture and arts from some of the finest representatives of Spain's intelligentsia of the 1960s, I also learned about the historical importance of Isabel and Ferdinand, Philip II, and the impact of Cortes and Pizarro.

HEMINGWAY

A few of the students and academics were either anarchists or sympathetic to anarchism. One was a mine of information on the subject of Ernest Hemingway, a writer who probably did more than most to prejudice his readers against anarchists by portraying them as simple-minded idealists or self serving criminals whose lack of discipline and pursuit of the social revolution allowed the fascists to win. Hemingway's hostile judgements on anarchists appear mainly in a brief passage in *For Whom The Bell Tolls* and in his play *Fifth Column*. Although he was apparently never a member of the Communist Party, Hemingway was susceptible to their flattery. *Fifth Column* was either a flagrantly dishonest or phenomenally naïve drama (which portrayed the Communist Party's Soviet-sponsored secret police organisation, the Servicio de Inteligencia Militar (SIM), as a heroic 'fascist-hunting' organisation, as opposed to a gang of killers dedicated to the summary murder of anti-Stalinists) which was apparently written in Gaylords, the Madrid hotel reserved exclusively for Russian officers and important Comintern and Communist Party officials.

Somewhat perversely – maybe it was a subconscious wind-up – I chose the Russian revolution as one of my special subjects for my History A Level. Don Benigno, the prison officer who controlled my correspondence, didn't take kindly to this. Indignantly, he explained that I would not be permitted to take this subject, as the required texts would not be allowed into the prison. My second choice was the history of the English working class in the eighteenth and early nineteenth centuries.

When the exam papers arrived, the prison authorities arranged for me to have a small classroom for myself, with Don Benigno as invigilator. For one of my Spanish language papers, I had to write an essay on one of three themes. As Benigno handed me the paper he said – with what passed for a smile in his book – that he knew which theme I would select. I looked at the three subjects, which were: 'A trip to the moon', 'What I would do if I had my life to live over again' and 'The pros and cons of dictatorship'. I grinned inwardly as I thought how right he was. I chose the last. Personally, I thought I was quite circumspect in my arguments and made no reference to Franco, but I did write scathingly and pointedly about the corporate states of Hitler's Germany and Mussolini's Italy.

Don Benigno's froglike features furrowed when he saw I had not chosen 'What I would do if I had my life to live over again.' He rebuked me, saying he thought I would have had more sense. This thought simply hadn't occurred to me.

The governor, Don Ramón, sent for me the following day. Don Benigno stood beside him with my exam papers on the desk in front of Don Ramón. The Director looked at me paternally, shaking his head with an overstated air of resigned sorrow. My answers, he said, would have to be sent for clearance to the Dirección General de Prisiones before they could be returned to the AEB in London, but he knew they would be 'very disappointed' in what I had written. Basically he was telling me that I could kiss goodbye to any thoughts of a presidential pardon or any further reductions in my sentence. But in the long run it didn't make any difference and I passed with reasonable marks in all three subjects, thanks to a sympathetic AEB who had made it all possible.

x x x

We tried to read changes in Franco's Spain in the light of what was happening in the rest of Europe. Every time there was a cabinet reshuffle we would spend hours trying to guess the implications of the changes; whether it had been a victory for the *aperturistas* (those seeking an 'opening up' of the regime), or the hard-liners, the *inmovilistas*.

The aperturistas appeared to be ahead on paper at least, with promises on the 'conditional' right to strike, new press laws and trade union legislation. Franco's age and the poor state of his health added to the uncertainty in the air, weakening even further the country's political and industrial stability.

Social and industrial unrest erupted again in January 1965 with the arrest of thirty railway workers charged with derailing and holding up locomotives and freight trains in Malaga. On 18 February more than 2,000 students from Madrid University, the privileged children of the Francoist elite, marched through the streets of the capital shouting slogans such as 'Democracy yes, dictatorship, no!' This was followed by angry student demonstrations across Spain, in Barcelona, Granada, Salamanca, Bilbao, Murcia, Valencia, Santiago, Seville, Zaragoza, Oviedo, Valladolid and La Laguna. In March the students showed their discontent with the state-run student unions by demanding more democratic and representative bodies. This led to demonstrations against police brutality and demands for civil liberty – events unheard of in the previous twenty-five years.

Franco's new constitution, the liberalish (in Francoist terms) Ley Orgánica del Estado, the Organic Law of the State, which attempted to deal with political life and governance after Franco, was finally approved in December 1966 by an enormous 95.9 per cent majority of the 19.4 million votes cast in a referendum.

Like everywhere else in Europe, young Spaniards were becoming increasingly unwilling to accept a system that didn't even pay lip service to basic human rights. As the year progressed, more and more students, intellectuals and professors such as José Luís López

Democracy Yes, Dictatorship No!

Aranguren, Enríque Tierno Galván and Agustín García Calvo came into conflict with the authorities and ended up in Carabanchel.

x x x

The prison saw an influx of Marxist-Leninists (the Maoists), ETA members (the armed Basque independence movement) and a handful of Trotskyists. But the closest friend I made was an old cenetista (member of the CNT) who arrived from another prison – Miguel García García. I had heard a lot about Miguel before he arrived.

Meeting Miguel García

Imprisoned for 22 months in 1939, after the war, Miguel was just one of the 16,000 or so political prisoners held in Barcelona's Cellular Prison, originally built to hold 1,000. Fourteen to sixteen people stood, sometimes lay, ate, slept and pissed and shat in a space meant for one. Miguel was one of the Tallión urban guerrilla group that operated in Barcelona from 1945 until their arrest 21 October 1949. Their downfall had resulted from one of the group attempting to sell a stolen gold watch to a police informer in the Barcelona flea market.

Miguel's speciality had been the printing and forging of documents (in which he told me he had been trained by the British SIS (MI6) during World War II). He later wrote about his experiences in his book *Franco's Prisoner*.

'When we lost the war, those who fought on became the Resistance. But to the world, the Resistance had become criminals, for Franco made the laws, even if, when dealing with political opponents, he chose to break the laws established by the constitution; and the world still regards us as criminals. When we are imprisoned, liberals are not interested, for we are "terrorists". They will defend the prisoners of conscience, for they are innocent; they have suffered from tyranny, but not resisted it. I was among the guilty. I fought, I fell, I survived. The last is the more unusual.'

As Miguel noted, he was one of the lucky ones; his sentence was commuted to twenty years on 13 March 1952. Many of his friends were not so lucky. The following morning five of his closest comrades were marched from their cells in the condemned gallery, the *cuarta*, in Barcelona to face a Francoist firing squad.

When I first met him in 1966 it was hard to imagine that Miguel had already spent seventeen years in prison. For a man in his late fifties Miguel had a clear and smooth complexion – which he swore was due to using lemon juice as aftershave – and such a fiery dynamism and optimism that one would have thought he had only just been arrested and would be out by the end of the week. The same energy and enthusiasm characterised Busquets and many others like them. The strength of their characters and morale was an inspiration.

My job as *practicante* meant I was able to wangle Miguel on to the sick list when he arrived. This allowed us to meet for the few days he had to spend in Carabanchel before continuing on his way to Soria via Zaragoza. Miguel had been learning English for some time, but I was the first British person ever with whom he had been able to hold a conversation. I explained to him a system I had for getting letters in and out of Carabanchel and gave him a spare bottle of diluted lemon juice I had for invisible writing. I discovered later he used most of this as aftershave.

My last words to him as he passed through the spiked gate were, 'Don't forget to look me up in London when they let you out.' Little did I know that three years later he would be living with me and driving me up the wall in Coppetts Road, Muswell Hill in north London, forever cooking tortilla española for supper and ruining my new Teflon-coated frying pan with a metal scourer!

x x x

The most significant 'propaganda of the deed'campaign of the time was that of the First of May group. This was in fact the continuation of the now self-dissolved Defensa Interior (DI), an official, albeit secret, branch of the CNT. Its militants were recruited from among the international anarchist movement, and had access to the same resources as the DI, but it operated as an independent and autonomous clandestine body outside the control of the official Spanish anarcho-syndicalist labour organisation.

The group first came to the world's attention on 1 May 1966, by

First of May Group

kidnapping Monsignor Marcos Ussia, the 40-year-old Spanish ecclesiastical attaché to the Vatican. They said Ussia would be released in return for the release of some political prisoners in Spain – including me – and a declaration in support of an amnesty for all Spanish political prisoners by the Vatican. The letter added that the kidnappers were averse to violence but had been compelled to act in this way owing to the world's indifference to the plight of Franco's prisoners. They eventually released him without harm, and although no prisoners were released in return, other demands (like improvement of some prision conditions) were met.

In the years between my arrest in 1964 and 1966, a heated debate had been going on within the anarchist movement over the question of the armed struggle against Franco. Apart from a bomb attack on the Spanish consulate in Naples on 2 January 1966, there had been very few organised actions since my arrest in 1964, although Spanish embassies, consulates and Iberian Airline offices throughout the world continued to be the target of demonstrations and acts of vandalism by people passionately opposed to Franco's unspeakable regime. The older generation looked on Franco as the last of the Axis powers, bound to fall if only his real nature could be shown to the rest of Europe. The new generation didn't see it that way – the tyrant would survive, thanks to the Americans. Spain had become an important strategic client state and military base, a proxy of the US.

To fight Franco meant taking on its sponsor, the USA, the daddy of all rogue states. The struggle against injustice had to be extended beyond anti-Francoism to challenge colonial interests, dictators and warlords everywhere and the US, Soviet and Chinese governments that sustained them in power.

This new generation demanded action that was exemplary, dramatic, spectacular, to capture the headlines of the world's press, radio and TV. The Ussia kidnapping was the first such propaganda by the deed action since the 1958 kidnapping of racing car driver Juan Manuel Fangio by the 26 July Movement in Cuba.

And of course this led to more anarchists in Carabanchel. London was a significant site for these actions. On 25 April 1967, the personal secretary of the Spanish Ambassador in London was taken at gunpoint from outside their home and held for a few hours by the First of May group, before being released with a warning of other actions to follow. Two days later, on 27 April, two members of the group handed in a letter to the legal attaché of the London Embassy explaining the reasons for the brief kidnapping 48 hours previously.

The intention was to make it clear that next time it would be for real unless their demands were met. The letter demanded that the 'Madrid Five' be tried by the civil authorities, and my early release. Late at night on on 20 August 1967, they raked the front of the US Embassy in London's Grosvenor Square with machine gun fire, knowing the building would be empty. Octavio Alberola had been declared public enemy number one by the BPS and their allies, taken to be the leader of the First of May Group. Thirty-five-year-old Alberola had already had eighteen years' experience in the revolutionary struggles of South America. He had worked closely with Guevara and Castro in the 'Anti-Dictatorial Front' of South America, the group that later gave birth to the 26 July Movement which overthrew the Batista regime in Cuba. He had also been active in the struggle against both the Trujillo dictatorship in Santo Domingo and that of Pérez Jiménez in Venezuela.

Less than a week later, on 1 May 1967 the bruised and tortured body of Octavio's father, 72-year old José Alberola Navarro, a highly respected professor of literature, was found bound, gagged and hanged in his Mexico City apartment. It had been no ordinary murder. It bore all the hallmarks of a ritual death squad killing similar to those carried out by the notorious Mexican 'parallel' police squad, the Brigada Blanca, or, possibly, Otto Skorzeny's 'Paladin Group', the BPS's preferred 'plausibly deniable' proxy killers.

The date of the murder, 1 May, was significant. The elderly José Alberola was no threat to either Franco or the Mexican state.

My Mum Writes to Franco

I was still petitioning to join the other political prisoners in the *sexta*. I got on well with most of the prisoners in the *quinta*. With a few notable exceptions most were fundamentally decent people. But what I found difficult to come to terms with, being young and idealistic with high expectations, was the fact that even the 'good' guys tended to be unreflective, crushingly pragmatic, and a good number were always looking for the 'edge', to gain the advantage on people. Life in the *sexta* would be, I felt, more 'Athenian', in the sense of good comradeship and stimulating intellectual discussion, especially now that Andrés Edo was there. In the *sexta* I would be with – and learn from – men who took ideas seriously enough to suffer the consequences.

On the other hand, in the *sexta* I would be cut off not only from good friends, but from the very people with whom, as an anarchist, I should have been sharing my ideas and values – 'extending outwards the area of sanity'. Nevertheless, I persisted with my petitions – threatening, amongst other things, a hunger strike – and eventually the governor relented.

The gallery, at that time, held its full complement of 120 prisoners, most of them CP members or union militants and strikers. It seemed as though the entire Spanish Communist Party was in jail. Political prisoners were not allowed to work, and this contributed to an almost insufferable sectarianism, with each faction attempting to score points off the others, or gain control of the gallery. The anarchist group passed its time writing letters, in discussion, or planning escape attempts.

I was not there long before, with no warning, I was transferred to another prison, perhaps because the authorities had got wind of an imminent escape.

Visitors from the British Embassy had been telling me for some time that high-level negotiations were currently taking place to secure my release and that they were optimistic. The outcome, they said, was 'almost a foregone conclusion'. The vice-consul, Mr Harding, asked me to suggest to my mum that she write a personal letter to General Franco asking for clemency. But I was to say nothing to her about the Embassy believing this had a particularly good chance of success. It looked as though this appeal might have something going for it, so I decided to leave for Alcalá without further fuss.

I was sad to leave Carabanchel. I had made many friends and learned much there; it also held lots of good memories, including my first shave. On the whole the place had provided lots of useful insights and my experiences there had been educational, stimulating and happy in their own peculiar way.

My next prison, Alcala de Henares, was much less of a hot-house, and there I resumed my printing career.

Alcala held a high proportion of the flamboyant and irrepressibly enthusiastic Andalusian gypsy prison population. To paraphrase Michael Caine in the film Zulu, '*Gitanos*', there were 'bloody fahsands of them'. They spent weekends and evenings bunched together at the most distant corner of the exercise yard. They were theatrical, ebullient and noisy.

It could have been a scene outside a Sevillian tobacco factory at closing time as they swaggered, gesticulated and shouted loudly and noisily at each other in *caló*, the gypsy language. The only time they shut up was when one of them broke into a hoarsely forlorn and interminable *cante jondo* accompanied by curt vocal flourishes and harsh, metallic *bulerías* as the guitarist built up to a frenetic climax. This was inevitably followed by raucous flamenco guitar music punctuated by countless '*Holás!*' in other unintelligible Andalusian-

Arabic-*caló* interjections and much strutting, posturing, heel clattering, thumb, forefinger and castanet-clicking and macho pirouettes – all to the painfully harsh accompaniment of *las palmas* (timpanous hand-clapping).

x x x

The campaign for my release was now building momentum. The British Embassy in Madrid was forwarding two or three postbags of letters and parcels a month from friends and sympathisers all over the world to Alcalá.

My appeal was now well under way and visitors from the Embassy kept reassuring me that this one would be successful. Why it would be successful nobody said, but a nod is as good as a wink to a blind man and I didn't pursue the matter. When the British Consul, Miss Forrester, came to see me we had the use of the governor's office, where he left us to talk alone in comfort and without observers. Twice she visited me at Alcalá with a Spanish marquis who was liaising with the Francoist authorities on my appeal.

Miss Forrester told me everything had been prepared for the appeal. I had to write to Mum and tell her the time was now ripe for another letter from her to Franco, petitioning him for my release. It appeared to me that she had written so many times to Franco they might have had a thing going.

At the beginning of August 1967, my friend Ross Flett wrote secretly bringing me up to date with moves to get me out of jail. Ross had been meeting regularly with my London solicitor Benedict Birnberg and he seemed very well informed. More and more articles pushing the British government to support my release were appearing in the broadsheets. George Gardner of the *Sunday Times* was the prime mover and his articles, which began in the early summer of 1967, were being picked up by other heavyweight broadsheets and MPs, who in turn were pushing the British Foreign Office to throw its weight behind my official plea for clemency. The Foreign Office had in fact been told by the Marqués de Villaverde, Franco's son-in-law and an influential power broker, that as I had now served over three years, a plea to Franco for a personal pardon was likely to be received positively, probably in light of the ongoing negotiations over Gibraltar, the Common Market, the importance of the British market to Spain, and the growing numbers of package holidaymakers on Spain's beaches.

The effects of the revived British press campaign were immediate. A fellow prisoner who worked in the prison administration told me that he had overheard a telephone conversation about me between the governor and someone at the Direccion General de Prisiones in Madrid. Apparently I was to be given VIP treatment and a delegation would be arriving from Madrid to inspect the conditions in which I was being held. That same afternoon I was pulled out from the printshop to the governor's office and asked what colour I would like my cell painted. Taken aback somewhat, I replied that white would be nice and added quickly that a desk, bookshelves, easy chair and bedside lamp would come in handy as well. The governor made some notes and then dismissed me. When I returned to my cell that night, it had been transformed into a desirable bachelor flat.

As the *Times* articles continued so too did the number of visits from the ministry men, and I began to feel like some rare animal in a zoological conservation project. As my twenty-first birthday approached on 10 July, I suggested half jokingly to the *jefe de servicio* that it might be a nice idea if I could have a proper birthday party to which I could invite my friends. He agreed, and after consulting with the governor it was arranged that I be given the use of the infirmary dining room.

A Spanish friend, a chef who worked in the prison kitchen, organised the menu. We had kid goat cooked in wine with roast potatoes, salad, coffee, cheese and ice cream. There was beer, wine and brandy. The cabaret was performed by a well-known Filipino rock star who was inside for murdering his agent, gypsies singing *cante jondo* and playing and dancing flamenco and the cook who sang Spanish ballads while accompanying himself on the guitar. The party lasted from two in the afternoon until eleven at night. It was noisy, good-humoured and everyone got absolutely legless.

x x x

The decision to pardon me by *indulto personal*, a personal pardon, was approved by General Franco in the middle of August. It was rubber-stamped by his Council of Ministers on Friday 18 August 1967, but was not made official until its publication in the *Boletín Oficial del Estado* on Thursday 21 September. This was the same day Admiral Carrero Blanco was appointed vice-president. The Spanish Ambassador in London, the Marqués de Santa Cruz, wrote a letter to Mum dated 16 September informing her that I would be released within a matter of days. The Ambassador continued:

'I am sure that this decision is owed in great measure to the dignity and motherly concern shown in your letter and also, if I may say so, to the restraint and propriety with which you have approached this unhappy incident right from the start. I cannot but stress that it is to you that the credit for Stuart's release must go, and that he could have had no better advocate than his Mother. With best wishes for your future happiness and that of your son. Santa Cruz.'

My release was also a move in the long game over Gibraltar. Tensions over the rock were running particularly high, and on 10 September 1967 a plebiscite took place on the question of whether Gibraltar should remain a British possession. Of 12,762 registered voters 12,138 favoured remaining British. 44 voted for union with Spain. The Francoist government needed some positive PR after that, and my release helped ameliorate the outside world's view of the regime.

x x x

News of my pardon had been one of the closest kept secrets ever in Alcalá. Everyone seemed to know, and the streets outside had apparently been crawling with Spanish and British reporters and television crews for three days, but no one told me a thing.

The regime milked it for all it was worth. The dictator had a heart after all and could respond to a mother's pleas for mercy. No one believed a word of it, but it was good political theatre and I wasn't going to complain. The first I knew of it, however, was when Miss Forrester came to tell me the news that I would be freed the following day. I was astonished and almost wiped out with an overwhelming sense of relief. Almost lost for words I gabbled my gratitude and rushed to tell my friends – but the cunning bastards already knew and were grinning all over their faces.

We had a celebration drink in the shade of the wall with a *botijo* of wine I had stashed, but it was tinged with real sadness. I was about to be freed and break up our little band of friends. We had reached a major fork in the road and the guys I was leaving behind were going to remain in jail for who knows how many years. I felt particularly bad for those who had no outside interest in their cases. Unless they were extremely lucky, those whose sentence had been commuted from death to imprisonment had to serve the full twenty-year tariff, the maximum consecutive time anyone could theoretically spend in a Spanish prison.

Following well-established prison tradition, I divided my belongings among my friends. In some way this ritual helped assuage the strange sense of guilt I felt at leaving friends behind while I went off to pick up my life in the outside world. When the time came we shook hands, hugged emotionally, and said our farewells. I went back to my cell, uneasy about my future, to be locked in and counted for the last time.

x x x

Before breakfast the following morning, Thursday 21 September, I packed up the few remaining books I wanted to keep and was escorted to the prison reception. When all the required forms were completed, I was released into the custody of two BPS men waiting to escort me to Madrid and hand me over to the custody of the British Embassy.

We were followed all the way to Madrid by a posse of press cars. Those who overtook us to take a photograph had their car numbers noted. I gathered from my minders that those involved would be receiving a visit within the next day or so. We lost most of them in the

Madrid traffic. The secret policemen sitting in the back with me had his arms resting on my Bergen. On top were my hastily packed books and as we went into a particularly sharp bend the top book fell out. The BPS man picked it up and looked at it. My heart stopped. It was the Penguin edition of *Mutual Aid* by Peter Kropotkin, still a banned book in Spain, possession of which could have got me another six years in prison. He then tucked it back into my rucksack, face down, without a word.

With Mum at the British Embassy. Miss Mildred Forrester, the British Consul, is on the left, and Nicholas Henderson, then British chargé d'affaires, is immediately behind me.

On arrival at the Embassy I was rushed up the stairs to Miss Forrester's office where I was signed over to British custody and my BPS escorts were handed a receipt for the safe delivery of one Scot. I was taken to meet Mr Harding, the consul, who was sitting with Mum and Benedict Birnberg. The *Scottish Daily Express* had flown Mum out the previous evening. Seeing her there in the flesh without any glass partition between us was an extraordinarily elating experience. Mum was beside herself with happiness, as was I. What could I say? I was at a loss for words. I was free and surrounded by English-speaking people for the first time in almost three and a half years. I was dazed by it all. Someone asked me a question in English and I found myself replying in Spanglish, English words and Spanish grammar.

Mum also broke the news to me that the *Scottish Daily Express* was now expecting payback for having paid her travel and accommodation costs on this and earlier trips. It wanted an exclusive. Two of the paper's reporters, Wilson Russell (known to his colleagues as 'Stashy Dan') and James Hastie, had accompanied Mum from Glasgow and had booked her into one of the most exclusive hotels in Madrid. Their strategy was to manipulate their way by means of psychological dependency into Mum's trust and confidence; I would be grateful for their financial and moral support and would give them my exclusive story.

I was appalled and angry that this moral blackmail was my welcome back into the free world. For a moment I wished myself back in the relative simplicity of the prison. Worse, Russell, I discovered much later, had been trying it on regularly with my Mum during

Stashy Dan

these trips, knocking on her bedroom door late at night and generally making himself a nuisance.

Word had spread among the journalists assembled in the library for a press conference that my story had been bought by the paper. This belief was reinforced by my circumspect replies of 'no comment' to the more direct and contentious questions. Exasperated, they asked me bluntly if the *Scottish Daily Express* had bought my story and if that was why I was refusing to commit myself to any specific answers. I replied quite forcefully that this was not the case. But the smug grins on the faces of Stashy Dan and James Hastie seemed to belie the truth of my statement. The fact that they themselves didn't ask me a single question throughout the conference but simply sat with their arms folded added fuel to the other journalists' suspicions.

245

The press conference contained no surprises. I was neither silly nor brave enough to say anything remotely controversial or hostile while still on Spanish soil. At the end of the press conference a woman journalist asked me to describe my feelings on being a free man again. I thought for a moment and the words that immediately sprang to mind came from a favourite Siegfried Sassoon poem in a dog-eared anthology of First World War poetry, *An Anthology of Armageddon*, I had lugged around with me. I replied, simply, that 'It felt as though "everyone suddenly burst out singing".'

John Rety, Christie-Carballo defence committee (C-C dc).

The scurrilous methods and lack of ethics of *Scottish Daily Express* reporters were legendary, so I assumed they would make their main move when we reached London. With this in mind I rang John Rety, an anarchist friend in London, from the Hotel Palacios in Madrid and explained my concerns to him. John said he would arrange for us to be met at Heathrow airport. Somewhat reassured by this piece of pre-emptive planning, I took advantage of my first evening of freedom to relax and soak in a hot bath in a real bathroom, on my own, without having to line up in file and march to a grey, concrete shower room.

x x x

Purged of the last of prison sweat and smells by the unique floral fragrance of Maja soap, I went downstairs for a celebratory dinner with Ben, Mum, Miss Forrester and one or two others from the British Embassy. Our party was watched over by four somewhat bored-looking officers of the Brigada Político Social who sat at a table in a far corner of an otherwise deserted restaurant. Their brief, presumably, was to ensure nothing happened to me, or alternatively that I did nothing embarrassingly dramatic while still on Spanish soil.

I slept like a log that night. It was the first time in over three years that I had slept on a soft mattress between clean linen sheets without a single *chinche* to feed on my blood. But nothing could beat the sense of exultation the following morning when I emerged from sleep to find myself in a comfortably furnished room with a handle on the inside of the door and no *recuento*! I was really free. It hadn't been a dream; I was out of prison and I felt as though the previous three years had been a nightmare.

The next morning we drove to the airport. By midday, Friday 22 September 1967, Mum, Ben and I and a good part of the British press were 30,000 feet in the air on board a BEA jet from Barajas airport and safely out of Spanish airspace. The two *Scottish Daily Express* reporters sat in their first-class seats fretting and fuming and plotting. They now knew for certain the story was not theirs, and that if they wanted to be players they would have to bid for it on equal terms, through Ben, like the rest of the press.

Meanwhile, Mum, Ben and I celebrated my flight into freedom with champagne. We toasted liberation and the future, whatever that might hold.

PART THREE

LONDON

The Scotsman's Return
from Abroad

As we fastened our seatbelts for the descent into Heathrow, Stashy Dan launched his assault, with a carrot and a stick. The carrot was a plane to Glasgow held back especially for me. I could be back in Glasgow that afternoon, if I spoke exclusively to the *Scottish Daily Express*. The stick was that if I didn't, I would disappoint my Granny, who had been campaigning for my release and was right now waiting by her door for my return. Imagine the headline, he said: 'The granny who waited and waited for the prodigal grandson who never turned up.'

I told him what he could do with his plane. When I returned to Glasgow to see my Granny, it was going to be on my terms, not those of Express Newspapers.

His veneer of civility peeled away. 'This is your last chance, Stuart,' he spluttered. 'If you don't come with us, by tomorrow afternoon you will be the most hated man in Scotland.' I told him that he was a piece of shite. The angry hack's face changed from blotchy beetroot red to patchy blush white as he turned and stomped back to his seat.

But in theocratic Scotland, it was no joke to invoke the power of a man's Granny. At the moment, the story of my release was my Granny's triumph, and I was a hero. If that story turned into Granny's shame, I could well be the most hated man in Scotland.

x x x

In spite of my continued refusal to have anything to do with them, the *Scottish Daily Express* wasn't giving up. We were ushered into a VIP lounge and asked to remain there until called – a special customs clearance the newspaper had arranged.

When eventually we were told we could leave, Mum, Ben and I made our way to the baggage hall and exit. As we came closer I noticed a large and noisy crowd of people jostling beyond the constantly opening and closing automatic doors. I recognised the smiling faces of old friends and realised this was John Rety's reception committee. Grinning broadly, and with Mum gripping my arm tightly, I made for the doors.

As we crossed into the main arrivals hall, two intimidating-looking men moved in on us, one grabbing my arm and the other my Mum's. My thug whispered not to worry, they would soon have us safely through the crowd where a fast car was waiting to take us to a quiet country hotel. Mum was getting the same story in her ear, but with the added proviso that if I did not want to go with them she was to come on her own. They were *Scottish Daily Express* 'minders'.

They were now trying to separate us. Mum was close to hysterics. 'Whit's goin' on, Stuart,' she shouted. 'Whit's happenin'?' She thought we were being kidnapped – which we were. As we passed through the automatic doors, straight into the waiting group of anarchist friends, I elbowed the man holding me to one side and called out that they were *Scottish Daily Express* heavies and were trying to kidnap us.

Pandemonium broke loose as the anarchist reception committee jumped on our would-be kidnappers from the front and behind. To add to the confusion, other waiting television and newspaper reporters thought that my friends had been hired by the *Scottish Daily Express* to prevent anyone else talking to us. A group of French hippies and assorted teeny-boppers waiting for a rock 'n' roll celebrity saw the commotion and rushed into the melee.

It was the late summer of 1967 – the 'summer of love.'

A *Daily Telegraph* reporter was punched on the nose by my friend

Mark Hendy, the secretary of the Christie-Carballo Committee. Mark was arrested, but fortunately the reporter decided not to press charges when it was explained to him that Mark thought he was from the *Scottish Daily Express*. Albert Meltzer – a twenty stone ex-boxer – stood at the top of the escalator, preventing anyone getting past until we were safely on the lower level.

The Christie-Carballo Committee

We made it across the hall to a waiting car by the exit. John Rety assured us that the driver was a safe and experienced 'getaway' expert – news that did little to reassure Mum, who was by this time convinced we were about to be murdered as seven or eight people tried to squeeze into the back seat of the car with us. All I was aware of was her muttering loudly to herself 'Oh, ma Goad!' and 'Whit's happenin', son?' I eventually persuaded her that everything was all right and we were among friends.

x x x

Aware that something like this might happen, I had rung my Granny from Heathrow to explain the situation with the press and that we would not be back in Glasgow that night. I also asked her to get rid of the *Scottish Daily Express* hacks who had been squatting in her front room for the past five days, ever since the news of my release had been leaked. Taking pity on them, she had invited them in to wait for me. Two had been sleeping on her sofa!

Once the *Scottish Daily Express* newsdesk absorbed the fact that I had no intention of returning to Glasgow and the story wasn't in the bag, they collected my Granny from Blantyre, and took her to their Glasgow office where they kept her for three hours in order to extort whatever distressed quotes they could. They began by working her into a real state of apprehension: 'We have bad news for you!' The *Scottish Daily Express* eventually ran the sob story of the ungrateful boy who refused to visit his 'poor auld granny'.

x x x

Sturdy though it was, our elderly Rover was never designed to act as a troop carrier. We had travelled only a mile or so when a rear tyre blew out, forcing us to crawl to a halt on the hard shoulder to change the wheel.

The car with Beaverbrook's boys pulled in behind us. They sat and watched as everyone piled out and lifted the car up to change the wheel, the driver having forgotten to bring a jack. Beaverbrook's men shouted they had one we could borrow. Our driver wandered over to speak with them. A minute or so later he stepped back and let a five pound note he held between his thumb and forefinger fly away in the breeze. It was like the final scene in Jacques Tourneur's 1957 film, *Night of the Demon* (based on an M. R. James story called *The Casting of the Runes*) when the cursed runes are blown down the railway line. While handing him the jack, a *Scottish Daily Express* man had tried to slip him a fiver to let them know where we were being taken. But our driver could not be bought – or certainly not for five pounds!

With the tyre changed, we set off again – this time minus some of our passengers, who we agreed to meet later. We managed to lose our pursuit car in the back streets of west London. Mum was still clutching my arm for dear life, and I could almost feel her glow of happiness.

The Summer of Love

I gazed out of the car window, mesmerised by the passing throng of people flooding the pavements of Earls Court. It was a balmy, sunny late September afternoon, and to me, having been in a Spanish gaol for three years, it was as though the circus had come to town. There were flower children with their faces painted in vivid psychedelic colours, long-haired people of indeterminate sex wearing pillar-box red Grenadier Guards jackets, and sensuous, confident-looking girls in skimpy tops, buttock-hugging miniskirts and thigh-length boots easing their way through the crowds. This was a very different Britain from the grey country I had left in the summer of 1964: wilder, younger, more free. It held the promise of a new world. Scott McKenzie's hippie anthem blared out from the car radio, telling us what to do if we were going to San Francisco. It felt like San Francisco had come to us.

x x x

We drove to the Earls Court flat of a Polish-Argentinian anarchist, Iain Kaliszewski, where a welcome home party of old friends, acquaintances and sympathisers had been organised for me. Mum appeared a bit more relaxed by this time, but perhaps she had just surrendered. Anyway, she was now chatting away quite the thing to all the weird and wonderful people who had popped by to say hello and wish us well. She had her wee boy back at last, and that was all that mattered to her.

During the party, Albert Meltzer offered me a job in his Coptic Street bookshop and anarchist press when I came back from Scotland. It was a promising start. But first I needed time out back home in Blantyre to see my Granny, collect my senses and get some perspective on the new situation in which I found myself.

ALBERT MELTZER

Albert Meltzer, who died in 1996, was possibly the most respected torchbearer of anarchism in post-war Britain. His sixty-year commitment to anarchism survived both the collapse of the Civil War in Spain and the Second World War. As a public speaker, campaign organiser, pamphleteer, author and publisher he was a crucial figure in fueling the libertarian impetus of the 1960s and 70s, and helping to steer it through the reactionary challenges of the Thatcherite 1980s and post-Cold War 1990s.

Born in London in 1920, Albert became an anarchist at the age of 15 when he first drew attention to himself by contradicting the speaker, Emma Goldman, by his defence of boxing.

The anarchist-led resistance to the Franco uprising in Spain in 1936 boosted the movement in Britain and Albert's activities ranged from organising solidarity appeals, producing propaganda, and working with Captain Jack White to arrange illegal arms shipments from Hamburg to the CNT in Spain. A lifelong trade unionist, he fought Moseley's Blackshirts in the

Battle of Cable Street and was involved in the Cairo
Muutiny in the British Army in 1946. His working
career ranged from fair-ground promoter, film extra,
second-hand bookseller to copy-taker on national
newspapers. His last employer, strangely enough, was
the *Daily Telegraph*.

His achievements include *Cuddon's Cosmopolitan
Review*, first published in 1965, the founding of the
Anarchist Black Cross and *Black Flag*, and the Centro
Iberico in Havelock Hill. The Kate Sharpley Library,
probably the most comprehensive anarchist archive in
Britain, is his most enduring legacy. His
autobiography, *I Couldn't Paint Golden Angels*, is a
unique portrait of the life of a working-class
anarchist.

The next morning, Mum and I began the trip back to Scotland in a
hired car. Ben Birnberg was dealing with the media to sell my story
and recover some of the legal expenses and the money Mum had sent
to me in prison. I had agreed to call him every hour, having told him
not to consider anything from the *Scottish Daily Express*. My
preference was for *The People*, whose reporter, Dennis Cassidy, had
behaved impeccably during the flight from Madrid, and by the time
we reached the first service station, Ben had agreed a deal for £600.
Ben told me to remain where we were, and that Dennis would be
leaving London immediately to join us.

That Friday night we booked into a small hotel near Luton. Dennis
and I didn't get much sleep. We had a lot of ground to cover as he had
to write his first article for that Sunday's paper. Next morning we
drove in Dennis's car to Luton airport and caught a plane to Glasgow.
The press was waiting for us at Glasgow airport, but Hugh Farmer,
The People's Glasgow stringer, was also there and we managed to get
away without being followed.

Home to my Granny's Mince an' Tatties

Fortunately, just before we arrived at my Granny's house in Blantyre, the hacks – who had been hanging around there for days – decided I wouldn't be arriving for a few hours and nipped off for a drink. We passed them at the end of Gran's street, but they didn't see us.

When Mum and I walked through the front door, it was quite a moment. I was half expecting a skelp across the ear from my Granny because of that day's headlines in the *Express* accusing me of neglecting her, and for running off to Spain and almost getting myself killed. Instead of a wallop, I was welcomed into her substantial bosom with a familiar smile that came from the heart, and a long tight hug. I breathed in the long-forgotten and comforting smell of Gran and her freshly-laundered clothes like the air of a fresh spring morning.

This display of emotion felt awkward at first. Our family, like most Presbyterian families of the time, mainly expressed emotion by the raising of an eyebrow. Raising two would have signalled the onset of hysteria. But now it felt like shedding the last defensiveness of prison. 'Ye'll no have had yer tea, then, son. Sit doon,' she ordered. Like the reporters, she hadn't been expecting us until later, and was mortified that she had nothing ready, apart from the mince an' tatties she had prepared for herself and the next-door neighbour. Like prodigal 'Bisto Kids', Mum, Dennis and I sat down to the homely smell and taste of steaming mince an' tatties. For a moment, it seemed as if I had never been away.

After lunch – with Dennis growing ever more fidgety about the imminent return of the Glasgow press pack – we were all taken off to a secluded country hotel near Renfrew, some 20 miles away, where the other reporters couldn't get to us – at least until *The People* story had appeared and the hue and cry had died down.

x x x

True to their word, the *Scottish Daily Express* had had a field day smearing me. Among their more imaginative headlines was 'The Secret Thoughts of Christie', which claimed that even now I was 'plotting the downfall of society'. It was not long before the *Express* was clamouring for my arrest again.

Dennis Cassidy's interview with me appeared in *The People*. It was the first of three instalments and I was to remain in what was effectively their protective custody until all parts had been published over three weeks. But any resemblance between what I told Dennis and what was published in *The People* was coincidental. I was portrayed as some sort of prison baron who led the life of a sybarite, waited on hand and foot by flunkies. All three instalments were written in a similar sensationalist vein. I had heated arguments with Dennis after each episode appeared; it was all a question of 'emphasis', they said. But it was a useful lesson on the workings of Fleet Street. I learned then that you need a long spoon if you want to sup with the devil.

The three issues of *The People* with my story ran their inevitable course from the newsagents' counter to chip-shop wrapping paper. The country had tut-tutted for a week or so about the Ealing comedy-type high jinks of the failed amateur assassin who had lived the life of Riley with his servants in prison, and remained an unreconstructed anarchist – then promptly forgot about me. I was yesterday's man and of no further interest. Francoist journalists went even further, one lyrically claiming that England had sent Spain a terrorist, and that they had sent back a good citizen – a vindication of Franco's penal system.

x x x

And so I left my luxury hotel in Renfrew to return to the normality of everyday life with my Mum and Gran in Blantyre. It was a difficult transition. According to the form book, I should have settled down to a steady job at nearby Colville's Steelworks, or looked for a regular milk round with the Blantyre Co-op. My fifteen minutes of infamy were over.

I was not too upset by the sudden show of disinterest; on the contrary, I had not really appreciated that my story was ever news, at least not in this personal sense. There had been lots of anarchists in Franco's prisons, some of whom had got much nearer the bull's-eye than I had, who had been freed without so much as a mention in the local paper. A huge number of political activists had passed through Franco's jails since 1939 – to say nothing of those who never came out, or were killed before they reached prison. Among these were quite a few non-Spaniards. But the image of the kilted, bagpipe-wielding youth who had innocently wandered into the murky ways of the anarchist resistance in Spain had proved too much for the British tabloid press to resist.

Back in Blantyre, readjusting to speaking articulate English proved difficult. I had emerged from an almost monastic world where I spoke little, and in Spanish, into a whirlwind of constant questions and expectations of seamless, gripping accounts of prison life and deeds of derring-do. It was a curious sensation – I was learning my native language over again. I also felt uncomfortable in large groups of people. Interestingly, when my friend Miguel García García came out of prison two years later, after spending more than 20 years in Franco's jails, he was unable to speak at all for about three months.

x x x

Even Blantyre had changed. Three years earlier I was called a 'pansy' for my long hair; now I was a freak because of the prison-issue short back and sides. The 'permissive' or 'alternative' society, with its focus on sex, psychedelics, kaftans, tie-dyes, public 'freak-outs', and bands like The Grateful Dead and Jefferson Airplane had swept the country in my absence. Nowhere had this been more noticeable than in

The Counter-Culture

Glasgow, which had long prided itself only on the preaching of the word, and a Calvinist one at that. I was a latter-day Rip Van Winkle, and while I had been asleep the so-called 'counter-culture' had taken over.

My first impressions were that this 'alternative' society was somehow part of the libertarian protest movement which was either going to sweep away or radically transform the political order. But that was far from being the case. This social counter-culture shared with political activism a revolt against traditional values and constraints, but it had no real political aims or methods. A few people attempted to set up apolitical communes. Really, the focus seemed to be narcissistic – the music, drug and leisure-oriented lifestyle was libertine, rather than libertarian. People trying to free themselves of their internalised order of oppression tend to reach for whatever tools are available, but for the most part it seemed to me people just wanted to get high, talk therapy and listen to Jim Morrison. Music for them became their outlet for hostility to the system and the focus for their generational solidarity. Hedonism was a metaphor for revolution, but it had become stuck at one step removed from reality – frying your brains on LSD became the issue, not fighting oppression.

In the first few months after my release I smoked any spliffs that were passed around, and sexual liberation could only be applauded, but unlike many of the people around me, I was never convinced this was going to change the world – at least, not for the better. The counter-culture was becoming an end in itself rather than a means to an end. On the whole they were a creative, colourful and cheery lot whose hearts were in the right place, but no way was racism going to be eliminated or the steadily escalating Vietnam War stopped by good vibrations alone.

x x x

After a couple of weeks of life in Blantyre and Glasgow, the initial euphoria and sheer pleasure of being out of jail and home with my family ebbed to a state of content, then shrivelling boredom and frustration.

The tectonic plates of history were on the move. The spectre of revolution was haunting Europe. Political and social movements were emerging way beyond the instigation and control of the political parties: had it been like this in England in 1648–9, in France in 1789, Europe in 1848, Paris 1870, Mexico 1911, Europe 1918–20 and Spain in 1936–7? Whatever was in the air, these were clearly defining times that would have an important impact on the future.

I kept thinking of the people I had left behind in Spanish jails: good friends and comrades like Juan Busquets and Miguel García, who had been in prison since 1949, or my old cell-mate, Luis Andrés Edo. It was time to galvanise and do something; organise material support and solidarity for those still in Franco's jails and bring their plight to the attention of those who cared – or I felt would care, if only they knew.

To most British people in the late 1960s, even the most committed of anti-fascists, Franco's prisoners were still as shadowy and unreal – if as tragic – as those in Stalin's Siberian Gulags. Yet I had gone in, and returned. They were not as remote and unapproachable as reputation had them. Prisoners had visiting days and postal deliveries, and people could get money from outside to spend in the prison canteen – and there were ways of getting information in and out. Both psychologically and morally, helping prisoners was a real way of helping the Resistance. They were the casualties of a continuing Civil War in which, if it was not immediately possible to act as a combatant, one could play a role by supporting those inside, and no one was better placed to do that than me. Also, Franco was still firmly ensconced in power – and that power had to be challenged.

I felt I had no choice but to return to London. I was now 21 years old. Nice as Blantyre and Glasgow were, they couldn't compare with London for hope, expectation, variety and emotional fulfilment. Telling Mum and Gran was difficult, and they were obviously disappointed, but they knew it was pointless trying to keep me in Scotland when I had clearly made up my mind to leave. I knew they sensed I would come to no good in London, Gran in particular; she had the second sight, but she was too wise a woman to push it.

x x x

GRANNY MADE ME AN ANARCHIST

The Britain I returned to that autumn was as restless and discontented as I was. Hippies were turning into politicised Yippies. Harold Wilson's Labour government, which had come to power shortly after my arrest three years earlier, was in full economic crisis with more than half a million people out of work, the highest unemployment figures since before the Second World War. Unrest was spreading. Angry students were protesting against the education system and the roles for which they were being groomed. Students had occupied Nanterre and Madrid Universities and the London School of Economics (LSE), and militancy was on the rise in industry. Almost every day there were news stories of unofficial 'wildcat' strikes by rank-and-file workers no longer prepared to accept the leadership of the traditional trades unions. This was hardly surprising. Union officials were there to compromise and negotiate token agreements on wage demands and conditions with the employers; they were not there to defend and advance their members' actual interests.

Dissatisfied, frustrated, and distrustful of established authority, people were taking to the streets in greater numbers. They were protesting against unemployment, poor housing, social benefits – and, increasingly, about America's Vietnam War. Anger was also building at the United States's attempts to build what George Orwell described as Oceania – the American Empire. On the other side of the fence, the Soviet Union was at the same time imposing its totalitarian hegemony on its own client states. Racist tension in Britain was also on the rise with the emergence of the newly constituted National Front, a merger between several 'Keep Britain White' factions including then the League of Empire Loyalists and the British National Party.

The world was turning upside down in 1967. At the beginning of the year, murderous Chairman Mao had faced rebellion in Shanghai. In Franco's Spain, workers and students had taken to the streets for the first time in many years to openly challenge the fascist regime. In Greece, in April, following the machinations of US Ambassador Talbot, ultra right-wing army colonels seized power, supported by the country's neo-fascist secret and military police. Global tension had escalated dramatically with the Six Day War in which Israel 'pre-emptively' attacked Egypt and Syria, annexed Gaza and the Golan Heights, and occupied the Palestinian lands west of the river Jordan in Jordanian territory. In June, large-scale demonstrations had disrupted the Berlin visit of the US-supported Shah and Empress of Iran.

A significant event occurred on 2 June 1967 during the biggest of the anti-Shah demonstrations, one that transformed the nature of the struggle against injustice from reformist street protest to revolutionary violence – the killing of Benno Ohnesorg, a young protestor shot dead in the street by an over-zealous German policeman. It was a signal from the institutions of power that they had reached the acceptable limits of protest.

Also in Berlin, the paranoid Springer press denounced in hysterical terms the anarchist Fritz Teufel and the Marxist student agitator Rudi Dutschke, leading to the latter being shot by a right-wing fanatic.

America's war in Vietnam with its rising death toll of American soldiers and innocent Vietnamese civilians was provoking ever-larger anti-US protests across the globe, leading to what was to become, possibly, the largest extra-parliamentary movement in world history. As in Germany, these demonstrations, with police provocation, were turning increasingly violent. In Washington that October 50,000 demonstrators were brutally attacked by soldiers and federal marshals, while in Britain 5,000 protestors responded angrily to heavy-handed police violence when they were refused permission to deliver a petition to the US Ambassador.

All this time and in the face of vociferous global opposition, US B-52 bombers were hammering away at the North Vietnamese cities of Hanoi and Haiphong, causing thousands and thousands of civilian deaths and injuries. In France, almost 100,000 students and striking workers marched together through Paris's Latin Quarter in protest against the war.

US Bombs Hanoi

X X X

This global radicalisation was taking different forms in different places – and among different generations and groups. As for the anarchist anti-Francoist action groups, the geo-political climate had changed since 1945, and the new generation of anarchists were no longer taking the 'anti-fascism' of the Allies at face value.

In July 1967 the First of May Group publicly committed itself to the principles of international revolutionary solidarity – that is, it offered help to any other movement that needed arms and explosives. Their actions were still intended not to harm people. After shooting up the US Embassy in London, they left a curt note in explanation: 'Stop criminal murders of the American Army! Solidarity with all people battling against Yankee fascism all over the world! Racism No! Freedom for American Negroes!' The communiqué was signed 'Revolutionary Solidarity Movement – First of May Group'.

Murder of Ché Guevara

Finally, in November, Ché Guevara was killed in Bolivia by local soldiers and US Rangers. The politicians who ordered Guevara's murder could not have known that in so doing they would create a powerful icon of revolt for a new generation of rebels. After his death, the name of Ché Guevara was to acquire an influence that spread far beyond the shores of Latin America, and way beyond any contribution he ever made to revolutionary socialism. In response, the First of May group carried out simultaneous bomb attacks on the Greek, Bolivian and Spanish Embassies in Bonn (the then capital of West Germany), the Venezuelan embassy in Rome, the Spanish, Greek and American embassies in the Hague, and the Spanish tourist office in Milan.

X X X

The Establishment was not passive. For the first time since the Curragh Mutiny in 1914, when high-ranking army officers had prepared to overthrow the Liberal government's plans for Irish independence, rumours emerged from the backrooms of Whitehall and the City of a possible military coup to topple the government of Harold Wilson – similar to that carried out earlier in the year by the CIA-backed colonels in Greece.

The plots and intrigues against Wilson had been building ever since he took over as Labour leader following the death of Hugh Gaitskell in

January 1963. Gaitskellites, ultra-right-wing MI5 officers and James Angleton of the CIA were all convinced Gaitskell had been murdered by the administration of some sort of toxin, and Wilson was the beneficiary. *Ipso facto*, Wilson was behind Gaitskell's death, directly or indirectly, and an agent of influence of the Soviet Union. By 1966, the right wing was paranoid about Wilson, mainly over the third sterling crisis and the Rhodesian deadlock. Cecil King, then head of the Mirror newspaper group and a director of the Bank of England, began talking for the first time of the need for a 'National Government' of non-politicians. (King first refers to the idea in his diary entry for 24 July 1966, following a meeting with Louis Franck, a former MI6 officer, and the chairman of Samuel Montague, the merchant banking house.) By early 1967 King and Hugh Cudlipp, his Daily Mirror editor, were holding regular Saturday morning seminars postulating the political, social and economic collapse of British society.

Thoughts of a coup were shared by a wider circle of the political, business and military Establishment, including the then US Ambassador, David Bruce. Some wanted a takeover by a coalition of the centre, others wanted a takeover of the right. The names of those involved mean little now, because nothing came of it, but they included top corporate bosses such as the heads of Associated Television (ATV), Lord Beeching, head of ICI and Lloyds bank, Lord Watkinson, ex-Conservative Defence Minister, and Field Marshall Lord Harding, ex-chief of the Imperial Staff, and director of various banks and defence industry company Plessey. Other arcane bodies such as the anti-socialist pressure groups Aims of Industry, Common Cause, and the Economic League were also involved to greater or lesser extents. These conspirators were to continue seething, plotting and intriguing for at least another eight or nine years before disappearing below the surface of British parapolitical life after Harold Wilson's unexpected resignation in April 1976.

Establishment Conspiracy

x x x

I had been working for Albert Meltzer in his Coptic Street bookshop since returning to London, assisting Albert and operating his printer.

Albert couldn't afford to pay me a great deal, but at least I was now working with a fairly dynamic group of people.

I had a polarizing effect on the anarchist movement. At my first meeting after my return, in the autumn of 1967, an Australian anarchist and pacifist accused me of betraying my supporters by allowing them to believe I was innocent of the charges laid against me in Spain. Some anarchists, like those involved with the newspaper *Freedom*, thought I should have admitted my guilt and accepted the consequences, in the nineteenth-century manner. My worldview was a bit more pragmatic. I wanted to live to fight another day. The majority of my friends and supporters in the Christie-Carballo Defence Committee and the SWF had a much more common sense approach to my defence and had known all along I was guilty, but that made them all the more determined to support me in what I did. And many who did not continued to support me once they knew the truth, believing as I did that the political point remained exactly the same. To some extent it was this meeting which marked the parting of the ways between what I would call the 'militant' and 'quietist' anarchists, the latter being those attracted to the anarchist movement because of their anti-nuclear and pacifist convictions, and the former determined to effect actual change.

The Anarchist Black Cross In this same meeting, we revived the Anarchist Black Cross, a prisoner support organisation originally set up in Tsarist Russia in the late 1800s, which we wanted to be an international prisoners' aid network to help people imprisoned because of their resistance to fascist and authoritarian states, irrespective of the crimes of which they were accused or convicted. Most of Spain's political prisoners were not supported by groups like Amnesty because they had been convicted of crimes involving violence. (Amnesty later changed their policy, realising that a large percentage of political prisoners were framed for violent acts they had not, in fact, committed.)

Our ethos was different: we believed that if an act was carried in furtherance of anarchist principles, then no matter what the act was, it was a political act, and needed our support. But our principal criteria were freedom and respect for human beings. We would not have lent support to any psychopath who killed or injured innocent people on the basis that he claimed to be an anarchist.

For the media and the politician the criterion is always the abstract word 'violence', not the dynamic in which events occur. The anarchists who tried to shoot Mussolini at various times throughout the 1920s and 30s, for example, were denounced in Italy as 'terrorists', which is not how the rest of the world looked at them, or how most people would now describe them. At various times, anarchists have supported violent action against individual tyrants or their functionaries (such as the gunmen hired by the employers to kill union leaders in Spain after WW1). The only difference is how one defines and classifies a dictator and a tyrant, not the quality of the action. And who decides who is a tyrant?

For the most part, anarchist violence since World War I has been aimed at buildings and property rather than people, while the violence of the state has been very personal – arrests, incarceration, beatings (and in Spain executions, degradations, torture) against its own citizens, carpet bombings, assassinations, invasions against the citizens of other countries. Perhaps violence is wrong, under any circumstances. But the state doesn't think so, and as a member of that state, neither do you.

The security services thought I would be one of the conduits through which violent ideas would penetrate the new generation of British radicals. In the end, murderous methods of protest did not enter European politics through anyone in the anarchist movement, but from neo-Marxist groups such as the Red Army Fraktion in Germany and the Red Brigades in Italy, and nationalist groupings such as the Provisional IRA in Ireland and ETA in the Spanish Basque country. But who could have foreseen that development?

x x x

To counter the climate of subversion, Sir Joseph Simpson, the Metropolitan Police Commissioner, increased the number of Special Branch officers to 300 and moved them into the purpose-built New Scotland Yard building in Victoria Street. For obvious reasons, I was put under surveillance.

Although we were very low on their list of priorities, the Foreign Office-controlled Secret Intelligence Service (SIS), or MI6, headed in 1967 by Sir Dick Goldsmith White, was concerned with the international activities and connections of the Anarchist Black Cross. The Foreign Office's priority was to maintain the delicate diplomatic balance that existed between Britain and Franco's Spain before the dictator finally shuffled off this mortal coil. Franco's regime, when it finally went, had to be replaced seamlessly by one acceptable to Western (i.e. US) interests. Nothing was to upset or deflect this process, especially embarrassing high-profile anti-Francoist direct action campaigns such as those carried out between the spring of 1962 and '65 by the Defensa Interior or the First of May Group in its various manifestations from 1966 to 1975. Protests which had previously been peaceful were now ending in violent confrontations with the police and attacks on US-related property targets. The tension seemed to be building relentlessly, and with what outcome nobody knew.

The radicalism of the time had a technological boost when Gestetner duplicators were replaced by the small offset-litho machine in the mid-1960s. The easy availability of this new and relatively cheap print technology meant that the number of radical publications mushroomed. Individuals and small groups could now try to take on the media establishment.

The press attention I received due to my Spanish history helped enormously in establishing the ABC. First, they paid me to write stories for them and, just as importantly, they were happy to use me as a source for stories about Spain and anarchism. A bemused Albert told me that during the Spanish Revolution, many anarchist workers had spent night after night at meetings and demonstrations to try to capture people's attention, so they could bring the facts about the Spanish Revolution to the workers in this country. Nothing could penetrate the wall of silence of the British press, which was instructed to sell the conflict as one of the Nationalists versus Reds, Democrats against Rebels, or even Fascists fighting Communists, thereby concealing the stunning successes, at the barricades and in the fields factories and workshops, of the popular organisations pledged to the cause of libertarian communism and workers' self-management.

The name anarchist was anathema to the press and was used only occasionally as a form of vile pejorative. By the 1960s they were getting over this, though my case embarrassed them a little. I was classed an 'unrepentant' anarchist, just as demonstrators who supported me were 'self-styled' anarchists. (When awaiting trial I had merely been an 'alleged' anarchist'!) Although the term came more into currency, the meaning was distorted – we were either throwing bombs and killing people for unknown reasons, or beautiful people that had more to do with trendy Christianity than politics.

Films as well as rock music, LSD and flower power played their part in creating the mood of 1967, and softening us up for 1968. Cometh the time, cometh the film. For me, the transcendental film of 1967 was *Cool Hand Luke*. It found absolute resonance with my generation. The reason it was so successful I think was because it was such a powerful human story about the passion for freedom, no matter what the personal cost. Paul Newman gave the defining performance of his career, playing the protagonist, Lucas Johnson, the stubborn but dignified rebel who, contemptuous of authority, refuses to submit to oppression and who the system can't break – it can only kill. As Luke points out to a 'kindly' screw putting him into the box until after his mother's funeral: 'Aw, callin' it your job don't make it right, boss.' The film also has the immortal line drooled by the sadistic redneck prison captain played by Strother Martin: 'What we have here is a failure to communicate. Some men you just can't reach . . .'

Lucas Johnson's multiple ambiguities said it all. Although anarchic, Luke, an apparently self-effacing guy, was an unlikely revolutionary role-model whose low-level defiance managed to restore hope and pull together the prisoners against the prison warders. It spoke on lots of levels about struggle, the human condition – and about 1967. Luke was the guy we all aspired to be.

'Paris Today, Hornsey
Tomorrow!'

Early in the morning of 27 February 1968, I was woken by group of plain-clothed policemen in my bedroom.

The CID officer in charge of the raid introduced himself as Detective Sergeant Ian Ferguson, with a warrant from Bow Street Magistrates Court to search my flat in Crouch End, north London, for explosive substances and weapons. His men then proceeded to rip up floorboards, dismantle my prized reel-to-reel tape recorder and the bed, rummage through cupboards and drawers, throwing everything into the middle of the floor. Trying to look behind the wallpaper, they nearly pulled down the ceiling. One even plunged his hand down the lavatory pan.

Pulling the bed away from the wall, they turfed out the cupboard behind. 'Chrise!' two of them cried in unison, 'Wossiss?' 'Leaflets,' I said. They had already passed over small packages of these in the drawers without comment. Seen in neatly stacked bundles of fifty at a time, done up with rubber bands, they seemed just what they were, innocuous political gimmicks. Seen in bulk, several thousand dollar bills have a traumatic effect on the viewer. They even had a traumatic effect on me and I had printed them.

The notes were propaganda leaflets to be used in a First of May Group action directed against the US Air Force base at Torrejón. They were printed on poor quality paper in the form of US dollar bills, but instead of 'One Dollar', the inscription said 'Una Vida' ('One Life') –

Una Vida Dollar Bills

overprinted in red, with the words 'Primero de Mayo' (First of May). Even the feeblest-minded Monopoly player would never have accepted these in payment for Liverpool Street Station. But as it turned out, the Metropolitan Police, the director of public prosecutions, Sir Norman Skelhorn, and the US Secret Service thought otherwise.

x x x

The police were investigating a mortar device found opposite the Greek Embassy. Their presumption was that the First of May group was behind it, but they were wrong. The device had nothing to do with the First of May Group, although I understand British libertarians were in fact responsible for the action.

DS Cremer, who was waiting for me in the car, knew that I was closely linked to Octavio Alberola, the prime mover behind the group, who had just recently been arrested. After some brief questioning at the West End Central Police Station, I was released. For the next week, a Hillman Minx was parked at the end of the road morning, noon and night with men taking notes and possibly photographs, of everyone who came and went. As Ross and I went out to work in the morning – Ross to Bassetts Liquorice Allsorts factory and me down to Coptic

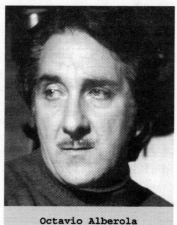

Octavio Alberola

Street – we would give them a smile and a wave, wishing them good morning.

Four days after the raid, the surveillance team was gone. Six closely coordinated explosions had occurred that morning in three countries, damaging the buildings of US military and Spanish diplomatic missions in London, The Hague and Turin. In London the Spanish Embassy and the US Officers' Club had been hit. All the actions had been claimed by the First of May Group.

It was obvious the police had advance information on the attacks, but not enough. Nor did the withdrawal of the Hillman Minx mean I was now cleared of suspicion. It was simply that they thought I was too cunning to get caught in such an obvious way. For them, I was the First of May Group's 'man in London', being the only reference point they had in Britain. They knew I was in regular contact with the group's principal activists in France, Belgium and Italy, but at the time that was insufficient evidence on which to arrest, charge and convict suspects, in Britain at any rate.

French newspapers like *L'Aurore* began warning of a 'red-hot summer', as did the more respected French weekly *L'Express*: 'Anarchists prepare a hot summer'. Something was in the air.

x x x

Octavio Alberola had been arrested in Brussels on 8 February, charged with illegal entry and illegal possession of arms. In the run-up to Octavio Alberola's trial there had been many international protests and demonstrations. Faced with such intense international and domestic pressure and the Belgian people's innate distaste for the Franco regime, the court accepted Octavio's defence that he was carrying two pistols for self-defence against the Franco regime, for which he received a nominal two months' imprisonment. Having already served this sentence waiting for trial, he was allowed to leave the court a half-free man. I say half-free because his application for political asylum had been refused and he was still liable for deportation to Spain. Of course this would mean his almost certain death.

Octavio was sent under 'area confinement' to a chateau near Liège in northern Belgium, where the cooperative movement had offered him a job as assistant director at a school for deprived children. The school's director was another Spanish anarchist exile, Francisco

Alberola's trial

272

Abarca, whose extradition had been sought four years earlier by the Swiss authorities for attacks on aeroplanes belonging to the Francoist state airline, Iberia. Octavio's partner, Ariane, being a French citizen, was expelled to France.

In Britain, the Anarchist Black Cross organised a campaign in support of Alberola.

x x x

March 1968 teemed with a sequence of seemingly unrelated global events, all of which appeared to be coalescing. New anti-hierarchical and libertarian movements were appearing in campuses all over the industrial world – in Madrid, Seville, Zaragoza, Santiago de Compostela, Bilbao and even the *Opus Dei* university in Navarre. Although the Vietnam War and students played an important part in what was happening, it was far from being an anti-Vietnam War or student phenomenon. In France, Germany, Italy, the Netherlands, and Japan, and in the United States, worker- and student-led strikes, demonstrations and protests were erupting quite spontaneously. Things were also moving fast in the Soviet sphere of influence, with major anti-Soviet demonstrations taking place in Poland and in Czechoslovakia where the so-called 'Prague Spring' was now under way.

When President Johnson announced on 16 March he was escalating the war by sending up to 50,000 more troops to Vietnam, the defiant response on the streets was immediate – and furious. Anti-war protestors took to the streets of every major city of the industrialised democracies, and the offices of US government buildings and corporations subjected to violent attacks. In Britain, the Trotskyist *ad hoc* Vietnam Solidarity Campaign (VSC) led by, among others, Tariq Ali, quickly organised what turned out to be a massively successful protest march for 17 March, which brought around 25,000 demonstrators to the US Embassy in London's Grosvenor Square. They were in the mood to batter down the gates of Troy, let alone the US Embassy. Mounted police were used to break up the demonstration violently, and there were at least 300 arrests. This led

Vietnam Solidarity

273

to the VSC demo being repudiated and denounced by both the Communist and Labour Parties; nor did it receive the support of approval of the trades union movement, or the Campaign for Nuclear Disarmament (CND), Britain largest anti-war grouping, then mainly controlled by the Labour and Communist parties. Clearly these bodies no longer represented a substantial portion of the population.

This was possibly the most significant and widely publicised demonstration of the 1960s, and one of the most confrontational. Assessing the 17 March demonstration's importance, the magazine *New Society* (21 March 1968) said: 'The demonstration was something new, something that indicates the pattern of major protests we shall have in the future . . . things cannot be the same again after Sunday. The time of the orderly peace platform marchers are gone . . . The departure from orthodox CND type marches could be seen in the demonstration's method of moving down streets, in its reaction to the police, in its speakers and in its platform . . . The 17 March demonstration had become street occupation . . . the idea was to seize the area, not march on the side of the road . . . the aim was maximum disruption . . . The main lesson was that the British tradition of polite politics is past.'

X X X

For the first time in many years there was a real threat of civil – perhaps even of revolutionary – disorder on the streets of Britain. The atmosphere in London was so thick with tension you could have cut it up and sold it as briquettes. Anarchists from all over Europe were turning up regularly at the Coptic Street bookshop or our print shop in Pentonville Road. Some would stay at my flat in Crouch End, including those involved in the Nanterre demonstrations.

In March, after a series of protests, anarchist and Trotskyist students from the Sorbonne and Nanterre campuses took over Nanterre's main administration building. The students were angry and frustrated. They had discovered that for the previous five months the Dean of Nanterre had authorised the surveillance and photographing of 'anarchist and Trotskyist troublemakers' by undercover policemen. The Dean responded to the student action by calling in the police. This was the first time French police had raided a campus since the days of the Vichy regime during the Nazi occupation. The students managed to drive off the first wave of police and retain control of the campus for another week, at which point more gendarmes were called in and the campus was officially closed.

That Easter many of the Nanterre anarchists – like anarchists from all over Europe – came to London, as they did every year, for the big anti-nuclear Aldermaston March. Rudi Dutschke, the German student spokesman, had been shot and seriously injured the previous week by a right-winger following a hate campaign orchestrated by the Springer press group. On reaching Trafalgar Square on the Easter Monday, 15 April, many of the protestors decided to continue the march to Axel Springer's offices in the *Daily Mirror* building at High Holborn to express their anger. The Springer conglomerate controlled around 85 per cent of the West German press output at the time and the climate of intolerance it created throughout Germany left people in no doubt as to who was responsible for the Dutschke shooting. Similar demonstrations against the Springer group were taking place all over Europe that weekend.

Estimates of the number of people in Trafalgar Square varied from 25,000 to 100,000. Jean Pierre Duteuil and Dany Cohn-Bendit, anarchists from the Nanterre group, told me they were amazed at the turn-out. They had been beavering away trying to generate anti-Vietnam War activity for the past six months in Paris and no way, they said, would it be possible to attract a fraction of the numbers on the streets of London that weekend. The French, they said, were apathetic and conservative.

It was soon demonstrated that they were very wrong indeed. In fact, in the Nanterre occupation, Jean Pierre and Dany had already set in train the sequence of events that was to bring France to the very brink of revolution.

x x x

On the night of 3 May, we had been out for a bevvy in our local, the

Queen's in Crouch End Broadway. Because my flat at 2a Fairfield Gardens was within a couple of minutes walk of the pub, people tended to drift back to my place after closing time with a carry-out to continue the 'cheneral hilarity', as Para Handy would say. It was sometime after 11 p.m. and someone turned on Radio Luxembourg, when there was a news flash – the Sorbonne had been shut, there was rioting in the streets of Paris, cars were burning and barricades had gone up in the Latin Quarter.

French Students Take Over the Latin Quarter

Earlier that day, several of the anarchists who occupied the Nanterre campus, including Jean Pierre Duteuil and Dany Cohn-Bendit, had been summoned to the Sorbonne to appear before the university's disciplinary panel. In solidarity, the Nanterre students had called for a protest demonstration in the Sorbonne courtyard. Hundreds of protestors from across the radical leftist political spectrum turned up to support them. The exception was the Communist students' union, who denounced it as a provocation.

The next provocation was provided by the Sorbonne rector Paul Roche, who panicked and called in the hated French riot police, the Compagnie Républicaine de Securité (CRS). The CRS waded in with their traditional heavy-handedness, beating up and arresting students for trespass, and the effect was catalytic. The police action had the immediate effect of bringing more people onto the streets. Within hours students and young workers had taken over the Latin Quarter, chanting slogans calling for the release of their arrested comrades, the reopening of the university and the withdrawal of the police from the Sorbonne. The CRS and the gendarmes tried to break up these demonstrations with baton charges and beating up literally anyone on the street. Violent street fighting followed.

Meanwhile, back in my flat in Crouch End, a crowd of maybe eight of us sprawled on the floor, the bed, the table and the one solitary chair, tightly clutching our cans of McEwans, enthralled by the noisy chants, the shouting, the whoosh of exploding petrol bombs, the sounds of breaking glass and police sirens broadcast direct from the streets of Paris. Was this the big one? Was it the start of an insurrection – a re-run of the Paris Commune of 1871, the Kronstadt

Republic of May 1917, the revolution of July 1936 in Spain? Whatever it was, it was a wake-up call, a break with the past, a defining moment – and who could say where it might lead?

Slightly pissed but euphoric and our hearts pounding with anticipation, everyone in the room jumped to their feet, grabbed the brushes and large cans of white emulsion and gloss we had bought to paint the flat, and raced downstairs, out the door and up Crouch End Broadway to Hornsey Town Hall to announce the birth of a new society. 'Paris Today, Hornsey Tomorrow!' was the slogan we scrawled across the full width of the building. There was no doubt about it. We would make sure that by the following morning the good burghers of Hornsey would know the revolution had begun. But by 10 a.m. the next day the forces of reaction in the form of Haringey Borough Council had stepped in and their cleansing department had almost obliterated our handiwork – almost, but not quite. The ghostly outline of that night's work remained for many years; it certainly outlasted our hoped-for revolution.

Les événements in Paris lasted a bit longer, six or seven weeks perhaps, but the extent, significance and importance of what began on the night of 3 May is still unclear almost forty years later. May 1968 certainly spelled the end of one period and the beginning of another. Within 24 hours what had begun as an exclusively student-oriented dispute had erupted into a much wider social and industrial struggle. Two days later, by 5 May, Paris was witnessing the worst street fighting since the Liberation in 1944, with up to 30,000 students, young workers and the unemployed confronting de Gaulle's CRS riot police across the barricades – always the best way to get a clear view of the enemy. The protests and demonstrations quickly spread to other French towns and cities. ^{The Events of May '68}

By 11 May the occupations had extended to secondary schools and colleges, with pupils and teachers marching in protest en masse through the Latin Quarter. The Minister of the Interior, Fouchet, and deputy prime minister Foux, ordered Paris police chief Grimoud to clear the streets – no matter what the cost. This order, in turn, sparked the infamous 'night of the barricades,' when protestors stood up to the hordes of black-uniformed CRS charging their way down the Latin Quarter's rue Gay-Lussac. Over a thousand people were injured that night, and at least 500 were arrested. When the TV and photographic images – burning cars, baton-wielding CRS goons attacking anyone and everyone in sight, young people throwing stones and Molotov cocktails, masked against the acrid fumes of CS gas – were flashed across France and the world they caught the imagination and inspired solidarity across the world.

On 13 May over a million French workers, employed and unemployed, and students marched through central Paris carrying the red and black flags of socialism and anarchism. The Movement of 22 March, the libertarian group from Nanterre who had started the ball rolling ten days earlier, announced that the 'struggle against repression' was now the 'struggle against the State'.

At this point, the French state made an important tactical decision. Prime minister Georges Pompidou ordered the CRS to withdraw from the Sorbonne, allowing the students to occupy it, and therefore isolate them from the escalating workers movement. The police were to ensure the students were contained in the Latin Quarter.

The occupation of the Sorbonne faculty led to an extraordinary intellectual explosion. Every lecture hall and seminar room was filled to overflowing, day and night, with people enthusiastically debating every conceivable political, cultural and social idea. The intensity and spread of the intellectual debate is difficult to recapture, but it is interesting to note that during the period May–June, the sale of books in Paris jumped by 40 per cent.

x x x

Situationism, Marcuse and Sartre One myth that has to be scotched here is that of Situationist influence on May '68, at least according to my Nanterre friends from the 22 March movement who were present at the birth. They assure me that although both Guy Debord's *Society of the Spectacle* and Raoul Vaneigem's *Revolution of Everyday Life* were both published in 1967 and surreal graffiti were on the walls, Vaneigem and Debord provided little if any intellectual inspiration during the uprising. Their main contribution came later. Certainly the writings of Herbert Marcuse play no part at the time. In a book published in 1970, *La révole étudiante*, Dany Cohn-Bendit wrote: 'People wanted to blame Marcuse as our mentor; that's a joke. Not one of us had read Marcuse. Some of us had read Marx, maybe Bakunin and, among contemporary writers, Althusser, Mao, Guevara and Henri Lefevre. The political militants of the 22 March group have almost all read Sartre.'

I should also add that although anarchist critiques of power, and libertarian ideas of self management and anti-hierarchical structures were prevalent throughout the events of May, and for a considerable time afterwards, the organised anarchist movement had little influence other than in Nanterre and the parts played by individual militants in the weeks that followed.

x x x

Something else happened around this time. Out of the acrid smoke fumes of the CS gas a fearless radical political culture was born which affected everyone: students, workers – intellectual, industrial, agricultural and professional – and the unemployed. Whatever it was that took hold, it was clearly radical ideas and values that were driving the May events, not economics. These events had a deep political and moral resonance, not only in Paris but across France. People who had previously been average militant trades unionists and obstreperous students, now began to perceive themselves as revolutionaries involved in a liberation struggle similar in a way to those taking place in South East Asia, South America and Africa. The war in Algeria still loomed large in the French political psyche, as did to a lesser extent France's imperial role in Indo-China. Who knows, perhaps the events of May provided an opportunity for people to redeem themselves for the things that had been done to oppressed people in the name of France. For whatever reasons, the police violence, the street-fighting and the tactical and strategic debates certainly gave participants and observers a practical and theoretical sense that revolutionary change was indeed possible, providing they could maintain the momentum and push the limits that bit further.

Quite spontaneously, people began to emerge from the narrow boxes and confines of their everyday lives and cross hitherto impenetrable social barriers, They began to discuss and conduct their affairs collectively. The human warmth, feel-good mood, fellow-feeling and common sense of purpose that swept across social and generational sectors was extraordinary. It was almost as though mankind was remaking itself. Jean Paul Sartre said of the May Days: 'They expanded the field of the possible.'

France On Strike

The strike movement itself took off on 14 May with the first major factory occupation by the *Sud Aviation* workers in Nantes. Interestingly, Sud Aviation's president was Maurice Papon, the Nazi collaborator and former head of the Paris prefecture, the man responsible for the cold-blooded police massacre of up to 200 Algerians in Paris on 4 October 1961. Over 122 factories throughout France were occupied by their workers. Factory occupations had last been heard of in 1936, under the Popular Front. The country appeared to be moving very close to the brink of revolution. By Tuesday 21 May over ten million workers across all sectors – public, private, agricultural, industrial, service and communications industries – had stopped work. France was in a state of almost complete paralysis.

The strike movement, which by 21 May had spread through every region and industry of France, began as a rank-and-file phenomenon, outside and beyond the control of the French unions. It was the members who had gone on strike, not the unions. This loss of control was a serious threat to the unions, and their apparatchiks immediately set about re-establishing control over their rank-and-file.

Neither of the two major French unions, the PCF nor the CGT, were ever on the side of the revolutionaries in any way; they merely used the situation as a bargaining chip in wage negotiations and to give them political leverage with de Gaulle and the French middle classes. The role played by the French Communist Party in May 1968 paralleled that played by the Spanish Communist Party during the Spanish Civil War; that is, counter-revolutionary. By the end of May the CGT had dissociated itself completely from the revolutionary movement.

Without a mobilised working class, no revolution was possible. And although there was an angry uprising in May 1968, there was no insurrection, no break with the past, and no attempt to dismantle the state. Unlike revolutionary Spain in July 1936, when state power was seized by the *barrio* committees and the militias, in France there was no grassroots movement to take over and collectivise the factories and the land, or to run the other key service sectors of public life.

x x x

President de Gaulle, meanwhile, refused to back down and flew in secret to Baden Baden in Germany on 28 May to seek the support of General Massu, the C-in-C of the French Army of the Rhine. Massu promised him the support of the army and de Gaulle then returned to Paris, dissolved the National Assembly and called for new elections. He then spoke on national radio and television to tell the French people that France was facing a Communist coup, that the army was with him, and he would not hesitate to call on it to restore order as and when necessary. He also authorised the Prefects of France's regions – as 'Commissioners of the Republic'— to use all the powers at their disposal to suppress subversion.

Hardly had de Gaulle's words 'Vive la France!' died away before a million loyal Gaullists and extremists of the centre and right were being bussed and trained into Paris from all over France to hit back at the leftists and demonstrate their support for 'law and order'. It ended in a huge and carefully staged march down the Champs Elysées. Not even the Countryside Alliance could have done better.

It was de Gaulle who was proposing a violent resolution of the situation, not the workers or the protagonists of the events of May. There never had been a Communist menace. de Gaulle's threat to call in the troops was directed not at the students and young workers, but at the trade unionists to frighten them into breaking the strike.

The strike movement continued into June, but was finally extinguished with the help of the CRS, the CGT, the PCF and de Gaulle. The last embers of revolt were extinguished by the CRS on

11 June when they forced their way into the Peugeot factory at Sochaux and the Renault factory at Flins. Two workers were killed and over 150 workers and students were badly injured at the hands of the police.

But the memory and legacy of May '68 lingered on.

Agitprop and the October Revolution

For the civil servants and politicians in the Whitehall Cabinet Office and for the captains of British industry, May 1968 was something they could not afford to ignore. The speed at which state, government and union authority had imploded when confronted with this totally unforeseen radical popular movement was shocking.

France 1968 was a dreadful warning to governments in almost every industrial country, East and West. Lessons needed to be learned. The core values of capitalism, state, government and institutional authority had been subverted. Uprisings and violent demonstrations were taking place everywhere that year: Mexico, Germany, Japan, the United States, Italy, East Germany, Poland, Czechoslovakia and so on, all fuelled by the war in Vietnam and popular hostility to US and, in the case of Eastern Europe, Soviet imperialism. What had happened in France in May could easily happen in Britain in October. The British government needed a contingency plan.

The rioting in London's streets during the 17 March 1968 anti-Vietnam War demonstration in Grosvenor Square, and now the breakdown of the established order in conservative France worried the Establishment. One of its key players, Cecil King, a director of the Bank of England and publisher of the *Daily Mirror*, was so convinced that the country was facing institutional meltdown by the threat from the left – compounded by his obsession that Prime Minister Harold Wilson was a Soviet asset – that he sent *Mirror* editor Hugh Cudlipp

An English
Coup

283

to an urgently arranged meeting with Lord Mountbatten on 5 May. This influential royal earl, the queen's cousin and her consort's uncle, had recently retired as chief of the defence staff and King believed that he would be amenable to supporting an army-backed plot to overthrow the Wilson government and replacing it with a so-called 'government of national unity'.

King had also been holding secret meetings with MoD officials and had addressed junior officers at Sandhurst military academy, calling on them to rise up against the Wilson government. Parallel with these covert activities, King had also been running a virulently anti-Wilson campaign on the front pages of his usually pro-Labour newspaper, demanding the prime minister's resignation in the face of the country's grave economic crisis.

King's conspiratorial foreplay somehow leaked out and he was sacked a few days later as chairman of the International Publishing Corporation (IPC) and director of the Bank of England. But King's fears certainly reflected the mood of the time within the Establishment. A senior army officer at Ashford Barracks, the home of the Intelligence Corps, was reported as saying that planning for the coup had got as far as designating the Shetland Isles a home for 'internees', and drawing up lists of trade union leaders acceptable to a 'government of national unity'. They obviously didn't think too highly of Shetlanders.

The *Mirror* wasn't the only newspaper involved in the coup machinations. In their book *Smear! Wilson and the Secret State*, authors Stephen Dorril and Robin Ramsay claim that 'Former *Times* editor Harold Evans is quite specific that the paper (*The Times*, under the editorship of William Rees-Mogg) encouraged Cecil King's lunatic notions of a coup against Harold Wilson's Labour Government in favour of a government of business leaders led by Lord Robens.' (Robens was then a director of *The Times*.)

MI5 chief Sir Martin Furnival-Jones later reported to Labour's new Home Secretary James Callaghan that the names of the conspirators included 'civil servants and military', including a Major-General. These were aided, according to Harold Wilson's political secretary, Lady Falkender, by Lord Mountbatten, whom she described as a 'prime mover' and assisted by 'elements in the city'. Mountbatten apparently had a diagram on his office wall showing how it could all be done. Callaghan never showed Furnival-Jones's report to Wilson or his Cabinet.

Faced with growing social disturbance and the rumours of insurrection fed by the Special Branch, Home Secretary James Callaghan (advised by James Waddell, head of Home Office security liaison, and Sir Edward Peck, Chairman of the Cabinet Office Joint Intelligence Committee) ordered the newly appointed Metropolitan Police Commissioner Sir John Waldron and MI5 chief Sir Martin Furnival-Jones to re-think the government's security strategy – and double quick. The enemy was no longer at the gate – it was among us.

x x x

Academics and intelligence and security experts were tasked to address this threat and come up with some answers. The conclusions they reached were to change, dramatically, the thinking and strategy of the Cabinet Office and the Security Service. The previously held theory that blamed social discontent on small manipulative groups of sad and frustrated malcontents collapsed overnight – at least as far as the Cabinet Office was concerned – although it was still a useful explanation to hawk around the press.

Ferguson Smith, the head of Special Branch, and Dick Thistlethwaite, head of MI5's 'F' branch, the counter-subversive department had, until then, been focusing their energies on running informers and agents within the trade union movement and the Communist Party. From the Spring of 1968, however, they shifted their attention to infiltrating the anti-Vietnam war movement and the anarchist and Trotskyist left.

The government was worried. They knew the events of May were not simply the result of student high jinks. It had been a genuinely pre-revolutionary situation. What had been viewed as separate economic, political and social grievances could suddenly and unexpectedly conflate and trigger a popular movement to destabilise the country. And this was a Labour government supported by the traditional left – Her Majesty's Communist Party and Trades Union Congress – so there would be no group to mediate.

The Cabinet Office authorised plans for counter-insurgency manoeuvres. MI5's threat assessment, prepared over the summer of 1968, was incorporated into a War Book exercise – codenamed 'Invaluable' – planned for that autumn. The cover they needed for this exercise was the much-heralded anti-Vietnam War demonstration called by the Vietnam Solidarity Campaign (VSC) for Sunday 27 October 1968.

x x x

From June to October, European media speculation about an imminent social revolution grew to near hysterical levels. False news stories were regularly planted in the press, with the newspaper editors' connivance, about 'Red' plots to destabilise and take over the country. These were variations on 'Russians seen in East Anglia with snow on their boots' stories of the 1920s. No story was too far-fetched. In Italy, the threat of subversion and the accession to power of the Italian Communist Party was taken so seriously that the Italian general staff set up a training camp and recruited neo-fascists.

Reds in East Anglia

Most of us on the receiving end of this media abuse were bemused by the outlandish stories whose plots and language looked as though they had been lifted straight from late Victorian potboilers. Every day the newspapers sought to outdo their competitors in the headlines of fear. In Grub Street the clocks were ticking inexorably towards midday in the film *High Noon*. The problem was, it was us, the 'good guys', who were being cast in the role of 'Killer Miller's killers'!

The only non-sectarian publication of the time which was respected by liberals, leftists and hippies was the weekly London listings magazine, *Time Out*. Another beneficiary of the offset-litho revolution, *Time Out* had been launched by Tony Elliott on 12 August 1968. Its editorial and Agitprop pages were to become essential reference points for finding out what and where marches, demonstrations and meetings were happening, And although Tony Elliott kept well clear of involvement with any particular group, he was on the side of the angels and the magazine quickly became the accepted voice of the non-aligned left. It also became the standard bearer of the new radical investigative journalism which began to explore the darker recesses of the secret state and capitalism. The only other publication doing anything comparable was *Private Eye*, particularly Paul Foot's 'Footnotes' column.

Spring, summer and autumn of 1968 was a time of great expectations of real political change – and not only in the industrialised democracies but in the Soviet bloc as well – as witnessed by events in Poland and Czechoslovakia that year. Wherever politicised people met there were heated discussions on the nature of authority, sexuality, equality, democracy and self-management. Government, party and trade union authority was being challenged at every level. The question was, how far could our optimism carry us before we provoked real resistance?

x x x

One evening in early September, Detective Sergeant Ferguson knocked on my door to let me know my trial for forgery was set for the following day at the Old Bailey. I had that night to prepare my defence.

Everyone assumed the trial was going to be a short one: I was up before Mr Justice Christmas Humphries, who despite being Britain's leading Zen Buddhist, was the man who had presided over the convictions for murder of the mentally incompetent Derek Bentley, executed in 1953, and the last woman to be hanged in Britain, Ruth Ellis. She was hanged in 1955.

The prosecution had flown in from Paris a US Secret Service agent, Brooks T. Kellner, to testify about international law and the fact that the words 'Una Vida' and 'Is this worth the slaughter in Vietnam?' were 'not usually found on genuine US banknotes'. And, to my outrage, my Spanish military sentence was admitted in court as part of my criminal record, despite the fact that Britain's own courts-martial are not considered criminal convictions. But in the end, evidence that I was going to start a job soon (fixed up by my flatmate Ross; Albert had been forced to close the bookshop by the most tyrannical power of them all – money) proved to Justice Christmas Humphries that I wasn't all evil, and to the disappointment of the Special Branch he bound me over for two years in the sum of £300. But for the Special Branch, the case confirmed me as an agent of the First of May Group.

x x x

As the build-up to the October demonstration grew, the media ratcheted up its attempts to instil more and more fear in the public mind. To show they were on the case, they identified some of those they described as the 'behind-the-scenes anarchist troublemakers'. I was one of those selected by the press as a leader.

Albert had been constantly pushing me to use my notoriety to get publicity for the anti-Francoist cause. Now I found myself not only a 'leader' in the cause of a Vietnamese authoritarian power struggle but, according to one issue of *News of the World,* a student leader into the bargain. The *News of the World* promptly denounced me in the next issue for never having been to a university myself, apart from once in a brief anti-apartheid protest in Aberdeen University in 1963 and again at the LSE in 1968.

The final countdown was taking place for what the press, at the Special Branch's instigation, was calling the 'October Revolution'. It wasn't a revolution at all. It was simply a major anti-Vietnam War demonstration to the US Embassy in Grosvenor Square organised by the Trotskyist Vietnam Solidarity Campaign (VSC). The anarchists didn't have much time for VSC. The various hues of Trots wanted the North to win whereas we wanted the people to be free of the lot of them – Ho Chi Minh and the Americans.

For the authorities, however, the 27 October VSC demonstration was a chance to implement their 1968 War Book counter-insurgency exercise, 'Invaluable'.

x x x

According to media and 'police sources', 'extremists' and 'anarchists' were planning a coup for 27 October, the cover for which would be provided by the enormous numbers of anti-Vietnam War demonstrators flooding into London for the VSC demonstration.

The newspapers, with the full connivance of the Cabinet Office, were interested only in creating a climate of fear to scare people off the October demonstration. The Special Branch claimed to have infiltrated people into 'anarchist and other extremist cells', and had uncovered the previously mentioned 'concrete evidence of a plot' to seize London. Clive Borrell and Brian Cashinella broke the story in *The Times* and the *Evening Standard*. It was immediately picked up by the rest of Fleet Street, as well as by the radio and TV. The day *The Times* published the story, Home Secretary Callaghan convened a secret meeting of Fleet Street editors and publishers at the Home Office to tell them he believed 'something' could well happen on 27 October, and that he had set up a 'hot line' with the Police Commissioner Sir John Waldron. He also told the press barons that he had authorised hurried firearms training for scores of police officers to cover any eventuality. A crime reporter on a quality 'Sunday' asked, in all seriousness, if it were true, as alleged by one of his security service sources, that the anarchists had – or were making – an atomic bomb.

All army, police and air force leave in the Home Counties was cancelled for the weekend of the demonstration. Some of the more rabidly right-wing newspapers covered up the names of their offices in Fleet Street, along the route of the march. And, for the first time ever, troops from the Parachute Regiment were posted on guard duty at Buckingham Palace and other royal homes. Massive police operations were carried out on the approach roads into London. Banner poles and marbles (used for rolling under the feet of the police horses) were removed from demonstrators, coaches were stopped and searched, including one or two bitterly protesting rugby teams who were taken for offensive radicals. Universities were raided, homes and offices of organisations broken into whether they were associated with the demonstration or not.

x x x

Waldron also held a series of private meetings with Fleet Street editors and proprietors to talk up the situation and to make sure the press took it seriously. It was essential, according to Callaghan and Waldron, that for political reasons the public should be fired up with 'anti-demonstration feeling'. It was a clear example of what Walter Lipmann called the 'manufacture of consent' by the manipulation of the attitudes and opinions of the masses.

Covering The Revolution But the Borrell–Cashinella story directly contradicted what *The Times'* News Team had been reporting over the summer. Ever since the events of May when the authorities began to circulate stories of anarchists and revolutionaries preparing a 'hot summer', the News Team had been investigating these reports. In fact, until Borrell and Cashinella appeared on the scene, *The Times'* News Team was the only group of journalists who were reporting the background to the national debate and the preparations for the demonstration. One of these journalists, Gary Lloyd, I knew from his coverage of the anarchist conference in Carrara the year before. They had done an enormous amount of research and legwork, and they concluded that the hysteria being generated by the rest of the media was totally unwarranted and grossly artificial – 27 October was simply going to be a big demonstration, and nothing sinister was being planned.

Suddenly, the *Times* News Team was disbanded. This struck me as suspicious, given that of all the British press *The Times* reporters had produced the most intelligent and insightful journalism on the preparations for the demonstration. Literally overnight the paper did a complete editorial U-turn, and its austere columns were turned over to sensational speculation under the bylines of Borrell and Cashinella. Their remit, they told me, was to 'cover the revolution'.

These reporters were on government business. Their job was to scare people witless and make them less likely to question government erosion of civil liberties and the draconian measures of the police and judiciary. There was no attempt to explain that popular anger on this scale about what the Americans were doing in Vietnam does not erupt from nowhere for no reason.

The *Evening News*, with a large readership in London and the Home Counties, was the most virulent of all the papers running scare stories.

In the last week before the October demonstration it ran a fiction serial about a group of agitators taking over London under the cover of a violent demonstration. The lines of distinction between fantasy and reality were becoming difficult to distinguish. The *News* responded to *The Times* and *The Times* fed off the *News*. Only a day or so before the demo, the *News* front-paged a story under Borrell's and Cashinella's bylines saying that they had information from a Special Branch contact that full-scale plans for insurgency were under way.

x x x

The trouble with disinformation is that it acquires a life of its own. Everyone involved in the demonstration, Marxists, Trots, Liberals and Christians, looked suspiciously at everyone else. Finally all of them came to the conclusion that no one was trying to – or capable of – pulling off a coup d'état. No one, however, could be sure about the anarchists. Consequently, I was approached a good many times and asked what the anarchists were up to. The answer was clear, at least as far as the *Black Flag* group was concerned. We would participate, but to wish a plague on both Washington and Hanoi. As the demonstration was being organised by the VSC under the banner 'Victory to the Vietcong', sophisticated journalists read our position as an evasion, especially since everyone knew from their 'newspaper reports' that lorry loads of explosives that had arrived in London.

One of Cashinella's reports, published on 5 September, had arms, ammunition, Molotov cocktails – everything except tanks being smuggled into London, with an anarchist plot existed 'to disrupt a major portion of central London by direct sabotage'. He continued: '. . . it was established beyond doubt that some extremist organisations as far apart as Liverpool, Scotland and South Wales were actively engaged in a scheme to plant bombs in Westminster and the City of London. Further, there was direct evidence . . . serious plotting was taking place on how to take over, on military lines, such institutions as the Bank of England, Lloyds, the Stock Exchange, Ministry of Defence major communications centres and even Scotland Yard itself.' Yet no one was ever arrested.

Borrell and Cashinella later admitted in their book *Crime in Britain Today* that they had been used by the police: 'The Special Branch then hatched up their own plot. They decided to "leak" their fears to the press and allow the situation to snowball. Public antipathy would do the rest, they reasoned. Certain Fleet Street journalists, including ourselves, were independently appraised of the situation through "the Old Boy" network. It was a story none could refuse coming from such an immaculate source. It was a story which no newspaper could ignore, and as article followed article, public reaction against the march grew. It was a clear case of the media being manipulated by the Special Branch to serve their own ends. But in our view it was totally justifiable, because the consequences otherwise could have been devastating.'

x x x

All over the country the police went on 'fishing' expeditions, ostensibly for these caches of much-hyped weapons, weapons of lesser destruction. But in fact these raids, unreported in the press, were to collect intelligence on the friendship and political networks thrown up by the anti-Vietnam War movement. They visited the homes and offices of activists in various political movements up and down the country, but no explosives were found, no weapons of mass or minimum destruction turned up, no arsenals were discovered – and no bombs went off. They only things they found were address books, names and the political sympathies of the occupants of the houses and flats they raided.

In addition to the raids, there were reports of mysterious 'burglaries' at addresses where, one presumes, warrants were difficult to get. The burglaries had one thing in common. The burglars were interested only in correspondence and address books, not in taking anything of value. I don't know whether or not I was ever burgled. Everything in my flat was always in such a mess it was impossible to know.

Despite the hysteria whipped up against the organisers of the proposed demonstration, the press had some difficulty in knowing who they were. They decided it was 'the students'. Tariq Ali became the mastermind of the whole affair and was appointed 'student leader' for the occasion by the *Daily Mirror*. Later, when they wanted him to write some articles, they promoted him to being 'leader of the revolutionary movement' in Britain. He was not, at that time, even leader of the Trots, nor even of his own International Marxist Group, which did very well from the publicity he brought them, and soared ahead in the student membership stakes.

The *Express*, possibly still smarting under the rebuff it had received from me on my return from Spain, informed the world that I was 'Number Two Anarchist' in London. In view of the anarchist opposition to leadership, this was not quite so much of an insult as being called Number One – but there was much amused speculation as to who Number One might be. It was assumed that even the numbskulls in the plate glass buildings wouldn't cast Tariq Ali in that role. Probably they had mistakenly reported a police spokesman, who had called me Alberola's Number Two.

Yet, curiously, in spite of all the media's attempts to traumatize people, on a practical level, hardly anyone felt threatened. There was no mass exodus of the bourgeoisie or the aristocracy to the Bahamas or the Riviera (perhaps they were already there); nor was there a run on the pound or a collapse of share prices. In contrast to the press, those who would have been threatened by a revolution – like those who would have benefited by one– took no steps at all. Not for the first time was there a gulf between what the public was offered as its daily consumption of media food, and what it accepted.

x x x

In the event, the 27 October demonstration came and went. Unlike the spectacularly successful 17 March demo, it proved a massive anti-climax for anyone who had believed the horror stories being generated by the press and Special Branch. Somewhere between 50,000 and 100,000 demonstrators turned up, but there were no bombings, no takeover of the Bank of England or the BBC TV Studios or even Marine Ices ice cream parlour in Chalk Farm. According to Borrell and Cashinella the plot was real, 'but was thwarted by the

27 October 1968

advance publicity it received'. The journalists claimed they had been 'in a unique position to know', as they had broken the story jointly in *The Times*, 'once the Special Branch was certain that it had concrete evidence of what was being planned.'

As the police obligingly held back the traffic, the demonstrators chanting and roaring 'Zieg Heil', 'US Out' and 'Ho Ho Ho Chi Minh' swept through London from Charing Cross along the Embankment, up Ludgate Circus and along Fleet Street into Trafalgar Square. The march then turned down Whitehall, past Downing Street, Parliament Square, along Victoria Street, Grosvenor Place to Hyde Park Corner then up Park Lane to Speakers Corner for a rally and speeches in Hyde Park.

Most anarchists had decided not to participate, but so many turned up to see what would happen that in the end they grouped, and found themselves to their amazement a force of almost a thousand strong rallying behind the red and black flags and banners. Had they organised a march themselves they would have been pleased to get seventy. Most wryly agreed, 'If we want any more demonstrations we'll agree first not to have one.' Predictably, instead of milling around in Hyde Park listening to the VSC platform speakers, a couple of thousand Maoist, Trotskyist, anarchists and other angry and hyped-up protestors broke away from the main march and headed for the American Embassy. The embassy was, of course, well defended by ranks of police. We linked arms, formed blocks and managed to break through the first police cordon into the square, but we were met with a much stiffer line of defence in front of the Embassy itself. People were chanting slogans, taunting the police, throwing the occasional firework, coins, marbles, poles and anything else at the Embassy, but it was all theatre and ended embarrassingly with some of the protestors linking arms with police and singing 'Auld Lang Syne'.

Other protestors were so angry and exasperated they ran down Park Lane smashing the windows of the Rolls-Royce car showroom in a final gesture of defiant outrage against one of the most ostentatious symbols of capitalism. What we would have done had we been able to get inside the US Embassy without being shot by the armed marines was anybody's guess – apart from maybe setting fire to the place, which had been talked about in moments of McEwans-fuelled wishful thinking. But no one who was there would have described it as unnecessary vandalism. Not after My Lai, the half a million Vietnamese dead, to say nothing of the raids, the strip-searches, the harassments, the press wind-ups.

x x x

From the point of view of the government, police, security service and army, it had been a highly successful exercise. After praising the police for their discipline and restraint, Home Secretary James Callaghan commended the demonstrators, saying that most of them had shown 'self-control', and that he doubted 'if this kind of demonstration could have taken place so peacefully in any other part of the world'. The moment of danger had passed and the authorities had been able to contain and control the demonstration without triggering a night of rioting in the streets and insurgency.

Certainly the protest movement changed that day. For many, the angry rhetoric and rituals of street protests now seemed empty and contrived gestures. To be lauded by the Home Secretary spoke volumes. May 1968 in France had ended in June with a whimper, while the October demonstration simply fizzled out. Some demonstrators left Grosvenor Square that day, disillusioned or burned out, to pursue their own agendas. Others, a minority, left convinced there had to be other more effective ways to put the politicians and the power system under pressure. It was definitely the end of the peer pressure show.

FRANK KITSON

A rising star in the British Army, Brigadier Frank
Kitson - who in 1968 was CO of the First Battalion of
the Royal Green Jackets and received an OBE that year
for unspecified services to the Crown - was seconded
by the Ministry of Defence to University College
Oxford in 1969 as a Defence Fellow to read counter-
insurgency.

Kitson, a 42-year old colonial warrior, was no
stranger to the practicalities of the subject. From
1953-5, he had been the Military Intelligence Officer
in Kenya responsible for organising the terrorist
counter-gangs during the emergency. He served similar
functions in Malaya in 1957 and Cyprus between
1962-4. His brief now, following the 'hot summer' of
1968, was to work out what could be done to the
natives of the home islands. His thesis on counter-
insurgency techniques, which he completed in 1970,
was published by Faber & Faber as *Low Intensity
Operations: Subversion, Insurgency & Peacekeeping*,
with a foreword by Chief of the Defence Staff General
Sir Michael Carver. By the time the book appeared in
1971, Kitson was C.O. of the 39th Infantry Brigade in
Northern Ireland where he was implementing the
policies and types of operations he had helped
develop in Kenya, Malaya and Cyprus.

Kitson's strategy, as outlined in *Low Intensity
Operations*, was threefold: penetration of the local
government structure, the institutionalisation of a
shoot-to-kill policy in ambush-type situations (later
euphemistically referred to as 'Observation
Post/Reactive - OP/React); and corruption of the

Common Law process by dispensing with jury trials. In Ireland this policy was implemented with the creation of the infamous Diplock courts in which the judge sits alone and interprets both the law and the facts.

Kitson admits that many regard subversion as being 'principally a form of redress used by the down-trodden peoples of the world against their oppressors', and 'there is something immoral about preparing to suppress it'. But, he continues: 'On the other hand subversion can be used by evil men to advance their own interests in which case those fighting it have right on their side ... Fighting subversion may therefore be right on some occasions, in the same way that fostering it might be right on others, and the army of any country should be capable of carrying out either of these functions if necessary, in the same way it should be capable of operating in other forms of war.'

'Anarchist Blows Up
Constable's Village'

Around this time, I made my second appearance in the studio of Malcolm Muggeridge's *The Question Why*, although my first on air. The programme was called 'Why Violence?' and it did not endear me to the authorities.

This time I appeared with, among others, Monica Foot, John Rety and David Triesman, confronting a team of senior police officers, with a dear old nun sitting in the middle to see fair play, though her sympathies were fairly obvious from the fact that she had an enormous depiction of a public execution hung around her neck. Her main contribution was to explain that the anarchists were wrong and that government came from God.

Somebody brought up, not very subtly I thought, the question of Glasgow thugs and what should be done with them. This feed provided me with my one *bon mot* of the programme – that the Glasgow thugs were only amateurs, whereas the police were professionals. At least two purple faces showed near-apoplexy.

x x x

'Why Violence?' Discussing violence as part and parcel of the political process is an emotive red herring. Like terrorism, violence can mean whatever you – or they – want it to mean. It's like discussing the existence of God. Everyone has their own idea as to when the use of violence for political, geopolitical, moral or ethical ends may or may not be legitimate. Little old ladies who are incapable even of upsetting a cat asleep on the chair they wish to occupy can be rabid supporters of flogging and hanging for those demonized by the *Sun* newspaper. Politicians have given the order to send hundreds of thousands of innocents to their deaths in carpet-bombing or 'shock and awe' air raids from Dresden to Baghdad, yet let an anarchist try to assassinate the vilest autocrat, and the same people will throw up their hands in horror. Horror at violence in this context is pure cant. It is objection to persons doing as individuals what the state legitimizes wholesale.

Positions on violence are usually taken according to where one stands in relation to those in power, and whether one is a target, protagonist or bystander. We are all conditioned early in life by the mass media, politicians, pundits and spin doctors to deplore the other side's violence. For most people, only violence sanctioned by the state can be 'legitimate' on the basis that it is 'just,' defensive' and 'liberatory'. After all, the state makes, interprets and upholds the laws, and defines and applies its own rules and standards in defence of the status quo. But for those people who have no redress in the face of injustice and are victims of the authority structure, or those who question its legitimacy and are critical and distrustful of it and its actions, and have reached the limits of legitimate and acceptable protest staked out by those in power – beyond which dissent must not extend, even to defend important human values – then they have no alternative but turn to whatever methods are available to them to resolve or ameliorate the situation. Their response can be seen to be either morally appropriate and proportional, or morally inappropriate and disproportionate, but as far as the state is concerned it is 'illegitimate'.

As for the anarchist position on the use of violence, all I can say is there is none, other than the normal human right to defend oneself and one's interests. Why, when and if men and women decide to take up arms is an entirely subjective and individual process – what is right for them – which can only be understood in the context and atmosphere of the time. Anarchists don't seek political power, only moral authority. Nor do they plot to bring down democratic governments through aimless acts of malicious, visceral, hatred; but they do seek to sideline them as much as possible by empowering people through education, example, and by fashioning events wherever possible to promote the general principles of mutual aid and self-management.

X X X

Buenaventura
Durruti I share the Spanish anarchist Buenaventura Durruti's attitude towards democratically elected governments. Asked about how the anarchists felt about the recently elected Republican government in Spain in 1931, Durruti said he knew it could not meet the expectations of the Spanish working people, but at least it should have the benefit of the doubt. The role of anarchists in relation to governments, revolutionary or otherwise, he said, was in opposition. But the degree of that opposition would be geared to the willingness of the Republic to confront the problems facing the Spanish workers. 'Our activities have never been and never will be at the service of any political party or any state. The anarchists and the trade unionists of the CNT, united with all revolutionaries and backed by pressure from the street, have as their goal to compel the people in government to carry out their mandate.'

You can't say fairer than that. If you can't vote the bastards out, make it as difficult for them as possible.

X X X

Prior to and during the October demonstration, the *Black Flag* and Anarchist Black Cross issued a joint leaflet reiterating arguments I had made in the *Telegraph* colour supplement about the futility of supposing that anything could come of a violent demonstration such as had been suggested by the Marxist organisers. Just because people were fed up with non-violent demonstrations, which the pacifists had been urging, it did not follow that violent ones would be better or more effective. What was needed was what we described as 'Monday militancy' – week-long commitment – rather than weekend protest.

(Incidentally, when we launched this leaflet at an Anarchist Black

Cross social in The Roebuck pub on Tottenham Court Road, an obvious undercover copper used the pretext of a film on the TV – Henri Georges-Clouzet's *Wages of Fear* (*La Salaire de la peur*) all about driving a truckload of nitro-glycerine across dangerous mountain roads – to try and start a conversation about the difficulties involved in transporting explosives. Three years later this encounter came back to haunt me, at what could have been a particularly damning moment of my life.)

x x x

One piece of cinema which contributed a lot to the mood of *If* combativity in the wake of May 1968 was Lindsay Anderson's surreal allegorical attack on the British class system and metaphor for Revolution – *If*. The story unfolds in a British public school, somewhere in the heart of England, building to boiling point with its mesmerising throbbing drum rhythms and harmonies of the *Sanctus*, the African Latin Mass from Missa Luba sung by a choir of young Congolese boys. The school's smug, self-righteous and arrogant teachers, support staff and prefects stood in for the ruling class and their acolytes. The headmaster who rules over this repressive parody of society sees himself as a man of integrity and good judgment who talks mince, thinks it's wisdom, and provokes anger and a determination for justice in the hearts and minds of Anderson's protagonists. The rebel heroes were anti-establishment and sympathetic and the hail of bullets they rain down on their oppressors in the final scene is both unexpected, humorous and heart-lifting – in a *schadenfreude* sort of way. The night I saw it, everyone in the cinema stood up and applauded enthusiastically.

x x x

In October 1968 I started work converting coal gas appliances to burn the new North Sea gas. My mate Ross got me started at the William Press training school in Mill Hill. For three weeks I learned the intricacies of dismantling, converting and even sometimes rebuilding gas cookers, gas central heating, water heaters and other sundry gas appliances. Because a shortage of qualified fitters meant Press had to pay top wages, many applicants claimed to be experienced tradesman. Later, when I asked one guy who had made a terrible botch-up on a job if he really was a fitter, and he replied, straight-faced, 'Yes, a carpet fitter.'

Because this was new technology, nobody really knew what would happen when we converted aging appliances from coal to North Sea gas. As even the experts were keeping their fingers crossed, praying that the nation's antiquated coal gas system wouldn't blow to pieces, three weeks' training qualified me as well as any of them. I passed the final exam and in no time at all was talking like an old time-served tradesman. I even learned how to take a sharp intake of breath. Conversion Unit Number 8, based at Brentwood in Essex, just to the north-east of London, was my new base. Our contract covered the whole of Essex, which we were converting community by community, turning up every morning in our convoys of bright-orange three-ton vans wearing our trendy bright blue overalls. It was a bit like the Durruti Column heading for Zaragoza in July 1936.

My first conversions were a complete disaster. My last house the second day was like Willy Lotts' Cottage, the location of Constable's 'The Haywain', an old chocolate box picture of a place with no electricity at all – even the lighting was gas. It was a job that had to be done as quickly as possible, so the elderly lady who lived there could at least make herself a cup of tea and have some light. I did my best. Even so I did not finish everything until eleven that night. When I asked where her meter was she led me by candlelight to a cupboard to show me. I remember thinking that it was an extra large governor, one I hadn't seen before, but paid no more attention – and started to adjust the valve cap as per normal.

Looking forward to the promised cup of tea and the prospect of getting home to bed, I suddenly became aware of low rumblings, like the sound of distant thunder. Either that, or an earthquake. It came from the meter. Although I had been warned of these devices, I couldn't for the life of me remember what to do if they went wrong. The noise grew louder and louder, and more menacing. Adopting my most nonchalant manner, I asked the old lady not to panic, and if she would mind stepping outside and moving as quickly as possible to the back of the garden. I also asked her to call across the garden fence to her next-door neighbours and ask them to do likewise.

The place consisted of only a few isolated cottages, miles from anywhere and neither the lady of the house nor her neighbours had a telephone. And I didn't have a radio. We were also miles from technical support – if we had any at all. A vision flashed through my mind of the whole area being blown sky-high. I could even see in my mind's eye tomorrow's newspaper headlines once they knew who was involved: 'Anarchist blows up Constable's village.'

The noise from the gas main had by this time reached crescendo point and had blown the mercury completely out of the valve. A powerful geyser of high-pressure gas was now gushing from a pipe on the outside wall right up the garden path. All it needed was one spark to turn it into a blazing inferno.

I went to make sure the old lady was safe with her neighbours who had gathered together in their back gardens. It must have brought back to them the dark days of the Blitz. I then climbed the fence at the back and hared across the fields to telephone for help. Half a mile down the lane I found a house with a phone. I eventually managed to get through to the Gas Board emergency service who said they would send someone right away. I then went back to the house where they were all standing at the bottom of the garden singing 'We'll meet again, don't know where, don't know when.'

Eventually, around midnight, the lights of a bicycle betokened the arrival of the gas emergency service. An elderly man propped his bike against the garden wall, walked into the house completely unperturbed, and turned off the supply at another cock which I had completely overlooked.

It took me some time to live down the events of that night. The women of the village had obligingly told the crews of every William Press van they came across. But in spite of all that I soon became a competent and conscientious workman.

x x x

It's an interesting stereotype that anarchists are not good, reliable workers, an image that historically has grown out of, first, the Russian nihilist movement and later, work-shy hippies. But the great anarcho-syndicalist unions which flourished throughout Europe from the end of the nineteenth century to 1939 would never have been able to negotiate unless their workers – skilled and unskilled – had been the best there were. The revolutionary worker taking on the state has to be good at his job. But in Britain, the labour movement was the happy hunting ground of authoritarians. No one thought of it as being part of a libertarian development.

The management at William Press, like everyone else, knew my history and politics. Few, if anyone, in the company believed that it was possible to be persecuted for having a different viewpoint from that of the government. They would say half-seriously that they didn't support it themselves, except by way of tax. The manager shook his head in bewilderment at being told he shouldn't employ someone who had been in a Spanish prison – and had not even been sent there by a properly constituted court – when they were regularly being asked by the Home Office to cooperate in resettling and rehabilitating British prisoners who had presumably had a fair trial. Just normal assumptions of fair play made everyone at work resent the police harassment of me. And they only saw a small part of it.

x x x

By this time I had repaid the Foreign Office for my fare home from Spain and had my passport returned. With the long weekends we had with William Press, and the company's generous travel allowance ostensibly to allow us to return home once a month (I had put down Glasgow as my 'home' address), I was making regular Friday-to-Sunday weekend trips to France and Belgium on behalf of the Anarchist Black Cross to discuss general anti-Francoist strategy with Octavio Alberola.

My name, however, was on the Special Branch's ports watch list and – as a 'code J' – these foreign comings and goings were closely monitored. The police always wondered where we got the money to pay for these trips. It never occurred to them, either, that both Albert and myself were working bloody hard and long hours to fund them.

The French and Belgian police as well as Scotland Yard were all concerned to know what I was up to. On one occasion when I got a sympathetic interview with the *Radio Times*, the journalist commented that I looked, and came over as, respectable, but that people shouldn't be deceived as I mixed with international anarchists. It seemed to be the mixing with foreigners that made you less than respectable. The intrinsic superiority of the British, even the anarchists, was somehow tainted or diluted through contact with Continental types. Obviously the police hadn't adapted themselves to that aspect of the era of the Common Market. In Brussels, Paris, Calais, Ostend, Brussels, Geneva and Milan the local political police were waiting and watching.

This and other minor forms of harassment were repeated up and down the country, wherever young radicals congregated. Young people had a voice, but everyone pretended it was a minority one. The politicians tried hard to sell the 'silent majority' idea, a weasel phrase that pretended that the majority of people supported the 'status quo'. The truth was very much the other way. A lot of people were getting angry at the post-October arrogance when the security forces seemed to imagine they had won a great victory. Sooner or later the anger was going to boil up. There only needed to be a minority that wasn't going to accept things to start matters off. It turned out to be sooner – and 'angry' was the key word.

x x x

My Granny died on 7 February 1969. She was 79 years old and had been ill for some time with bone cancer, diabetes and other lesser illnesses and infirmities that accompany old age. Granny hadn't feared death, which made her passing all the easier, not only for her but for Mum, Olivia and myself. She had seen too much of death to be afraid. There had been pain, but the doctors had given her some morphine-based drug which appeared to keep it at bay. She showed signs of weariness, but other than that she was the same spirited woman up to her last breath.

I had been going backwards and forwards up to Scotland whenever I could, which wasn't often enough, to spend some time with her.

Mum, Olivia (my sister) and Gran

Towards the end, before they took her to Hairmyres hospital, I would sit in the evenings in a chair at the foot of the bed we had made up for her in the corner of the room. She didn't like the light on so the room was lit only by the flickering flames from the open coal fire in the grate. It was very peaceful. We didn't talk much, just the occasional couple of words; we didn't really need to say more.

I wasn't with her when she passed away early one morning, something which I regretted. The fact that she wasn't there any more made me quite melancholic, but grief is the price of love and it has to be paid. I also knew that she would have wanted us all to get on with our lives. She had left behind warm memories to treasure which helped transform that sadness and sense of loss into an optimistic appreciation of her life and the example she set others, particularly me.

> 'Weep not for her!
> Her memory is the shrine
> Of pleasant thoughts, soft as the scent of flowers,
> Calm as on windless eve the sun's decline,
> Sweet as the song of birds among the bowers,
> Rich as a rainbow with its hues of light,
> Pure as the moonshine of an autumn night;
> Weep not for her!'

D. M. MOIR, *A DIRGE*

x x x

With the domestic political situation in Spain continuing to deteriorate, First of May Group bombings of Francoist institutions became more frequent through 1969. I was questioned regularly in connection with these incidents, irrespective of where I had been, or indeed which country they happened in. The closest I came to being connected with a violent incident was on 15 March 1969, when Alan Barlow and Phil Carver – anarchists who lived in room below me in Fairfield Gardens – were arrested for putting a bomb through the letterbox of the Banco de Bilbao, a Spanish bank, in Covent Garden.

Alan Barlow and Phil Carver

The police found a note in Alan's possession, when arrested, claiming the bombing was being carried out on behalf of the First of May Group. The device was set with a short fuse to ensure it went off early in the morning when the premises were empty and passers-by were unlikely to be injured. Unfortunately, for Alan and Phil, this particular fuse was too short and the device exploded as they were running away, straight into the arms of the police who apparently had the premises under surveillance, following information received from the Spanish secret police via Interpol.

Phil claimed just to have been accompanying his friend into town, a story supported by Alan, and was eventually given a suspended sentence; Alan went down for a year. No conspiracy charges were brought, just the unlawful use of explosives.

At precisely the same time as Alan and Phil's trial – on 5 July 1969 – during which it was being argued that were these two to be locked up, British society would become an immeasurably safer place, bombs similar in every way to that which they had thrown into the Banco de Bilbao went off at the Spanish Embassy and Spanish National Tourist Office.

Again, I was questioned about these First of May Group explosions, but fortunately I had an alibi, having just returned from Scotland visiting my Mum and my sister Olivia, who were still grieving for Gran.

x x x

In the summer, my partner Brenda and I took a holiday to Italy. We had intended to hitch-hike to Sardinia, but it turned out to be more of a relay tour, visiting one group of anarchists after another all the way from Paris to Marseilles, Genoa, Milan and Rome. Not only did they put us up, they also made sure that we made it safely to our next destination. Most of these connections had been made through the Black Cross.

When we arrived in Italy, the political tension was reaching its peak. Since the beginning of the year the European press had been prophesying another long hot summer of riots, strikes and terror. It proved to be a self-fulfilling prophecy. Since the early spring of 1969 there had been a series of bomb attacks in northern Italy – 32 according to the Italian ministry of the interior and 140 according to non-governmental sources. To anyone who knew anything about the anarchist movement it was obvious that the attacks had nothing to do with any comrades.

Bomb
Attacks in
Italy

These explosions were directed against premises where ordinary people went about their everyday occupations, a classic technique of fascist and nationalist terrorists to create a climate of fear and panic among the wider general population. The most damaging ones had been a bomb that exploded on Liberation Day, 25 April, on the Fiat stand at the Milan Trade Fair and another the same day at the Bureau di Cambio in the Banca Nazionale delle Communicazione in the city's central station. Both bombs had been designed and timed to injure or kill. No one died, but dozens of people had been seriously injured.

The right-wing press and the policemen and investigating magistrate leading the hunt for the perpetrators – Special Branch Inspector Luigi Calabresi, his superior, Antonio Allegra, head of the Milan political police, and Judge Antonio Amati – immediately blamed the anarchists. Fifteen anarchists were pulled in for questioning and, of these, six were charged with the Fiat and bank bombings. All six – Eliane Vincileone, Giovanni Corradini, Paolo Braschi, Paolo Facciolo, Angelo Piero della Savia and Tito Pulsinelli – strenuously denied the charges. Giovanni Corradini, an architect, and his partner Eliane Vincileone were Calabresi and

Amati's main suspects, being the best-known anarchists and, presumably, in the police view, best filled the role of the brains behind the operation. What probably damned them was the fact they were close friends of the wealthy and influential left-wing Italian publisher Giangiacomo Feltrinelli.

The comrades with whom I had discussed the Anarchist Black Cross in Carrara the previous August – Amedeo Bertolo, Umberto del Grande, and Giuseppe Pinelli from the Ponte della Ghisolfa anarchist group – had not hung around; they had set up the *Croce Nera Anarchica* (CNA) in March that year. By the time we arrived all their energies were being taken up with the defence of the six anarchists who had been held in San Vittorio prison since 2 May.

Since the previous summer Pinelli and other comrades had been monitoring neo-fascist activities. As he had told me then, Italian neo-fascists were travelling regularly to Greece, ostensibly invited on cultural exchanges, and were returning to Italy describing themselves as anarchists and Maoists. In these guises, they tried to spread fear and disorder, thus preparing the ground for a right-wing military junta to take over in Italy, just as it had done in Greece. The Italian comrades also discovered that the neo-fascists were organising paramilitary camps around the country where their members were given quaint names derived from Tolkien's *Lord of the Rings* trilogy, such as Hobbits, and received ideological indoctrination and training for insurgency and attacks on leftist militants and offices. As Amedeo Bertolo and Giuseppe Pinelli explained, the vast majority of the bomb attacks and outrages that year had been the work of these right-wing extremists, attempting to move public opinion against the anarchists. The Italian neo-fascists were so close to the police, security and intelligence services as to be almost indistinguishable. Although we didn't know it at the time, we had arrived in Italy slap bang in the middle of the birth of what came to be known as the 'strategy of tension.' The principal eminence gris behind this campaign, we discovered much later, was Federico Umberto D'Amato, the head of the Confidential Affairs Bureau of the Interior Ministry.

Both Pinelli and Bertolo were convinced something major was

Giuseppe Pinelli.

afoot, and that there was a real possibility of a right-wing coup in Italy. As elsewhere in Europe, much of the conservative and extreme right genuinely believed they were living in a pre-revolutionary period. Pinelli voiced his fears in the second issue of the CNA bulletin: 'Where there is an authoritarian regime in place, in the lead-up to some important event, special checks are carried out and hotheads, subversives and anarchists are detained by the police – some to help with inquiries, some on criminal charges: all as a precautionary measure. So, in this ghastly year of 1969, we wonder – what on earth is going on in Italy?'

The truth about the sinister machinations that were in train in Italy and the preparations for a coup d'état did not begin to unravel until December that year.

X X X

Brenda and I went to Sardinia – a beautiful, rural, rugged island, still more or less a land of peasants and bandits, but above all of kindness and courtesy. It was not free from the tension that infected the rest of the country (Colonel Gadaffy had just gained power in Libya and ordered the closure of the American bases there, so Sardinia was strategically more important than ever), but it seldom affected our time there.

In early September we returned to the mainland and went directly to Milan to catch up on the latest developments. As Pinelli described it, the fascist plot was gaining momentum. The number of bombings for which anarchists were being blamed had now apparently jumped from 140 or so to almost 400. The Milanese anarchists weren't particularly worried about the prospect of a coup, which they thought unlikely to succeed, and would be strongly resisted, but the bombings and anti-anarchist propaganda did cause them concern. That was the last time I saw Pinelli, standing outside San Vittorio prison, where the six comrades framed for the Milan Trade Fair bombing were being held. As it turned out, it was Pinelli who prevented the coup, but literally over his dead body.

Later that year, Leslie Finer, a former Greek correspondent of the *Observer* managed to obtain and publish in that newspaper an extraordinary secret document from his contacts among exiled Greek opponents of the colonels. This dossier had been compiled in May 1969 by an Italian-based Greek secret service agent of the KYP (the Central Service of Information). Sent originally to Giorgio Papadopolous, then president of the Greek council of ministers (and a CIA asset), the memo reported on the results of the Greek-funded terrorist campaign mounted in Italy in 1968–9 with the connivance of various Italian fascist organisations along with 'some representatives from the Army and the Carabinieri'. A copy was forwarded on 15 May to the Greek ambassador in Rome, Pampuras, by Michail Kottakis, head of the diplomatic office of the Greek foreign ministry. The report speculated on the chances of success of a right-wing coup d'état as a result of the escalation of the ongoing terrorist campaign. It also assessed the activities of Luigi Turchi, an MSI (fascist) deputy, and a Mr P., possibly Pino Rauti, but, more sensationally, it referred to the problems they had faced with regard to the bombings at the Fiat stand at the Milan Trade Fair and the central station and why they had been unable to do anything prior to 25 April. It was as clear an admission of guilt as one could hope for. It also referred to a major escalation of terrorist actions should Greece be expelled from the Council of Europe.

Leslie Finer gave me a copy of the entire Greek dossier which I forwarded at once to Pinelli in Milan. But the magistrate, Antonio Amatti, refused to admit the dossier as evidence in the Milan bombing case and the six remained banged up until they were finally acquitted on 28 May 1971, two full years after their arrest. The real perpetrators of the 25 April bombings – and the August 1969 railway bombings – were Franco Freda and Giovanni Ventura, two neo-fascists and Italian secret service agents who were finally sentenced in 1981. They each received 15-year prison sentences for their part in planning and carrying out the bombings.

Early in December I sent Pinelli the Greek document. On Friday, 12 December, a further four bombs exploded in Rome and Milan. One of these, planted in the Banca Nazionale dell'Agricoltura in the Piazza Fontana in Milan, exploded a little after 4.30pm, claiming the lives of sixteen people and wounding 100. Another, in the Banca Nazionale del Lavoro in Rome, injured fourteen, while two planted at the cenotaph in the Piazza Venezia wounded four. It was a day of massacre – a state massacre, as it turned out.

The Piazza Fontana Massacre *(margin note)*

X X X

For Inspector Luigi Calabresi of the Milan Questura and his boss Antonino Allegra there was, again, no doubt that anarchists were responsible. Among 100 or so anarchists arrested during the course of that night and the following day, twenty-seven were taken to San Vittorio prison, the rest being held for interrogation in Milan police headquarters in the Via Fatebenefratelli. Among those held were a number of CNA members, including Giuseppe Pinelli. After more than 48 hours in police custody the 41-year old railwayman was finally taken to Calabresi's room for questioning late in the evening of 15 December. Police officers present were Luigi Calabresi, Vito Panessa, Giuseppe Caracuta, Carlo Mainardi, Pietro Mucilli and Carabinieri lieutenant Savino Lograno.

The Death of Pinelli *(margin note)*

Around midnight, Aldo Palumbo, a journalist from *L'Unita* was having a smoke in the courtyard when he heard a series of thuds. Something was bouncing off the cornices as it fell from the fourth floor. He raced over to find the body of Pinelli sprawled in the flower bed. According to the duty doctor Nazzareno Fiorenzano he had suffered 'horrific abdominal injuries and a series of gashes on the head'. The autopsy showed that he was either dead or unconscious before he hit the ground. A bruise very much like that caused by a karate blow was found on his neck. No one was brought to trial for his death, the ramifications of which shake the Italian political scene to this day. The Milan magistrate, Gerardo D'Ambrosio, closed the official file on Pinelli in 1975. According to the finding, the anarchist died as the result of 'active misfortune', the 'misfortune' being his having 'fallen' from a window. All the policemen indicted for his death were absolved.

Luigi Calabresi, the political policeman leading Pinelli's interrogation, was shot by an assassin on 17 May 1972, and so what he knew will never be disclosed.

On 13 March 1995, after more than 25 years and countless court cases and appeal hearings, Judge Salvini indicted twenty-six Italian neo-fascists and secret service officers for their involvement in the Piazza Fontana massacre.

x x x

Back from Italy, Brenda and I moved from Crouch End to Muswell Hill. The flat in Fairfield Gardens had never recovered from the probing the police gave it the morning they found the agitprop dollar bills.

Everywhere that summer and autumn there was anger and tension: strikes, anti-Vietnam War protests, trouble building in Ulster, factory occupations, and spreading frustration with formal politics. It felt that to remain silent and stand back was to give comfort to the politicians, and be complicit in their crimes and injustices.

Things were also heating up in West Germany. President Nixon's visit to West Berlin was marked by massive anti-Vietnam War demonstrations and an unsuccessful bomb attempt on his motorcade, with explosives thoughtfully provided by a German secret police agent, Peter Urbach. Government offices throughout the country were targets for bomb attacks. In the USA, an activist offshoot of the Students for a Democratic Society (SDS) played a decisive part in the massive resistance to the Vietnam War including promoting draft-dodging. In October 1969, vowing to 'bring the war

Days of
Rage
home', the Weathermen took to the streets of Chicago. During October's 'Days of Rage' several hundred activists with helmets and clubs rampaged through the streets, attacking the buildings of the big corporate multinationals and clashing with the police. By the time the 'Days of Rage' had ended, 284 people had been arrested and fifty-seven police officers hospitalised, and over $1 million's worth of damage done. At a Weatherman 'council of war' to draw lessons from the Days of Rage, the participants decided to go underground and engage in a clandestine, armed struggle. An explosion in a Greenwich Village house in early March, which killed three Weathermen, signalled the start of an armed protest campaign against their own rogue state.

x x x

In November, the American investigative journalist Seymour Hersh broke the news that the US army had tried to keep secret: Lieutenant My Lai William Calley had led his platoon into the Vietnamese village of My Lai where the soldiers had opened fire on a group of defenceless women and children, massacring 109 people, including a two-year-old child. The impact of this story on American public opinion was enormous, and was a major contributory factor in eroding support for the war. That same month Salvador Allende was sworn in as Chile's new president, promising, to the US administration's horror, 'socialism within liberty'.

The newspaper campaign of fear was having an effect, at least according to the newspapers. It was the time of the 'Brolly Brigade', the name given by the press to angry middle-class commuters who poked railwaymen with their umbrellas during the railway go-slows and strikes. At a time when rail workers were endeavouring to boost their wages by industrial action, city gents were being encouraged by the press to attack them. This was considered great stuff – 'the middle-class backlash', the 'right-wing backlash' were heard over and over again. The papers reported with great glee, making much out of nothing, when railwaymen – usually those still going about their duties – were attacked and abused by stockbrokers. Similarly, the

WHAT ROUGH BEAST ...

TURNING and turning in the widening gyre
The falcon cannot hear the falconer;
Things fall apart; the centre cannot hold;
Mere anarchy is loosed upon the world,
The blood-dimmed tide is loosed, and everywhere
The ceremony of innocence is drowned;
The best lack all conviction, while the worst
Are full of passionate intensity.

What rough beast, its hour come round at last, was
slouching towards Bethlehem to be born?

W.B. YEATS

National Front was on the rise, giving the supporters of Powell and Mosley a direct line to fascism.

But there was no revolution in 1969 either. By the end of what the press was calling the 'hot autumn' of 1969 the revolutionary *tsunami* thought to have been triggered by May '68 seemed to be receding. What had happened? The protests against the war in Vietnam continued to grow, but in spite of the high profile debates and militant demonstrations, the vast mass of people in society remained untouched by what was to many thousands of militants a highly charged political atmosphere. Traditional loyalties to the Labour Party and the unions had never been completely swept aside, anti-capitalist consciousness didn't take off and political apathy ebbed back into everyday life. The old left reasserted themselves and regrouped.

Others including 'revolutionaries' accepted the state and the system for what it was and chose 'pragmatism,' to work with or within it – some for genuine, albeit piecemeal, reform; others notably for self-advancement. Revolutionaries can be opportunists and careerists, too. Position and tenure are big motives everywhere – look at what happened to Marxism.

x x x

The student movement, which had provided much of the New Left's dynamic, had peaked with the events of May 1968. Most students were satisfied with the levels of democracy offered them in student assemblies and representation in educational institutions; others imploded into the alternative, self-defeating culture of the 'underground'.

The New Left's cohesion had started to crumble from late 1968 onwards, gathering pace after the US invasion of Cambodia and particularly after the killing of four students at Kent State University by the US National Guard in May 1970. The beatniks, hippies and weekend dropouts of the 'alternative society' who had identified with the radical political movement turned instead to the parallel 'cultural revolution' of psychedelic acid rock, the maharishi and spiritual enlightenment, hash, LSD and freak-outs at UFOs. They simply gave up on radical politics, not necessarily because they were afraid of the increasing violence, but because they thought their protests were going unheard and they were banging their heads against a political brick wall. If you can't beat them, turn on and drop out.

This was the Woodstock generation. The main item on their political agenda was the legalising of cannabis.

What we thought was prologue turned out to be a short and unsatisfactory one-act Play for Today. The bubble just burst. What was left of a genuinely libertarian and spontaneous movement of young workers and students was now distinctly Leninist, in the Trotskyist sense – that is, elitist and authoritarian – and had become part of the International Socialists (IS, later the SWP) and the International Marxist Group (IMG). It didn't take long before the 'responsible' student leaders joined the system: David Triesman, Jack Straw, Kim Howell and Peter Hain to name but a few. Divisions were further aggravated by the fragmentation of the movement into more exclusive black power, feminist and other single-issue political organisations.

But it wasn't all negative. Certainly there were some gains from May '68. I do believe that for a lot of people it led them to live more wisely and with greater concern for others, and with a greater confidence in what shop-floor activity could achieve. Perhaps, too, it promulgated a key anarchist idea – distrust whoever seeks power. I'm glad to say we've never quite recovered from that.

A Chance Meeting in
Angel Alley

In October 1969, shortly after the Liverpool conference, my old friend
Miguel Garcia Garcia was released from Soria prison in Spain. He had
served a sentence of twenty years and a day. This term was the legal
limit for a consecutive sentence in Spain. He intended staying in
Spain once he was free, but I helped talk him out of the idea. They
would soon have had him back inside had he remained. Miguel felt
that at sixty-five it was too late for him to begin again in a foreign
country, but he soon relented and came to stay with us in Muswell
Hill.

The impact of life on the outside for Miguel was traumatic. Within
days of his release he had completely lost his voice. It took him a good
couple of months for him to recover fully. I suggested to him by letter
that he stop off in Liège, on his way to England, to meet Octavio
Alberola who would brief him on the recent demise of the FIJL (to
which Miguel had belonged as a young man) – another victim of the
post-May '68 depression – and the consequent reorganisation of the
First of May Group which had taken up the new generation of
resistance fighters. Miguel had made it clear to me in jail and in his
letters that his resistance days were far from over. Octavio also
arranged for him to see a throat specialist about the loss of his voice.

Miguel arrived in London early in December 1969. I was amazed at
how well he looked. He was tall, well-built, apparently as fit as a
butcher's dog apart from an occasional shortness of breath (due to TB

as we discovered much later), with jet black hair tinged with grey round the temple, a square jaw and a flawless complexion. Twenty years of prison beds had also affected his back to the extent that he couldn't sleep on a sprung mattress. He kipped on the floor until we were able to get hold of a wooden board that he could place on his bed at night.

Miguel's spoken English was extraordinarily good for someone completely self-taught and who had never been to an

Miguel Garcia Garcia

English-speaking country in his life. He had gleaned it entirely from books and patio conversations with people like me. He was ideal for the role of international secretary of the ABC and immediately plunged himself into the task of helping the prisoners he had left behind. His contribution was invaluable. Charismatic and – when he recovered his voice – a natural public speaker, he gave regular talks on the anti-Francoist resistance and his experiences in prison that were received enthusiastically by packed audiences up and down the country.

One of these meetings was held at the Freedom Press meeting hall in Whitechapel's Angel Alley. Miguel's voice still hadn't fully recovered so I translated for him. It was a highly emotional occasion and the audiences listened, spellbound, as Miguel recounted his struggle then and his struggle now. Miguel's story was a living cause, revolutionary and exemplary. By the end of the evening, the Spanish Civil War was no longer an abstract historical event to most of Miguel's captivated audience. Here was an experienced urban guerrilla and activist who had spent the best part of his adult life in Francoist jails, a man still deeply involved in the revolutionary struggle, whose belief had never dimmed.

x x x

Among the hundred or so people who came to meet and hear Miguel speak that night in February 1970 was a group from Powis Square in Notting Hill. These young people had been involved in a number of self-help community groups, such as the East London Squatters' Movement, the Claimants' Union and the Notting Hill People's Association which had been heavily involved the previous year in the opening up of the local squares around W11. Until then the private landlords had controlled the squares with big wire fences preventing non-residents getting into them.

After the meeting, two of the Powis Square group, John Barker and Hilary Creek approached me and Miguel, wanting to know more. John and Hilary had not come across any anarchists whose ideas they could relate to before. They had been impressed by the way the Anarchist Black Cross was not only organising assistance and solidarity for political prisoners throughout Europe, but also connecting it to the wider international and domestic struggles that were going on at the time. They agreed with our ideas and arguments and had no truck with conventional politics, but didn't think of themselves as anarchists.

Like lots of others, they didn't believe that anarchism had any roots in the working-class struggle in Britain. I argued that the opposite was the case. Up until the late forties and early 1950s, the anarchist movement in Britain had been primarily working-class and dynamic. It had been sidelined partly by post-war apathy, and partly by the fact that in 1946 the main weekly anarchist newspaper, *Freedom,* came under the control of Vernon Richards and his coterie of Tolstoyan and Gandhi-influenced middle-class pacifists and academics: people like George Woodcock, Reg Reynolds, Ethel Mannin and Herbert Read, who used the paper to argue the case for permanent protest – as opposed to class struggle – and who believed the idea of revolution 'outdated.'

The readership they attracted tended to be middle-class, liberal and arty. When Herbert Read accepted a knighthood for 'Services to

Literature' in 1953, the editors of *Freedom* published an 'explanation' of Read's action, but this proved too much for one working class anarchist, Glaswegian Frank Leech, who dropped dead of a heart attack after reading the article, aged only 53.

x x x

I felt an immediate empathy with John Barker, who reminded me of Roxy music singer Brian Ferry, with his dark hair constantly flopping over his eyes. He was well-read, confident, and articulate with a wry sense of humour. He and Hilary lived in a basement flat at 25 Powis Square, Notting Hill. John had been a student at Cambridge University, where he had been active politically – but not in the Kim Philby Dining Club, as has been alleged. John had moved from supporting the Labour Party in the 1964 elections to libertarian socialism. Like the Nanterre students, he was concerned by the roles for which students were being groomed in the outside world.

At Cambridge, John became friendly with Jim Greenfield from Widnes, Lancashire. Jim, the son of a long-distance lorry driver, was ginger-haired, pale-faced and freckled with intense piercing eyes. He struck me as a bit moody and emotionally coiled. Originally he had intended to read medicine at Trinity, having gone up there on the same day as Prince Charles, but had switched to economics when he found he couldn't get on with the aggressively conservative medical students. In Cambridge both had been become involved in radical street theatre and the Campaign Against Assessment, and had walked out of their final exams – having first ripped up their exam papers in a gesture of protest against the elitist nature of the system of which Cambridge liked to see itself as the pinnacle.

Hilary Creek had been living with John since early 1970. She had gone to Essex University from Watford Grammar School to read economics. After a month she changed to Russian, which she studied for two years. Hilary had short dark auburn hair framing an almost cherubic face, intelligent eyes with an ironic smile. Her Welshness showed in her reserved and occasionally flinty character. She had met John and Jim while working with homeless families in London's depressed East End. Besides the squatters' movement, Hilary was active in the women's movement, and in the anti-voting campaign in the run-up to the elections of June 1970.

X X X

Meanwhile, Jim Greenfield had formed a relationship with Anna Mendelson, a friend of Hilary from Essex University. Anna, a former head girl at Stockport High School, had studied literature and history at Essex and was from a Mancunian Jewish working-class background. Her dad was a Labour councillor and a market stall trader. Anna was dramatically beautiful and looked as though she had materialised from an Edward Burne-Jones painting. Unlike Hilary, Anna was outgoing and demonstrative. Maternal, warlike, proud, all she lacked to be the embodiment of Marianne, the symbol of revolution, was a Phrygian bonnet.

Hilary and Anna had also grown disillusioned with the superficiality of university life and values and left without completing their degrees. One of their friends, Ian Purdie, a Scot, had just been sentenced on 10 February to nine months for petrol bombing the Ulster Office in Savile Row. Their seriousness, integrity and unambiguous opposition to capitalism impressed me. But we didn't know just how important that first chance meeting in Angel Alley in Whitechapel was to be to the net about to be cast around us.

X X X

Brenda and I moved to a larger and more convenient flat in Fonthill Road, Finsbury Park, while Miguel Garcia moved to Suffolk to stay with some Anarchist Black Cross comrades, Ben and Libertad Gosling, who had been sending him food parcels and money when he was inside. But the English countryside proved too quiet for Miguel who soon returned to London, taking a flat of his own close to us in Upper Tollington Park, next to Finsbury Park, where he began writing the book on his experiences in Spanish jails, *Franco's Prisoner*. Albert moved in with him shortly after. They made an odd couple indeed, but a great double act.

While Miguel was writing his book in 1970, the First of May Group – which had been more or less inactive throughout 1969 apart from Alan and Phil's arrest and the 25 May bombing of the Spanish Embassy in Bonn – regrouped and launched a fresh series of actions These attacks were organised on an international scale, the main targets being Spanish banks, diplomatic centres and Iberia Airlines, the Spanish state airline. They were to be a statement to the world that while Franco remained in power, protests would be heard everywhere. But, unfortunately, they did nothing to halt the ever-growing wave of economically important tourists to the beaches of Franco's Spain.

On 3 March, 1970, three First of May Group members (Juan Garcia Macarena, 24; Jose Cabal Riera, 21; and Jose Canizares Varella, 35) were arrested in France and charged with conspiring to kidnap Spain's permanent delegate to UNESCO, while in April an Italian anarchist, Ivo della Savia, had been arrested in Belgium on an arrest warrant issued by the Italian government on charges of involvement with First of May Group actions in Italy.

On 10 May, small firebombs ignited on a number of aeroplanes of the Francoist airline Iberia at different airports throughout Europe. These coordinated actions were carried out by the First of May Group. Scary, but not lethal, the devices were not a danger to the safety of passengers or the plane itself. Donald Lidstone, a senior member of the Home Office Explosives Department at Woolwich Arsenal, described the firebombs thus: '. . . after giving off an intensely hot flame for a second and a half, it then gave off a large amount of black smoke – enough to impair the pilot's vision.' All airlines and airports were notified of the bombs before the planes took off.

The police 'leaked' a story to the *Daily Express*. The man responsible, according to 'police sources', was a person readily identifiable as yours truly. Unfortunately, libel actions are only a rich man's way of getting richer. Had I been Randolph Churchill I could have walked off with enough money to live without working for the rest of my life. As it was, I continued converting the Home Counties – to natural gas – and limited my response to a statement issued through

323

my lawyer, Ben Birnberg, denying any involvement in the actions. On the afternoon in question, I had been at a garden party at the home of two close friends in Crouch Hill, Valerie and Graham Packham. One of my 'alibis' was a senior police officer who lived next door.

Surveillance was intensified. DS Cremer was now a frequent visitor at John and Susan Rety's shop in Camden High Street. Part of Cremer's job as a skilled 'speciality' officer was to establish friendly and sympathetic relationship with the people the Branch was targeting. Cremer would pop in unannounced and suggest a game of chess. He had played, it was said, against the Russian spy Gordon Lonsdale – after his arrest, presumably in the hope of getting him to talk. Cremer explained to John that the police really had nothing against me except my libertarian views. 'I don't think myself the anarchists are as black as they're painted,' he said between pondering over a bishop and a rook. 'I think they are honourable, idealistic and reasonable people . . . but the sort of things that are going on are giving them a bad name in the view of people higher up.' He pronounced 'higher up' as though this was not a view he shared.

x x x

In June 1970, Edward Heath won an unexpected victory in the general election. Although Wilson's government had been having constant trouble with the unions and proposed fining them for 'wildcat' strikes, Labour was expected to be returned to office. Instead, the apparently genial Heath stole a victory while no one was looking.

But Heath confused his surprise win with a mandate to pursue his radical championing of the free market – what Wilson had ridiculed as Selsdon Man policies. These were ideas that the electorate hadn't properly examined, and their consequence – four years of blunt and aggressive confrontation of the union movement – was not something the population had signed up to. Heath tried Thatcherism before Thatcher (it was only prevented from being Heathism by factors beyond his control, like the OPEC oil price shock). Conservative journalist Peregrine Worsthorne later remarked that his mistake might have led to civil war.

It came as a surprise to many, including most journalists, to realise that the long confrontation with the workers was reaching such a pitch. But not to Heath. Addressing the UN General Assembly just after he came to power, he warned: 'Today we must recognise a new threat to the peace of nations, indeed to the very fabric of society. We have seen, in the last few years, the growth of the cult of political violence, preached and practised not so much between states as within them. It is a sombre thought, but it may be that in the 1970s, the decade which faces us, civil war, rather than between nations, will be the main danger we face.' The Heath government's confrontational response to genuine social discontent was to turn his prediction into a self-fulfilling prophecy.

Heath's State of Emergency

I doubt if the leaders of British industry wanted so headlong a clash; they knew from their own experience how much safer and easier it was to buy trade union leaders and to incorporate them into the establishment. Behind the new Tory Government, however, other forces were at work, representing a new trend – government not by the profit-making capitalists, but by accountants, lawyers and the people who lectured on the ideology of self-interest and the need for profit-making capitalism. They were academics and theorists rather than practitioners. Consequently they opted for the easy solution: go for the militants, what they called the 'far and wide left'. But the trade union leaders knew only too well the principle so well established in Nazi Germany, that if everyone to your left is shot then you end up the extremist.

Heath's government developed an Industrial Relations Bill, under Secretary Robert Carr, that, like Wilson's 'In Place of Strife' White Paper, placed punitive restrictions on trade union rights. The result was enormous demonstrations throughout the industrial centres of Britain, with the highest number of walkouts since the general strike of 1926, particularly in the docks, local authorities and electricity. Heath announced a state of emergency. Both sides seemed to have declared war.

x x x

I was travelling abroad a lot and being interviewed by the police with increasing frequency. An interview with DI Palmer-Hall and DS Balmain from the Special Branch in September 1970 appeared on the surface more or less typical, but from their probing there were things they weren't telling me – and they didn't have anything to do with Franco.

Balmain asked my lawyer Ben Birnberg to arrange an interview with me at Ben's office in Borough High Street. He wanted to know what I knew about bombs that had exploded on Sunday 27 September, at various airports – Heathrow, Le Bourget and Le Touquet.

'Nothing.'

Did I have a car? I had the use of Mr Meltzer's Corsair. (Fortunately, he didn't ask me if I had a licence to drive it.) Why had I gone to Brussels, Liège and Namur recently and whom had I seen? I did not know the people I met there well enough to put names to their faces, nor did I know where they lived. (They knew perfectly well I had gone to meet with Salvador Gurruchari in Brussels and Octavio Alberola in Namur, but why should I tell them anything. They would only use it against me, and perhaps against them.) Did I remember the night of 29–30 August 1970 – a Friday night? Did I know the Roehampton area? I didn't and wasn't quite certain where Roehampton was. How about 7–8 September 1970? I didn't keep a diary.

'There was an explosion that night in the South West area.'

'These things happen all the time nowadays.'

'What do the names 'The Wild Bunch' and 'Butch Cassidy and the Sundance Kid' mean to you?"

'Great films. All about honour and redemption, friendship – and sticking it to the bad guys.'

When the interview ended I told him that, like Frank Sinatra, it was the last one I would give. Already the management at William Press were complaining that I spent more time being interviewed by police than I did working. In future they would have to charge me with something or get off my case.

'Butch Cassidy and the Sundance Kid' and 'The Wild Bunch' were the names used on communiqués received following unreported bomb attacks on the homes of both the Metropolitan Police Commissioner, Sir John Waldron on 30 August and, a week later, that of the Tory Attorney General, Sir Peter Rawlinson.

More attacks on Establishment figures occurred in the following months: Attorney General Rawlinson's house was bombed again in October; there were simultaneous and coordinated attacks on Italian government offices in London, Manchester, Birmingham and Paris – all claimed by groups calling themselves variously, Butch Cassidy and the Sundance Kid, The Wild Bunch, the International Revolutionary Solidarity Movement, and Lotta Continua (the last on behalf of the murdered Giuseppe Pinelli); a bomb exploded in the offices of Greenford Cleansing Department during an industrial dispute; another blew up a BBC Outside Broadcast van covering the Bob Hope-compered Miss World Contest at the Albert Hall; in December, the Spanish Embassy was machine-gunned when international demonstrations of solidarity with six Basque nationalists on trial in Franco's courts were taking place.

Miss World Bomb

x x x

The day after the shooting at the Spanish Embassy, 3 December, the main newspapers received the following hand-written one sentence note, stamped with a John Bull printing kit:

Communiqué 1 The Angry Brigade

'Communiqué 1, The Angry Brigade:

'Fascism and oppression will be smashed. Embassies, High Pigs, Spectacles, Judges, Property (Spanish Embassy machine-gunned Thursday).'

This was the first time the name 'The Angry Brigade' had been used.

Six days later, on 9 December, the Department of Employment and Productivity in St James's Square – the ministry responsible for the imminent, much hated Industrial Relations Bill – was bombed. The explosion occurred just after the police had completed a search of the building. Communiqué number two from the Angry Brigade was sent to the underground newspaper the *International Times*, where it was published in its issue no. 93. Again, short and to the point, it said, simply: 'Success. Min. E & Prod.' It was stamped, 'Communiqué 2, The Angry Brigade', with the now familiar John Bull printing kit. A third communiqué was sent to *IT*, extracts from which were published in issues 94 and 95. The note described the bombing of the Department of Employment as part of 'a planned series of attacks on capitalist and government property'. It ended: 'We will answer their force with our class violence.'

Who were Butch Cassidy, the Wild Bunch and, lastly, the Angry Brigade?

'We Attack Property, Not People'

The day the Industrial Relations Bill passed into law I had been working in North Ruislip and didn't arrive home in Finsbury Park until shortly after ten in the evening. Around the time I was parking my car, two bombs exploded outside the Barnet home of Robert Carr, then Secretary of State for Employment in the government of Prime Minister Edward Heath – the man responsible for the Bill.

Brenda and I were sitting down to dinner when a television news flash announced the explosion.

'Serves him right,' I said.

'Who do you think will get the blame?' said Brenda. I nearly choked.

Our upstairs neighbours Pete and Val came down later to share a few bottles of cider and asked if we had heard the news. 'Oh well, maybe you won't be the fall guy,' said Pete. 'They only blame you for things to do with Franco, don't they?'

x x x

Who did it? That evening, those claiming to lead the attack on Robert Carr's Bill queued up for slots on the TV or radio to deny they attacked his house. Someone claimed that no trade unionist could have had anything to do with it. The Trotskyists were especially vehement in their denunciations, calling the whole event a 'fascist provocation'. Their most frequent argument – apart from 'the time is not yet right' – was that armed or 'propaganda-by-deed actions' were 'substitutes' for the mass mobilisation of the working class. These were the people who insisted that only a disciplined Marxist organisation could 'lead' the working classes to socialism. Someone suggested Carr had engineered it himself, and compared it to the burning of the Reichstag. Responsibility was claimed the next morning. The press announced that a letter had been sent to *The Times*, postmarked Barnet. It said simply: 'Robert Carr got it tonight. We're getting closer.' It was signed and stamped Communiqué 4, The Angry Brigade.

The police were later to allege that the Carr bombings were the eighteenth in a series of small-scale, high-profile attacks by the same group of individuals. This group initially called itself the First of May, then by a variety of tongue-in-cheek names inspired by current outlaw-friendly films such as Butch Cassidy and the Sundance Kid and The Wild Bunch, finally settling on the Angry Brigade. The choice of name was an ironic reference to the middle-class 'Brolly Brigade' who had been winning the hearts and minds of middle England by attacking striking railway workers with their umbrellas.

The probing in DI Palmer-Hall's line of questioning now became clear. Before Carr's house was bombed, only the police and a few newspaper editors, including me, had heard of the Angry Brigade. The name had been used only a month before in the note to the underground newspaper *International Times* claiming responsibility for a machine-gun attack on the Spanish Embassy on the night of 4 December. *Black Flag* had received the communiqué, but we chose not to publish it knowing it would lead to further visits from the police.

The machine-gun used in that attack, a Beretta M1938-42, was one of the connections with the First of May Group – it was the same one used in the First of May Group attack on the American Embassy in Grosvenor Square three years earlier.

After the Angry Brigade announcement, the country was awash with shock and *schadenfreude*: shock from the politicians, the mandarins, the broadsheet and tabloid leader writers, and, of course, 'decent people everywhere' who rushed to express their outrage, but *schadenfreude* from a good part of the rest of the country, who had felt 'they had it coming'.

x x x

The day after the Carr bombs, Conservative journalist Peregrine Worsthorne attended a lunch at the Savoy given by Granada Television for their annual presentation of newspaper awards. William Whitelaw, Heath's first Secretary of State for Northern Ireland, was the guest of honour who took advantage of the occasion to make a speech deploring the attack. 'Instead, however, of his words being greeted by that fierce rumble of assent which might have been expected from an audience wholly at one with the speaker,' a taken-aback Worsthorne reported '(they) were received, for the most part, in the cold silence of scepticism.'

The real shock was that MI5 had failed to sound any warning. Despite the investment of money and time in spying on the radical left, no one had any idea these attacks were being planned. Immediately, the Angry Brigade became the top priority of the security services. Detective Chief Superintendent Roy Habershon led the investigation, under his regional senior officer, Commander Dace. Habershon immediately recruited a team of around thirty officers from the Flying Squad (SO9) and the Special Branch (SO12), a group which later became known as the 'Bomb Squad', and later still the 'Anti-Terrorism Branch', (SO13).

The 'Bomb Squad'.
l/r: Commander Robert Huntley;
Commander Ernest Bond; Detective
Inspector George Mould and
Detective Constable Ron Smith.

x x x

The Angry Brigade's Communiqué No. 5 explained in more detail the reasons for their choice of targets, and to draw attention to the previously unpublicised attacks on the Attorney General and the Commissioner of the Metropolitan Police.

COMMUNIQUÉ NO. 5

'We are not mercenaries. We attack property, not people! Carr, Rawlinson, Waldron, would all have been dead if we had wished. Fascists and government agents are the only ones who attack the public – the fire-bombing of the West Indian party in South London, the West End cinema bomb (references to two serious bombings that had killed two people and injured many more). British democracy is based on more blood, terror, and exploitation than any empire in history. It has a brutal police force whose crimes against the people the media will not report. Now its government has declared vicious class war. Carr's Industrial Relations Bill aims to make it a one-sided war. We have started the fight back, and the war will be won by the organised working class with bombs.'

The leader writers expressed due disgust at the idea that senior officials were being held personally responsible for their actions. In denouncing these bombings, the newspapers allowed their indignant patriotism full rein. The *Daily Mirror* offered a reward of £10,000 to any person providing information leading to the arrest of the culprits. Would-be sleuths were assisted by the Beaverbrook Press (perhaps still mindful of its old vendetta) which supplied helpful clues as to the 'identity' of a certain Scotsman involved. The *Evening Standard* of 14 January also gave a hint – the police were after 'a young Scottish anarchist', experienced in explosives, who had been imprisoned in Spain. Who could they have meant? The *Scottish Daily Express* led the subsequent tally ho with the headline 'Carr Bombs, Hunt for Scot':

'Nationwide police checks were being made last night to flush out a known bomb anarchist – a Scot in his early twenties whom the Special Branch have put at the top of their wanted list in connection with the double bombing of Employment Minister, Mr Robert Carr.'

I was not the only Scottish anarchist, as the Beaverbrook Press would have been quick to assure a court. And Spain had lots of anarchist prisoners, though admittedly the Scottish ones might be a little thin on the ground – but again, what reputation did I have to lose anyway?

Curiously, it was at exactly the same time the police were said to be looking for me that the long line of Hillman Hunters, Hillman Minxes and military motorcycles disappeared from around the North Thames Gas Board base at Harrow. Nor was there any further surveillance on my flat in Finsbury Park. They could hardly monitor my comings and goings if they were giving out the story that I was missing, and they couldn't arrest me because they had no evidence.

A rich man would have marched off to the libel courts; I had no option but to sit it out.

Much later, the Angry Brigade was made out to be a collection of quintessentially English amateur bunglers, in an attempt to retrospectively deny a threat existed; the view at the time was the reverse. 'Scotland Yard and security officials are becoming increasingly embarrassed and annoyed by the activities of the Angry Brigade,' said *The Times*. 'They cannot now be dismissed as a group of cranks. Some senior officers credit the group with a degree of professional skill that has seldom been experienced.'

Talk of 'professional skills' is interesting, and indicative. Professional in what way? Is there a way you can earn your living by putting the wind up Cabinet Ministers? Unfortunately, no one pays for agitation except professional politicians and commercial interest groups. The police had in mind, or wished to portray, professional conspirators. But just because the Angry Brigade couldn't be dismissed as a group of cranks, it didn't follow that they were professionals, or a group, or, in fact, that the incidents were linked in any way, expect by the common political effect they were desired to have.

x x x

Late in January, I agreed to an interview with Nicola Tyrer, the recently appointed educational correspondent of the *Evening News*. She wanted to do a series on young people and thought I might make a good subject. We arranged to meet in a Hornsey restaurant that Thursday evening.

That Thursday, Paul Foot blew the whole Fleet Street crossword puzzle sky-high in his *Private Eye* column 'Footnotes', by naming me and completely debunking the national press stories of international police searches for the missing Scot. Unfortunately, apart from exposing the whole of Fleet Street as liars, the publication of Foot's story meant they could now mention me by name.

Reporters from every national daily and Sunday paper converged on Harrow-on-the-Hill to besiege the North Thames Gas Board yard where I was based. I was out on sector at the time. The yard supervisor chased them out, but they congregated outside like hungry scavengers waiting for my return.

I agreed to take a week's holiday. That night I met Nicola Tyrer as arranged. It was her first assignment as educational correspondent of the *Evening News* and it turned into a front-page scoop. The headlines shouted 'Christie – Bombs, I Deny It!', and the paper printed the whole story of the police harassment and my fear that I would be framed by the police. The *Evening Standard* was ignominiously reduced to quoting from its rival.

x x x

After the *Evening News* story appeared, Habershon – in a bland how-preposterous-for-Mr-Christie-to-think-otherwise statement – announced he had 'no special interest' in me. But in a raid on Ross's house on 24 January he netted my address book, and crowed that it was 'A Glossary of International Revolutionaries' – a description that hardly fitted Malcolm Muggeridge whose name and address was among those listed. Habershon backed off from me, at least publicly, and began looking for other suspects. The name he came up with – and remarkably quickly – was that of Ian Purdie, also a Scot, but someone unknown to me.

Ian had been released from Albany prison on the Isle of Wight the previous June after serving a nine month sentence for petrol bombing the Ulster Office in August 1969. Purdie's flat in Bedford Gardens had been raided by the 'Bomb Squad' just three days after the Carr bombs, but he was in Edinburgh, and had been there, and Manchester, since the day of the bombing. He returned to London on 18 January and two days later gave a voluntarily statement to DI Palmer Hall as to his movements. Coincidentally, the day Purdie gave his statement, 20 January, two uniformed

Jake Prescott

policemen on patrol in Notting Hill's Talbot Road arrested a man they claimed had been walking in an unsteady manner. When they searched him back at the police station they found some cannabis resin – and three stolen cheque books. The man's name was Jake Prescott, with previous for burglary and possession of a gun. Like Purdie, he too had recently been paroled from Albany Prison.

Prescott was banged up in Brixton Prison first with one other prisoner, Mr 'B', then, two days later, a third prisoner, Mr 'A'. Like Prescott, they were in for dishonest handling and other petty offences. Prescott proved a talkative cellmate. In the week they were together he opened up to his new friends about the revolutionary circles in which he was now mixing. He also told his cellmates in considerable detail about how he had been involved with another man, whom he identified by name, and two women in the Carr bomb, as well as the earlier bombings at the Department of Employment and the Miss World contest. He boasted of addressing the envelopes which had accompanied the Angry Brigade communiqués. Prescott also talked about me, saying I had been told to 'get out of the way' on a couple of occasions, presumably to establish an alibi, although he had never met me himself.

Unfortunately for Prescott – and for everyone connected with him, directly and indirectly – Mr 'A' was also a registered police informer who worked for a local Brixton CID officer, DI Peck. Sensing remission and the £10,000 reward on offered from the *Daily Mirror*, Mr 'A' contacted Peck who, in turn, got in touch with DCS Habershon. Habershon was sufficiently impressed with what Mr 'A' had to say that he immediately asked for Prescott's personal belongings to be sent from Brixton to Barnet to be examined by forensic scientists.

Prescott's address book was to be Habershon's crock of gold, Rosetta Stone and Enigma machine rolled into one. The handwriting was the same as that on the envelope containing Carr bombing communiqué. Habershon knew of Prescott's prison connection with Ian Purdie from Mr A, but the diary also provided Habershon's team with a first circle of suspects. The following day, 3 February, Habershon withdrew police opposition to bail and Prescott was released and placed under 24-hour surveillance.

X X X

Much of the investigation centred around a 'commune' at 29 Grosvenor Avenue, a large four-storey house in Highbury, Islington, inhabited by, among others, an anarchist printer called Chris Broad and his partner Charlotte Baggins. It had been Prescott's first port of call after his release on bail from Brixton. Ian Purdie had also lived there for a time.

Chris was a pleasant, well-mannered guy who had been left money by his parents and who wanted to contribute something. His way of doing that was to set up a radical print-shop in the basement of number 29 (where, amongst other publications, he printed *Black*

Flag). The Broads and their friends hoped the 'commune' would provide a model of alternative, collective behaviour. (To me the place was a mad-house and as far removed from an anarchist commune or practice as was possible to get. There was no privacy, no doors on the toilets and no bannisters on the stairs – a failure that to me verged on the criminal in a house teeming with unmonitored babies, and unchecked and indulged toddlers and children.)

Prescott was one of the regular Grosvenor Avenue 'hangers-on'. Fortunately, he was one of the many I never met. But for Habershon, the convergence of both Prescott's connection and mine with Grosvenor Avenue was a plus. The names in Prescott's address book were cross-checked against those in mine.

Habershon raided Grosvenor Avenue on the afternoon of 11 February, almost exactly a month after the Carr bombing and the same day three of the women living at Grosvenor Avenue were appearing at Bow Street Magistrates' Court charged with disrupting the Miss World contest (they had been throwing flour bombs and jeering at the presenter, Bob Hope). At the same time a BBC Outside Broadcast van covering the event was blown up by the Angry Brigade. Habershon sensed a connection and arrested four of the Miss World women defendants in the precincts of the Court, and had them taken to Barnet for questioning, before going to Grosvenor Avenue where the raid was already underway.

Prescott and a Dutchman, Jan Oudenaarden, who had been seen leaving Grosvenor Avenue earlier, had been arrested earlier coming out of a nearby pub and were already at Barnet Police Station. All were denied access to their solicitors.

X X X

Habershon's interrogation of the women confirmed that both Purdie and Prescott had indeed been staying at Grosvenor Avenue.

Prescott was no match for Habershon. He finally admitted to addressing three envelopes, but claimed he was ignorant of their contents. The stolen cheque books he had used, he said, the day after the Carr bombing to buy a ticket to Wivenhoe for a friend, Anna

Mendelson, and three return tickets – for himself and two other persons,whose names he couldn't remember – to Manchester, where he had stayed in a house in Cannock Street, in Moss Side for a couple of days. He could only remember the Christian names of the people who lived there: Jim, John, Chris and Hilary.

Habershon immediately requested the local Drug Squad/Special Branch to raid Cannock Street on a drugs or explosives charge, whichever was easier, to discover the political sympathies of the occupants. It proved a fruitful strategy. In the house at Cannock Street lived John Barker, Hilary Creek, Kate McLean, Chris Bott and three others. All were marked down as the sort of literate young militants who might well be involved in the Angry Brigade. Nothing of direct relevance to the Carr bombing was found and nobody was charged, but address books, letters, newspapers, magazines and a typewriter were taken away for closer scrutiny. The house and its occupants – John, Hilary, Kate and Chris – were placed under police surveillance.

x x x

By holding Oudenaarden and Prescott without charge, Habershon was acting in clear breach of habeas corpus, which the two men's lawyers and those of the National Council for Civil Liberties (NCCL) all protested. Oudenaarden was released after three days. He later told the press it was 'the most frightening experience of my life'. On 13 February, Jake Prescott was charged under the 1883 Explosive Substances Act with conspiracy to cause explosions; an open-ended charge which carried a twenty-year prison sentence.

Prescott
charged

The raids throughout London and the provinces increased in intensity, and spread to Scotland. It later emerged that Habershon's two main suspects were Purdie and me, and he was searching for evidence to connect us.

Habershon had spent a considerable time in the Fraud Squad, and emphasised that Prescott's stolen cheques, and others like them, could be a way of finding the other members of the Angry Brigade. In a cheque fraud, seemingly unrelated facts can be brought together to provide an overall picture of the 'conspiracy'. He believed that the

Angry Brigade or people close to its activists were supporting themselves through cheque fraud and by following the paper trail he would find his leads and his evidence. Other than myself, his main suspects appeared to be unemployed so they had to be supporting themselves by illegal means,

In the police theory, the Angry Brigade was a British section of the First of May Group and I was the facilitator. The conspiracy they had constructed began even before my return to Britain in 1967, before most of their other suspects had left school or university. But I didn't fit in with the stolen chequebook-strategy. I was clearly not involved in any cheque-kiting, was holding down a responsible job, working long hours from early morning until late at night, didn't live in a commune and didn't smoke dope.

x x x

On 19 February 1971, less than a week after Jake Prescott was charged with conspiracy, *The Times* published communiqué number 6 which they had received through the post from the Angry Brigade. It was probably the Angry Brigade's most important statement.

COMMUNIQUÉ NO. 6

'Fellow Revolutionaries ... We have sat quietly and suffered the violence of the system for too long. We are being attacked daily. Violence does not exist only in the army, the police and the prisons; it exists in the shoddy alienating culture pushed out on TV, films and magazines; it exists in the ugly sterility of urban life. It exists in the daily exploitation of our labour. The system will never collapse or capitulate by itself. More and more workers now realise this and are transforming union consciousness into offensive political militancy. Our role is to deepen the political contradictions at

> every level. We will not achieve this by
> concentrating on "issues" or by using watered-down
> socialist platitudes. Our attack is violent – our
> attack is organised. The question is not whether the
> revolution will be violent. Organised militant
> struggle and organised terrorism go side by side.
> These are the tactics of the revolutionary class
> movement ... until the revolutionary working class
> overthrows the capitalist system.'

No one with a traditional anarchist background would have expressed these ideas in quite this way, but the writers were clearly libertarian socialist. (The defining thing about the politics of the Angry Brigade was a scrupulous avoidance of all sectarian and institutional labels – anarchist, Marxist, and, particularly, Situationist.) And clearly the Angry Brigade, like the First of May Group, was moving from the political to the revolutionary, from simple anti-fascist solidarity to class-war solidarity, and therefore to confronting the state. The idea behind every Angry Brigade action was that politicians, industrialists and financiers were personally responsible for their actions. The Angry Brigade attacks were not intended to kill or injure people. The picture of the bombings has become distorted by the way similar devices were used with very different objectives by the Irish, Basque and Islamic *jihadist* groups in subsequent years. When the Irish campaign moved to mainland Britain not long after this, it struck blindly at 'the enemy', conducting an irregular version of 'total war', a strategy only different in scale from that of Al Quaida in targeting New York's Twin Towers using civilian aeroplanes. The Irish nationalists and *jihad* warriors failed to see that their cause would have been much better served by targeting not the 'innocent', but that term's implied correlative, the 'guilty'. The Angry Brigade and those who acted in its name tried to pinpoint and limit their actions to the 'guilty' without taking life (although clearly not without the implication that they could if they decided to).

Nor was the purpose to negotiate for specific political ends, bypass the democratic process, or even launch an urban guerrilla campaign in the hope it would lead to an insurrection. The constituency or community needed for a successful urban guerrilla campaign simply didn't exist, and certainly couldn't be created artificially. The Angry Brigade's actions were intended purely to complement the social struggle of the time by dramatically articulating the anger felt by many at the injustices of the system, the chicanery of politicians, and the people's apparent powerlessness in the face of so many assaults on their standards of living, their dignity and sense of fairness. By articulating this anger, they believed that other voices would join theirs.

And other voices did. In addition to its anti-working class legislation, the Heath government had just posted unemployment figures of 814,819, the highest since May 1940. Discontented people up and down the land followed up the Angry Brigade's offensive by attacking Tory Party and government buildings and Army Recruitment offices and with communiqués, letters and telephone calls. Not only this, but the police repression was fanning the flames of discontent among a wider section of the non-aligned left and radical hippiedom (although of course some of this was directed against the Angry Brigade itself). According to one newspaper report, in January 1971 alone there had been thirty unpublicised attacks on Establishment properties, banks, various Conservative Party offices and the home of Conservative MP Duncan Sandys. These were obviously not coming from one group. In fact, even the idea of a 'group' – let alone the idea of a leader – was becoming hazy. People were acting spontaneously, from similar sets of ideas. This drove the police into a confused frenzy – they were trying to find an organisation that increasingly appeared not to exist, but because they lacked any other understanding about how society might work, they were forced to continue searching for a traditional organization, with a leader, a membership and fixed plans. And in the end they had to invent one.

x x x

Habershon was being attacked from the left for his authoritarian excesses, and from the right for his lack of results. He announced he was after twelve main suspects. At last on 6 March Habershon arrested Ian Purdie at a house in Lavender Hill, South London.

Ian Purdie's arrest.

Unlike Prescott, Purdie gave nothing away during inter-rogation. Totally uncooperative throughout the questioning his replies ranged from 'No comment', to 'Work it out for yourself'; 'When are you going to charge me instead of giving me all this shit?'; 'Haven't you heard of Judge's Rules?'

Humiliatingly for Habershon, a week after Purdie's arrest there was a major explosion at the main offices of the Ford Motor Company at Gants Hill, Ilford, Essex. Again, no one was hurt. The explosion, which occurred during a major strike at the Ford works, was accompanied by a thousand-word communiqué commemorating the hundredth anniversary of the Paris Commune.

The March Ford bombing sparked yet more raids on Purdie's friends and associates, and other known anarchists. John Barker's circle was the focus of these. But still Habershon could come up with no substantial evidence of the gang he was after.

The case against Prescott and Purdie was postponed and postponed, against the furious protest of human rights lawyers, until, at last, on 22 April, it was impossible for the police to procrastinate any longer. The evidence presented at the six-week committal proceedings was extremely flimsy – non-existent in Purdie's case –

COMMUNIQUÉ NO. 7

'Our Revolution is autonomous rank-and-file action –
we create it ourselves. We have confidence now ... we
don't have to wait for them to dangle something
tempting like a (Enoch) Powell, a Bill, or a bad
apple in front of our faces, before we jump like
rabbits. We don't clutch desperately at the illusion
of Freedom. Our strategy is clear: How can we smash
the system? How can the people take power?

   '... We must attack, we cannot delegate our desire
to take the offensive. Sabotage is reality, getting
out of the factory is not the only way to strike ...
stay in and take over. We are against any external
structure, whether it is called Carr, Jackson, IS, CP
or SLL is irrelevant – they are all one and the
same ...'

Communiqué 7, The Angry Brigade.

but eventually the two were committed for trial at the Old Bailey.
Among the ten other suspects Habershon had in the frame was Chris
Bott, a resident of Cannock Street. Habershon had him picked up in
Manchester on 26 April and taken to London where he was charged
with fraud, then released on bail.

'Public Enemy Numer One'

On 1 May 1971 another bomb went off. This time it was in the trendy
Biba boutique in Kensington. (This and the Miss World bombing were
perhaps the only two truly Situationist-feminist bombings carried out
by the Angry Brigade.) Biba had a long tradition of exploitation of
their young shop assistants, who were paid miserable wages, as were
their cutters, but the Angry Brigade intended it as an attack on trendy
consumer capitalism:

> 'In fashion as in everything else, Capitalism can only go
> backwards – they're dead. The future is ours . . . The only thing you
> can do with modern slave houses called boutiques is wreck them.
> You can't reform capitalism and inhumanity. Just kick it till it
> breaks.' Communiqué 8, The Angry Brigade

(On 4 May, shortly after the Biba bombing another bomb was found
attached to the chassis of a car belonging to Lady Beaverbrook, but it
was never attributed to the Angry Brigade, either by themselves or by
the police.)

x x x

Two weeks later, on 22 May the Press Association received a
telephone call: 'This is the Angry Brigade. We've just done the police
computer. We're getting closer.'

The computer in question was the police computer at Tintagel House on the South Bank of the Thames, a device whose full potential and importance were just beginning to be realised. The explanation for the attack came in a slightly more surreal Communiqué 9.

COMMUNIQUÉ NO. 9

'We are getting closer. We are slowly destroying the long tentacles of the oppressive State machine ... secret files in the universities, work study in the factories, the census at home, social security files, computers, TV, Giro, passports, work permits, insurance cards. Bureaucracy and technology used against the people ... to slow up our work ... to slow down our minds and action ... to obliterate the truth. Police computers cannot tell the truth. They just record our "crimes". The pig murders go unrecorded. Stephen McCarthy, Peter Savva, David Oluwale. The murder of these brothers is not recorded on any card. We will avenge our brothers. If they murder another brother or sister, pig blood will flow in the streets. 168 explosions last year, hundreds of threatening phone calls to government, bosses, leaders.

'The Angry Brigade is the man or woman sitting next to you. They have guns in their pockets and hatred in their minds. We are getting closer. Off the system and its property. Power to the people.'

That same May night there were simultaneous explosions in Paris at British Rail HQ and the showrooms of two prestigious British car firms – Rolls Royce and Rover. The Paris bombings were accompanied by a communiqué in the form of an open letter to Prime Minister Heath, then visiting Paris to develop and consolidate

Britain's role in the Common Market. The communiqué also protested against the arrests of Ian Purdie and Jake Prescott and was collectively signed by the Angry Brigade, Group Commune 71, Groupe Marius Jacob and the International Revolutionary Solidarity Movement – the last being the umbrella name for the European anarchist action groups, including the First of May Group.

Tintagel House was not only the location of the Scotland Yard computer, it was also the new home base of the recently formed and still secret 'Bomb Squad'. Sir John Waldron, the Metropolitan Police Commissioner, had recently authorised an increase in the 'Bomb Squad' to thirty officers, relocated it from Barnet to Tintagel House, and given it a new permanent Commander to ensure it had the necessary precedence and clout. The name of this Commander was to be kept secret; he was to be referred to as 'Commander X'.

Commander X's identity wasn't much of a secret. I learned his name through journalist sources within days of his appointment – he was Ernest Radcliffe Bond who, although officially appointed to head the investigation on 23 June 1971, had been involved in the case for some time. He had been present during the interrogation of Jake Prescott in Barnet in February. But the Metropolitan Police needed some good press and this was one way of regaining the PR initiative. In fact, the real reason for Bond's identity being kept secret was to avoid the embarrassment of his home being bombed, like that of the Police Commissioner and the Attorney General.

On 22 July the Essex home of the hardline anti-trade union managing director of Ford's Halewood plant, William Batty, was bombed – as was one of the transformers at the firm's Dagenham plant. The explosion at Batty's home blew out the French windows of his study at 2 a.m., while he and his wife were asleep in the bedroom upstairs. Both were unharmed. Prime Minister Heath, Home Secretary Maudling, the Cabinet and the press were outraged. 'The police have been ordered to treat the Angry Brigade as Public Enemy Number One,' stated the *Sunday Telegraph*. Increasingly, the linguistic style of the Angry Brigade, the newspapers and police converged.

In fact, the 'public' – at least the working class – and the Angry

Brigade were on the same side, and the jubilation at next bombing confirmed that.

In July, John Davies, Edward Heath's Secretary of State for Trade and Industry, announced the closure of the Clydebank and Scotstoun yards of the heavily state-subsidised Upper Clyde Shipbuilders, and the mass layoff of almost 9,000 workers. A third shipyard was to be operated with a greatly reduced workforce taking a pay cut. This was a deliberate move by the Heath government to attack the union movement. Despite close police protection on all of Heath's Cabinet Ministers, the door of Davies's Putney flat was damaged by a bomb blast on 31 July and reported extensively in the national press. This attack was accompanied by Angry Brigade Communiqué 11.

Dad

The following day, 1 August 1971, the workers of Upper Clyde Shipyards began a protest occupation of the yards that was to last almost two months. I was in Glasgow at the time, having gone up to visit my Mum and my Dad who were now reunited, after the unexpected reappearance of the latter after twenty years. Mum had written to him asking for a divorce and he turned up on the door one day in Blantyre suggesting that they 'Mak a kirk or a mill o' things', meaning should they give the marriage another go. Mum thought, why not? and that was that. Dad had been living with another woman in Aberdeen for some time, but that relationship had ended for some reason. I never asked him why. Personally, I think he had come home to die as it was around this time he was diagnosed with cancer of the bowel, but he didn't tell anyone about his condition until closer to the end.

The atmosphere in the Glasgow shipyards was loaded. Trade union and Stalinist Communist Party spokesmen who had publicly denounced the Angry Brigade's 'irresponsible' act during their negotiations were howled down when brought face to face with the shipyard workers. (In the end, though, the 'pragmatic' union officials agreed to surrender thousands of jobs and accept a no-strike clause.)

x x x

I had been in regular but discreet contact with John Barker since the Freedom Press meeting the previous year, keeping him and the others in touch with the work of the Anarchist Black Cross and the literature we were producing. The ongoing harassment from the Manchester police had persuaded them to move back to London, to a flat in Stamford Hill.

By now the police knew where I was living in Fonthill Road and the constant police surveillance and the daily expectation of a raid or possible arrest were also having an effect both on Brenda and on me. We decided to move to somewhere we couldn't easily be found. Our upstairs neighbours and friends, Val and Pete, had moved recently to a small cottage in Drift, outside Penzance, on the road to Land's End. We rented a cottage nearby and Brenda moved down, with the two cats and all their offspring, in a journey enlivened by Brimstone's deciding to have another litter half-way there. My intention was to move to Cornwall permanently as soon as the gas conversion contract opened up in the West Country. In the meantime, I moved back into a flat in Nightingale Lane, Hornsey with Ross, sharing it with another mate and his girlfriend, who held the lease.

John Barker was an occasional visitor to the Nightingale Lane flat. On one occasion he came to borrow a drill, and to let me know they were moving from Stamford Hill to Amhurst Road in Stoke Newington. He was also going to France for a short break and wanted Guy Debord to contact Guy Debord, the French Situationist, with a view to translating some of his work into English. I gave him some addresses in Paris where he might make contact through mutual friends, and told him to let me know how he got on when he returned. (Not that I had much time for Debord: he had some insightful cultural and analytical ideas, but the man was a total arsehole in his everyday relationships, like Karl Marx, and I like the idea of at least some degree of proportionality between people's thoughts and actions.)

I didn't see John again until 28 July, when I returned from Cornwall and took him, among other publications, Miguel Garcia and Luis Portillo's account of *Unamuno's Last Lecture*. (Luis was the father of Michael Portillo, the Conservative MP and a Maggie Thatcher protégé.) I did not stay long at Amhurst Road. We went to our usual rendezvous in a

Amhurst Road.

pub in Stoke Newington High Street, where John told me he had heard on the grapevine that some people had been considering a kidnapping in the name of the Angry Brigade should Prescott and Purdie be convicted.

The 'Bomb Squad' raided 359 Amhurst Road at 4.30 in the afternoon of Friday 20 August. (Habershon was on holiday at the time, and missed the raid and – not interrupting his break – the interrogations.)

Amhurst Road Arrests

The police had hit the jackpot, claiming to have found two sub-machine guns, an automatic pistol, ammunition, thirteen detonators – the number turned out to be important – and explosives. They also found documents and other paraphernalia, including a John Bull printing set, all of which was relevant to the investigation.

Habershon's men had not only found Jim Greenfield and Anna, but also John Barker and Hilary Creek. They had what they believed to be the core of the Angry Brigade. Except one. At the police station, both men were badly beaten up by DS Gilham's two young detective constables, Sivell and Ashenden. It's unlikely the beating was an

ANGRY BRIGADE, MOONLIGHTER'S CELL

On 11 August, the Northern Ireland government introduced internment without trial in the Six Counties and arrested 450 suspected republicans and members of the left-wing socialist People's Democracy group. The government's action provoked an immediate outcry and protest demonstrations throughout the UK. The response of the Angry Brigade came four days later when it bombed the Army Recruiting office in London's Holloway Road. It was followed by a communiqué signed 'Angry Brigade, Moonlighter's Cell'.

attempt to extract a confession from the two men; it was more likely punishment, maybe just anger, at John and Jim for what they represented. As they were beating the two men they told them that when they were finished they were going to the women's cells to beat up Anna and Hilary. Neither of the women were beaten up, but they were humiliated by being stripped naked, their clothes removed and given an old blanket to wear all the time they were there. Nor were they given any food or water.

x x x

For me, that Saturday had been one of those days when nothing seemed to go right. It began with trouble and worked its way up to disaster.

I had crashed Albert's car on Friday night, and had no money to fix it. Ross had been robbed on a night out in the West End. The nearest person I knew who might be able to help was John Barker in Stoke Newington. At the back of my mind was the thought that I was at least postponing the evil hour when I had to go to my friend and confess

I'd smashed up his car and ruined the weekend he had planned in Wales. I remember the car radio was playing R Dean Taylor's song *Indiana Wants Me* as I drove. I hummed along and joined in the chorus.

The battered Corsair was still drivable – just – albeit in a sorry-looking state. Out of habit, I parked several streets away from Amhurst Road and walked up the row of terraced Victorian houses to number 359, the very last house in the street. The front door was ajar, but thinking nothing of it I ran up the three flights of stairs to the top flat and was slightly taken aback to find that door too was open. I walked through the hallway and into the front room, shouting 'anyone in?'

I looked around. What had been a lived-in room a few days earlier had been stripped bare of furniture. Suddenly, I became aware of a man stretched out at the far end of the room, below the two sash windows, which were fully open. In spite of my shout, the man was still fast asleep and snoring, with a copy of the *Daily Express* spread over his chest and his feet up on one of the remaining chairs.

I walked over and shook the sleeper awake. 'What's going on here?' I demanded. He spluttered and nearly fell off the chair with surprise. With a sinking heart I saw hanging above him on the wall a two-way police radio. It crackled into life with voices, static and white noise. A creaking sound behind me made me turn round. A knot suddenly tightened in my stomach. There, framed in the doorway, stood Detective Constable Claude Jeal, a Special Branch officer who had been on my case for some years. DC Jeal smiled with barely concealed delight. I'd walked into a trap they didn't even know they'd set. A quarter of a million pounds worth of Special Branch expenditures was about to be justified.

The snoozing policeman quickly regained his composure and produced his warrant card in reply to my question. It was Detective Constable Daniels of the Special Branch. He asked me why I had come to that address. Not being certain what exactly had happened, the wisest thing was not to answer any questions – not even to confirm my name, despite the fact that Jeal and Daniels knew perfectly well who I was. Daniels then arrested me in connection with what he described as property removed from the flat the previous night by police officers. I said I thought it a bit over the top to charge me over what had gone before I got there. But at the same time I was wondering what the hell I had walked into – and how I was going to get Brenda some money and Albert his car.

x x x

In the charge room at Stoke Newington Police Station, they removed all my possessions, including the car keys. They even took my cigarettes, though Jeal did give me a few of his own in compensation. I asked him to buy me some more out of the money I had on me, which he did.

August was not my lucky month. I had been arrested in Spain around the same date seven years earlier. Not normally given to displays of emotion, once that cell door banged shut behind me with its ominous reverberation, all my frustration and anger at events over the last twelve hours – the last twelve weeks, or months, or years – boiled over. Suddenly, I started kicking the cell door and shouting for my solicitor.

After I'd been told to shut up a couple of times, two young CID Detective Constables attached to the 'Bomb Squad', Sivell and Ashenden, charged in and grabbed my arms, doubling them behind my back, and frog-marched me through the charge room out into the yard to a waiting police car, us exchanging curses all the while.

As I was being manhandled past the police garage in the yard, I noticed the Corsair parked there with a large sign in front 'Wanted for Fingerprinting. Do Not Touch.' As we passed it, one of the coppers said, 'Right you bastard, you're going to go down for twenty years for this little lot.' They wore the smug grins of men who know something I didn't. I knew that could only mean they had planted something in the car, but wasn't to know what until later that afternoon.

We were joined in the car by the senior officer who had led the raid the night before, Detective Sergeant Andrew Gilham. As we drove to Albany Street Police Station, the field HQ where Commander Bond had set up his travelling forensic circus, I gathered from the needling of the two younger detectives that I had been arrested because I was the 'leader' of the Angry Brigade, and that they had found an arsenal in Amhurst Road with all 'the evidence' they needed to put me away for years. I didn't rise to the bait. DS Gilham finally told them to be quiet.

An Arsenal in Amhurst Road

At Albany Street it struck me that if all this show of power came into operation just to deal with a minuscule outfit like the Angry Brigade, what would British democracy be like if it was confronted with an insurrection? I wasn't expecting an answer to this mental and metaphorical question, but it came a year or so later, postmarked Belfast.

The charge room was as busy as a Saturday afternoon in Sauchiehall Street. The crowd of inquisitive uniformed and plain-clothes police officers parted to make way for my escort and me. I was booked in and taken to the cell block in the basement.

Much later in the afternoon when things had quietened down a bit, I heard John's voice shout, 'You all right, Jim?' A grunt in the affirmative came from Jim's cell, which turned out to be two up from my own. John went on, 'Did you hear they brought Stuart in?'

'Stuart who?' said Jim. 'I haven't heard anything.'

'The evidence'.

'They did!' I shouted. They had also arrested Chris Bott when he called at the Stoke Newington flat later that day and he, too, was brought down to the cells. We couldn't sustain much useful conversation shouting along a darkened corridor where anyone could have been listening. The atmosphere must have been like that in the steerage dormitory of the Titanic as it was going down. To cheer us up a bit I began a singsong – a rousing but discordant rendition of 'See what the boys in the backroom will have' from the Marlene Dietrich film *Destry Rides Again*.

After the singing died down and in between the sporadic one-liners that passed for conversation, every so often we'd hear the sound of a cell door being unlocked then banged shut and steps echoing along the corridor. Someone was being taken away for interrogation. After an hour or so they would return and someone else would be taken away. Finally, they came for me at about 7:15 pm.

x x x

I was escorted to the second floor office by Detective Sergeant Davies, a big fat cop with a round chubby face and a thick black droopy moustache. As we were about to enter the interrogation room, I saw the familiar figure of DS Roy Cremer come out of an office. As we passed, he gave me a friendly smile in his inimitable manner, as if to say simultaneously that he was sorry to see me there, that it was really nothing to do with him, and he looked forward to many more pleasant chats. Davies looked back at him as he disappeared down the corridor. 'Bloody Special Branch!' he said. I breathed again. He sounded almost as though we had something in common – a dislike of the political police.

The interrogation room was painted in institutional cream, brightly lit with fluorescent tubes. Davies joined three other men seated at a table against the wall, two at each end. I was in the middle. Davies did the introductions. On my left was DC Michael Doyle. On my right was DCI Riby Wilson of the Special Branch and my interrogator-in-chief, Commander Ernest 'Ernie' Bond.

A stockily-built thick-necked man in his early fifties, Bond was smartly-dressed in a chocolate brown pin-stripe suit, brown shoes and matching tie. His skimpy, thinning brilliantined hair was slicked back from a broad forehead. A bulbous nose, thin lips and high cheekbones drew attention to his deep-set stony-eyes and boxer's ears. His appearance suggested an ageing Buenos Aires tango dancer.

DC Doyle was the exhibits officer. The exhibits – documents, cheque books, passports, driving licences, sub-machine guns, an automatic pistol, ammunition, sticks of dynamite, and a box of detonators, all allegedly removed from Amhurst Road and my Corsair – were stacked high on the table in front of me.

Bond looked at me. His eyes dilated for a just a moment. I tried to read his face; it was inscrutable. Not a hint of triumphalism. Then he spoke. The tone of his voice was monotonous, as though he had launched into a set-piece monologue. He began with the time-honoured formula: 'I presume you understand why you have been brought here?'

'No,' I replied 'you presume wrong, I have no idea.' Apart from a few abusive remarks made by his subordinates I had been told nothing. I reminded him that it was on record that I would not give any more interviews to the police, not even in the presence of my solicitor, and it seemed to me that even for them this was going a bit far in investigating political activities.

Special Branch Interrogation

Bond agreed that I was not obliged to assist the police with their inquiries, but said there were still a number of questions he needed to put to me. I said he could do so, but I would prefer to have my solicitor present. There was one thing I would say, however – at this all ears stood up – and that was a criticism of the outrageous lack of amenities in the police station. I had been held eight hours without a bite to eat and the very least they could do was provide us with a regular cup of tea and something to eat now and again.

Bond turned to Riby Wilson and asked if he could arrange for me to have a regular cup of tea. He then cautioned me and began his questions. To everything that was put to me I either made no reply or asked for my solicitor. Bond then explained that he was making inquiries about the Angry Brigade. 'What we have found leads me to believe that those connected with the flat are associated with the Angry Brigade,' he said. This then was their way out of the definitional problem of who was in the Angry Bridage – they had determined that the Angry Brigade would be those people found with explosives.

'Look at these (Free Prescott and Purdie) posters found in your car.'

'I didn't know possession of posters was a crime. I would like to consult with my solicitor on that fact.'

'This *Time Out* magazine is yours – do you sympathise with the Angry Brigade? There's a picture in it which refers to them.'

'I don't edit *Time Out*. My sympathies are my own.'

'You have publicly admitted being an anarchist, haven't you? '

I replied 'Yes, I have. My solicitor can tell you all about it.'

Bond rummaged through the large pile of plastic bags on the desk and produced one they said contained what had been taken from my car. I was asked to separate what was mine from what was Albert's. Bond then leaned down to open his desk drawer, not to the pile on his desk, from which he produced a little cardboard box with two detonators sticking out from a bed of cotton-wool. Here was the magician producing the rabbit from his hat.

'In the boot of your car police officers found these two detonators. What have you to say about these?' His face was expressionless.

I stared in disbelief at the detonators and looked at Bond. For some reason I couldn't believe they would be so crude as to plant detonators on me, or anything else so obvious. It seemed that this was their card that trumped my ace. It was now for a jury to decide whether it had come out of Bond's sleeve or the boot of the Corsair.

At the end of the interrogation, just as I stood up to go, the music of *La Marseillaise* blasted loudly from the street outside. Wilson and Bond jumped from their seats and rushed to the window to see what was happening outside. It was an ice-cream van. Riby Wilson turned to me with a laugh, saying he thought for a moment French revolutionaries had come to rescue me. I don't know if they really expected that within a few hours French revolutionaries could have got over to London to attack a small police station near Regent's Park complete with municipal band. In my cell, I thought about Bond's conduct of the interrogation. Clearly, he had not been looking for a confession. He was simply going through the motions for the Court. He was telling me 'like it was'.

Ben Birnberg came to my cell early next morning. Ben agreed with my decision not to give a statement, but he did suggest I cooperate in giving a handwriting sample and to allow them to take swabs from my hands to verify whether I had handled explosives recently. I did both.

Later that afternoon I was taken upstairs for another brief interview with Bond, largely about the names in my address book. Bond pointed out the sinister significance of Barker, J., and Chris B. I referred him to the not-so-sinister Malcolm Muggeridge.

That evening, in the cells, Sir John Waldron, the outgoing Police Commissioner himself, came to gloat with a posse of high-ranking police officers and civilians. For a few seconds he and the others peered in at me, silent and expressionless, through the hatch of the cell door then walked down the corridor to look at the others.

x x x

Monday morning was my second morning in captivity, and the third for the others. One by one the four of us were marched out to a small sink in the charge room where we were allowed to have a quick freshen-up with cold water, surrounded by half a dozen policemen, and then taken outside to the high-walled police car park for a brisk twice around the yard walk, so we couldn't say we hadn't had any fresh air. It felt like being a prisoner in Fort Apache with all the cops on the roof and the guards on the door. Anna and Hilary, who were still without clothes, were kept locked up until finally some old prison uniforms were provided in order for them to be brought into the charge room. We were then all marched into the charge room and lined up. This was the first sight I had had of the others since our arrest. Jim and John were bruised on the face and had been badly beaten up. Anna and Hilary both looked tired but cheered up enormously on seeing John and Jim.

The full line-up of those the authorities had decided were the Angry Brigade was John Barker, Anna Mendelson, Hilary Creek, Jim Greenfield (all arrested at Amhurst Road), Ian Purdie, Jake Prescott (both of whom they had had for some time, and were held separately), me, and Chris Bott, the last to arrive. Not the twelve Habershon had promised, but eight would have to do.

We were lined up according to the severity of the charges against us. Jim and Anna were first on the list, then John and Hilary. Chris Bott and I brought up the rear. I whispered to him that it was rather like a double wedding with us as best men.

The room was packed with policemen, lowly and senior. It was obviously an historic occasion. The charges against us were read out one by one by the Station Inspector. When he came to my name I shouted that I had been framed. Everyone looked at me, slightly embarrassed. It was as though someone objected to the wedding.

The Inspector, nonplussed, noted my objection and proceeded to read out the property sheets. I refused to sign my list, which included the two planted detonators. This created a problem – the Inspector didn't want to have to type out the list again. Bond stepped in at this point and saved the day by initialling the two offending items. They formed a striking contrast to the other rubbish in the car, which included a half-eaten bag of peanuts.

Hilary and Anna

X X X

At ten o'clock that Monday night, as I was settling down to sleep, the cell door flew open and I was dragged from my bunk by a flurry of uniformed policemen, handcuffed and quickly frogmarched through the police station and bundled into one of six Black Marias waiting in the yard, one for each of us.

Our police escort had been told not to speak to us so we didn't know where we were being driven at such high speed through the night. Our destination turned out to be

THE ANGRY BRIGADE

No one knew who the angry Brigade was, or how many
people were involved, and it's unlikely ever to be
known. I certainly don't know. What I can surmise is
that those involved were a relatively disparate group
in their early-to-mid-twenties who had reached the
imposed limits of protest. Some of the people on
trial had indeed taken part in Angry Brigade actions
(as John Barker put it later, in his case 'they had
framed a guilty man'); some had not. Our various
defences all lay in the lack or suspect nature of
police evidence.

The sense of anger, frustration and outrage
everyone felt wasn't unique to Britain. Much the same
degree of angry militancy was being reached all over
the world around the same time: the Weather
Underground in the States, the 2nd June and Red Army
Fraktion groups in Germany, the GARI and MIL in
France and Spain, the Partisan Action Groups and
nascent Red Brigades in Italy, and so on.

Unlike Pallas Athene, this milieu of young radicals
who came to be known as the Angry Brigade did not
spring forth in 1970, fully armed from the cloven
head of some sinister Zeus. The Angry Brigade was a
creation of its time, an *ad hoc* collection of
dissatisfied young people who, politicised by
America's war in Vietnam, and the aggressive anti-
working class bias and anti-trade union policies of
the Conservative government of Ted Heath, felt that
the failure of the parliamentary and party political
system left them no options to make their point than
by exemplary direct actions - propaganda by deed. The

strategy was not urban guerrilla warfare leading to insurrection, or even pre-emptive regime change. It was a signal that lines were being drawn, ends of tethers reached, and that at least some people were angry about what was happening in the world and were prepared to highlight the wrongs and injustices through the psychological impact of victimless symbolic attacks. In spite of the rhetoric of the communiqués, their immediate aim was not revolution – although they all considered themselves revolutionaries – but to complement the bitter social struggle that was going on at the time and act as a spur, pushing back the boundaries of illegitimate state power by a more combative approach to protest. Apart from wanting greater political accountability and democratic control over their lives and what was being done in their name by the permanent government, in their sights were all the concentrated weaknesses and flaws in society, including predatory capitalism, anti-working class legislation, racism, sexism, colonialism, the consumer society, the nuclear state and US and Soviet imperialism – to name but a few.

the police cells at Clerkenwell Magistrates' Court where we were going to be remanded in custody the following day. The move was a security measure to make sure the 'International Anarchist Conspirators' couldn't find our whereabouts and break us out in the dead of night.

The IAC must have been having the night off.

After a breakfast of stewed tea and bland porridge, we were marched into the adjacent courtroom. The dock was so small we couldn't all squeeze in so Chris Bott and I had to stand at the side. I looked around at the equally tight squeeze in the public gallery, friends and comrades who had braved the formidable police pressure and searches to crush in. I was elated to see Brenda trying to lift her arm out of the scrum and give me an encouraging wave. I signalled to her to go to the back of the court for a visit afterwards, and waited to hear what the magistrate had to say.

The magistrate wasted no time listening to protestations of innocence. The police had brought us there and charged us, and were convinced of our guilt. As he put it, he was 'small fry'. All he could do was legalise our being locked up until we could prove our innocence before a judge and jury. In the event, we would not be given that opportunity for a year and a half.

Doing the Brixton Shuffle

Anna and Hilary were sent to Holloway; the rest of us went to Brixton.

I was sent to maximum security, as they had me down as a 'recidivist' for some reason. (Although I did try to avoid this. The reception screw asked if I had ever been in prison before. 'I have never been in a British jail in my life,' I said, Jesuitically. 'You're the fucker who was sentenced to twenty years in Spain,' I was told.)

Over the next three months we made gruelling, weekly journeys to magistrates' courts, processions which began as huge productions when the police still suspected a rescue attempt would be made for us, but then obtained a blander tone as time wore on. This routine is a consequence of the acclaimed *habeas corpus* – nobody can be kept imprisoned without coming before the court, so people have to keep coming back and back and back to court until finally the authorities decide they had scraped together all the evidence can to chance a trial. At least it prevented us joining the ranks of the 'disappeared'.

All the allegations against us were predicated on the possession charge. In my case the alleged possession of two detonators; in the case of the four from Amhurst Road, the alleged possession of arms – and in the case of Chris Bott, nothing at all. Chris was tacked on to the Amhurst Road 'possession of the explosives and guns' charge, despite the fact everything had been removed before he arrived there.

x x x

On one occasion, a Trotskyist screw (yes, there are such things, unsurprisingly) asked if I had read Kropotkin's *In Russian and French Prisons*. In fact, I hadn't. It was a rare item because the Tsarist authorities had bought up edition after edition of the book when it first appeared, to prevent it being known, but it has been reprinted since then. 'You ought to write *In Spanish and English Prisons* one day,' he said, half jokingly. He took it for granted, as did many of my friends, that the Spanish prisons would be much worse, but it is a sad commentary on English liberalism that this just wasn't true. When I discussed this with Miguel Garcia, my friend and former fellow prisoner, he agreed that it was the soullessness of British prisons that made them outstanding in the history of penology. National characteristics come into it as well. Cold cabbage, muddy fishcakes, soggy sponge with lumpy custard and gnats' piss for tea would be considered a provocation diet in Spain. The authorities offering it would be expecting a riot. British prisoners have probably been conditioned by years of factory canteens, greasy spoon cafes and now Macdonalds.

But there was another striking difference between the two countries: British jails were run on a system of state socialism, where you get what you are given. ('Incentives' and 'earned privileges' are now the system.) Spanish jails in Franco's time were run along on much more humane lines inasmuch as there was some degree of choice involved. You could work and earn more, or – and this is a punishment – not work and scrape by if you were prepared to do without things like fags and Serrano ham sandwiches. You could have money sent in from outside and spend it in a canteen or the prison restaurant. Thus responsibility for the individual's quality of life in prison became his own, that of his comrades or his family.

Like money everywhere, its circulation in jail leads to corruption, but it is also the one thing that eases tyranny. Corruption certainly exists in English jails – albeit fitfully. In Spain it was built into the system. But for those who have illusions as to what can be achieved by the parliamentary system, a comparison of Spanish and English prisons would be interesting.

Some might think this flattering for Francoist jails. It is not intended to be. Ultimately conditions in all prisons come down to what a government feels it can get away with. In Franco's Spain they had had more or less the whole nation locked up at one time or another, so that the guards had to live with the prisoners. In Franco's jails many of the inmates were taken out and murdered. But as the jails there gradually settled into becoming part of the furniture of the regime they became less unbearable, simply in order to avoid the constant tension and cycle of reprisals. If people spent Francoist-length sentences in Brixton under Home Office rules, the place would be ripped apart.

X X X

Prescott and Purdie's trial had been due to start on 6 September. The prosecution failed to have it attached to ours – Prescott had already been in gaol six months and Purdie five – but the motion in any case delayed the trial to 10 November 1971.

One of the claims made by the police was that the Angry Brigade was now 'smashed.' Unfortunately for them, on 24 September, a month after our arrest, Albany Street barracks, just down the road from where we had been held, was bombed. The Angry Brigade claimed responsibility in calls to the press. Another bombing followed on 19 October, at the home of Chris Bryant, one of the Midland's biggest lump employers (whose employees were all theoretically self-employed, paid no taxes or National Insurance contributions and received no protection in terms of health, security or safety) who was then in the middle of a major industrial dispute. It was accompanied by Communiqué 13 which, apart from explaining the reasons for the bombing, stated that those of us then in custody were political prisoners in the ongoing class war. It added: 'We are not in a position to say whether any one person is or isn't a member of the Brigade. All we say is: the Brigade is everywhere . . . Let ten men and women meet who are resolved on the lightening of violence rather than the long agony of survival; from this moment despair ends and tactics begin.'

Attacks
Continue

X X X

Later attacks were directed at Chelsea Bridge opposite the barracks, Everton Street Army Tank HQ, the officers mess in Dartmoor Prison, and the Post Office Tower. British government offices and institutions in Amsterdam, Basle, Barcelona, Rome and Paris were also bombed and the attacks claimed on behalf of the Angry Brigade, and in support of Ian and Jake and those of us arrested subsequently. As far as I am aware neither the Angry Brigade or First of May Group were involved in the spate of letter bombs that were being sent at this time.

x x x

The final Angry Brigade Communiqué 14, Geronimo Cell, was published in *International Times* (no. 144) on 14 December 1971.

ANGRY BRIGADE COMMUNIQUÉ 14, GERONIMO CELL

'... Friends ... it's time to weigh the balance between revolutionary advances and the gains of repression ... No revolutionary group can carry on regardless. We are not military generals or a ruthless elite. If the more the Angry Brigade bombs, the more innocent people are framed, then revolutionary solidarity demands second thoughts and different actions. THE WORKING CLASS HAS MANY WEAPONS MORE POWERFUL THAN BOMBS. By halting the bombing we threaten something worse. Our worse will always be aimed where it hurts the bosses most, their precious property.

'We have shaken the bosses and scared cabinet ministers. We have given them a small dose of their own medicine, a little taste of their own violence. But now is the time to silence capitalist cynics and revolutionary fools. The present spate of letter bombs has absolutely nothing to do with the People's movement, or any cells of the brigade. Letter bombs are a desperate tactic, the product of frustration and impatience. We condemn those who use bombs against civilians, fanatics who care little for human life. Zionism will not be destroyed by killing a few businessmen. We feel for the Arab movement, we support their aims to liberate the Middle East, but the present campaign is indiscriminate and unproductive.

'Again, we totally support the liberation struggle of the Irish people. But do not believe that the Provisional IRA are its best supporters. THOSE WHO BOMB WORKERS BOMB THEIR OWN ARMY ... This communiqué is addressed to all our comrades in Ireland ... The Angry Brigade suggests that the Irish people make it clear to the Provisionals that, apart from our class enemies LIFE IS NOT EXPENDABLE. Random terror is the rule of law and order. In the name of socialism, we deny any connection with those who commit inhuman acts.

'ALL ANGRY BRIGADE ATTACKS HAVE AND WILL BE DIRECTED AT RULING CLASS PROPERTY ... WE ARE NOT MERCENARIES, WE ATTACK PROPERTY NOT PEOPLE ...'

These bombings did not challenge the police definition of the Angry Brigade. They described all subsequent events as 'copy-cat' actions, or perhaps the work of sympathisers. In fact, the people who carried out these actions were as much (and in my case much more) a part of the Angry Brigade as the people locked up. As the famous saying goes, you can't imprison an idea.

x x x

In Brixton I spent my days and nights reading, writing and thinking – pacing up and down or lying on my bunk. If it didn't rain we were banged up for 23 hours a day with half an hour's exercise in the morning and afternoon, doing the Brixton shuffle around the figure-of-eight path in the small grassy compound outside 'A' wing. If it was raining we were inside for 24.

As in Carabanchel, it was fascinating to chat to my fellow prisoners and find out how they had got there. A regular companion on the 'A' wing shuffle was 'Bang-Bang' Charlie Cowden. Charlie was a fellow Glaswegian, a distinguished-looking one at that, with his mane of silver hair and patrician good looks. He looked every inch a Guards officer. He had been an armed robber forced by ill-health into a life of charlatantry and confidence frauds, at which he clearly had no natural talent, having notched up almost 600 offences. On this occasion he was inside for bigamy. The extraordinary thing was that both wives were still bringing him food hampers every week, one from Harrods and the other from Fortnum and Mason, delivered in Rolls-Royces. Brenda used to chat with both the wives in the waiting room.

A couple of guys on my landing had probably escaped hanging only because there was no longer a death penalty. There were toughs, toffs, hare-brained drug-dealing hippies and genteel middle-class fraudsters. Most of 'A' Wing prisoners were serious hard-men, professional robbers of security vans, banks, post offices and building societies. They faced long prison sentences. Mind you, so did we.

x x x

The 'glory days' of the old-time East End gangsters were over by the time we arrived in Brixton. They had shared the same values and morality as the Metropolitan CID who pursued them, coppers like Commander Bond. The two sides were parasites living off each other, particularly what was then the Flying Squad. Those who had ended up in Brixton were usually Tories, whose cell walls were decorated with Union Jacks and photographs of the Queen. By the early 1970s the new serious criminal tended to be younger and more independently minded, with no respect for 'Law and Order' as part of the natural order of things. As in every other strata of society, the age of deference had gone. By 1971, the photos on the wall were more likely to be of Ché Guevara than the Queen.

Brixton's screws, as in most British prisons, were recruited mostly from the north of England. The job offered security and a roof over their heads. Mostly they were reasonable people. They didn't bother us if we didn't bother them. But there was also a less likeable hard core of fascists who wanted to run the place under the regime of the National Front-dominated Prison Officers' Association and did what they could to make life unbearable for prisoners in general, and for us in particular.

There have been lots of published commentaries on prison life. Presumably they are read for pure titillation, for the reforms over the last 100 or even 50 years have been negligible. Possibly the prisons have got worse, and certainly the same ones have got older. I was better off than most, since Brenda was able to work half-days and visit me with meals. Still, she couldn't have done it without a lot of help. The Anarchist Black Cross had set up a defence fund for us, but it could never have managed to raise enough to keep Brenda going while she spent so much time and money visiting me. When I came out I had a look at the books and found someone had been putting a fiver a week in and even more. I couldn't find out who it was. For some time I suspected a deep ruse of the Special Branch, as Albert in his usual self-effacing way said it was anonymous, until he finally confessed he was the donor. Of course my gratitude for both of these acts of support cannot be expressed. Even Habershon and Bond could scarcely forbear expressing admiration for Brenda after daily visits had stretched into a year or so . . . a cheer indeed from the ranks of Tuscany.

Another regular visitor with expensive food parcels was Simon Watson Taylor, an exotic survivor of the old London Anarchist Group, secretary of the London Surrealist Group in the 1940s and translator of Alfred Jarry's *The Ubo Plays.* Simon had the soul of a hippie and the dress sense of a fop when he had to impress. He carried a silver-topped cane on which his name was engraved. Asked by the screws to identify himself as he handed in his Fortnum hamper, Simon whacked his cane down on the desk and said 'Take it from there, my man!' Wrong attitude. The screws got their own back – on me – by dumping all the expensive food on to one plate and covering it in custard, which was in fact Advocaat.

George Melly, who had been looking after Simon's collection of surrealist paintings while the latter was on his travels to India in the 1960s, sold one of these at Simon's request to raise money for the Stoke Newington 8 Defence Committee. It went for about £10,000.

x x x

They wouldn't allow me out of 'A' wing, so after a lot of argy-bargy with the Governor and the Home Office, Jim, John and Chris were transferred to 'A' wing to prepare our joint defence. After more pressure Hilary and Anna were brought over from Holloway on a couple of occasions. No one interfered with our notes during these conferences, but Anna and Hilary had all their papers taken away and read by the authorities every night they got back.

I had no idea whether or not my co-defendants were guilty either of possession, of conspiracy or of the specific bombings: I didn't ask and I didn't care. We were, however, on the same side and in the same dock. If we were to stand any chance of acquittal we had at least not to allow ourselves to be divided against each other. It was a case of hanging together, or hanging separately. From the start we agreed we should not be divided against each other, but neither should we be subjoined to the point where conspiracy was easy to prove. The mere fact that the police and the Director of Public Prosecutions (DPP) insisted we were all in the dock together facing the same conspiracy charges was something over which we had no control.

We began to understand the pitfalls of the conspiracy laws under which we were charged. The prosecution didn't need to prove that we all had had possession of weapons, or that we had any direct link to the bombings – just that there was probably an 'agreement' and if we knew what that 'agreement' was we were conspirators. It didn't even need any explanation or exchange of words; the 'agreement' could be effected by a 'wink or a nod'. Kafkaesque or what!

We agreed we would all act individually, with separate counsels. John, Anna and Hilary chose to defend themselves. This way we hoped to force the prosecution to spell out its charges, and in being more specific, appear less plausible. We all knew only too well that the prosecution would drag in my Spanish experience and contacts as part of the conspiracy charge against me, and this would form the basis of the case against everyone else.

Ben Birnberg chose Kevin Winstain as my barrister. At first I thought it an odd choice. Kevin was very different from the other young barristers who were launching their radical careers on the back of our case: Mike Mansfield and Iain McDonald. His manner appeared downright reactionary and sexist. I was mistaken. Not only had Kevin a brilliant mind, his arrogance and cutting wit was a defensive armour plating hiding one of the kindest, most sympathetic human beings imaginable. In the end there was only one QC on the team, Lawton Scott, who acted for Chris Bott.

x x x

The air of discontent in British society had permeated even the walls of HMP Brixton. The spring and summer of 1972 were hot. As the temperature rose, so too did the tension among the remand prisoners. A riot situation was building up. There had been reports of sit-downs and rooftop protests in other prisons. I can't remember what exactly triggered the first sit-down protest in our prison that summer, but the general agreement amongst the prisoners was that we had had enough. I was among those delegated to negotiate with the prison authorities. The main conditions prisoners wanted improved were food, the right to associate, and proper visiting facilities. And at the heart of our protest – being remand prisoners – was the bail system. The average period spent on remand in 'A' wing at that particular time was nine to twelve months.

Some of these demands were met; the majority were not. I was hauled in front of the governor and received a warning. The prisoners' movement spread throughout the country, not due to us (it had started before we arrived) but because of the intolerable conditions that provoked anger, protest, and, often, violence.

x x x

The British state denies holding any political prisoners. The German state, pressed to reveal how many political prisoners it had, coyly admitted to one in its history – Rudolph Hess. In their definition, there is no such thing as a political prisoner, just criminals. But a political prisoner is never distinct from a criminal. In Nazi Germany, Spain, Russia, Greece, Brazil, Turkey, Baghdad, Tehran, and Guantanamo Bay, political prisoners are incarcerated, and worse, because they have broken the law of the land. The state is the arbiter of what is legal – therefore by definition those who oppose it are criminals. Some states, though, are smarter than others, and recognize that they should separate political activists from unpoliticised prisoners who are disgruntled with the unfair distribution of wealth and class justice.

It is curious that one aspect of hypocrisy has defeated another. The insistence that there were no political prisoners in this country, despite the existence of a political police force such as the Special Branch and the domestic surveillance activities of MI5's F-branch, not to mention political offences, contributed to the defeat of what would have been the usual Establishment-type reform that was later granted in Northern Ireland, and which successfully divided the struggle – the meaningless classification into political and non-political.

x x x

One grey and wet Sunday afternoon, the cell door was unlocked for the tea orderly on his rounds with the large metal container with the grey-brown liquid that passed for tea in Brixton. The screw who unlocked the door had moved on to open the next cell; the one following behind was still closing cells further down the landing. Looking around he whispered that he had an important message for me from a mate I spent some time with on exercise, a security van robber, to make sure I saw him in the yard during afternoon exercise.

When exercise time came round and the doors unlocked, the Navy Lark was just starting so I decided to stay in to listen to what was one of my favourite programmes. I couldn't be bothered to traipse around in the rain, thinking that whatever my friend wanted it could wait. Later, that afternoon, after evening tea, I heard a commotion, some shouts, banging of doors being unlocked, scuffles and the echoing sound of feet running down the iron stairwell. Suddenly there was a tremendous cheer from the cells ... it was a breakout! The whole wing erupted: radios were turned up full blast. At the time I had my radio tuned into Radio Albania. My choice of listening had nothing to do with that station's editorial content, it was purely to hear the signature tune of the station's English language broadcast – *The Internationale*. Turning up the volume full blast to hear the Red Army choir echo throughout the wing was a wonderfully satisfying wind-up and quite exhilarating.

Next day I was given a blow-by-blow account of the escape from one of the friends who failed to get over the wall, but had managed to get back to his cell and bang himself up before he was discovered. They had planned to go to Spain and because of my contacts and knowledge of the language they wanted me to go with them. The two screws on evening slop-out duty had been tied up and locked in the cell. They opened the cell doors on the top landing of those involved in the escape, overpowered another officer, and made for the adjacent control room where they smashed up the radio and alarm system. They then went through the kitchens, over the wall with a ladder (most of them spraining ankles getting down the other side), and nicked a Mini from a couple returning from holiday.

For the next month or so the press was full of stories about 'hobbling bandits' limping gingerly into banks, post offices and building societies, grabbing cash and hobbling out again. We had no doubts who they were, and within two months they were back inside on the 'fours' charged with additional offences of escaping and armed robbery.

They were arrested the very day they were due to fly out to Spain. One of the gang was a bit on the flash side and had taken to driving around town in a Jaguar E-type. On the fateful day, he'd been driving down Charing Cross Road when the plaster cast on his foot was stuck on the accelerator and he plunged straight into the front of the Hippodrome theatre. No one was hurt, but he was arrested and the whereabouts of the others discovered.

'Look how useful you'd have been Stuart, if you'd come with us,' he said. 'We would have needed someone who could speak the language.' I am sure that my return to Franco's Spain with a mob of armed bandits would not have been the wisest of moves. Thank goodness for the Navy Lark.

In the Dock at the Old Bailey

In both the Prescott and Purdie case and our own, the prosecution attempted to argue that they were not ready to proceed. But because they refused us bail (I managed to raise over £100,000 in sureties, including £25,000 from Malcolm Muggeridge, but the police opposed bail at any price), they had to proceed with the trials.

Prescott and Purdie's trial opened on 10 November 1971 at London's Central Criminal Court, better known as the 'Old Bailey'. It lasted almost three weeks. The presiding judge was Mr Justice Melford Stevenson, a man who had been threatened by the Angry Brigade, and was a favourite object of attack because of his extreme right-wing views and prejudiced decisions. According to the legal code he should never have participated in the case, other than as a witness.

Justice Stevenson insisted that he was not holding a political trial. Political trials, he claimed, were unknown in the United Kingdom, which meant that the defendants were not allowed to respond to the political police's evidence with answers in terms of their politics, which might be favourably received by the jury.

Ian Purdie took the wise decision – which may have needed long deliberation, considering the possible interpretation placed upon it – of not giving evidence in his own defence. This had the effect of making the prosecution case stand or fall on the lack of evidence they had against him. As quickly became apparent, they had nothing.

The case against Prescott was based on two pieces of evidence. He had 'confessed' all to two prisoners who had shared his cell for a week in Brixton, Mr A and Mr B, neither of whom was named or whose evidence convinced the jury. Justice Stevenson instructed the jury that these anonymous informers had to be believed, or else it must be admitted that they had conducted 'a really wicked conspiracy with the police'. Which is precisely what the jury believed, given that Prescott was cleared of all charges relating to specific acts of bombing.

The second charge was based on the envelopes in which the Angry Brigade communiqués had been sent to the press. Jake Prescott did not deny addressing the envelopes. He claimed at the time that he did not know what they had been used for – if indeed they had been used at all. The judge directed the jury that if Jake had handled or addressed the envelopes, then he was guilty of conspiracy. On this charge, the jury followed the direction of the judge, though in my view it was a highly dubious piece of reasoning, but explicable when one considers Mr Justice Melford Stevenson's role as a possible victim in the case.

At 7.46 pm on 1 December the jury returned with their verdicts: Ian Purdie, not guilty on all charges; Jake Prescott, guilty of conspiracy, but not guilty on the two specific charges as allegedly admitted to Mr A and Mr B. He was sentenced to fifteen years.

(After Prescott left prison, having completed his sentence, reduced to ten years after the Stoke Newington 8 trial, he wrote to Robert Carr and his family apologising for his involvement in the bombing of their house, an apology that Carr accepted.)

Ian Purdie, acquitted on all charges in the Angry Brigade case, was sent back to prison, having been refused bail, to await trial for forging a cheque for £240. He eventually was granted bail on 23 December.

To bring him up to the promised twelve, Habershon added four names to the conspiracy charge against the six of us. Angela Weir, a teacher in her mid-twenties, was arrested on 11 November; Chris Allen, a Notting Hill play leader and Pauline Conroy, a university lecturer were arrested a week later; and finally, on 18 December 1971, so was Kate McLean, a twenty-one year old former art student from a small village in Kent, then living at 29 Grosvenor Avenue where she worked in Chris Broad's printshop. Kate's dad, Tony McLean, had fought in Spain with the International Brigades during the Spanish Civil War in 1936–7.

x x x

And so, on 3 January 1972, just over a month after the end of the Prescott–Purdie trial, ten of us went forward to the Crown committal proceedings at a new venue in Lambeth Magistrates Court.

On the first day we learned that charges against Pauline Conroy and Chris Allen were to be dropped on grounds of 'insufficient evidence'. Pauline Conroy had been on bail because she had a baby to look after – and she had to fight tooth and nail to get that concession – while Chris Allen had been in Brixton with us.

The crown committal proceedings meant we, the accused, could at last see the prosecution case against us. The magistrate, Mr Herbert Christopher Beaumont MBE, did not go as far as to say that this was not a political case, but he did say that the role of the political police must not be discussed. He did not want the fiction that we had no political police exposed and directed the Special Branch officers not to answer questions on their activities or the interests of their organisation put by any of the defence counsel.

Britain's Political Police

Without an understanding of the role of the Special Branch the trial would be meaningless. It would not just be Hamlet without the ghost, it would be Hamlet with no reference to the murder of Hamlet's father in case it embarrassed the King of Denmark. The outcome of the trial therefore depended on how far counsel and those defending themselves could outwit this stratagem.

The committal outlined a graded conspiracy in which I was cast in the pivotal role. It went back to a period when my co-defendants were still at school in some cases, or just starting at university in others. I had apparently cast my net wide, and linked the First of May Group with the people in the dock, whom the prosecution claimed constituted – or in part constituted – the Angry Brigade.

Our dilemma was that none of us wished to disown the actions of

377

the Angry Brigade. Had we done so, all those who represented what we most despised politically would have been delighted, and I'm not sure that the sentences wouldn't have been greater than they were. Certainly we were revolutionaries. Among those in the dock, I was the only one who defined myself as an anarchist; those of the others who called themselves anything described themselves as libertarian socialists. Our common ground was self-management, anti-capitalism, anti-imperialism and, most importantly, a belief in direct action. We didn't believe people should submit passively to oppression and injustice, and we did believe that they should respond to confrontation. Part of our defence was that these were the very reasons we had been charged – but that did not mean we were guilty.

Then the trial proper began.

x x x

The Edwardian baroque façade of the Old Bailey had been rebuilt in 1907 from the stones of the notorious Newgate Prison, a sink of human misery for hundreds of years, which was only demolished in 1902. It had been the setting for the most infamous cases in world criminal history.

No grand entrance for us, though. Around 9 o'clock in the morning of 31 May 1971, we arrived by van through the prisoners' entrance, round the back and down the ramp into what looked like a supermarket loading bay and into holding cells. At around 9.45, we were taken from our cells through labyrinthine passages, ending in a small oak-panelled room containing a bench and narrow and steeply-inclined wooden staircase, such as you might expect to find in a yacht. This staircase led into the dock of Number One Court. We were about to follow in the footsteps of defendants in the most publicised criminal cases in English history – some appalling, some tragic, and some political: Daniel Defoe, Oscar Wilde, Dr Crippin, Lord 'Haw-Haw' (William Joyce), John Haigh, Derek Bentley, Timothy Evans, my namesake John Reginald Christie, Ruth Ellis, George Blake, James Hanratty, the publishers of *Lady Chatterley's Lover*, and the Kray twins.

x x x

The dock of Number One Court at the Old Bailey could just about hold the eight of us, along with two male and two female dock-officers – twelve in all. We were on the same eye-level as the judge who sat directly across the well of the court. We were surrounded on three sides by a glass screen, presumably to minimize our chances of escape or assassination. On our left, by the main public doors from the Great Hall into the courtroom, was the jury box with two stepped rows of benches for twelve men and women. Between the jury and the judge was the witness box. Directly below the jury was the court reporters' box, with room for perhaps half a dozen hacks. In the centre was the well of the court with tables and chairs for the Clerk of the Court, his bewigged and black-gowned officers and ushers and senior police officers. In the first row of stepped benches to our right sat the prosecution and defence lawyers.

Behind the barristers was a gloaters' box, slightly smaller than that in which the jury sat, reserved for VIPs. Above the VIPs was the steeply raked public gallery where friends and interested parties could watch the mills of British justice grind slow and small. Directly behind the dock was the area reserved for family members of the accused

On special days in the legal calendar of the Corporation of the City of London, Old Bailey judges carry small nosegays of flowers as a smelly reminder of the times when they could hang, draw, quarter, disembowel and burn the entrails of people like us. (The last man to be hanged and beheaded for treason was Colonel Despard in 1803. The authorities remitted the disembowelling and the rest purely to prevent an insurrection among his pro-democracy supporters in post-French Revolution Europe.) The flowers masked the stench of death, disease and decay of Stewart, Hanoverian and Victorian London. This was one of those days – 31 May 1972.

x x x

The Clerk of the Court told everyone to rise, which we did. The buzz of conversation died away. From the door on the right-hand side of the judicial stage emerged a procession of men in fancy furry hats, wigs, ermine-collared crimson robes, gowns and gaiters, in single file. They were led by a clerk wielding an enormous ceremonial sword, which was hung on the wall behind the judge's bench like a sword of Damocles. The medieval flummery came as a surprise to us in the dock and it took me all my time not to laugh out loud. Here was the power of the body politic in its fanciest frocks, as though it was anxious to show that *every* trial was a political trial.

The line-up on the judicial bench consisted of the Lord Mayor of the City of London and his acolytes; the Recorder, the principal legal officer of the City; the Common Sergeant, the legal adviser to the Court of the Common Council; various aldermen – and our trial judge, Mr Justice James. Judge James had been personally selected for our trial by Lord Chief Justice Parker and Edward Heath's Lord Chancellor, Lord Hailsham, because he was a man less obvious in his political leaning than Justice Stevenson.

The Lord Mayor took what appeared to be the best seat in the house, under a wooden canopy, with the presiding judge seated at an unpretentious desk to his right. The Recorder, the Common Sergeant, his City colleagues and the Sheriff sat to the left of the judge.

The Clerk of the Court stood up and read out the charges in the case Regina *v.* Greenfield and others. When he came to my name, the first charge was read out: 'On or about 20 August 1971, at Sydnor Road (where I had parked the Corsair), knowingly had in his possession or under his control certain explosive substances, namely two detonators and a screwdriver, in such circumstances as to give rise to a reasonable suspicion that he did not have them in his possession or under his control for a lawful object.'

As soon as this charge was read out, I shouted loudly that I was innocent and that the detonators had been planted on me by police officers acting under the instructions of Commander Bond. The Clerk politely told me to shut up, and that my defence would be heard in due course. The judge and other dignitaries on the bench looked at me blankly, or maybe they were embarrassed. It was difficult to tell at such a distance. After the arraignments, we sat down and the trial began.

x x x

Not a lot of people knew at the time that defendants had a right of veto over jurors. Seven refusals each, totalling 56: a virtually free hand in rejecting people who might be prejudiced. We tossed them all out one by one – the middle class, the trendy liberals – and focused on trying to empanel a solidly working class jury.

In an unprecedented challenge to the political bias of the courts, we even managed to oblige Mr Justice James to ask jurors if they were members of the Conservative Party, or if they had a relative who was serving in Northern Ireland, a police officer, a member of the judiciary, an employee of Securicor or were prejudiced against anarchism – if so, this might meant they could not give the defendants a fair trial.

In total we challenged fifty-four would-be jurors. The prosecution challenged two. In the end we got more or less the sort of working class jury that we hoped for, one that we hoped would look at the case from our point of view.

When the jury was finally empanelled, John Barker invited them to ask questions directly of the defendants. Mr Justice James nearly had a fit at this attempt to short-circuit the system and ruled against it, insisting that all questions from the jury be passed through him.

The prosecution case revolved around our politics. None of us was prepared to disown the Angry Brigade, which, we believed, was at least doing something – however gestural – to fight back. On the other hand we didn't want to admit responsibility, just because the police had selected us as 'likely candidates' for guilt and fabricated their case accordingly. Our strategy, from the start, was to challenge everything the prosecution said. As Brigadier Frank Kitson had pointed out in his recently published work *Low Intensity Operations*: 'The Law should be used as just another weapon in the government's arsenal, and in this case it becomes little more than propaganda cover for the disposal of unwanted members of the public. For this to happen efficiently, the activities of the legal service have to be tied into the war effort in as discreet a way as possible . . .'

x x x

The trial started in earnest at ten the following morning when the chief prosecuting barrister John Matthew QC (who had also led the prosecution case in the Purdie-Prescott case) rose to give his opening speech to the jury.

'Now members of the jury, the allegation in this case is that these defendants, these eight defendants, calling themselves revolutionaries and anarchists, under various names, sought to disrupt and attack the democratic society of this country, with whose structure and politics they apparently disagree, to disrupt it by a wave of violent attacks over quite a lengthy period, that is, by causing explosions aimed at the property of those whom they considered to be their political or social opponents.'

The allegation was that between March 1968 and August 1971, nineteen bombs were successfully detonated, mostly in London, to damaged buildings; and six further bombs were unsuccessful. On two occasions shots were fired at buildings, namely the Spanish and American Embassy buildings in London. It was the Crown's case that these twenty-five incidents were all linked, and that responsibility for them could be shown to emanate from a common source. They wanted to show that we were all 'part or parties' to that common source, but not necessarily that we were all involved in all of them.

John Matthew spent eight hours delivering his opening speech, only 45 minutes of which were reserved for Angela Weir and Kate McLean, and even less for Chris Bott. I could see a puzzled look on Chris Bott's face as he wondered what the hell all this had to do with him. The idea behind having three people in the dock with absolutely no evidence against them was so that in the event of a hung jury, a compromise could be reached between those for a guilty verdict and those against. It would be a balm for their consciences. I was portrayed as the British contact for the mastermind of global revolution, Octavio Alberola.

John Barker, Hilary Creek and Anna Mendelson were defending themselves. Jim Greenfield, the first name on the indictment, was represented by Ian McDonald. Kevin Winstain and Patrick Mullen acted for me. Ted Glasgow and Joe Harper appeared for Kate McLean, and Mike Mansfield for Angela Weir.

x x x

John Matthew's opening remarks were given huge press attention, but then the blanket of silence descended. Media coverage in favour of the defence was only lifted when Alex Comfort, anarchist poet and scientist, challenged the *Guardian* as to the reasons for the silence, a challenge that was taken up by radio and TV. It was broken again with the presentation of a birthday cake to Anna, an event far too significant for the press to miss out on, even if they could afford not to report that the prosecution case was being bowled over like ninepins – while all the country was assuming that 'the Angry Brigade have been caught . . . they will all get twenty years . . . they ought to get life'. If I was the mastermind, Jim was cast in the role of technical expert; John Barker was the ideologist. Anna, for want of anything better against her, was Jim's moll. (Indeed, had she been his legal wife, they would have had to acquit her; a husband and wife cannot be guilty of conspiracy together.) Hilary they had down as a courier, since it could be proved that she went to France and therefore she must have brought the explosives back with her. In the eyes of the prosecution, the women were never seen as activists in their own right, they were secondary players without any autonomous political identity.

Other than the explosives the police claimed they had found in the flat, there was very little evidence to link any of us to the actual explosions. The prosecution therefore tried to rely on scientific evidence that linked all the bombings to each other and to the materiel supposedly discovered in Amhurst Road. The police called their experts; we called our experts. We reached stalemate, and Matthews more or less gave up on scientific evidence, telling the jury to rely on common sense instead.

x x x

The prosecution case took so long – well into July – that once it was finished it was almost time for the judge's summer holiday. Bewigged, red-robed and ermine-collared, he looked benignly around the courtroom and announced that everyone needed a rest. Even those of us in the dock were politely asked what we thought, despite the fact that for us a holiday was not on the cards. Personally, I was most in favour because I felt August was never my lucky month. However, we were all fed up with the routine – getting up in the morning at seven, washing, shaving, slopping out the piss-pots, going straight from the cells at eight to the Old Bailey, and getting no exercise nor any fresh air throughout the week – week after week. We also had to cart around with us all our worldly goods: books, papers and a mountain of legal depositions, while handcuffed to someone else. This went on for six months. A change is said to be as good as a rest, so a few weeks in god-forsaken Brixton, without going to the Old Bailey each day, came like a month's holiday in Spain . . . certainly the way I remembered it.

x x x

Returning to the Old Bailey after our five-week long holiday was like returning to school for a new term, with all the old familiar faces; the banter among ourselves as to how this juror or that juror was taking it, and jokes about the judge and persecution team. But the exams were upon us instantly – it was our turn to make our case.

John, Hilary, Jim and Anna's defence was that the explosives and weapons in the Amhurst Road flat had been planted by the police. The defence's cross-examination of the police witnesses delved deep into their motives for lying, the psychology of the bomb squad – and underscored the fact that individual innocence or guilt had no bearing whatsoever on the results of a police investigation which had been ordered at Cabinet Office level to get results. A conspiracy had existed, they told the jury, but one that had taken place in smoke-filled back rooms in Whitehall with the object of finding the most 'likely candidates' and getting them into the dock.

John Barker questioned all the police witnesses about similar cases of planting explosives, referring in particular to the collapse that June of the high-profile Saor Eire arms trial at the Old Bailey when the provocateur role of the Special Branch became known. Every time

John mentioned this trial Mr Justice James angrily put him down, telling the jury to disregard what they heard.

But references to specific cases of police corruption in the defence's cross-examination more often than not caught the police witnesses unawares, making them come across as decidedly flaky.

John, Hilary and Anna successfully opened up to the jury about their everyday lives and their politics, about their work in the Claimants' Union and the squatting movement and their research into the activities of property tycoons such as Freshwater. (So effective was this approach that John Matthew made the point to the jury in his summing up that they should disregard any feelings they might have about 'capitalist landlords' and stick strictly to the law.) They also put the question of violence into perspective by comparing the damage done to Robert Carr's kitchen with the fact that 529

John Barker
(Roy Knipe)

building workers died on building sites every year, yet these deaths are neatly reclassified as 'industrial accidents' and buried far from the front pages of the national press and rarely mentioned on the radio or television news.

x x x

A large part of the case against me relied on the perjured testimony of a friend of Ross's called Lisa Byers. She had responded to a newspaper's promise of £10,000 for evidence against the Angry Brigade, and had told Habershon that she had found a machine gun magazine in the glove compartment of my car (actually Albert's car).

Habershon

She thought it might have fitted one of the machine guns the police showed her. As a member of the jury pointed out, 'I've been in the Army and I couldn't recognise what clips fitted that gun. How could that woman, a barmaid, recognise them?' She was lying anyway.

The second thread of their case was my international connections through the Anarchist Black Cross.

Finally, there was the question of a single bullet found in my flat in Fonthill Road, over a year earlier. I hadn't paid much attention to this piece of evidence at the time, thinking nothing of it. I assumed it had been thrown in as general incriminatory makeweight evidence. Not at all. What the bastards had done was take the unfired bullet from my flat in June 1970, load it into the chamber of the Browning 7.65 automatic allegedly taken from Amhurst Road in August 1971 and then eject the unfired and previously pristine bullet, thereby providing an invaluable forensic link between the bullet, the gun and me. When I heard this I almost choked. The brazenness of the fit-up quite took my breath away, and I made the point quite forcefully from the witness box. But I think Matthew was also embarrassed and realised how questionable this piece of evidence was as he didn't pursue the matter and made only a passing reference to it in his summing up of the case against me.

Eventually my turn came to take the witness stand.

x x x

Kevin, my counsel, took me through my life history in the hope that this would allow the jury to see that the motives which had governed all my actions, including my trip into Spain, had been honourable ones. Most accused people avoid mentioning previous convictions when taking the stand; I had thought it best to make my involvement in the Spanish Resistance and the fact that I had been convicted for my part in a plot against Franco's life clear from the start. I hoped it would give them a better idea as to why the police were so determined to get a conviction in my case.

Jim Greenfield
(Roy Knipe)

I told the court of my life since returning from Spain, hoping to show them that a man under constant surveillance by the police and the security service (a fact accepted by the judge and the prosecution counsel alike) and working extremely long hours on the gas conversion contract would not have much opportunity, let alone inclination, to do what was alleged by the police. Then we tackled the evidence. Fellow workers and managers from William Press came to the stand in succession to say that they travelled in my car regularly and that they had never seen anything remotely resembling guns, detonators or magazine clips. They also testified to police harassment, and gave me sterling character references.

The most difficult part of the case against me was a letter found at Amhurst Road, written by me in Spanish and signed Edy. The prosecution wanted to know why I would use a pseudonym, and what the other acronyms, abbreviations and coded references used referred to. Were I to give these names in court, Scotland Yard would have passed them on within hours to their colleagues in the Directorate General of Security in Madrid. The people concerned would have been immediately arrested, tortured and possibly even executed. So I stressed that the letter had to do with the anti-Francoist resistance, and had nothing to do with bombing campaigns.

The detonators had been planted in my car by the police; a fact I had stressed from the moment Commander Bond produced them from his desk drawer, 45 minutes into his interview with me. This protest had been faithfully recorded in the police notes of my interview with Bond. What appears to have happened came out during John Barker's cross-examination of the exhibits officer, DC Michael Doyle, when he said originally thirteen detonators had been 'found' in Amhurst Road. Yet, later it emerged that eleven were 'recovered' from the flat, and one of those was on the floor.

Kevin Winstain, my barrister, put the matter to Sergeant Gilham who had led the raid on Amhurst Road: 'Human beings are often subject to temptation, are they not? And isn't it right that you pocketed two detonators? For a later time, against another suspect who might not have incriminating material in his possession or in his home?'

Hilary Creek
(Roy Knipe)

'Not at all,' replied Gilham.

'And,' continued Winstain, 'with that little touch of nervousness that such an enterprise might induce in a person, you dropped the 11th, having picked up three.'

'I did not, sir.'

'And that's how it dropped on the floor?'

'No, sir.'

Winstain then accused Gilham outright of either planting the detonators himself in the boot of my Ford Corsair, or getting his two junior officers DCs Ashendon or Sivell to do so. Gilham denied doing any such thing. It was down to the jury to decide whom they believed, Gilham, Ashenden, Sivell – or me.

x x x

Now it was the turn of the Crown to question me. Matthew's delivery was very low-key, sometimes sarcastic, sometimes deadpan. He began by describing my anti-Francoist activities in Spain, then examined me on my friendships with Spanish anarchists. These questions had been prepared by Habershon with information provided by the Francoist secret police; the implication being that my association with these men was a crime in itself. The point he was making was that I had done this sort of thing before, and therefore even if not actually guilty of the alleged charges, I was still the sort of character who would have done such things and should therefore be put away for a considerable period of time.

He went through a few of my connections – Alain Pecunia, Alberola – and some of my articles in *Black Flag* that supported various First of May actions. But after a couple of hours he sat down. I was surprised. He had been nowhere near as hard on me or as sarcastic as he had been with the others. In fact he had been extremely straightforward.

Habershon sat strangely impassive throughout the rest of my cross-examination. Every time I looked towards John Matthew to reply to his questions all I could see was Habershon's egg-shaped face staring up at me emotionlessly from the well of the court. He looked slightly out of place among the black robes and stony grey wigs in his green tweed suit.

After two and a half days in the witness box I was asked to stand down, which I did with a sense of relief. It was over, for better or worse. As I came down the steps I looked at Habershon. As our eyes met I wondered what thoughts were going through his brain at that moment. His face was inscrutable, but I had a feeling he knew then that he'd lost the jury in my case.

x x x

Chris Bott, like Ian Purdie, did not take the stand. It had already been submitted for him that there was no case to answer, and no evidence to suggest he was in any way involved other than his friendship with John and the fact that he had turned up at Amhurst Road the morning after the raid. There was even less evidence against Kate McLean so she too did not go into the witness box. Angela Weir did go into the witness box and produced evidence to the effect that she was not the person who had accompanied John Barker to France the day before the raid. She had been in London attending a Gay Liberation demonstration in Fleet Street.

Anna Mendelson was the first of the self-defendants to address the jury. Tired and ill, she had to take several breaks during her closing remarks, the thrust of which was to refute all the charges against her.

John Barker's summing up of his case for the defence was a truly brilliant piece of advocacy, worthy of Tom Paine. Everyone commented admiringly on the way he handled his case. One lawyer observed that people were paid a king's ransom for making cross-examinations and closing speeches like his.

John first challenged the absurd idea – central to the prosecution's case – that associating with people who might be involved with the Angry Brigade meant that you were conspiring with them. Then he moved on to the explosives, which he claimed had been planted. In reply to Matthew's question as to why this issue had not been mentioned before the trial, John said:

'If you make allegations in a magistrates' court, the response is "that it is for the jury to decide", and that is absolutely right. It is for you to decide and not for anyone else. And that is why I have waited, sometimes patiently, to put my side of things to the people who matter. You are the twelve independent people who live in the real world. And you are the people with the power. You are the first people I have come across in any of the courts who have the power to acquit or convict. So the question of a plant is for you.'

Answering Matthew's charge that the bombings had stopped since our arrest (which in fact they hadn't), John Barker argued that perhaps the Angry Brigade had decided that it was not worth continuing if the price of bombing was the arrest of eight innocent people. Maybe the Angry Brigade had decided that bombings were no longer relevant or appropriate, especially with the miners' strike and the dockers' actions around the Industrial Relations Bill:

'Perhaps they now feel that bombs are completely irrelevant, and that the class war is being fought, and that the Angry Brigade doesn't have to make symbolic gestures with bombs to make it real – because it is real!'

Hilary Creek then made her final address to the jury. She talked about other aspects of the inconsistencies in the police case and the fact that most of the materials they claimed were evidence of conspiracy such as notebooks with names and addresses, directories and information from Companies House, were only materials used to research the nature of power. She spoke to the jury as human beings, rather than as functionaries of the state:

'We have all been sitting here for six months, and I think you know us. We have talked about ourselves, our politics, and how we carried them out. We told you that that was not by bombing. You have seen us react to questioning. You have heard me speak. I am not an actress. If I am, then I must be

Anna Mendelson
(Roy Knipe)

the finest in the world and am due for an Oscar to have done what I have done for the past six months. You see, the Bomb Squad is still in existence – the same as it was sixteen months ago. It is also admitted that they are still looking for four people. Although they might have been getting close with us, the fact still remains they got the wrong people – and that's not good enough.'

x x x

Finally Mr Justice James began his summing up. He started by saying that there were not many trials in which a political motive was something of importance, but it was here: 'Finding people with the right political motives has been one of the main focuses of the police investigation in the Angry Brigade bombings.' However, he went on: 'This is not a political trial. I direct you to have none of it.'

In reference to the defence claim that the police had planted guns, ammunition and explosives, and furthermore had lied throughout their testimony, Judge James said 'It is true that in such a large organisation as the Metropolitan Police there are bound to be a few black sheep. But, the vital question for you, members of the jury, is: did what is alleged happen in this case? You will make up your minds on the evidence taking into account your assessment of the witnesses involved.'

They were told to weigh carefully the allegations of brutality by the police. It was up to the jury to decide whether in fact Jim Greenfield had been grabbed by the testicles by Ashenden, bounced from wall to wall and given a black eye and bleeding nose. They had to decide if it were true that John Barker had been suspended upside down in a toilet while the other police officers punched and kicked him in the cells at Albany Street.

At last he came to the core of the trial: the conspiracy. The offence, he said, lay in the agreement. Even if the agreement was not put into effect, it remained an offence. The Crown did not have to prove that any of the eight of us actually caused any of the explosions, simply that they agreed to: 'You have to be satisfied that the prosecution has proved that there was one agreement to cause explosions, to which each of the accused had made himself a party, to return a verdict of guilty on that charge.

'As long as you know what the agreement is, then you are a conspirator. You needn't necessarily know your fellow conspirators, nor need you always be active in the conspiracy. All you need to know is the agreement. It can be effected by a wink or a nod, without a word being exchanged. It need have no particular time limit, no particular form, no boundaries.'

Judge James noticeably avoided any reference to a shake of the hand, presumably to avoid upsetting the freemasons present such as Bond, who appeared to be shifting uncomfortably in his seat at this definition of conspiracy.

The Spanish element, which the prosecution had began by making so much of, was dropped.

x x x

Judge James finished his massive summing up on Monday 4 December 1972, after eight days and an estimated quarter of a million words.

By now, our trial had entered the Guinness Book of Records as the longest trial of the century. The jury filed out to their room at lunchtime to consider the 109 days of evidence and the millions of words spoken in the court during that period. We were ushered out of the dock to wait. It was, to say the least, nerve-racking.

By 4.30 the jury still had not reached a conclusion so the judge adjourned them for the night. I spent most of that time pacing up and down in my cell wondering what verdict the jury would reach, and what the consequences would be, to me and those I loved. A second twenty-year sentence would not be easy to get through, especially as there was unlikely to be a prolonged international campaign trying to secure my early release.

Emotionally exhausted and filled with trepidation, we filed up the stairs into the dock of Number One Court at 10 a.m. the following morning. We all wondered if this would be the last day of the trial – and the first day of the rest of our lives. The jury still had not reached a verdict and again we were packed off downstairs to while away the time, chatting, playing cards, but all the time thinking of what the future held.

Eventually, twenty-two hours after retiring, the jury returned to the court with a question for the judge. They wanted to know why the area of Amhurst Road had not been evacuated during the police

search – a telling question indeed. By late afternoon the jury still had
not been able to reach a verdict. It meant another sleepless night in
Brixton.

x x x

The film shown on television that night was one of the all-time great
courtroom movies –*12 Angry Men*. It was a powerful drama about a
jury's deliberations in an apparently open-and-shut murder case, one
in which the defendant has a weak alibi. Eleven of the jurors
immediately vote for a guilty verdict, but one juror – Henry Fonda –
refuses to accept the prosecution case at face value and holds out for
a not guilty verdict, gradually persuading the others to vote likewise.
Habershon, Bond and the Bomb Squad rank and file were apoplectic
the next day. They were convinced this film had been deliberately
dropped into the broadcasting schedules at the last moment by Angry
Brigade sympathisers in the BBC to sway the jury against the police
case. If only! But it was certainly fortuitous from our point of view,
and no doubt it added something to the unfolding deliberations in the
jury room.

x x x

Perhaps to eliminate the Henry Fonda, eventually the judge called the
jurors in from the jury room and said, 'You have spent a long time
giving your consideration to this matter. When I asked you to retire to
consider your verdict I told you to return a unanimous verdict.
Having regard to the passage of time, will you please retire again and
seek to arrive at verdicts in respect of those counts upon which at
least ten of you can agree.' The members of the jury were sent back to
their room and we were returned to the dungeons of the Old Bailey.
Thoughts of a hung jury and another six-month retrial flashed through
my mind.

As the afternoon wore on, we grew quiet and introspective. Late in
the afternoon Judge James assembled the court and told the jury that
he would not be sending them to a hotel that night. The court would
sit until a verdict was decided. It was a crude attempt to pressure

them into reaching a decision. The jury went back to their room again, visibly tired from their wrangling. We went downstairs for our daily visits. I had just sat down to chat reassuringly with Brenda when one of the prison officers tapped me on the back and said we had to go back into court – the jury was coming back with its verdict. This was it.

'Not Guilty, Your Honour'

Until the moment I went into the witness box, most of the barristers and solicitors present, with the exception of Kevin and Birnberg's team, thought I was certain to go down. Even after that strangely muted prosecution case, a guilty verdict was always a possibility, but I felt optimistic about my prospects.

The police witnesses' account of finding the two detonators in the Corsair was flaky, to say the least. The dates they had concocted for the conspiracy charge started immediately after my return from Spain – a haste which would have bespoken a man even crazier than the one they saw before them – and during which time most of the others in the dock were still at school.

And in one way the length of the trial, and of each of our testimonies, was in our favour. The juries had, as Hilary said, got to know us. The police wanted to paint me as an evil mastermind; but for six months they had seen an average working-class guy, who worked long hours with very ordinary working-class mates, and who was being persecuted for the ideas he held about the way society could be better.

x x x

It was early evening when we climbed the steep, dark rickety flight of stairs to the dock to await the jury's return and their verdict. The court was packed. The press benches – which had remained empty for so long apart from the Press Association man, David May of *Time Out*, Bea Campbell of the *Morning Star* and *Guardian* reporter, Jackie Leishman – were full of reporters already working out the following day's headlines. One agency reporter – agencies are supposed to supply factual and unbiased information to the press – was overheard saying, 'I hope they all go down.' The public gallery was overflowing, as was the area behind us reserved for relatives, all nervously waiting to hear what the jury had decided.

Finally, the wood-panelled door leading to the jury room opened and the twelve men and women edged their way to their benches. It was 5.15 p.m. The foreman, seated closest to the judge, was the last to take his place. We scanned the jurors' haggard faces, anxious for some hint as to the verdicts they had reached. Their faces were inscrutable, but it didn't look good. They were avoiding our eyes. The judge asked them if they had reached a verdict. The foreman, a middle-aged working-class man still in his shirtsleeves, self-consciously answered, 'Yes.' The Old Bailey's Chief Administrator, Leslie Boyd, took him through each charge and each name on the indictment. The first and most important charge was that of conspiracy to cause explosions.

The atmosphere was electric. We could hear and feel our hearts pumping. Then came the verdicts. We strained to hear every quietly spoken word.

'James Greenfield – guilty of conspiring to cause explosions;

Anna Mendelson – guilty of conspiring to cause explosions;

John Barker – guilty of conspiring to cause explosions;

Hilary Creek – guilty of conspiring to cause explosions.'

Then it was my turn. I steeled myself as the Judge asked the foreman how they had found against me.

'Not guilty, your honour.'

x x x

My first thought was that I hadn't heard correctly and was in some altered state of consciousness. I could hardly believe it. Apart from the planted detonators all the evidence against me was circumstantial.

As for the detonators, it came down to my word against Detective Sergeant Gilham's. The jury had believed me and not Gilham.

I only just registered, peripherally almost, that Chris, Angie and Kate had also been acquitted.

The feelings of euphoria I experienced were tempered by the desolate faces of John, Anna, Jim and Hilary. For them it had been a defeat, tempered by a little victory. It could so easily have gone their way. However, they would not be leaving the courtroom that day as I would, through the front portals into the real world. Their exit would be in handcuffs, through the back gate in a cellular prison van and driven through the sodium-lit streets of London to Holloway Jail and Wormwood Scrubs for who knew how many years.

After delivering the thirty-one verdicts, the foreman was so overcome with the emotion of the moment that he had to sit down, having been given a glass of water by the usher. Recovering his composure, the foreman stood up again and turned to Judge James to make a courageous plea: 'Us members of the jury would like to ask your lordship for – I believe the word is leniency, or clemency – but that is what we would like to ask.'

x x x

It was a ten-to-two majority verdict. The mainly working-class jury initially failed to agree on convicting the first four. In the end they reached a compromise. Ten jurors wanted to convict the first four – but only if the others were acquitted on all charges. Two of them stuck out for a complete acquittal of all eight of us, but were over-ruled by the other ten.

For three days the jury had been divided seven to five – five for acquittal on all charges. In the end, a majority verdict had led to a squalid compromise. But despite the guilty verdict, it had still been a victory for those who had defended themselves. They had made a powerful and moving case against the system, without using the tools of the system itself, and had come as close as they ever could to being acquitted.

The jury could well understand why someone would want to blow up Franco – and why, in that case, he would be a target for conservative-minded policemen pursuing a right-wing agenda at the behest of Edward Heath's Cabinet Office.

x x x

Judge James told the four of us who had been acquitted we could leave the dock. John, Jim, Hilary and Anna turned to embrace us before we were taken downstairs for the last time. They had to remain behind to hear their sentences. It was an extremely emotional moment. My heart thumped with happiness at my imminent freedom and my gut churned with guilt at leaving them to their fate. This was no play – it was for real. The curtain would not come down and rise later with these four people walking happily out hand in hand, as they had walked in, or taking a bow before an applauding audience. During the interval which was to follow, they would be locked away in cells and grow older, their young lives drained away in sacrifice to the state.

Still defiant toward the court, the four offered no mitigation in their defence. They put on a brave face and managed sardonic smiles as Justice James launched into his sentencing speech, saying how sorry he was to see 'educated people' in their situation. He added that 'undoubtedly a warped understanding of sociology' had brought them to their present state.

'The conspiracy of which you have been convicted had as its object the intention of disrupting and attacking the democratic society of this country. That was the way it was put by the Crown, and that is the way it has been proved to the satisfaction of the jury once the suggestion of planting of evidence had been got rid of on overwhelming evidence. *Sentencing the Angry Brigade*

'For the purposes of sentence, I propose to disregard any of the incidents which occurred before responsibility is claimed by the Angry Brigade communiqués. That shortens the period and reduces the number of explosions.'

Judge James continued: 'The means you adopted could have been even more lethal than they were, but I am satisfied on the evidence that the devices you used were not deliberately designed to cause death or serious injury, but rather damage to property ... Your participation arose because you objected to the orderly way of society. One of the most precious rights is that an individual should hold his opinions and be able to express them and be able to protest, and when one finds others who set out to dominate by exercising their opinions to the extent of enforcing them with violence it undermines that precious right ... Undoubtedly, you have in many of your interests sought to do good, and have done good, and I count that in your favour. But when all is said and done the public is entitled to protection ... I am going to reduce the totality of the sentences, by reasons of the jury's recommendation, by five years.'

He then proceeded to weigh off all four to various sentences on the different charges of conspiracy and possession. As he went through them the years started to mount up – fives, eights and tens. At the end he added the crucial word – concurrent – making a total of ten years. With remission for good behaviour they could be out in seven years.

x x x

As John Barker later reflected, in his case, 'they had framed a guilty man – and there were plenty holes in the frame.' But equally, John said of the later actions, when they knew they had become the focus of the Angry Brigade investigation, '. . . it was fucking madness. We continued out of stubbornness, the Angry Brigade having a dynamic of its own, and most of all from a naïve, romantic sense of loyalty. Two comrades who had been arrested should not be deserted, left on their own, even though our addresses or names had been in a captured address book. Continuing in these circumstances was not being serious taken to a new level, it was foolhardy; the youthful feeling that nothing very terrible could happen to us and fuck them, we'll show them.'

Anna was the first to speak before leaving the dock. She thanked the two jury members who had consistently held out for an acquittal. Jim, John and Hilary added their voices to this sentiment before they too were led downstairs to the prison vans waiting to take the men to

Wormwood Scrubs, the allocation jail for first-timers, and Hilary and Anna back to Holloway.

The trial had lasted 109 days, involved more than 200 witnesses, 688 exhibits and more than 1000 pages of depositions and statements. The judge's summing up alone ran to 250,000 words. After seven months of debate, the verdict, the judges remarks and sentencing took only 45 minutes.

Jake and Ian

Jim and Anna were the only two in the dock charged with causing explosions, one at Paddington Green Police Station and another at the Italian Consulate in Manchester, but the jury acquitted them in both cases. But all four, like Jake Prescott, were convicted on the main count of conspiracy. According to Mr Justice James, all that was required for proof was a nod, a wink, a state of mind, an opinion, a secret thought . . . On this basis they could have arrested and charged hundreds if not thousands at the time. It was a judgment against the whole radical movement – everyone was a conspirator.

x x x

In spite of the jury's verdicts, Habershon and Bond remained adamant that everyone who had stood in the dock was guilty. In reply to question at a press conference, Bond said: 'How do we know that the eight did not do it?' He made a number of unfavourable comments about the eight of us as a whole, and then made a pointed reference about me in particular. 'The evidence presented during the trial showed quite clearly the defendant's international links. The explosives came from France and Christie had contacts there and in Spain ... Christie has admitted being an anarchist.' Someone interjected: 'But that is not the same as being a member of the Angry Brigade.' Bond answered, 'What's the difference?'

The best post-trial press comment in a mainstream newspaper came from the London *Evening Standard*. In an article headlined, 'The Red badge of revolution that is creeping across Britain', its leader writer wrote: 'These guerrillas are the violent activists of a revolution comprising workers, students, teachers, trade unionists, homosexuals, unemployed and women striving for liberation. They are all angry ... Whenever you see a demonstration, whenever you see a queue for strike pay, every public library with a stock of socialist literature. . . any would be a good place to look. In short, there is no telling where they are.'

I couldn't have put it better myself.

There was no victory for either side, and no defeat either.

The only victory was for the jury system itself. The jury had carried the day by showing that trials are about justice as well as evidence. By rejecting much of the prosecution case the jury – as John Barker described it, 'the critically intelligent citizenry in action' – had shown that the conduct of Bond and Habershon's officers had left something to be desired.

Releasing The Angry Brigade

The Lord Chancellor, Lord Hailsham, ordered an immediate post-trial inquiry – which took place between 14 December 1972 and 17 January 1973 – to 'learn the lessons of the case and to prevent a similar outcome arising in future', particularly with regard to jury selection. Never again would defendants be allowed to choose a jury of their peers. Also, thereafter, most major trials of a political nature were held outside London, in places in the commuter belt like Winchester, where the Crown could be reasonably certain of a comfortably middle-class jury list to ensure the conviction of the enemies of the state. Winchester Crown Court happens to be the only Crown Court in England where the majority of the population is employed by the Ministry of Defence. The most famous example was the 1973 trial of the Winchester Eight: Delours and Marian Price, Gerry Kelly, Hugh Feeney and four others. The eight IRA members were sentenced to life imprisonment, plus twenty years, for the Old Bailey and Great Scotland Yard Police Station bombings in Whitehall in March 1973. One person died and around 200 were injured in the Old Bailey blast. The last trial in Winchester that I recall was that of three IRA members charged in 1988 with the attempted murder of Tom King, the then Minister of Defence.

The Winchester Eight, 1973

Looking at the Angry Brigade case in context, apart from cheering up the powerless with dramatic gestures, the six-month trial was probably its most enduring achievement. As well as a vindication of the jury system, the trial provided an extraordinary public forum that allowed us – particularly John, Hilary and Anna who defended themselves – to speak directly to twelve ordinary men and women about ourselves, our ideas and our motives. We were people who didn't want to see the planet run forever unchallenged by fools and knaves – yet the trial showed that these were the only ones who wanted to govern it.

x x x

Free again and outside the court I was happily reunited with Brenda. With Kevin Winstain, Ben Birnberg and Jenny (my solicitor's clerk who had done most of the foot-slogging legal work in my defence case) we hailed a taxi and headed for the King's Cross offices of the London weekly *Time Out* where the Stoke Newington Eight Defence

The Stoke Newington 8

The trial.
(Roy Knipe)

Committee had organised a press conference and to announce a demonstration to Holloway Jail the following day. Tony Elliott, the publisher of *Time Out*, and David May, its news editor, had been consistently supportive of the Stoke Newington Eight Defence Committee since our arrest, and had laid on champagne for the four acquitted and the SN8 defence group. After Chris Bott, Angela Weir, Kate McLean and I answered the media's mostly obvious questions, Brenda and I took off to spend the first night of my regained freedom in a nearby hotel.

Metaphorically speaking, we had left the corpses of our comrades Jim, John, Hilary and Anna lying on the battlefield. As I was exploring the mini-bar, Jim and John were being inducted into the dour surroundings of Wormwood Scrubs' 'C'/'A' Wing, and Hilary and Anna were trying to come to terms with who knows how many years in even worse women's prisons up and down the country.

Now it was the turn of the vultures. The scavengers of Fleet Street screeched around to pick the bones not only of the fallen, but, in an unprecedented attack of spite, of the survivors as well.

Rupert Murdoch's *Sun* had clearly prepared its story on the assumption that we would all be found guilty. It claimed that the house in which most of my co-accused had lived in Wivenhoe, Essex years before had been used for drugs, sex and orgies. They squawked: 'most revolting of all their activities was ritual slaughter. Turkeys stolen from a local farm were torn and slashed to pieces ... Afterwards the revellers, drugged, drunk and exhausted, collapsed on the kitchen floor to sleep off their orgy in a ghastly mess of blood and fragmented flesh.'(The reality was more prosaic. One year Jim Greenfield stole a turkey for their Christmas dinner and was arrested by the local police, who followed the trail of feathers from the still-squawking bird from the nearby farm to their cottage.)

And of course they trolled out the Fleet Street version of my past.

The *Daily Express* was equally vicious in its appraisal of the trial and the four condemned young people, but slightly more cautious in dealing with those of us who were acquitted.

x x x

The better class of papers, such as the *Daily Telegraph*, went for a more sophisticated version of the same rubbish. The Tory broadsheet was scornful of the fact that the Angry Brigade had killed or injured nobody. This made them a 'pale imitation' of the anarchists they admired – 'figures like Ravaschol (sic) or Hosea (sic) Garcia Oliver'. Presumably believing that Juan Garcia Oliver was some long-dead anarchist and not alive and living in Mexico City and capable of legal action (I sent him a copy of the *Daily Telegraph*) – he went on to say that 'Hosea' Garcia Oliver had 'boasted' that his was the hand that killed 253 men.

Juan Garcia Oliver

The press could not forgive the moderation of the Angry Brigade, protesting vigorously that they were amateurs, and not a patch on the 'old anarchists'.

Even the local rag in Blantyre had a go at me, which I saw when Brenda and I went home to see my parents. The lead article in the *Blantyre Advertiser* – in fact it looked like the only article – carried the banner headline that read 'Christie in Blantyre'. By the tone of the article it should have read, 'Dracula back in the Carpathians'.

Anyone deluded enough to believe their guff must have remained under the illusion that I wanted people to accept freedom from government by obliging them to do so under force of arms. I had never believed or argued in any way, at any time, in any pub or publication that violence was an effective way to change society. The only groups consistently using coercion, violence, weapons and explosives to impose their will or as a form of political argument are those allied to governments. Although anarchists may attempt (sometimes successfully) to kill a tyrant and those who serve him with their brutality, thereby resisting illegitimate authority by violent means, no anarchist would dream of using violence to impose views which have at their heart voluntary cooperation. In fact, most anarchists I know who have been in prison have been there in punishment for non-violent protest against their rulers' resort to violence.

x x x

Our case concluded, Edward Heath and his Cabinet handed out the glittering prizes to their good and faithful servants. Mr Justice James was appointed a Lord Justice of Appeal, Detective Chief Superintendent Roy Habershon – who wept in court on being commended for his loyal service to the Crown by Judge James – was promoted to Commander and seconded to the Home Office's Research and Planning Office in 1973. In 1974, he headed the investigation into police involvement in the death of Warwick University student Kevin Gateley in Red Lion Square on 5 June 1974. His report absolved the police of all responsibility. In April 1975, Commander Habershon replaced Robert Huntley as head of the Bomb Squad.

Commander X did well. Bond was awarded the Queen's Police Medal and made Deputy Assistant Commissioner, responsible for all CID operations for the whole of the Metropolitan Police, retiring in 1976 to pursue his hobbies, DIY and freemasonry.

The Home Office, too, drew lessons from the trial. Sir John Waldron had been retired as Metropolitan Police Commissioner in April 1972 and replaced with Heath's appointee Sir Robert Mark, a new broom for the Yard. Mark immediately authorised the expansion of the Special Branch to around 500 detectives. He also appointed a new head of the Branch to take over from Ferguson-Smith, Deputy Assistant Commissioner Victor Gilbert.

The security service also had an urgent makeover. Sir Martin Furnival-Jones stood down as head of MI5 and his place was taken by another Heath appointee, the ultra-reactionary Sir Michael 'Jumbo' Hanley, chosen in preference to the more liberal Home Office candidate James Waddell. MI5's 'F' Branch, responsible for domestic counter-subversion, became the pre-eminent department within the security service with Hanley pouring in men and resources to root out, as he described them, the 'far and wide left'.

A new anti-terrorist section, F3, was set up to deal with the emergent threat from groups such as the Angry Brigade, and FX set up to infiltrate them and run informers throughout the trade unions, the universities, extra-parliamentary pressure groups and the media. K Branch, the department responsible for monitoring the state's former public demons – Soviet spies and Comintern fifth columnists in government – was downgraded, sidelined and hung out to dry. The new enemy within was both the red menace and yellow peril rolled into one.

x x x

The Angry Brigade was an ad hoc creation of its time. To me, and I suppose quite a few other people, it appeared a natural and spontaneous response to the ideology of selfishness, arrogant management rhetoric and the punitive anti-working class legislation introduced by Edward Heath after his election in June 1970. It struck a lost chord which found resonance at a particular moment in time, in spite of all the blustering in the media in their crude attempts to roll back dissent. Throughout this period, thousands of people wore Angry Brigade badges on anti-Tory and anti-Vietnam War demonstrations up and down the country.

The attitudes and values which shaped the ends of the Angry Brigade were overtaken by events. On 9 August 1971, ten days or so before our arrest, Edward Heath's government had arrested and imprisoned 342 people in Northern Ireland – not because they had committed a crime, but because of their background, friends or likelihood of political resistance to the government. This had provoked one of the last Angry Brigade actions before our arrest, the **Bloody Sunday** bombing of a British Army recruiting office in the Holloway Road. Six months later, thirteen citizens of Derry were shot dead by British soldiers during a peaceful civil rights demonstration. The effect of this was to trigger a serious ongoing Provisional IRA bombing and murder campaign over many years in which countless numbers of innocent people would be killed, suffer serious injury, or be subjected to grief and bereavement.

x x x

Nationalists and religious zealots do not discriminate between those they see as their enemies. Everyone – capitalists, generals, princes and workers alike – is 'the enemy', and as there are more of the last it is mostly the ordinary people who are hit. Anarchists have a 'bad name' in the media, not because they can point to one indiscriminate massacre by anarchists – there have been none – but because the one thing holders of power fear is that they personally should be held responsible for their own actions.

An IRA sympathiser with whom I used to pass the time of day in Brixton's exercise yard talked half-jokingly about all the wicked things anarchists had done in the past. One had thrown a bomb at the King of Spain on his wedding day, others had done all sorts of terrible things to the French bourgeoisie in the 1890s. He forgot to mention what terrible things the bourgeoisie had done to the workers after the annihilation of the Paris Commune. 'One thing I notice though,' I told him, 'the victims of the anarchists you're talking about do have names and histories, and a context . . . they are not just any innocent passers-by.' His answer was: 'Those are the fortunes of war.'

Following the Angry Brigade trial, the police cast all pretence of due process to the winds, particularly in cases involving the IRA which began stepping up its mainland bombing campaign in March with two large car bombs, one at the Old Bailey itself and the other outside the Ministry of Agriculture and Fisheries in Whitehall Place. The Judges' Rules were thrown out the window: the Winchester Eight charged with the 3 March 1973 Old Bailey and Whitehall bombings, for example, were kept naked in their cells for days with no access to a lawyer while they were being interrogated.

Henceforth Europe's police forces co-operated openly and without concern for public opinion or civil liberty. After all, there had been no outrage expressed about the use of the conspiracy laws in our case. It had been accepted without a murmur, as had internment and sensory deprivation – officially sanctioned torture – in Northern Ireland, and later the use of British troops in a policing role on the streets of Britain. The last pretence that Interpol and Scotland Yard did not concern themselves with political affairs had been brushed aside.

x x x

Prison took a far greater physical and psychological toll on the women than it did on the men. Anna Mendelson was the first to be released, on parole, on completion of the obligatory six years of her sentence in 1977. There was a great outcry in the media: 'They are releasing the Angry Brigade.' The press swooped on her as soon as the news broke. The story, having broken over Anna, ceased to be newsworthy and the others came out one by one. Hilary, the youngest, was released six months after Anna, her eyes weakened by a six month spell in a permanently-lit underground isolation cell. John and Jim, who both refused to apply for parole, came out in 1978, and Jake Prescott, first in, last out, early in 1979. (It seemed logical that after the ten-year sentences passed on John, Jim, Hilary and Anna, Jake Prescott's should be reduced, which the Appeal Court eventually did, bringing his sentence down from fifteen years to ten years.) Several of those acquitted had still had to face cheque-kiting charges. But as they had already served more than enough time for such relatively minor offences, they were released on conviction.

x x x

After the euphoria of acquittal came the dustcart of everyday life. I had an officially cleared character and £2.50 in cash. I contacted William Press's personnel manager to ask for my old job back. After a few weeks I received an official reply saying: 'Due to a change in programme we have now suspended all recruitment on the central London contract.' I tried other jobs, but as soon as the prospective employers heard my name and remembered in what context they'd heard it before, all doors politely closed on me. If they hadn't heard of me, they asked what I'd been doing for the last eighteen months.

After spending a couple of weeks in Blantyre with my recently reunited Mum and Dad, Brenda and I moved back to London, to a small flat in Wimbledon – Allington Close at the top of Wimbledon Hill. It had been Brenda's Granny's flat in an ostlers tenement attached to nearby stables.

Although I was jobless, I wasn't idle. As well as applying for work everywhere I could, I had finished a translation of a biography of Francisco Sabaté Llopart— '*Sabaté: Guerrilla Extraordinary*', who had been killed in a dramatic ambush by Franco's Civil Guard on 5 January 1960. I was doing the rounds of London publishers trying to interest them in the book, but I was having no success. There was little sympathy for books on anarchism, anarchists or anti-Francoists, because it was thought there was no market for them, unless written by reputable academics.

Sabaté: Guerilla Extraordinary

This rejection first put the germ of the idea into my head of setting up an anarchist publishing house and breaking through the censorship barriers that way.

The idea for the publishing house took firm root during the

summer of 1973. After being cooped up for eighteen months in Brixton I was in desperate need of exotic food in interesting places with old and new friends. Brenda and I arranged to spend July and August travelling through Europe, camping and staying with old friends and comrades. Before heading off on our travels, I visited Octavio Alberola in Liège to discuss developments in Franco's Spain.

No One's Blood on
My Conscience

The Anarchist Black Cross had been hit badly by the Europe-wide repression of the previous year, mainly in Germany where *Berufsverbote*, the witch-hunt depriving leftists of their professional employment, had reached almost McCarthyite proportions. Georg von Rauch, founder of the Anarchist Black Cross in Germany, had been shot dead by West Berlin police in December 1971. He was unarmed and had his arms in the air. Two months later Tommy Weissbecker, the Anarchist Black Cross's 23-year old secretary, was also shot dead by police in an Augsburg street while producing his ID. He had been under surveillance for some time. But it wasn't entirely a one-way process. In May, Milan police inspector Luigi Calabresi – the man widely believed to have been responsible for the murder of Italian Black Cross secretary, Giuseppe Pinelli – had been shot dead outside police headquarters. Not by an anarchist, but by a member of the Marxist Lotta Continua group, a group he had been suing for defamation of character.

Being in Europe again and talking with those still suffering the consequences of Franco's rule restored my energy after the Angry Brigade trial. Franco Leggio, an old friend, had run a one-man press for years in Sicily – *La Fiaccola* – and his publications had made a considerable impact throughout Italy. Albert Meltzer had been doing much the same in London, also against all the odds, but specialising mainly in duplicated pamphlets and papers. He too had lots of experience to draw upon, especially when it came to the uncertain financial times – and there were lots of those to come. Without Albert our publishing project could never have survived as long as it did.

The Birth of Cienfuegos Press

I decided to call the imprint Cienfuegos Press, after Camilo Cienfuegos, the popular libertarian Cuban revolutionary who died in mysterious circumstances in 1959. So I went out and leased an IBM Selectronic typesetting machine and reinvented myself as a publisher. Apart from Cienfuegos Press's books, the IBM machine also meant we could now typeset *Black Flag* and transform it from a short-run, shabby, duplicated publication, printed on poor quality paper and held together by staples, to a smartly-produced newspaper with clear photographs and sharp text set in Bold, Medium and Roman Helvetica – the only set of IBM golfballs we had – and printed on Albert's new Gestelith offset-litho on crisp white paper.

x x x

We had much to write about in *Black Flag* that autumn. In Bristol, two young anarchists, Dafydd Ladd and Michael Tristam, had been arrested and charged on 14 September with bomb attacks on fascist Portugal's vice consulates in Bristol and Cardiff, and the British Army's officers' club in Aldershot. They were sentenced to seven years and six years respectively the following February. And in December Edward Heath introduced the three-day working week.

On a more explicit level of brutality, Chile's President Allende had been killed in a US-backed coup and at least 5,000 leftists and liberals had been arrested, tortured and killed – 'disappeared' – in the repression that followed. Over a million Chileans had gone into exile. In Spain, things were also taking a turn for the worse. On 20 December, Franco's prime minister, Admiral Luis Carrero Blanco, was killed in his car in a Madrid street by an ETA commando with a massive culvert bomb. The blast was so enormous it blew his car over the roof of the church where he had just attended mass. Had it been Ascension Day it would have added a nice touch of irony. Carrero Blanco had been pivotal in Franco's plans for the succession and continuity of his regime and Franco never fully recovered from

Luis Carrero Blanco Assassinated

Carrero's death. The hard-liners were beside themselves with rage and almost lost the plot completely. Carlos Iniesta, the fundamentalist Director General of the Civil Guard, immediately ordered his men 'to repress subversives and demonstrators energetically without restrictions on the use of firearms'. Carrero Blanco's place as prime minister was taken by Carlos Arias Navarro, the 'butcher of Málaga', the man responsible for the mass summary executions in that city in early 1937. Three anarchists in custody were sentenced to death and one executed by garrotte. Hearing of this judicial murder and the manner of his death was a horrific sensation. I kept running and re-running the whole scene in my mind's eye. The response of anti-fascists around Europe was immediate, with protest marches, pickets, petitions, and bomb attacks on Francoist institutions around the world and railway lines into Spain blocked or sabotaged by protestors. More arrests followed. By April 1974 there were sixty anarchists awaiting trial in Franco's public order courts, and fourteen facing a military tribunal and possible death penalties.

I went to Paris and Brussels a couple of times to discuss how to try to prevent these executions with Octavio Alberola and other close comrades. The police in France, Belgium and Italy kept me under close surveillance whenever I travelled abroad. My mail and telephone were closely monitored and I was under similar scrutiny from the 'watchers' in Britain. The anarchist response (which did not

The Suárez
Kidnapping involve me) came on Friday 3 May 1974 when Angel Baltasar Suárez, the 43-year old director of one of the most important international Spanish banks, the Banco de Bilbao, was kidnapped in Paris. On 7 May, the *Grupos de Acción Revolucionario Internacionalista (GARI)*, the continuation of the now renamed First of May Group, issued its demands: that the Francoist government release all anarchist prisoners and apply its own law of conditional liberty (parole). This would have meant the immediate release of over 100 political prisoners being held unlawfully. There was also another, unpublicised, demand: the repayment of the majority trade union (CNT) funds seized in 1939 by the Francoist generals and their supporters and beneficiaries – including the Banco de Bilbao.

The ransom was paid and Suárez released unharmed, but there had been a spy in the group. As soon as Suárez's release was confirmed, the French police arrested seven anarchists – Octavio Alberola Surinach (Spanish, 46); Ariane Gransac Sadori (French, 32); Jean Helen Weir (Scottish, 29); Georges Riviere (French, 25); Annie Plazen (Spanish, 24); Lucio Urtubia (Spanish, 44); Annie Garnier (French, 32) – and recovered a substantial part of the three million French Francs (£300,000) repayment of the union funds paid to the kidnappers.

It had been Dad's birthday on 15 May so I was up in Scotland at the time, visiting him in Hairmyres hospital. He was 59 and dying of cancer of the bowel. It was an understatement to say Dad was monosyllabic. It was always difficult to engage him in conversation, even when he wasn't sedated in hospital, as he pondered deeply and long – sometimes as long as five or ten minutes – before replying to most questions. He was extraordinarily philosophical about life and death. Maybe that had something to do with a life lived on and close to the sea, and the tradition of generations of fishermen for whom danger and death were commonplace. We never spoke about our missing years, and he never apologized for not being there, but we had a comfortable relationship at the end. As I left for the last time, I kissed him on the brow. His last words to me were, 'Never fear, the sun will shine again tomorrow.'

So Brenda was alone in the Wimbledon flat when Chief Superintendent Ronald Page visited with an extremely aggressive French investigating magistrate. Brenda refused to answer any questions on my behalf. They left empty-handed.

Protests were mounted everywhere, with those in France and Belgium becoming particularly violent with high explosive and petrol-bombings of Francoist targets becoming a regular occurrence throughout the summer and autumn of 1974.

x x x

As anti-Francoist militancy intensified inside Spain itself throughout 1974, the repression of workers and students was growing harsher.

The regime felt under siege. On 13 September 1974, a bomb in the Café Rolando in the Puerta del Sol, a meeting place for BPS officers from the security headquarters, killed twelve people and injured seventy more. This was the same café where I had sat contemplating the facade of Franco's security headquarters just over ten years earlier, minutes before my arrest. No one ever claimed responsibility for the bomb, but it was probably carried out by ETA, the Basque separatist organisation.

Whether or not the kidnapping of Suárez worked no one knows, but the two anarchists were not executed. They were sentenced on 24 July to 48 years and 21 years respectively. The political repercussions in France of this new wave of Francoist repression led to the collapse of the kidnapping case. GARI quickly evolved into the French equivalent of the Angry Brigade.

In Britain, despite the fact that the 'Angry Brigade' was allegedly no more and its key members were safely behind bars, bombings and attacks on industrial and right-wing political targets, particularly Conservative clubs, continued up and down the country. A similar movement began in Ireland.

January and February 1974 had been the dying days of the Heath government. Following a four-month state of emergency – the fifth of his government – Heath had had enough. He called a snap election and went to the polls on 28 February with the slogan: Who runs Britain – the government or the miners? The miners, people replied, and Heath lost the election, making way for Harold Wilson – again.

X X X

Wilson Back in Power, 1974

To some Establishment cold warriors, Wilson back in Downing Street was like having Stalin back in the Kremlin. Britain under Labour meant either bloody revolution or Soviet government by proxy. Unemployment was rising and by April 1975 it had passed the million mark, with the biggest monthly increase since the Second World War. Despite the dire economic situation, Wilson was re-elected in October, but this time with the tiniest of majorities. Labour Home Secretary Roy Jenkins was unable to control the increasingly delusional security services and even Wilson's Defence Secretary Roy Mason found it difficult to get the army to implement Labour policy in Northern Ireland, with senior officers claiming it was not prepared to break what was effectively an insurrectionary strike by Protestant loyalists in Ulster.

Shortly after Labour's second election victory, the prime minister's home was burgled, a move widely believed to have been the work of the MI5. A form of mass paranoia about Wilson appears to have reigned within the upper echelons of the security service and the military at the time. Senior officers in Sir Michael Hanley's totally unaccountable MI5, led by Peter Wright and his CIA mentor, the counter-intelligence chief James Angleton – the 'smoking man' in the *X Files* – were convinced Wilson was a soviet agent. Not only that, they also believed that his predecessor, Hugh Gaitskell, had been bumped off by the KGB to get Wilson into power. This belief was shared by a whole cabal of Tory and neo-fascist ne'er-do-wells around the Carlton Club and the Special Forces Club at 8 Herbert Crescent, Knightsbridge. All these people were convinced Wilson was a traitor and that their loyalty to the Queen meant getting him out, by hook or by crook. The means by which they hoped to achieve this coup was by the 'Unison Committee for Action' group, headed by the former senior MI6 officer George Kennedy Young and retired General Sir Walter Walker, KCB CBE DSO, former NATO Commander-in-Chief Allied Forces Northern Europe.

x x x

Another conspiratorial parapolitical organisation of former and serving spooks, army officers, civil servants and policemen was David Stirling's Great Britain 1975 Organisation (GB75). This was a 'volunteer army' of **GB75** patriotic strikebreakers and right-wing conservative vigilantes brought together as a contingency measure for the government of Britain, in the event of its collapse – which they predicted would take place in December 1975. Ernie Bond, incidentally, was a close friend of David Stirling from the early days of the SAS and through his ongoing involvement in the SAS Regimental Association, but whether or not he was one of the sinister group of shadowy intriguers clustered around Stirling is a matter for conjecture. This 'parallel' government had been built on the back of Stirling's 'Better Britain Society' and' Greater Britain League', both anti-trades unions and anti-leftist organisations. Stirling had formed the latter after Wilson was returned to power in 1974.

But this near-hysteria was not confined to the extremists of the far-right. Fear of a General Strike, the collapse of law and order and possible insurrection had permeated the whole of establishment culture. In April 1974 a major conference on 'Revolutionary Warfare' was held at Lancaster University with twenty-six senior army officers, including the GOC Commanding North-West District, nine senior police officers, including three Chief Constables, two Royal Navy and four Royal Air Force officers, six professors and five more academics. Similar conferences and seminars were occurring on an international level with titles like the Trilateral Commission's *Task Force Report on the Governability of Democracies*. As in 1968, the smoke-filled backrooms were again buzzing with talk of a coup and 'pre-emptive' action.

x x x

In the spring of 1975 Brenda and I were still in Wimbledon when there was knock on the door of our small second storey flat.

The caller was a police inspector, who must remain nameless. It was a 'friendly' visit. He advised me that 'a number of people' were extremely annoyed that I had 'slipped the net'. He said it would only be a matter of time before they managed to put me 'back in the frame'. In the strongest possible terms, he recommended that I would be well advised to get out of town, the implication being that the next time I went down it would be for a long time – or perhaps worse.

Who could refuse advice like that? So, sensing that in this case discretion was the better part of valour, there wasn't much point hanging around for the convenience of Scotland Yard or Leconfield House, and so we decided to move out of London. He who fights and runs away and all that, or a strategic withdrawal as the political-military euphemism has it.

But it wasn't just the Special Branch or MI5 threat. Brenda and I had been thinking for some time that it would be nice to move out of London to somewhere green and pleasant. Brenda's best friend had moved to Slaithwaite in the Colne Valley, on the outskirts of Huddersfield in West Yorkshire. When we visited, it turned out the registrar of Honley, in the Holme Valley also near Huddersfield, was selling his office. We bought the house for £1000.

It was also in the attic of this very house that a group of Huddersfield Luddites had hidden in April 1812, after shooting and fatally wounding William Horsfall, a mill owner and member of the hated Manufacturers Committee Against the Luddites – a nineteenth century employers' *posse comitatus*. Three young Huddersfield men, George Mellor, William Thorpe and Thomas Smith, were hung for his murder on Friday 8 January 1813. The name Luddite came from the signed communiqués activists left behind: 'Ned Ludd' or 'General Ludd' as opposed to 'Butch Cassidy' or 'The Angry Brigade.' Unseen forces were at work here.

x x x

Black Flag and the Cienfuegos Press publications were published from Honley. Brenda and I did the typesetting and handled the day-to-day correspondence – bills, prisoners and contributors – while Albert, Miguel and Phil Ruff did the bulk of the editorial work in London. I was beginning to understand the financial complexities of running a publishing house. It wasn't just about finding and publishing interesting books, then repeating the process, with one book paying for the next. They also had to be marketed and sold, something I hadn't really thought through. We made some pretty horrendous and expensive mistakes, running up enormous bills in the process. In spite of these set-backs, we managed to stagger along from – and through – one financial crisis after another.

Two other members of the London *Black Flag*/Anarchist Black Cross group joined us in Huddersfield: New Zealanders Graham Rua and Iris Mills. They had not been in England long. Graham and Iris had met in a New Zealand courtroom following his arrest at an anti-

Vietnam War demonstration. Iris had been his probation officer. Before long, we had an active group in the town, with our own premises. Prisoners from all over the world were writing to us as the Anarchist Black Cross about their cases, their treatment and the conditions in which they were being held. A number of these came from the notorious Long Kesh prison in Northern Ireland.

Among our correspondents was Ronan Bennett, a young Irish Republican brought up in Belfast, though born in England of an English father. As a teenager, Ronan had gravitated to the 'Stickies', or 'Official' wing of the Republican movement. Arrested and charged with the murder of a Royal Ulster Constabulary inspector during an armed robbery in Belfast in September 1974, Bennett was convicted in May 1975 – on very shaky identification evidence of a Loyalist woman who changed her story three times – to ten years for the robbery and 'life' for the police killing. He was eighteen years old.

The 'Stickies' split while Ronan was in Long Kesh prison and a shooting war erupted outside between the Official IRA and breakaway members. Inside Long Kesh, Ronan went with the breakaway Irish Republican Socialist Party (IRSP). Ronan then appealed against his sentence and, unexpectedly, was successful. The woman on whose evidence he had been convicted changed her mind again and admitted she wasn't sure if Ronan was the man she had seen or not. He was released in December 1975. He couldn't remain in Ulster, where his life was under threat from Royal Ulster Constabulary vigilantes and protestant paramilitaries, so he came to Huddersfield to live, moving in with Iris and Graham, with whom he had been corresponding. Needless to say, the Irish connection did not pass unnoticed by the F4 Division of the Police Department of the Home Office.

x x x

I was soon to find out that the doors of a number of countries were closing against me. Responding to an invitation from the German Trade Union organisation, I was turned back at the German border and handed over the Dutch police, who kept me in the cells until after the last train into Germany that night had gone. I was then told I would be released into the custody of a Dutch citizen, Bas Moreel, the European distributor for Cienfuegos titles. When I tried to enter Germany the next day, with £200 cash brought by the German comrades to show I was a respectable citizen, I was turned back at gunpoint. The orders had come directly from the Ministry of the Interior. I had been declared an 'enemy of the state' and they stamped my passport accordingly, and annotated it in fine Gothic script.

By the end of the summer and early autumn of 1975 the Franco regime was in Alamo mode. Between 28 August and 17 September, drumhead Francoist courts martial had passed death sentences on five members of the Basque separatist group ETA and eight members of the Maoist *Frente Revolucionario Antifascista y Patriotica (FRAP)*.

Franco was indignant in the face of appeals for clemency which flooded in from around the world, including those of Pope Paul VI, all the Spanish bishops and even Don Juan, the king in exile, through his son. As far as Franco was concerned, world opinion with regard to his governance was manipulated by left-wing masonic conspirators working in indecent concubinage with Communist-terrorist subversives. And so, a bitter and vengeful Franco, ignoring all pleas for mercy, confirmed five of the death sentences – three members of FRAP and two Basque members of ETA – who were executed by firing squad on 27 September. Their deaths were his blood price for the killing of Carrero Blanco.

Franco's Final Executions

The executions provoked the greatest wave of protests against the regime since Franco's victory in April 1939. Fifteen European governments recalled their ambassadors, including France. The case against the eleven anarchists in the Suárez kidnapping was complicated even further. Franco's embassies throughout the world were subject to angry demonstrations and violent attacks. In Holland the Spanish Embassy was set on fire and a bomb exploded outside the Embassy in Ankara. The President of Mexico even called for Spain's expulsion from the UN and Sweden's Prime Minister Olaf Palme denounced Franco and his government as bloody murderers.

x x x

Franco's
Death

Franco's days were numbered. He began to die on 1 October 1975. His death was hastened by the cold autumnal winds that blew down from the Guadarrama Mountains, during what turned out to be his last public appearance at the Palacio del Oriente. It was presaged by a series of minor heart attacks on the 15th, 20th and 24th of October. By 30 October his health had deteriorated to the extent that his appointed successor, Don Juan Carlos Borbon y Borbon, was named provisional head of state. Within days it seemed as though the deluge of innocent blood he had shed during his 37 years in power had returned to haunt him. On 2 November he suffered an intestinal haemorrhage that drenched his bed, carpet and parts of the wall in blood. Hooked up to banks of life-support machines he was kept alive and in pain for seventeen more days. Every so often he would recover consciousness, muttering how hard it was to die. Jesus clearly didn't want him as a sunbeam.

Legend has it that as he lay dying his wife, Dona Carmen Polo, opened the curtains of his darkened room then whispered to him that thousands of Spaniards had come to the Palacio de Oriente to say goodbye. Franco slowly raised himself up and asked: 'Why? Where are they going?'

On 19 November 1975, Franco's daughter Nenuca decided he be allowed to die and at 11.15 pm the tubes and wires keeping him alive were disconnected. The shabby figure of this once mythically evil man died shortly afterwards, in the early hours of 20 November.

King Juan Carlos Borbon y Borbon's first official duty was to preside over Franco's burial in the Valle de los Caidos, the mausoleum *el Caudillo* had commanded to be hewn out the mountain by slave labour. The only other head of state present at the funeral was Chile's General Agustin Pinochet. The oration was read by Prime Minister Carlos Arias Navarro, the butcher of Málaga. He read out Franco's political testament calling on the Spanish people to offer his successor the same affection and loyalty he had enjoyed, and to be constantly vigilant against the ever-alert enemies of Spain and Christian civilisation. The transfer of political power was seamless. Not one of Franco's enforcers, such as General Eduardo Blanco, my nemesis and the head of the dictator's secret police, or any of the countless thousands of people responsible for the barbarous and legal spoliation of Spain and its people since 1939, was ever brought to justice. It is only now, forty years after the dictator's death, that the crimes of the Franco regime are beginning to be addressed in Spain with the exhumations of the unmarked mass graves of its victims, 'the disappeared'.

x x x

Far away in Honley that late November evening, the 'enemies' of Franco's Spain congo'd down to the local off-licence and bought an enormous carry-out; 1975 had been a momentous year and it was time for a party to mark some kind of closure. We had much to celebrate: the defeat of the Americans; the end of the Vietnam War; and now a long overdue death. It was to be a wake for the tens of thousands of brave men and women who fought, suffered, died and lost loved ones in the cause of resisting the reactionary, priest-ridden, gun-and-prison backed regime that had been Francoism. The ghosts to whom we raised our glasses were the forgotten dead of a previous generation to whom my generation at least owed a profound obligation of remembrance and a duty of commemoration.

As the delicate warmth of Glenmorangie spread through my being, I reflected with a profound sense of relief and satisfaction on the fact that I at least had no one's blood or life on my conscience – not even Franco's.